SECOND EDITION

Mr. Cheap's® Atlanta

The Mr. Cheap's® Series:

Mr. Cheap's® Atlanta, 2nd Edition
Mr. Cheap's® Boston, 2nd Edition
Mr. Cheap's® Chicago, 2nd Edition
Mr. Cheap's® New York, 2nd Edition
Mr. Cheap's® San Francisco
Mr. Cheap's® Seattle
Mr. Cheap's® Washington D.C., 2nd Edition

SECOND EDITION

Mr. Cheap's® Atlanta

Bargains, factory outlets, deep discount stores, cheap places to stay, cheap eats, and cheap fun things to do

Corey Sandler
with Michael Lawrence

previous edition written by Mark Waldstein

Adams Media Corporation
Avon, Massachusetts

Copyright ©2002, Adams Media Corporation.
All rights reserved.
This book, or parts thereof, may not be reproduced in any
form without permission from the publisher; exceptions are
made for brief excerpts used in published reviews.

Published by
Adams Media Corporation
57 Littlefield Street, Avon, MA 02322 U.S.A.
www.adamsmedia.com

ISBN: 1-58062-692-0

Printed in Canada.

J I H G F E D C B A

This publication is designed to provide accurate and authoritative information with regard to the subject matter covered. It is sold with the understanding that the publisher is not engaged in rendering legal, accounting, or other professional advice. If legal advice or other expert assistance is required, the services of a competent professional person should be sought.
—From a *Declaration of Principles* jointly adopted
by a Committee of the American Bar Association
and a Committee of Publishers and Associations.

Many of the designations used by manufacturers and sellers to distinguish their products are claimed as trademarks. Where those designations appear in this book and Adams Media was aware of a trademark claim, the designations have been printed in initial capital letters.

*This book is available at quantity discounts for bulk purchases.
For information, call 1-800-872-5627.*

Contents

An Economical Introduction to the Wit and Wisdom
of Mr. Cheap 9

Shopping / 11

Antiques and Gifts 12
Appliances 17
Beds and Mattresses 23
Books 29
CDs, Records, Tapes, and Videos 36
Cameras and Photographic Supplies 44
Carpeting and Rugs 48
Clothing-New 53

> *Men's Wear—General, 54; Women's Wear—General, 56; Men's and Women's Wear—General, 59; Bridal and Formal Wear, 63; Children's Wear, 64; Accessories, 66*

Clothing-Used 68

> *Consignment and Resale Stores, 68; Vintage Stores, 72; Thrift Stores, 74*

Cosmetics and Perfumes 77
Discount Department Stores 81
Electronics 89

> *Audio/Video Equipment, 89; Computers, 92*

Factory Outlet Centers 95
Flea Markets and Emporia 99
Flowers and Plants 101
Food Stores 106
    Bakeries, 106; Candy and Nuts, 109; Coffees and Teas, 110; General Markets and Prepared Foods to Go, 111; Local Farmer's Markets, 117; Health Food and Vitamins, 118
Furniture 121
    New Furniture, 121; Used Furniture, 128; Office Furniture, 130
Home Furnishings 132
    Decorative Items, Kitchenware, Lighting, Linens, Paint, Wallpaper, 132
Jewelry and Crafts 136
Liquor and Beverages 143
Luggage 148
Musical Instruments 151
Party Supplies 155
Pet Supplies 159
Sewing and Fabrics 164
Shoes and Sneakers 167
Sporting Goods 180
Stationery, Office, and Art Supplies 185
Toys and Games 191
Unusual Gifts 194

Entertainment / 199

Arts Centers 200
Art Galleries 202
Children's Activities 209
College Performing Arts 212
Comedy 218
Dance 221
Festivals 225

Movies 228
   Drive-In Theaters, 231

Museums 231

Music 235
   *Classical, 235; Jazz/Blues, 237; Folk/Coffeehouse, 238;
   Dance/Disco, 239; Rock/Pop, 240; Latin/Salsa, 240;
   Eclectic, 241*

Outdoor and Sports Activities 241

Theater 246

Walks and Tours 251

Restaurants / 257

Atlanta Northeast/Decatur 258
Buckhead 274
Downtown Atlanta/Southeast & Southwest 287
Little Five Points 291
Midtown 297
Perimeter Suburbs 303

Lodging / 313

Hotels/Motels 314
Alternative Lodging 319

Index / 323

Alphabetical Index 323
Subject Index 331

About the Author 335

An Economical Introduction to the Wit and Wisdom of Mr. Cheap

Let's get something straight right at the top: Being cheap doesn't mean wearing rags, eating leftovers, and living in a cardboard box.

Instead, I prefer to think of being "cheap" as being very smart about how I spend my money. Put another way, my goal in life is to live a lot better than the next guy on the same annual income . . . or less.

Henry David Thoreau, who knew quite a lot about living well on less, put it well: "That man is the richest whose pleasures are the cheapest."

I like to eat well but pay a reasonable grocery bill. I love to travel almost as much as I love knowing that my family is paying thousands of dollars less than the folks in front and in back of me. We dress well but spend less.

Writing these books is a natural extension of my interests. For the past dozen years or so, I've written the *Econoguide Travel Book* series, now published by the Globe Pequot Press. In those books I've helped hundreds of thousands of readers travel around the world in high style and at a reasonable price. Another one of my books, *Buy More Pay Less*, from Prentice Hall Direct, explains how to buy just about anything anywhere.

I've traveled to Atlanta dozens of times as a travel writer and a newspaper reporter. I've come to realize that many visitors and residents see the trees but not the forest. In recent decades Atlanta has grown from a sleepy southern city all but invisible to the outside world to a thriving capital city on the U.S. and global map. Atlanta is now known to the world by a lot more than the small print on the Coke can; think CNN, the Atlanta Braves, the Summer Olympics.

My gold medal relay shopping team, lead by Michael Lawrence with cocaptains Janice Keefe and Maureen Moriarty; and long-distance runners Carol J. Bryant, Matt Zorivitch, Art Murray, and Barbara Parker joined me in walking the streets of Atlanta, working the telephones, and trawling the Internet in search of tens of thousands of deals and details. We built our book on the foundation laid by the original Mr. Cheap, Mark Waldstein, and his team.

We're proud of what we've uncovered, but it is important to issue a few important user's advisories: Things change; stores close, or move, or change their philosophy. Prices go up and down and menus can be transformed overnight.

Consider the write-ups of stores, restaurants, hotels, and attractions in this book as guideposts. When we discuss a specific product, it's to give you an idea of the type of item we found on the shelves when we did our research; you may or may not find the same thing when you visit.

Make a phone call or check out a Web site when listed in the book before you make a major expedition to one of the places we write about. Tell them you read about their business in *Mr. Cheap's Atlanta* . . . and please tell us how they treat you and about your shopping experience. We'll share your comments the next time we gather in these pages.

To contact Mr. Cheap, write to:
Econoguide
P.O. Box 2779
Nantucket, MA 02584

Please enclose a stamped, self-addressed envelope if you'd like a response.

You can also send us e-mail, at info@econoguide.com

Now go forth and shop.

Shopping

You can buy it new. You can buy it used. You can buy it imperfect. And you can buy it marked down. But please, don't buy it for full price. You wouldn't want to disappoint Mr. Cheap, would you?

The hundreds of stores in this section are all places that will save you money in one way or another. They cover a broad spectrum of discount shopping, from the latest designer clothing to thrift shops, new furniture and used, major brands and second-rate imitations. Think of the listings in this chapter as a roadmap for shopping, not as a catalog.

The prices quoted are based upon items Mr. C found at the time of his research. You shouldn't expect to find the same items at the same prices when you shop; these are just examples of sales philosophies and strategies. Even as prices and products change over time, this book will help you chart your course.

Many stores that sell several kinds of merchandise have been cross-referenced for you, appearing in each appropriate chapter; but remember to consult "Discount Department Stores" and "Flea Markets and Emporia" for many of the same items that have their own chapters.

Okay, enough talking-go to it!

ANTIQUES AND GIFTS

There's little Mr. and Mrs. Cheap like better than heading out for a mellow antiquing expedition in their vintage minivan with a rusty roof rack—mostly blue except for the right-front door panel—and decorated with Mr. Cheap's favorite automotive accessory: a bumper sticker that reads, "Don't laugh. It's paid for."

There's another important saying: "one person's junk is another person's antique." The trick, Mr. Cheap has learned, is to pay for antiques at junk prices.

Antique City

- 5180 Peachtree Industrial Boulevard, Atlanta; ✆ (770) 458-7131

This delightful emporium, conveniently located just off I-285, saves gas money. One of the largest antique stores in Atlanta—some 15,000 square feet, 3,000 of which is dedicated to fine rugs—it's a one-stop shop for all sorts of junk, er, antiques and collectibles.

Antique City is a great shopping experience, with more than a hundred dealers selling jewelry, books, magazines, stained glass, collectibles, home furnishings, and other quality merchandise. This is not a flea market—the antiques sold here tend to be upscale, but you can still find plenty of incredible values due to the massive selection.

Antique City also sells classic reproductions of antique furniture, and the rug portion of the store features high-quality Orientals and Persians, as well as other varieties.

The store holds sales at least twice a year—usually in the spring and fall—where all the dealers get together to offer their merchandise at discount. You'll also find seasonal and holiday sales here, so get on their mailing list or give them a call.

Overall, you'll find it hard to beat Antique City's winning combo of selection and value. Store hours are 10 a.m. to 6 p.m. Monday through Saturday, and noon to 5 p.m. on Sunday.

A Flea An'Tique

- 222 South Main Street, Alpharetta; ✆ (770) 442-8991

Question: Is this a flea market or an antique store? Answer: Yes.

More than thirty vendors have banded together to create a wonderfully eclectic shop, filled with antique furniture dating back to the early 1800s—Art Deco, Victorian, Empire, French Provincial, standard well-loved mahogany—as well as collectibles, glassware, mirrors, lamps, records, jewelry, pottery plates, and quality used furniture for every room in the house,

It's a clean, bright, and friendly place, a good spot for all home decorating needs, and a great place to have some fun treasure hunting. It's got the best prices in the area and a high turnover of goods, making it worth repeat visits.

A Flea An'Tique is open Monday through Saturday 10 a.m. to 6 p.m. and Sunday noon to 6 p.m.

Antiques & Beyond

- 1853 Cheshire Bridge Road N.E., Atlanta; ✆ (404) 872-4342

Here's another large antique "mall" where El Cheapedo has found great

SHOPPING: ANTIQUES AND GIFTS

values and unparalleled selection, about 14,000 square feet of great antiques and collectibles.

There are at least 50 vendors here, offering used and antique furniture, Art Deco furniture, mirrors and prints, linens, collectibles, and other decorative items for the home.

Senor C was offering a Wright Table Company huntboard that sold for $1,395, and this is a piece that can easily be sold for $4,000. All the linens are antique—everything from tablecloths to napkins (all of which range in price from $5 to $50).

The store features many collectibles such as Depression glass, pottery, art glass, figurines, and Coca-Cola memorabilia. And there is at least one vendor who sells new furniture at discounts of about 15 percent off retail.

Antiques & Beyond is open 7 days a week, from 11 a.m. to 7 p.m.

Beverly Bremer Silver Shop

- 3164 Peachtree Road, Atlanta; (404) 261-4009; (800) 270-4009

- www.silvershop.com

If you're looking to match a pattern from an inherited silver service, get an appraisal, or just want to pick up some beautiful, discount-priced flatware and hollowware from a large selection, you'll definitely want to check out this shop.

Located in an old 1930s-style strip mall called Peachtree Plaza, Beverly's is packed to the rafters with tables of secondhand tea sets, centerpieces, goblets, punch bowls, pitchers, and more, all at discount prices. There's also a much smaller selection of new pieces.

The small shop is jammed but neatly organized, with the freshly polished merchandise set out for your perusal on shelves and in display cases.

After more than 27 years in business, proprietor Beverly Bremer has built a loyal customer base that includes folks not only from the Atlanta area but from all over the country and beyond. She says about half of her sales are mail order.

Beverly and her well-trained staff know their stuff. They're adept at appraising and acquiring quality pieces at good value, so they can pass those savings on to you. They can identify and match old patterns from weddings gone by and get you the piece or pieces you need—a goal that would be very expensive if you were trying to locate "new" silver.

Generally, you can expect to save 50 to 75 percent on many pieces and patterns. For example, Mr. C spotted a Chantilly 4-piece place setting that would go for as much as $200 at other stores, available for only $99 here, and there are many, many other similar opportunities.

Silver is beautiful and appreciates with time, so there's really nothing not to like about this place.

Beverly's is open 10 a.m. to 5 p.m. Monday through Saturday.

Big Shanty Antiques & Flea Market

- 1720 N. Roberts Road, Kennesaw; (770) 795-1186 (next to the Cowboys dance club)

Mr. C loves this place, even though they refused to make a bid on his "antique on wheels" minivan. The reason Cheapo keeps coming around is that it's possible to find incredible deals here on all kinds of collectibles—from furniture to primitives, antique toys and books, pottery, glass, paintings, dishes, coins, and much, much more. In fact, you could classify many of the bargains as outright "steals."

Size has a lot to do with the values that can be had here, as Big Shanty boasts more than 150 vendors covering a vast show floor of a former Kmart.

These vendors have varying degrees of knowledge about what it is they are offering, and there are scores of underpriced pieces here that can be snapped up by the savvy antiques shopper. The Cheapster has it on good authority that recently an old pitcher worth more than $450 was acquired by a wily aficionado for only $40! A rolltop desk worth hundreds was purchased for just over $100. A vintage armoire was purchased for only $200!

Even if you're not the world's greatest antiques expert, the vast array of offerings at this place means that you can find unusual gifts and outfit your entire house with classic and elegant pieces for less than what you'd pay for much more nondescript items in a typical store.

Big Shanty Antiques is open 10 a.m. to 6 p.m. Monday through Saturday and from noon to 6 p.m. on Sunday.

Chamblee Antiques Row

- 3519 Broad Street (at Peachtree Road), Chamblee; (770) 455-4751

Save your soles! Within short walking distance of the corner of Broad Street and Peachtree Road in Chamblee you'll find an interesting collection of quaint buildings dating from the mid-1800s. Within about ten of them reside more than 200 antique dealers ready to offer you high-value deals on a wide assortment of antiques and collectibles. Mr. C likes this setup because it offers the same huge selection of some of the large "warehouse" antique markets, but you can still shop like you're at a "mom-and-pop" shop.

Antiques Row is open 10 a.m. to 5 p.m. Monday through Saturday. They're also open occasionally on Sunday, but call ahead to be sure.

Georgia Antique Center & International Market

- 6624 I-85 North Access Road, Atlanta; (770) 446-9292

Here's another of Mr. C's favorite mega-antique and flea markets. Open primarily on the weekends, this extravaganza features over 200 merchants selling jewelry, silver, oriental rugs, pottery, rare coins, books, furniture, and more. With that kind of selection, you'll discover plenty of good gift ideas, and save a bundle.

The Flea Market is open from noon to 7 p.m. on Friday; 10 a.m. to 8 p.m. on Saturday; and noon to 7 p.m. on Sunday. Some merchants are open during the week.

Hill Street Warehouse

- 2050 Hills Avenue N.E., Atlanta; (404) 352-5001

This warehouse store is packed full of home decorative accessories including antiques, Italian ceramics, and terra cotta. Store hours are 10 a.m. to 5 p.m. Monday through Saturday.

Lakewood Antique Market

- 2002 Lakewood Way, Atlanta; (404) 622-4488

Once a month, The Cheapster dons his best polyester leisure suit and tools on over to the Lakewood Fairgrounds, adjacent to the Coca-Cola Amphitheater. Here more than 1,500 vendors gather in a massive antique and flea market to sell everything under the sun, including antique furniture, vintage clothing,

SHOPPING: ANTIQUES AND GIFTS

books, pottery, dishes, glass, paintings, coins, housewares, and just about anything else you can imagine. This is another case where bigger is better: the vast selection of wares for sale among the fairground's five buildings and outdoor areas means that you'll find plenty of bargains.

There's also plenty of food on the premises, mostly of the county fair variety: stuff like corndogs, candy apples, popcorn, and Coke are big sellers. There's also more substantial fare, including sandwiches and barbeque.

This extravaganza is held the second weekend of every month. The hours are 9 a.m. to 6 p.m. Thursday through Saturday and 10 a.m. to 5 p.m. on Sunday. It will cost you about three bucks to get in, but you'll probably save that amount many times over, and the fee is good for the entire four days.

Main Street Antique Market

- 133 South Main Street, Alpharetta; (770) 521-1555

If you're looking for a more traditional antiquing experience, you'll enjoy this smaller antique mall of about 25 dealers located in the center of quaint and historic Alpharetta. These folks specialize in all kinds of quality furniture in oak, pine, mahogany, cherry, and walnut, and they also offer a variety of collectibles. You'll find deals in porcelains, china, silver, lamps, dolls (including accessories and repairs), flower arrangements, container art, and many other items.

The Cheapster usually cruises up to Main Street in the spring and fall, when he can snatch up quality pieces at 15 to 40 percent off their normal prices.

The store is open Monday through Saturday from 10 a.m. to 6 p.m. and Sunday from 1 p.m. to 6 p.m.

MR. CHEAP'S PICKS

Antiques

Beverly Bremer Silver Shop— Looking for quality silver? This place is packed to the gills with tables of secondhand tea sets, centerpieces, goblets, punch bowls, pitchers, and more—all discounted.

Big Shanty Antiques and Flea Market— More than 150 dealers offer incredible deals here on all kinds of collectibles—from furniture to primitives, antique toys and books, pottery, glass, paintings, dishes, coins, and much, much more.

Lakewood Antique Market— Talk about mega-selection! Here, one weekend each month, you'll find some 1,500 vendors selling everything under the sun, including antique furniture, vintage clothing, books, pottery, dishes, glass, paintings, coins, housewares, and just about anything else you can imagine.

My Favorite Place

- 5596 Peachtree Industrial Boulevard, Chamblee; (770) 452-8397

See the listing under *Used Furniture*.

Pride of Dixie Antique Market

- 1700 Jeurgens Court, Norcross; (770) 279-9853

Here's another antique market extravaganza, this one featuring 800 dealers and held on the fourth weekend of every month at North

Atlanta Trade Center. You'll find the usual assortment of collectibles, glass, art, jewelry, and furniture. Pride of Dixie doesn't hold any formal sales, but the sheer size of the market means good pickings for great values. Admission is about $4, and you can usually find a reduced price coupon in the weekend section of the *Atlanta Journal-Constitution* the week before the event.

Pride of Dixie is open Thursday from noon until 6 p.m., Friday and Saturday from 9 a.m. to 6 p.m., and Sundays from 11 a.m. to 5 p.m.

Red Baron's Antiques

- 6450 Roswell Road, Atlanta; (404) 252-3770

Nothing here is actually cheap, okay? Red Baron's is actually more like a museum where you can buy the artifacts on display—at an average ticket price of $30,000. These pieces include stained glass; 18th-, 19th-, and 20th-century furniture; bronze, marble, and stone sculpture; antique automobiles; jukeboxes; carousel art; and more.

So why does Mr. Cheap use up precious ink and paper to tell you about it? Because three times a year (usually the second weekend in February, June, and October) Red Baron's holds an auction where everything in the store sells—sometimes at surprisingly low prices. During this extravaganza, which draws bidders from all over the world ("like Wall Street meets Bourbon Street," according to the manager), early birds can pick up some museum-quality pieces for $100–$150. Don't come too late, however. By the middle of the day Saturday, the big-ticket items ($60,000 and up) will be in play. Probably not for you, but it's still a good show.

So if you're interested in a world-class collectible, by all means check out Red Baron's during an auction. If that is still a little too rich for your blood, walk on over to the Queen's Garden Gallery across the street, which has more reasonably priced items from the same collection.

Red Baron's is open Monday through Friday from 9:30 a.m. to 6 p.m. and Saturday from 10 a.m. to 4 p.m.

Scott Antique Market

- 3650 Jonesboro Road, Jonesboro; (404) 361-2000

- www.scottantiquemarket.com

Housed in two very large buildings at the Atlanta Expo Center on the second weekend of each month, this megamarket offers the enthusiastic antiquer just about anything under the sun . . . or the indoor lighting. Here you'll find up to 1,500 dealers from across the country selling the usual (and often unusual) assortment of furniture, accessories, jewels, books, pottery, dishes, glass, paintings, coins, and other collectibles.

The market is open on the second weekend of the month on Friday and Saturday from 9 a.m. to 6 p.m. and Sunday from 10 a.m. to 4 p.m. You'll pay about three bucks to get in.

Tara Antiques

- 2325 Cheshire Bridge Road, Atlanta; (404) 325-4600

After Mr. C has sated himself with a cheeseburger at the Varsity Junior drive-in, he tools his vintage VW bus just down the street to Tara's Antiques. Tara boasts about 150 dealers selling a broad selection of quality antiques, including furniture, jewelry, 1950s dishes, glassware, ceramics, rugs, clocks, and other collectibles. The merchandise here tends to be more high-end and less "flea market," but because of the multitude of dealers and the large selection, you can always find some good values here.

Twice a year Tara's holds a storewide sale, when you'll be able to get even better bargains on their substantial collections. The spring sale is outside, and the fall sale is indoors.

Tara's is open 11 a.m. to 7 p.m. seven days a week.

The Wrecking Bar

- 292 Moreland Avenue, Atlanta; (404) 525-0468

Mr. C has never seen anything quite like this huge mansion with an antique mall inside. Covering about 18,000 square feet in the historic Victor Kriegshaber Home, the Wrecking Bar boasts a huge inventory of antique doors, stained glass, beveled glass, carvings, mantels and fireplace accessories, columns, brass hardware, and decorative wrought iron. Many pieces are of museum quality.

The Wrecking Bar is open 9 a.m. to 5 p.m. Monday through Saturday.

APPLIANCES

There are lots of places to save money on appliances and electronics in and around Atlanta. Some, unfortunately, are as far below repute as they are below retail. When it comes to high tech, including cameras, camcorders, and computers, be especially careful to understand the difference between authorized products and those on the gray market or the black market.

An authorized product comes with a warranty and repair policy from an importer in the United States (or Canada, or wherever you reside). Read the warranty and be sure it is of value to you.

A gray-market product is a device that has been imported by someone other than an authorized reseller. The product *may* be the same as the device sold by the authorized importer, or it may have some different features; watch out for devices that are not set up to work with electrical voltage or television standards in your home. If there is a warranty at all, it may require you to ship the product to another country, which may not be a realistic option.

Another form of gray market involves something that used to be called "railroad salvage." These are devices that were scratched, dented, or otherwise damaged in shipping. The importer may allow them to be resold but without a warranty.

A black-market product is either a device not meant to be sold in this country, or not meant to be sold to consumers. It may also be something that "fell off the back of the truck," which is a somewhat-nice version of "this is stolen property."

Should you buy a gray-market device if it is sold at a tremendous savings? Maybe. I would never recommend buying an expensive device (more than $500, let's say) that doesn't come without a real guarantee of a reasonable service life. But if we're talking about inexpensive devices, it may be a worthwhile gamble. Just be sure to inform yourself about all the details before you make a purchase.

Remember, you are perfectly within your rights to inquire about the warranty and to explore the provenance of any product in a store before you make a purchase.

AAA-ALL American Appliance

- 5625 Mill Race Court, Dunwoody; (770) 396-5904

Hey, you've got to give these guys credit: In the brutal competition for the top spot in the Yellow Pages, they've got their A's in gear. Located in the Chamblee Village shopping center, AAA-ALL sells and installs a broad range of large and small appliances at competitive prices. They supply and service heating and air conditioning systems from York and other major brands, as well as refrigerators, ovens, stoves, refrigerators by GE, Maytag, Whirlpool, Kenmore, and other manufacturers. (In fact, they say that they'll get you any make or model you want.) You can regularly save 20 to 25 percent off selected appliances, especially during beginning-of-season specials. Service calls are regularly discounted.

AAA-ALL is open from 9 a.m. to 6 p.m. Monday through Friday.

AA Ideal Used Appliances

- 4118 Old Dixie Highway, Habeville; (404) 361-4445

Ideal, indeed. You'll be hard-pressed to find better bargains anywhere, with savings from 40 to 60 percent off retail prices on used appliances from Whirlpool, Hotpoint, Kenmore, and other big brand names. Customers have responded to the deals, allowing AA to move to Habeville and double its size to 6,000-square feet, allowing for a great selection of merchandise. Washers and dryers are priced at $100 and up; Carrier and Kenmore air conditioners start at about $75, and you'll find ranges and ovens starting around $125. Trash compactors, stoves, and freezers are similarly priced, according to age and wear.

There's a 30-day money-back guarantee on parts and labor (fix-ups are done in the store), and delivery is available for a fee.

The store is closed Sundays.

Appliance Warehouse

- 1012 Iris Drive S.W., Conyers; (770) 922-2267

- www.homeappliances.com

Located in a nondescript strip mall on the south access road of I-20, Appliance Warehouse offers solid deals on all the major brands. These folks have been in business for 40 years, so they've built up a large base of steady customers who have come to appreciate their reliability and great service. Rather than discounting during special sales like Sears, the owners of Appliance Warehouse like to say that they offer sale prices all year long. Other stores' specials are indeed about the same as the standard ticket price here, which averages about 30 percent off retail. And the

SHOPPING: APPLIANCES

deals are sweet: for example, here you can pick up a Frigidaire washer-dryer *pair* for just $525. Refrigerators start at $399.

The store is open Monday through Friday from 9 a.m. to 6 p.m., and Saturday from 9 a.m. to 2 p.m.

Ashby Discount Sewing Machines

- 2990 Canton Highway, Marietta; ✆ (404) 427-9947

See the listing under *Sewing and Fabrics*.

Baumann's Home Appliance Center

- 987 Chattahoochee Avenue N.W., Atlanta; ✆ (404) 605-0200

Smack dab in a lovely warehouse neighborhood, Baumann's offers personalized service and a large selection of competitively priced washers and dryers, disposers, dishwashers, ranges, cooktops, and other large appliances from such manufacturers as Maytag, GE, Whirlpool, Kitchen Aid, Asko, and Jenn-Air. For you aficionados looking for commercial-quality kitchen appliances, they also carry Viking.

Baumann's regularly carries rebate offers from all the major distributors and manufacturers, and you'll usually find a number of floor samples that you can pick up at low cost. Each year around the third week of January they hold a storewide sale where you can save about 25 percent on everything in stock. And they service everything they sell.

Store hours are Monday through Friday from 8:30 a.m. to 5:30 p.m.

Best Buy

- 1201 Hammond Drive N.E., Atlanta; ✆ (770) 392-0454

- 470 Flat Shoals Avenue S.E., Atlanta; ✆ (404) 581-0105
- 1568 Bankhead Highway N.W., Atlanta; ✆ (404) 792-7856
- 470 Flat Shoals Avenue S.E., Atlanta; ✆ (404) 581-0105
- 1568 Bankhead Highway N.W.; Atlanta; ✆ (404) 792-7856
- 2035 Martin Luther King Jr. N.W., Atlanta; ✆ (404) 756-9509
- 4145 Lavista Road, Tucker; ✆ (770) 939-7660
- 2460 Cobb Parkway S.E., Smyrna; ✆ (770) 859-9266
- 1201 Hammond Drive N.E., Atlanta; ✆ (770) 392-0454
- 1576 Southlake Parkway, Morrow; ✆ (770) 968-0884
- 1950 Highway 85, Jonesboro; ✆ (770) 719-9990
- 1450 E Park Place Boulevard, Stone Mountain; ✆ (770) 469-9848
- 5506 Buford Highway, Norcross; ✆ (770) 448-7090
- 1875 Pleasant Hill Road, Duluth; ✆ (770) 381-9494
- 850 Cobb Place Boulevard N.W., Kennesaw; ✆ (770) 424-7868
- 975 North Point Parkway, Alpharetta; ✆ (678) 339-1321
- 2780 Horizon Ridge Court, Suwanee; ✆ (770) 614-6668
- 3379 Buford Drive, Buford; ✆ (770) 614-0533
- 3205 Woodward Crossing Boulevard, Buford; ✆ (770) 614-0533
- ✐ www.bestbuy.com

The Cheapster thought Best Buy was just for home electronics and tech gear until the day he got lost searching for the men's room and stumbled into the appliance section. And what a section it was! The gleaming high-tech ambiance of the rest of the store carries over here, where major brands of refrigerators, dishwashers, washer-dryers, ranges, and other home essentials are displayed three deep and available at decent discount. Mr. C spotted a side-by-side refrigerator for $999, a built-in dishwasher for $189.50, an upright freezer for $279, an electric range for $299, and an electric dryer for $269.

From time to time, Best Buy also offers no-interest financing, so there's a way to save even more money!

Store hours are 10 a.m. to 9 p.m. Monday through Saturday, and 11 a.m. to 6 p.m. on Sunday.

Discount Appliances

- 3718 Bankhead Highway, Lithia Springs; ✆ (770) 819-8129

If you don't mind "pre-owned" appliances, then this could be the place for you. This used appliance store, located next door to Flowers Showers in a shopping center, carries quality merchandise from all the major brands, offering a 30-day warranty on everything they sell. They don't usually know what they're going to get in from one day to the next (they pick up a lot of their merchandise from people who are relocating out of town), but you can be sure that they'll have just about anything you'll need, as long as you aren't too picky about a specific set of features. Discounts vary, but prices run from $175 and up for washers, dryers, and stoves, with GE refrigerators going for about $200. TVs start at $100, VCRs at $50.

Store hours are 9 a.m. to 6 p.m. Monday through Friday. They're open 9 a.m. to 4 p.m. on Saturday.

Bob Carroll's

- 2122 North Decatur Plaza, Decatur; ✆ (404) 634-2411

Anyone with the slightest fetish for home appliances will reach satisfaction with the superb selection Mr. C found here, where the showroom floor is littered with gleaming specimens from GE, Maytag, Jenn-Air, and Hotpoint. Best of all, Carroll's sells them all at discounted prices. On one surveillance, the Cheapmeister scoped out a side-by-side GE refrigerator with ice dispenser for under $199, and "specialty" Jenn-Air ranges with downdraft vents and indoor grills for $999.

Mr. C also found a Hotpoint dishwasher selling for $239 and a Maytag unit selling for $399, a savings of $60 off the list price. Be sure to take a look at Carroll's closeouts and floor samples, too.

Cherian's

- 751 Dekalb Industrial Way, Decatur; ✆ (404) 299-0842

If you're shopping for small appliances and are willing to search a

---

MR. CHEAP'S PICKS

Appliances

AA Ideal Used Appliances— With all the big brands for sale at 40 to 60 percent off, you can't go wrong here.

Bob Carroll's—Awesome selection and prices.

Clayton Appliances—Chock full of name-brand appliances at near-wholesale prices.

bit, you may find some surprising bargains here. Catering to Decatur's Indian community, Cherian's features a mishmash of small appliances, many imported from overseas. So, along with bags of rice and tea and other grocery items, you'll find budget-friendly name-brand electronics and small appliances.

Be sure to carefully check the voltages on electronic items before you buy; some are not compatible for use in this country. Because Cherian's is a direct importer, some products sold here are meant for customers who travel overseas, or for those who send them back to family members in foreign countries.

The store is open 11 a.m. to 9 p.m. Monday through Saturday and 12:30 p.m. to 9 p.m. on Sunday.

Circuit City

- 3400 Woodale Drive N.E., Atlanta; (404) 233-2060
- 1968 Greenbriar Parkway S.W., Atlanta; (404) 349-5422
- 4512 Memorial Drive, Decatur; (404) 299-2001
- 5495 Jimmy Carter Boulevard, Norcross; (404) 662-0557
- 1241 Morrow Industrial Boulevard, Southlake; (404) 968-1211

Yes it's a faceless national chain and the sales personnel are sometimes as well informed as Mr. C's Shetland sheepdog, but Circuit City really does have a good low price guarantee. After purchasing an item if you find the same product selling locally for a lower price, Circuit City will refund 110 percent of the difference. (If the difference is $50, for example, they'll pay you $55.)

One of the super bargains that Circuit City found was a 13-cubic-foot Kelvinator refrigerator/freezer—good for a dorm room or undercounter bar—for a mere $37.

The stores are open Monday through Saturday from 10 a.m. to 9 p.m. and Sunday from noon to 6 p.m.

Clayton Appliances

- 200 N. 85 Parkway, Fayetteville; (770) 461-8331

Chock full of name-brand appliances at near-wholesale prices, Clayton's is one of Mr. C's favorite places to shop and, of course, a "best pick." Here in a sprawling 50,000-square-foot showroom, The Cheapster found such deals as a top-of-the-line 21-cubic-foot KitchenAid refrigerator, regularly priced at $1,099, ticketed at only $795. A self-cleaning Whirlpool gas range was marked down to $799 from $552, and a GE dishwasher was available at closeout for just $169. Countertop microwaves were priced starting at $149, and you could get a 5,000 BTU window air conditioner for $199.

This place probably has the best deals in town on fireplaces, with scores of models, starting at $525, displayed right on the showroom floor. Hmmm . . . a loaf of day-old bread, a screw-top jug of bargain burgundy, a discount fireplace, and the lovely Mrs. C. What a deal!

Clayton also offers installation, service, and parts on everything it sells.

Located in the North 85 Business Park, just north of Home Depot and next to the Dazzles skating rink, Clayton is open Monday from 9 a.m. to 6 p.m., Tuesday through Friday from 9 a.m. to 7 p.m., and Saturday from 9 a.m. to 5 p.m. They're closed on Sunday.

Monroe Power Equipment Company

- 2117 Pace Street, Covington; (770) 784-5880

Ah, the American Dream: a chain saw, chipper, and a leaf blower in every garage. Although His Royal Cheapness wouldn't call this a discount store, he is quite sure that you'll find Monroe to be the definitive place to buy almost any kind of power lawn and landscaping equipment, including tillers, lawn mowers, chipper-vacs, chain saws, and leaf blowers. The store opens its doors Monday through Saturday at 8:30 a.m. and closes them at 5:30 p.m., except on Wednesdays and Saturdays, when they close early, at 12:30 p.m.

Parkway Used Appliances

- 4915 Canton Highway, Marietta; (770) 516-0191

If you like good deals on a wide selection of major-brand washers and dryers, refrigerators, and stoves, you'll like Parkway. Here you can pick up pre-owned, totally refurbished appliances at a fraction of their new cost.

When you walk into the store, you see four long aisles of about 50 gleaming specimens with nameplates like Whirlpool, GE, Frigidaire, Amana, and Maytag. Even the older models have been repainted and look more-or-less brand-new. All these have been checked out and refurbished, and the inventory even includes some brand-new units that have been slightly dented or scratched. Prices on washers and dryers begin in the $150–$175 range; refrigerators start at $175 and range up to $800. Everything comes with a 30-day store warranty.

And remember: even if you buy a perfect new unit at full price, within a week or so it's going to have a few scratches and dents.

Regular store hours at Parkway are 7:30 a.m. to 5 p.m. Monday through Friday. They're occasionally open on Saturdays, too.

Sears

- 809 Ralph David Abernathy Drive, Atlanta; (404) 753-5683
- 1500 Cumberland Mall S.E., Atlanta; (770) 433-7525
- 2201 Henderson Mill Road N.E., Atlanta; (770) 934-3511
- 2478 Atlanta Rd S.E., Smyrna; (770) 432-5184
- 1300 Southlake Mall, Morrow; (770) 961-7110
- 2301 Mountain Industrial Boulevard, Tucker; (770) 621-6890
- 600 Shannon Mall, Union City; (770) 969-3261
- 2100 Pleasant Hill Road, Duluth; (770) 476-6691
- 400 Ernest W Barrett Parkway N.W., Kennesaw; (770) 429-4155
- Highway 400, Alpharetta; (770) 667-6700
- 5153 Highway 278, Covington; (770) 786-3434
- 1617 N Expressway # B, Griffin; (770) 227-9402
- 1219 W Spring Street, Monroe; (770) 267-4180
- www.sears.com

Sears has appliances? You don't say!! Well, this may be stating the obvious, but no self-respecting Cheapster could shop for washers, dryers, refrigerators, lawnmowers, and other homeowner necessities without at least taking a gander at that icon of American retail history! Sears carries its own "house" brand,

Kenmore, as well as many other brands including Amana, Frigidaire, GE, Maytag, Whirlpool, and others.

On a recent visit Mr. C spotted a built-in dishwasher for just $188, a top-load washer for $277, a food disposer for a measly $39.99, a self-cleaning range and oven for $359, and a canister vacuum cleaner for $179. Craftsman lawn mowers could be had for about $220, while gas grills started at $149.

Mr. C has gotten into Cajun cooking (his specialty is blackened toast), and maybe you have too. If that's the case, you'll join me in celebrating prices for charcoal smokers as low as $39.99!

Store hours can vary by location and season, but you'll usually find Sears open Monday through Saturday from 10 a.m. to 9 p.m. and Sunday from noon to 6 p.m.

Singer Sewing Products

- Lindbergh Plaza, 2581 Piedmont Road, Atlanta; ✆ (404) 261-4240
- 🖳 www.sewingmachine.com

Betsy Ross would have loved this factory service store, where you can find both new and high-quality used sewing machines for sale. The impressive, previously owned selection includes built-in table models by brands like Pfaff, Brother, and, of course, Singer. Repairs are done in the store, and their work is guaranteed. Particularly popular these days seems to be Singer's complete line of both new and used embroidery machines, now available starting at $500.

Meanwhile, you can also find used vacuum cleaners here by Singer, Eureka, and other brands. Mr. C saw a Kirby upright, several years old but still in great shape; selling for $400 when new, it was on sale for just $99. And a Singer 6.5-amp vacuum with headlight, originally offered for $139.95, was only $89.95.

Singer is open Monday through Saturday from 8 a.m. to 6 p.m.

BEDS AND MATTRESSES

A Bed Depot

- 595 Roswell Street N.E., Marietta; ✆ (770) 218-3028

Mr. C has seen some dedicated bedding merchants in his day, but these guys take the cake! They're relentless in their pursuit of great mattress and beds, often buying large quantities from other less fortunate retailers going out of business. In this way they manage to get merchandise at less than wholesale, and then pass on the savings to the customer—usually 50 to 70 percent off retail.

In fact, the Depot dudes claim they have the lowest mattress prices in Georgia. Mr. C has certainly slept around; he's not sure if somewhere, someone might offer him a place to sleep for less, but it would be a close race.

This is not a huge store (the showroom is 1,500 square feet), but the hundreds of low-priced mattresses here are literally stacked to the 14-foor ceiling on special shelves constructed by the owner. Sealy, Corsicana, Golden, and sometimes Serta are the major brands you'll find, along with a wide selection of headboards and beds.

Pillowtop mattress sets (normally $699 at most mall stores) can be had here for as low as $399. If the design or color of the mattress doesn't quite match the box spring, you'll save even more. And, everything is brand-new: A Bed Depot doesn't deal in used or rebuilt merchandise.

Store hours are 10 a.m. to 6 p.m. Monday through Friday and 10 a.m. to 5 p.m. on Saturday.

Best Buy Mattress

- 1950 Highway 85, Jonesboro; (770) 719-9990

This medium-sized store located in a strip center next to J&R Clothing deals in factory-direct clearance items for such major brands as Serta, Corsicana, and Symbol—priced as much as 50 percent off retail. All items are brand-new (no "seconds" or damaged merchandise) and carry full manufacturers' warranties.

On the Cheapster's last visit to Best Buy he spotted an ultra-premium pillowtop Symbol mattress set, complete with a 20-year warranty, for an astounding $499. (The typical retail price for this would be about $1,000.) He also grabbed a few winks on an extra-firm premium set that is sold elsewhere for about $600. Here it was ticketed at $299 and came with a 15-year warranty. Best Buy also carries futons, including frames and mattresses, priced at about $169, and bunk beds are also available at comparable great deals.

Just a word about those warranties, though: mattress warranties are very much like tire guarantees. If something happens to your bed in the first few thousand miles—make that the first year or two—the warranty will give you a reasonable rebate of the purchase price. In the twentieth year of a 20-year promise, a used mattress will probably be worth less than the sheets that are on it. Still, a longer warranty is better than a shorter one or no warranty at all.

Best Buy Mattress keeps their doors open from 10 a.m. to 7 p.m. Monday through Friday, and from 10 a.m. to 6 p.m. on Saturdays. They're closed on Sunday.

Conyers Mattress Outlet

- 1509 Old Covington Road NE, Conyers; (770) 922-3838

Conyers specializes in high-quality, full-warranty mattress sets, made by Sealy, Serta, and Lady Americana, priced at up to 60 percent off standard retail. With 45 to 50 beds on the floor, and a big warehouse out back, you're likely to find a great selection to go with the good deals here.

Conyers' standard prices regularly beat those of full-price competitors by $200 or more per set, and you can take advantage of even greater savings during frequent promotional and discontinued sales. Their most expensive queen set goes for $999, but that particular Lady Americana model has more springs and twice the warranty as a $5,000 equivalent from Stearns & Foster! Middle-range sets are priced in the $299 to $499 range (discounted from $599 and $699). These folks also carry bunk beds and futons ($199 with frame and pad), sold mostly from books and delivered within a week.

In fact, they also sell a lot of dining room and bedroom furniture from books, all with one-week delivery. In fact, you can outfit an entire bedroom for as little as $450.

Located next door to the Sonic Drive-In, Conyers Mattress Outlet is open Monday through Friday from 9 a.m. to 7 p.m., Saturday from 9 a.m. to 6 p.m., and Sunday from 1 p.m. to 5 p.m.

Discount Mattress Zone

- 1014 Iris Drive, Conyers; (770) 483-6580

- 2130 Hamilton Creek Parkway, Dacula; (678) 546-7196

SHOPPING: BEDS AND MATTRESSES

This 2,700 square-foot showroom features mattress sets from Sealy, Stearns, and Restonic, for prices lower than you'll find for these brands at mainstream retailers. You can regularly get $75 to $100 off on a queen-size set, with additional discounts of up to $100 possible using the coupons that Discount Mattress regularly distributes through local newspapers and mailers. An added bonus is that all previous customers get an extra 10 percent off the sale price.

Mr. C spotted a Restonic queen set, usually priced at for $699, for $549. A $100 discount was also reflected on a Sealy King ticketed at $1,199. Futons? They've got 'em: You can have your choice of 6", 8", "jumbo," or innerspring mattresses, matched up with 20 to 25 frames, starting at $129 and ranging on up to $450. Bunk beds are also for sale at $179 to $600. Keep your eye out for coupons that often offer additional discounts of $45 to $100.

Store hours are 10 a.m. to 7 p.m. Monday through Saturday, and Sunday from noon to 6 p.m.

Home Store Futon Gallery

- 1111 Euclid Avenue, Avenue, Atlanta; ✆ (404) 586-9647

- 80 Powers Ferry Road Southeast, Marietta; ✆ (770) 973-1474

A lot of folks think that this is the *only* place to get futons and other quality mattresses. The reason may be that the HSFG focuses on its main product like no place else. In business for nearly 20 years, this place actually makes its own mattresses, priced from $109 to $379, with eight variations to choose from and a lifetime guarantee on construction. After a bit of sleuthing, Mr. Cheap discovered that this establishment actually gets

> ### MR. CHEAP'S PICKS
>
> *Beds and Mattresses*
>
> **A Bed Depot**—With a great selection of brand-new mattress sets from Sealy, Corsicana, Golden, and sometimes Serta at up to 70 percent off, this place is hard to beat!
>
> **The Mattress Firm**—Combine deep discounts (50 percent or more) with the convenience of more than 20 stores in the Atlanta area, and you've got good odds to find a place to sleep.
>
> **Mattress Liquidators**—These folks have built a reputation based on personalized service and great deals. Even through they're a small store, they have an amazingly full range of offerings of "imperfect" items from the big name brands.

a lot of business from sleep-serious customers in Alabama, Tennessee, North Carolina, and elsewhere. Mr. C also perused a number of tasteful and well-constructed bedroom accessory items such as clocks, lamps, tables, shelves, and desks.

Mabelton Mattress Liquidators

- 5584 Mabelton Parkway S.W., Mabelton; ✆ (770) 944-7606

Here's a great mattress store with a personal touch. Owners Richard and Randy Sailors have been running the business for a while now, offering low prices on such major brands as Sealy and Stearns & Foster. The catch here is that the merchandise has small imperfections—slightly scuffed or scratched, labels sewn on wrong . . . you get the idea. (Who's going to notice that stuff under a mattress pad and sheet, anyway?) The upshot is that Richard and Randy can get these at high discounts and offer them to savvy bargain hunters for about a third off the regular retail price.

Store hours are Monday through Saturday from 10 a.m. to 6 p.m.

The Mattress Firm

- 6270 North Point Parkway, Alpharetta; ✆ (770) 410-0007
- 1155 Mount Vernon Highway, Atlanta; ✆ (770) 399-5115
- 3158 Peachtree Road, Atlanta; ✆ (404) 869-0510
- 1757 East-West Connector, Austell; ✆ (678) 945-1000
- Mall of Georgia, 3310 Buford Drive, Buford; ✆ (678) 546-6680
- 1544 Dogwood Drive, Conyers; ✆ (770) 388-0537
- 2442 Pleasant Hill Road, Duluth; ✆ (678) 473-0397
- 955 Barrett Parkway, Kennesaw; ✆ (770) 425-2666
- 875 Lawrenceville Suwanee Road, Lawrenceville; ✆ (770) 237-2337
- 1696 Cobb Parkway, Marietta; ✆ (770) 916-1045
- 1825 Mount Zion Road, Morrow; ✆ (770) 960-0819
- 6410 Dawson Boulevard, Norcross; ✆ (770) 798-9344
- 5448 Dawson Boulevard, Norcross; ✆ (678) 966-0144
- 1195 Woodstock Road, Ste. 900, Roswell; ✆ (678) 461-5744
- 1905 Scenic Highway, Snellville; ✆ (770) 985-3315
- 3630 Peachtree Parkway, Suwanee; ✆ (770) 476-0810
- ✇ www.mattressfirm.com

These guys sell only Sealy and Stearns & Foster products, and they guarantee that they'll beat anybody's price on a Sealy mattress set for sale at any retail competitor. With stores in 39 states, and over 20 locations in the Atlanta area alone, "bigger is better" seems to be the business strategy here: They're the #1 retailer for the Sealy and Stearns brands, and there are over 40 beds displayed on the showroom floor.

They have one sale or another going on all year long here. The Cheapster checked out the store during an "Ultimate Sale" when he was offered savings of up to $200 off Stearns & Foster queen sets. Mattresses generally ranged from $287 on up.

The Mattress Firm also gives you a 30-night trial, and usually offer no-interest financing, which is music to Mr. C's ears. They regularly run coupon-based offers on their Web site and in local papers, offering such deals as $50 off any full mattress set, $75 off any queen set, and $100 off any king set.

Store hours are 10 a.m. to 8 p.m. Monday through Saturday, 10 a.m. to 6 p.m. on Saturday, and noon to 5 p.m. on Sunday.

Mattress Liquidators

- 3106 Buford Highway, Duluth; ✆ (770) 813-0504

This place is a great find for anyone looking for bed products or furniture. In business for eight years, Mattress Liquidators has built a reputation based on personalized service and great deals. Even through they're a small store, they have an amazingly full range of offerings.

SHOPPING: BEDS AND MATTRESSES

In the mattress department, they carry "imperfect" items from most of the big name brands, including Simmons, Serta, and Sealy. These might be items where a label is on backwards or upside down, or perhaps have a scuff or other small cosmetic flaw that most people would never notice. You can pick these up for an incredible half to one-third of normal price, with king sets (including mattress and box springs) ranging from $199 to $599. These are sets that would be selling for $1,400 to $1,600 at mainstream mattress stores just down the road!

The manager says he doesn't get a lot of twins and fulls, so they also have some beds manufactured for them, all of which are brand-new and high quality, at the same super-deal prices.

You'll find plenty of futons here as well. These are high-quality sets, all wood, sometimes with inner springs, starting at $189 to $399. You'll also find brand-new Comfortaire air mattresses with a 20-year warranty at half price of what you'll find at the mall.

This relatively small store is also packed with floor displays of new, tasteful furniture. To save room and keep prices down, they might display one piece of a bedroom group, along with a color photo of the entire set. They pick up merchandise from local distributors, so you don't have to wait weeks for your order. All the furniture is brand-new, in the package, much of it ready-to-assemble. The furniture ranges from the "promotional" variety (made of lower-quality particleboard, tubular steel, imitation brass, etc.) to $10,000 bedroom groups that are available for half price!

Store hours are 10 a.m. to 7 p.m. Monday through Friday, 10 a.m. to 6 p.m. on Saturday. They're closed on Sunday.

Mattress King Discount Sleep Superstores

- 3651 Piedmont Road N.E., Atlanta; ✆ (404) 233-4662
- 1670 Cobb Parkway S.E., Marietta; ✆ (770) 956-7010
- 6470 Dawson Boulevard, Norcross; ✆ (770) 416-8554
- 11007 Alpharetta Highway, Roswell; ✆ (770) 552-0231
- 2277 E. Main Street, Snellville; ✆ (770) 736-8220
- 5220 Highway 78, Stone Mountain; ✆ (770) 469-9704
- 4783 Jonesboro Road, Union City; ✆ (770) 969-3001

You can pick up some pretty regal bedding at Mattress King. These stores specialize in selling major brand mattresses and box springs, with a good selection of styles and firmness, at impressively low prices.

Buying direct from this manufacturer allows the stores to pass savings on to their customers. Mr. C spotted a queen size "Dreamer" bed and box spring set for just $349; to go with it, you may like a four-poster maple bed frame by Leggett & Platt for $399. Other selections at Mattress King include Simmons queen-size mattress for $399 (a $599 retail) and a Serta Perfect Sleeper for $499. All mattress sets include a 10-year warranty and a 30-day comfort trial.

Back on the subject of frames, a brass-plated bed frame was $339 in queen size and $499 in king, while metal twin size headboards for children, painted in red, blue, black, white, and pink, were just $29.99. The "Sweetheart" twin frame, with its pretty scrolled metal headboard, was seen selling for $159. And an ornate oak-finish queen-size Leggett & Platt wood bed frame was $439.

Store hours are Monday through Saturday 10 a.m. to 8 p.m., and Sunday 12 p.m. to 6 p.m.

Rhodes Furniture

- 4370 Peachtree Road NE, #100 (corporate office), Atlanta; ✆ (404) 264-4600
- 3655 Memorial Drive, Decatur; ✆ (404) 289-2136
- 2540 Hargrove Road, Smyrna; ✆ (770) 434-8911
- 4715 Ashford Dunwoody Road, Dunwoody; ✆ (770) 395-1812
- 4363 Northeast Expressway, Doraville; ✆ (770) 934-9350
- 1972 Mount Zion Road, Morrow; ✆ (770) 471-2200
- 114 Pavilion Parkway, Fayetteville; ✆ (770) 719-0856
- 2340 Pleasant Hill Road, Duluth; ✆ (770) 476-1890
- 870 Cobb Place Boulevard N.W., Kennesaw; ✆ (770) 425-4275
- 6050 N. Point Parkway, Alpharetta; ✆ (770) 475-1656
- 1416 Dogwood Drive S.W., Conyers; ✆ (770) 922-9971
- 5955 Stewart Parkway, Douglasville; ✆ (770) 489-5300
- 2338 Henry Clower Boulevard, Snellville; ✆ (770) 972-8289
- ✍ www.rhodesfurniture.com

You don't need to be a Rhodes scholar to know that this place is jam-packed with great values. From mattresses to dinette sets, you'll save plenty here. These students of sleep supply have been in business for more than 125 years; they must be doing something right. In bedding, you'll find Sealy, Stearns & Foster, Jamison, and Simmons.

The last time we checked, if you pay in cash and your order is above $1,000 these guys automatically took 15 percent off the price. They even offered a free bed frame with the purchase of any queen set $599 or above. Pick-up and disposal of old bedding is free with the delivery of new bedding.

El Cheapster thinks their queen-sized sleeper sofas are priced right, too: as low as $699 complete. (Mr. C has seen furniture of similar quality offered for as much as twice that price.) Also for the bedroom, Rhodes was offering Simmons "Slumber Rest" queen mattress and box spring sets for just $599, and the same model set in twin-size for just $399. And a Danish-style bedroom group, with dresser, mirror, chest, and headboard, was almost $100 off retail at $577. Rhodes is also a great place for coffee tables, recliners, daybeds, hutches, and more.

On their nifty Web site (see above), Rhodes provides a specific criteria search in choosing the right bedding, allowing you to roll your own bed, choosing from twin to king, pillowtop to firm, and everything in between.

One of the bonuses about shopping is a 30-day satisfaction guarantee: If you're not happy with your purchase, return it within 30 days for a full refund or exchange, period.

The stores are open from 10 a.m. to 9 p.m. Mondays through Saturdays, and from noon to 6 p.m. Sundays.

Rich's Furniture Clearance

- Cobb Center, 2144 South Cobb Drive, Smyrna; ✆ (770) 433-4790
- ✍ www.richsonline.com

This clearance center sells close-outs, samples, and floor models from the company's many stores around the Atlanta area.

Major brands of indoor and outdoor furniture, as well as bedding, rugs, lamps, and accessories are sold here at reductions of 30 to 50 percent off original retail. To keep things moving, an additional 10 percent is knocked off the price every 45 days, until the item sells.

Some of these pieces are slightly damaged and are sold "as is," but, if you're not too fussy, you can find incredible deals on furniture for every room in the house, and even patio furniture for outdoors. And just like appliances and shoes and almost everything else, within a week or so a "perfect" item looks just like something sold at "seconds" prices.

Mattresses are sold in sets only and are rated in overall firmness and quality as "good," "better," "best," and "top of the line." In full size, these range from $199 for a good set to $369 for better, $449 for best, and $599 for top-of-the-line. Delivery on any item is available for a fee. The store will not hold an item for you, nor does it offer layaway plans.

This clearance center is open the same hours as Rich's Furniture stores: Monday through Saturday from 10 a.m. to 9 p.m., and Sundays 12 p.m. to 7 p.m.

BOOKS

You can save extra money on books by shopping for used editions. Remember, though, that only a brand-new copy of *Mr. Cheap's Atlanta* carries the full blessing and psychic support of the author.

Atlanta is blessed with enough used-book bookstores to give the hungriest bookworm indigestion; several are mixed into the listings below. Save even more by bringing in books that you no longer want. Most stores will give you a choice of cash or in-store credit; you'll usually get a higher figure by choosing the credit. It's a good, cheap way to check out new authors and to keep your library lean.

A Cappella Books

- 1133 Euclid Avenue N.E., Atlanta; ✆ (404) 681-5128.

Looking for an intellectually stimulating book at a no-brainer price? This full-service new, used, and out-of-print bookstore has been located in the heart of Atlanta's bohemian district, Little Five Points, since 1989. They stock up to 30,000 paperbacks and hardcovers, ranging from the common to the quite scarce. Their specialty books reflect the personalities of the funky Little Five Points neighborhood, and to varying degrees, the staff. But don't be fooled—they really have something for everybody who loves books.

A Cappella also prominently features classic works by Southern authors such as Flannery O'Connor and William Faulkner. Mr. C was thrilled to find O'Connor's *The Complete Stories*, listed at $8.95 for the paperback, for just $4.50 in like-new condition. Tom Robbins' *Skinny Legs and All*, listed at $5.95 for the paperback, may be found for $3.

Among the other interesting finds: *Fiction of the Fifties*, with short works by Saul Bellow, James Baldwin, and others, in good shape for $4.95, and *The Andy Warhol Diaries*, listed at $29.95 in hardcover, for $15. Clement Eaton's fascinating hardcover biography of Jefferson Davis could be had for $12 while Taylor Branch's *America in the King Years, 1954–1963* was reduced to $12. There's a good selection of Civil War titles, too.

Store hours are Monday through Thursday 11 a.m. to 8 p.m.; Friday and Saturday from 11 a.m. to 10 p.m.

Atlanta Book Exchange

- 1000 North Highland Avenue N.E., Atlanta; ✆ (404) 872-2665

One of a pair of related bookstores, this outlet specializes in new and used books of a fairly highbrow nature—humanities, history, architecture, and the arts. This store also has hard to find and out-of-print books. Every book in the store is discounted 50 percent because the wily owners take advantage of closeouts, remainders, and overruns of new books

MR. CHEAP'S PICKS

Books

A Capella Books—A huge selection of rare and used books at discount prices.

The Book Nook—Lose yourself in these aisles of secondhand books, CDs, videos, and just about anything related.

Chapter 11—Even if you're filing, you can afford recently remaindered bargain books here. Witty, knowledgeable staff.

This store has a particularly good selection of fine-art books (the oversized, color-plate coffee-table type), such as one on Monet, reduced from an original $75 to a more reasonable $40. And H. W. Janson's *History of Art*, probably known to every college art history student, was recently spotted for just $29.95. Ah, if only you'd thought to look here before going to the campus bookstore!

Not everything at ABE strikes such a scholarly tone. Mr. C also found a copy of Lewis Grizzard's enjoyable *Elvis is Dead and I Don't Feel So Good Myself*, in a used hardcover copy marked down from $11.95 to $5.95.

The store is open Monday through Saturday from 10 a.m. to 10 p.m., and Sunday from noon to 8 p.m.

Atlanta Vintage Books

- 3660 Clairmont Road, Chamblee, GA 30341; ✆ (770) 457-2919

- ✍ www.abebooks.com/home/AVB/

This awesome establishment made Mr. C's head spin when he considered its 60,000 titles in nearly every conceivable genre, including modern first editions, religion and philosophy, travel and exploration, civil war, military, juvenile series, children's illustrated, decorative covered Victorian books, Modern Library, Americana, and more. They also have African tribal art and antiquities and illuminated manuscripts.

They're open 10 a.m. to 6 p.m. Monday through Saturday, but you can also get in after hours by appointment.

Barnes & Noble Booksellers

- 2900 Peachtree Road, N.W., Atlanta; ✆ (404) 261-7747
- 7660 North Point Parkway, Alpharetta; ✆ (770) 993-8340
- 4776 Ashford Dunwoody Road, Dunwoody; ✆ (770) 393-9277
- 2952 Cobb Parkway, Atlanta; ✆ (770) 953-0966
- 120 Perimeter Center West, Atlanta; ✆ (770) 396-1200
- Southlake; 1939 Mount Zion Road, Morrow, ✆ (770) 471-2227
- Gwinnett Place Mall, Fayetteville Square, 1415 Highway 85 North; ✆ (770) 716-7640
- 2205 Pleasant Hill Road, Duluth; ✆ (770) 495-7200
- 50 Ernest W. Barrett Parkway, Marietta ✆ (770) 422-2261
- 1415 Highway 85 N., Fayetteville; ✆ (770) 716-7640
- 3333 Buford Drive, Buford; ✆ (678) 482-4150
- ✍www.bn.com

Mr. C not only writes books, but he can read, too. In fact, he is rarely seen without his nose in a book. And though he loves the quirky and wondrous charms of independent bookshops, sometime you just can't beat a national chain for great buys *and* selection. Hey, they have cozy lounge chairs for on-the-spot research, poetry readings, story times for children, author and book signings, creative writing workshops, and book groups tailored to some very specific interests and backgrounds. Books on the *New York Times* bestseller list are sold at 30 to 40 percent off the cover price.

Some stores even have cafes or coffee shops. All in all, B&N provides a relaxed and refined setting. You can make it an evening out, especially if there is a music event.

You can locate nearby stores on the company's Web site, and if you burrow down a bit further to the store listings you'll find a listing of many local events at the stores. Of course, you can always call for schedules.

You can join Barnes & Noble Readers' Advantage for $25 a year, which offers members a 10 percent discount on everything in-store and a 5 percent discount on merchandise purchased online, and that's on top of already discounted prices. If you're an avid book buyer, you'll more than make up for your investment.

Special ordering at B&N is a breeze, and B&N's own publishing house offers classic hardcovers in easily readable print at super savings. Their edition of Thoreau's *Walden,* for example, is only $4.98; same deal for titles like *Jane Eyre* and many other great works of literature. And any art lover will appreciate B&N's *The History of Art,* an oversized, glossy edition bargain-priced at $24.98.

B&N also usually has a bargain section where you can get more super deals than in most other bookstores in town. The Cheapster recently picked up some new hardcovers at great prices: Stephen King's *The Girl Who Loved Tom Gordon* was only $5.98, Anne Rice's *The Vampire Armand* was just $7.99, and Michael Crichton's *Timeline* was tagged at $7.99. P.J. O'Rourke's *Eat the Rich* was on sale for an amazing $4.98, and Deepak Chopra's *The Wisdom Within* was priced at a cheap $6.98.

Store hours are Monday through Saturday 9 a.m. to 11 p.m., and Sundays 9 a.m. to 9 p.m.

B. Dalton Booksellers

- Lenox Square Shopping Center, 3393 Peachtree Road N.E., Atlanta; ✆ (404) 231-8516

- 24 Peachtree Street S.W., Atlanta; ✆ (404) 577-2525

- Gwinnett Place Mall, 2100 Pleasant Hill Road, Duluth; ✆ (770) 476-8742

- Perimeter Mall, 4400 Ashford Dunwoody Road, Dunwoody; ✆ (770) 394-4185

- Town Center Mall, 400 Ernest Barrett Parkway Kennesaw; ✆ (770) 425-2817

- Northlake Mall, 4800 Briarcliff Road, Northlake; ✆ (770) 934-9292

- Cumberland Mall, 1317 Cumberland Mall Road, Smyrna; ✆ (770) 435-3297

Barnes and Noble now owns B. Dalton, which operates mostly as a smaller version of the larger stores in malls. Each location tailors their stock to fit their customers' needs. However, you get the same discounts here as you do at the Barnes & Noble superstores.

Be sure to check out the bargain table. Among the remainders and closeouts scoped out by El Cheaperoonie is the *Rodale Illustrated Encyclopedia*, brought to you by the people who publish *Prevention* magazine, at the reduced price of just $14.98. He also spotted *The American Heritage Picture History of World War II* for $19.99.

Store hours at B. Dalton generally coincide with those of the malls. However, hours may vary according to location, and hours are usually extended later during the holiday shopping season in November and December.

Beaver's Book Sale

- 696-A Cleburne Terrace, N.E., Atlanta; ✆ (404) 876-1068

The flip side to Atlanta Book Exchange, Beaver's has a larger variety of more pop-oriented subjects. This shop gets lots of closeouts on recent fiction and nonfiction, plus used books, so that at least a third of the shop's offerings are under $4.

You can get 60 to 90 percent off the price of most of the books in the store, plus there's lots of stuff for various hobbies and activities, such as cooking and gardening. A range of Chilton's car repair guides, including books for older model years, were available at $3 to $12 each. You'll also find cheap tomes on business, travel, and software, as well as lots of children's classics, note cards, and classical CDs—all for bargain prices.

Mr. C found an almost-new hardcover copy of Sebastian Junger's *The Perfect Storm* for only $6.95. Tony Hillerman's acclaimed Navajo novel, *Listening Woman,* was selling for just $3.25, and John Nance's *Pandora's Clock* could be had for $3.50. There are special $1 sections with older major titles, plus shelves and shelves of used paperback mysteries and science fiction, selling for half the cover price. Even comic books, same deal!

Located on the tiny side street that runs between the Majestic Diner and the Plaza Center, this Beaver is busy from 11 a.m. to 10 p.m. six days a week, plus Sundays from noon to 8 p.m.

The Book Nook

- 3342 Clairmont Road N.E., Atlanta; ✆ (404) 633-1328

- 6569 Church Street, Riverdale; ✆ (770) 994-3444

SHOPPING: BOOKS

- Rosswell Road at Cobb Parkway, Marietta; ✆ (770) 499-9914
- Highway 29, Lilburn; ✆ (770) 564-9462

Mr. C has seriously been considering pitching a tent at the Book Nook, or perhaps living out of his vintage VW bus in the store's parking lot. Why? This is simply one of the most incredible stores any book or music lover could ever hope for. These folks sell, buy, and trade used books, comic books, books on tape, videos, DVDs, records, tapes, and CDs. They've got so much of everything (more than 10,000 used CDs at the main Atlanta shop), they had to expand from their original Clairmont Road location and open three more stores just to hold all the stuff. Perhaps best of all, they're open late every day of the week, presumably because it's so hard to stop browsing and leave.

The book section, about two-thirds of the store, is a homespun warren of shelves from floor to ceiling. Rolling stools, those little round ones you see in libraries, are used more as a place to perch and read than for actually climbing. Unlike libraries, or any other bookstore for that matter, books are strewn throughout the aisles like the droppings of bookworms. Curiously, only one aisle is kept neat as a pin: the one for serial romances. Here, new and used paperbacks are arranged in catalog order, by series: Harlequin, Bantam, Silhouette, and all the rest. Amazing.

Used paperbacks are generally sold at 40 percent off the cover price. Used hardcovers are marked on the inside, with even greater reductions. Hardcovers are in the minority here, though there are still quite a few. Most are recent and in very good condition. Magazines and new books are not discounted.

With more than 300,000 used books and 10,000 used CDs at the main Atlanta shop, Mr. C easily spotted plenty of recent and not-so-recent bestsellers (including the wonderful but very-outdated previous edition of this tome!) as well as tons of computer how-to manuals. He saw lots of new and used children's books too, like *The Phantom Tollbooth* for only $1.80.

Book Nook is also a haven for comic book fanatics, both for its selection of the latest releases. There are no discounts on new comics, but they sell the pre-owned models at either 50 cents or half price each, randomly mixed for maximum browsing potential.

You can also sell your old books, comics, videos, and music, depending on condition and market demand; you may get a better deal if you choose what the store calls "universal credit," good on anything in the store, new or used, except new magazines. Or, better still, consider swapping, which the store will do in almost any medium.

The store has been around since 1973. In the early 1990s they began opening up their other locations, including the Book Nook II in Lilburn, focusing primarily on the music side of things, with nearly 30,000 records, tapes, CDs, and videos. Note also that the Marietta store has no records or comics.

Store hours for the Atlanta location are 9 a.m. to 10:30 p.m. Monday through Saturday, and 10 a.m. to 10:30 p.m. on Sunday. The Lilburn store keeps its doors open from 10 a.m. to 8 p.m. six days a week, and noon to 6 p.m. on Sunday. Riverdale's hours are 11:30 a.m. to 7:30 six days, and 1 p.m. to 7:30 p.m. on Sunday. In Marietta, you'll find the store open from 10 a.m. to 8 p.m. seven days a week!

Borders Books & Music

- 3637 Peachtree Road N.E., Atlanta; ✆ (404) 237-0707
- 650 Ponce de Leon Avenue N.E., Atlanta; ✆ (404) 607-7903
- 1605 East-West Connector Road, Austell; ✆ (770) 941-8740
- 1705 Mall of Georgia Boulevard, Buford; ✆ (678) 482-0872
- 6594 Douglas Boulevard, Douglasville; ✆ (770) 577-9787
- 3555 Gwinnett Place Drive, Duluth; ✆ (770) 495-4043
- 4745 Ashford-Dunwoody Road, Dunwoody; ✆ (770) 396-0004
- 605 Ernest W. Barrett Parkway, Kennesaw; ✆ (678) 581-1243
- 8000 Mall Parkway, Lithonia; ✆ (678) 526-2550
- 4475 Roswell Road, Marietta; ✆ (770) 565-0947
- 1929 Scenic Highway, Snellville; ✆ (770) 982-0454
- 3101 South Cobb Drive S.E., Smyrna; ✆ (770) 612-0940
- ✍ www.borders.com

Another major book chain that needs no introduction, Borders regularly offers sales on hundreds of the typical 80,000-plus titles on hand at each location, ranging from poetry to medieval history to "Esoteric Studies." They also offer a large selection of music CDs, videos, kids books, author events, and an extensive collection of foreign language magazines and out-of-town newspapers. (Just for the record: The Borders Group is the parent company of Waldenbooks.)

There are plenty of deals to be had here, including 30 percent off the current bestseller list, all the time. In addition to that nice little perk, your head will spin from the other specials that rotate from day to day. The last time Mr. C strolled into the store, selected recently published computer books were marked down 30 percent, and a large selection of music CDs were available for just $8.99. VHS movies were offered at 50 percent off with the purchase of two others at regular prices, and they were offering a "three for two" sale on Dr. Seuss titles.

While you're almost always guaranteed good savings at Borders, the bargain books section is definitely a bonus. On a recent visit, pictorials on Claude Monet and Frank Lloyd Wright were available in the $4 to $9 range, *Life* magazine historical pictorials were priced at $5.99, and beautiful hardcover cookbooks that usually sell for $50 when first published were priced $5 to $7. A Wayne Gretzky biography was only $4, and a number of formerly bestselling hardcover novels could be had for $5 each. Lots of children's books were priced at $2 to $5.

And speaking of kids, Borders has plenty of additional deals for them, such as $5 off the next purchase after buying ten children's books. Also, remember that Borders' in-store events, which include author readings and book signings, cater to the younger set as well: Children's book characters—or at least people who dress up like them—such as Barney the Dinosaur, Peter Rabbit, and even Harry Potter, make occasional appearances for book readings.

Borders has a number of membership programs that can save you even more money: All teachers can get 20 percent off any book, and corporate accounts can get big discounts on bulk purchases.

SHOPPING: BOOKS

Most Borders locations are open Monday through Saturday from 9 a.m. to 11 p.m., and Sunday from 9 a.m. until 10 p.m., though specific store hours may vary.

Chapter 11 Books: The Discount Bookstore

- Ansley Mall, 1544 Piedmont Avenue N.E., Atlanta; (404) 872-7986

- Briarcliff Village, 2 100 Henderson Mill Road N.E., Atlanta; (404) 414-9288

- 2091 North Decatur Road, Atlanta; (404) 325-1505

- 2345-A Peachtree Road, Atlanta; (404) 237-7199

- 3509 Northside Parkway, Atlanta; (404) 841-6338

- 10945 State Bridge Road, Alpharetta; (770) 667-0023

- 1910 Highway 20 South, Suite 80, Conyers; (770) 761-0161

- 1210 Thompson Bridge Road NE, Gainesville; (770) 535-6699

- Highland Plaza, 3605 Sandy Plains Road, Marietta; (770) 971-0744

- 2900 Delk Road, Marietta; (770) 984-1449

- 885 Woodstock Road, Suite 300, Roswell; (678) 461-0650

- 6237 Roswell Road, Atlanta; (404) 256-5518

- Snellville Plaza Shopping Center, 2280A Highway 78, Snellville; (770) 736-0502

If you don't act responsibly, you could go broke shopping at Chapter 11 stores. All books here are sold at 11 percent off the cover price at all times; reductions are taken at the register. This reduction doesn't apply to their drastically reduced remainders, but these are so cheap (most hardcover novels are in the $5 range) that you'd hardly notice. *New York Times* bestsellers, like *Band of Brothers* by Stephen E. Ambrose, are always slashed 30 to 40 percent off the list price!

Many of the books on the discount table are remainders and overstocks and may be a couple of years old, but they're also up to 75 percent off. Chapter 11 stacks and shelves even these closeout books neatly, keeping them in good shape. This is one bookstore that gets kudos from Mr. C for organization!

The staff members at Chapter 11 Books tend to be voracious readers themselves, specializing in of out-of-the-mainstream books; be sure to check out their "Recommended Reading" displays to get ideas from their personal favorites. To give you an idea of just how much these folks enjoy reading, Mr. C would like to point out that there is even a "Recommended Book of the Day." Now, that's serious!

All Chapter 11 Books locations are open Monday through Saturday from 10 a.m. to 9 p.m., and Sunday from 12 p.m. to 6 p.m., with some exceptions, so call ahead.

Old New York Book Shop

- 660 Spindlewick Drive, Atlanta; (770) 393-2997

- www.gaba.net/oldny.htm

If you have a fetish for rare and collector's editions, you'll want to check out Cliff Graubert's Old New York Book Shop, which he runs out of his home in Dunwoody. You can't just pop in, however: You'll first need to make an appointment to peruse his collection of more than 7,000 rare and scholarly hardcover books, which specializes in modern first editions, economics, art, literature, history, music, and Southern and African-American literature. Mr. C recommends that you first do some homework by checking out Graubert's spiffy Web site, from which you can search for your desired tome by title, author, publisher, key words, and binding.

CDs, RECORDS, TAPES, AND VIDEOS

You can save extra money on music by shopping for used items. Like used book shops, many of the stores below will allow you to trade in music you no longer want. Alas, they won't take just anything; used LPs, in particular, have become less marketable except to collectors. Most stores will give you a choice of cash or in-store credit; you'll usually get a higher figure by choosing the credit. It's a good, cheap way to check out artists you might not take a chance on at full price.

Barnes & Noble Booksellers

- The Peach, 2900 Peachtree Road N.E., Atlanta; (404) 261-7747
- 7660 North Point Parkway, Alpharetta; (770) 993-8340
- 4776 Ashford Dunwoody Road, Dunwoody; (770) 393-9277
- 2952 Cobb Parkway, Cumberland; (770) 953-0966
- 120 Perimeter Center West, Suite 300, Perimeter; (770) 396-1200
- Southlake; 1939 Mount Zion Road, Morrow; (770) 471-2227
- Gwinnett Place Mall, Fayetteville Square, 1415 Highway 85 North, Duluth; (770) 716-7640
- 2205 Pleasant Hill Road, Duluth; (770) 495-7200
- Town Center Prado, Marietta; (770) 422-2261
- 50 Ernest W. Barrett Parkway, Marietta; (770) 422-2261
- www.bn.com

Mr. C hates to start this section with a store that everyone already knows about, and one that is mainly known for books! Still, it's his duty to emphatically note that B&N isn't just for books any more. Indeed, most B&N superstores these days have entire sections devoted to music CDs (from classical to folk to show tunes to rock) and videos. You'll always save a few bucks on new releases here. You can join Barnes & Noble Readers' Advantage for $25 a year, which offers members a 10 percent discount on everything in-store and a 5 percent discount on merchandise purchased online (www.bn.com), and that's on top of already discounted prices.

Store hours are Monday through Saturday 9 a.m. to 11 p.m., and Sundays 9 a.m. to 9 p.m.

The Book Nook

- 3342 Clairmont Road N.E., Atlanta; (404) 633-1328
- 6569 Church Street, Riverdale; (770) 994-3444
- Rosswell Road at Cobb Parkway, Marietta; (770) 499-9914
- Highway 29, Liburn; (770) 564-9462

SHOPPING: CDs, RECORDS, TAPES, AND VIDEOS

Mr. C has already extolled the wonders of this store under "Books," but it deserves its own mention here in the music aisle. These folks sell, buy, and trade used books, comic books, books on tape, videos, DVDs, records, tapes, and CDs.

Like the books here, used music makes up a great deal of the business. Used records and compact discs, in particular, offer almost as much selection as any full-price store; yet CDs are priced at 99 cents to $8.49, with double CDs priced up to $12.99. Used LPs are generally $2.50 to $4.50, depending on their condition. There is also a good selection of (new) books, magazines, and even sheet music covering everything from rock to Broadway.

There are plenty of used video movies on VHS tapes, with lesser quantities in DVD format. Browse around and you'll spot top titles like *E.T, A Passage to India, American Beauty, Almost Famous,* and many others. VHS tapes are almost all priced at $4.99 to $8.99, while DVDs are priced in the $10.99 to $13.99 range.

Store hours for the Atlanta location are 9 a.m. to 10:30 p.m. Monday through Saturday, and 10 a.m. to 10:30 p.m. on Sunday. The Lilburn store keeps its doors open from 10 a.m. to 8 p.m. six days, and noon to 6 p.m. on Sunday. Riverdale's hours are 11:30 a.m. to 7:30 six days, and 1 p.m. to 7:30 p.m. on Sunday. In Marietta, you'll find the store open from 10 a.m. to 8 p.m. seven days a week.

Borders Books & Music

- 3637 Peachtree Road N.E., Atlanta; (404) 237-0707
- 650 Ponce de Leon Avenue N.E., Atlanta; (404) 607-7903
- 1605 East-West Connector Road, Austell; (770) 941-8740
- 1705 Mall of Georgia Boulevard, Buford; (678) 482-0872
- 6594 Douglas Boulevard, Douglasville; (770) 577-9787
- 3555 Gwinnett Place Drive, Duluth; (770) 495-4043
- 4745 Ashford Dunwoody Road, Dunwoody; (770) 396-0004
- 605 Ernest W. Barrett Parkway, Kennesaw; (678) 581-1243
- 8000 Mall Parkway, Lithonia; (678) 526-2550
- 4475 Roswell Road, Marietta; (770) 565-0947
- 1929 Scenic Highway, Snellville; (770) 982-0454
- 3101 South Cobb Drive S.E., Smyrna; (770) 612-0940
- www.borders.com

Borders is another major book chain that also offers a large selection of music CDs and videos. The last time Mr. C strolled into the store, he noted that a large selection of music CDs were available for just $8.99, and VHS movies were offered at 50 percent off. It's hard to beat that.

Most Borders locations are open Monday through Saturday from 9 a.m. to 11 p.m., and Sunday from 9 a.m. until 10 p.m., but specific store hours may vary.

CD Warehouse

- 2280 Peachtree Road, Atlanta; (404) 351-7005
- 2997 Cumberland Circle S.E., Atlanta; (770) 803-9947
- 3550 Highway 138 S.E., Stockbridge: (678) 289-9140

- 3605 Sandy Plains Road, #150, Marietta; (770) 509-0588

- 50 Barrett Parkway, #1240, Marietta; (770) 425-3472

- 2180 Pleasant Hill Road, #B14, Duluth; (770) 623-1552

- www.cdwi.com

This national chain features about 10,000 CDs for $8.99 or less, which is music to Mr. C's enlarged ears, and they also offer discounts of up to 75 percent on DVDs and games! As if the everyday low prices weren't enough (and they're never enough for El Cheaperino), CD Warehouse also offers a free CD Card that lets you earn a free CD for every ten CDs, DVDs, or games you buy.

CD Warehouse also offers an "Advantage Card" that gives you $1 off every CD, DVD, or accessory, and $2 off every boxed set, double CD, or video game.

Listening stations are set up around the massive sales floor where you can check out any of the CDs before you buy. If in some amazingly rare instance these folks don't have the CD you're seeking, they'll take a special order and promise to have the object of your attention in-house within three days!

They also give you up to $5 of cold, hard American cash for your used CDs, games, and DVDs, or let you trade them in for new product. Amazingly, they also fix scratched CDs for a minimal charge—sometimes while you wait.

Everything in the store has a seven-day guarantee: If your CD is scratched, skips, or has some other flaw (other than you're tired of listening to the music), the store will refund your money as long as you still have the receipt.

Store hours vary by location but are generally Monday through Saturday from 11 a.m. to 10 p.m., and Sunday from noon to 6 p.m.

Circuit City

- 4512 Memorial Drive, Decatur; (404) 299-2001

- Cumberland Mall, 968 Cobb Pkwy SE, Smyrna; (770) 955-6866

- Southlake Mall, 1906 Mount Zion Road, Morrow; (770) 210-6670

- 365 The Landing Drive, Douglasville; (770) 947-7197

- 3850 Venture Dr, Duluth; (770) 476-8172

- 1185 Ernest W Barrett Pkwy NW, Kennesaw; 770) 590-8544

- 6290 N Point Pkwy, Alphareta; (770) 664-0395

- 200 Big Shanty Rd, Marietta; (770) 420-2561

- 2940 Old Norcross Rd, Duluth; (770) 564-9000

- 225 Chastain Meadows Ct NW; Kennesaw; (770) 425-6480

- www.circuitcity.com

You probably don't need Mr. C to tell you about megastores like this, but Circuit City can certainly save you some bucks on music, the equipment to play it on, and more. After all, the chain's vast product line includes TV, VCR, DVD, camcorders, car stereo, home stereo, computers and home office products, CDs, tapes, and cellular phones.

Circuit City's low-price guarantee insures that they'll match any lower price for the same item advertised in newspapers, flyers, and on radio or TV. So if you prefer not to take the "used" route to save money on CDs, cassettes, and videos, this is a good place to consider.

Circuit City always offers about 40 of the top CDs for $11.99 each. They also regularly price a substantial rotating selection of older releases at just $8.99. Mr. C was able to pick up The Who's *The Millennium Collection* and Eric Clapton's *Time Pieces* with his last remaining $20. Long live rock and roll!

Of course, Circuit City is also "DVD Central," with lots of popular movies usually available for less than $20. The last time the Cheapster cruised the aisles he noticed *Bridget Jones's Diary* priced at $17.99, with *The Mummy Returns* and *A Knight's Tale* both available for only $19.99.

Need something to play those DVDs on? Circuit City can save you money there as well, with a selection of name-brand players priced in the $99 range.

Store hours are 10 a.m. to 9 p.m. Monday through Saturday, and 11 a.m. to 6 p.m. Sunday.

Circuit City Express

- 3393 Peachtree Rd N.E. # 4110, Atlanta; ✆ (404) 812-1799

The Cheapmeister thinks of this establishment as a "mini-Circuit City." It has a great CD and DVD selection, as well as all of the deals and policies as Circuit City, but without a lot of additional computers and electronic equipment sold in the big stores.

Hours are 10 a.m. to 9 p.m. Monday through Saturday, and noon to 6 p.m. on Sunday.

Corner Compact Disc

- 1048 North Highland Avenue, Atlanta; ✆ (404) 875-3087

- ✎ www.cornercd.com

> **MR. CHEAP'S PICKS**
>
> ### CDs, Records, and Tapes
>
> **Eat More Records**—One of the best local music selections around, at affordable prices.
>
> **Wax 'n' Facts**—A great place for suitably cheap CD and cassette selections in jazz, classic rock, soul music, reggae, dance (like hiphop and techno), indie classic rock, new rock, gothic industrial, free jazz, R&B, and folk.
>
> **Wherehouse Music**—Although this chain doesn't have the atmosphere of the other, smaller shops, this is good bet for huge selection at competitive prices. From country to jazz to world beat, Wherehouse Music will most likely have your target tunes.

This Virginia-Highland treasure vault of music has a huge selection of both national and local artists and is one of Mr. C's favorite places just to hang out while browsing and checking out new tunes at the plentiful listening stations scattered around the store. All genres are represented here, and Corner seems to have hit on the right formula for balancing a great selection of the big-name artists with a varied and informed stock of more obscure offerings. The combination of this setup and their knowledgeable staff makes this a great place to discover new music.

Store hours are Monday 10:30 a.m. to 9 p.m., Tuesday through Thursday 10:30 a.m. to 10 p.m., Friday and Saturday 10:30 a.m. to 11 p.m., and Sunday 11 a.m. to 7 p.m.

Criminal Records

- 466 Moreland Avenue N.E., Atlanta; ✆ (404) 215-9511

It's a crime that other stores don't offer bargains as good as those The Cheapmeister found at Criminal Records, a fantastic store smack dab in the middle of Little Five Points. This store has moved and doubled its size since the last time we checked it out.

This is the place for hard-to-find import CDs, arranged with impeccable organization. New CDs are priced at $14.99 and used CDs range between $7.50 to $8.50. The majority of the CDs are rock with some country thrown in, but there are also are some hip-hop, dance, and jazz selections.

Criminal's security system (kinda funny to say, isn't it?) is another way the store keeps prices low. Each CD is displayed for customers in a glass case and the staff will take them out of the case if customers are interested, foiling would-be shoplifters—an expensive problem for many stores.

The store has a listening system with a huge database that stores songs that Criminal Record calls free samples. There are three listening posts where customers can listen to any song for 60 seconds, including new releases.

Criminal Records also has a pretty large collection of new and used DVDs, ranging in price from $19.99 to $76.99, with used DVDs stickered between $9.99 and $17.99.

Another addition is the large selection of comic books, and they even sell toys to go along with the comics. They also have one of the largest selections of magazines Mr. C has ever seen–you name it, they've got it, from boogie boards to tattoos to fashion. Some of the publications are from major publishers and others are amateur 'zines.

Store hours are Monday through Saturday 10 a.m. to 10 p.m., and Sunday noon to 7 p.m.

Earwax Records

- 1052 Peachtree Street N.E., Atlanta; ✆ (404) 875-5600
- ✍ www.earwaxrecords.com

Mr. C wouldn't want to belong to any club that would have him as a member. Still, every time he checks out Earwax he feels like he's part of a very exclusive membership just because the incredibly knowledgeable and enthusiastic staff here make him feel so welcome and so…well, worthy. They not only help find the best CDs, but also love to talk about music.

Visiting Earwax is kind of like hanging out in your best friend's den, except that they have a great selection—everything from Tony Bennett to Jennifer Lopez, and they have great prices: as low as $7 for new CDs; $2 to $5 for used.

Earwax is open Monday through Saturday from noon to 8 p.m.

Eat More Records

- Carter Rockbridge Shopping Center, 1210 Rockridge Road, Suite K, Norcross; ✆ (770) 717-8111

You can show your good taste by shopping at Eat More Records, located across from Green's Corner. In business for some 22 years, this is one of those little shops where the sales staff seems to be as happy to talk about music as they are to sell you copies. If you are interested in upcoming music concerts, check the posters displayed in the window.

Eat More Records carries new and used recorded music in just about every genre. They've got imports, mostly new, like Beta Band and Radiohead, for $11.99 to

$24.99 and some used imports for $5.99 to $11.99.

The store's collection of CDs consists of almost everything: folk, country, rock, R&B, oldies, jazz, world beat, and soundtracks. New CDs are priced at $11.99 to $17.99; used merchandise at $6.99 to $8.99. EMR has a very large selection of LPs, including collectibles (check out EMR on Ebay and Gemm.com) that range from $4.00 to $75.00, as well as new LPs, depending on whether they are import or domestic range, from $10.99 to $24.99,

Still hungry for more vinyl? EMR has about 20,000 45s (that's a lot of 45s), both original labels and reissues, which are priced $2.50 and up. Tasty!

You can shop more hours at Eat More Records, too, since they're open seven days a week: 11 a.m. to 9 p.m. Monday through Friday, 10 a.m. to 9 p.m. Saturday, and noon to 7 p.m. Sunday.

Full Moon Records

- 1653A McLendon Avenue N.E., Atlanta; ✆ (404) 377-1919

Seemingly out of nowhere, in the midst of this quiet Candler Park neighborhood one mile east of Little Five Points, you come upon a block of funky storefronts —like an enclave that somehow is frozen in the Sixties. Among these is Full Moon Records, a secondhand shop that manages to pack a lot into its tiny space. They carry just about every genre—rock 'n roll, jazz, rap, world beat, R&B, reggae, folk, country, classical, soundtracks, even some opera and new age music!

The pricing couldn't be much better, whether your musical find is new or used, with many CDs priced around $7.99. Unless marked otherwise, all LPs are under $10.00, with many available for a measly buck. Cassettes are $3.99 each and all compact discs are $7.99 each.

The store also boasts several discount bins with albums for $1 and CDs for $3 that are just fun to browse through, and prices can't be beat. In fact, the same can be said of the store in general.

Hours are noon to 8 p.m. Tuesday through Saturday, and noon to 6 p.m. on Sunday. They're closed on Mondays.

Target

- 2400 North Druid Hills Road, Atlanta; ✆ (404) 325-3211
- 3535 Peachtree Road N.E., Atlanta; ✆ (404) 237-9494
- 2201 Cobb Parkway S.E., Smyrna; ✆ (770) 952-2241
- ✐ www.target.com

In his never-ending quest for good deals, Mr. C is not averse to dipping deep into the bubbling caldron of lowbrow Americana, even to the extent of taking his aging minivan over to that millennial icon of budget-minded consumerism: Target. Sure, the whole place is oh-so-middle-of-the-road, but you can't knock their CD sales. New releases normally priced at $14.99 are often stickered as low as $11.88 during weekly sales. Mr. Cheap found classic CDs like B.B. King's *Greatest Hits* available for as little as $7.99.

Store hours are 8 a.m. to 10 p.m. seven days a week.

Tower Records

- Lenox Shopping Center, 3400 Wooddale Road N.E., Atlanta; ✆ (404) 264-1217
- ✐ www.towerrecords.com

Open until midnight every single day of the year, Tower is the place to run to if the baby won't stop crying and you think that playing a Frank Sinatra song just might put him to sleep, or if you've just got to have *Liberace's Greatest Hits* at 11:59 p.m.

Tower's top-selling CDs, (based on the top 25 in store sales) are always discounted about 35 percent off list price. Newer releases, rising up the charts, also tend to be marked down—usually to about $13.99 for CDs and $11.99 for cassettes. And be sure to check the cut-out bins, where overstock music is always drastically reduced. You can usually find all varieties of music represented, from Patsy Cline to Fleetwood Mac to P. Diddy. The store also stocks a bowling-alley-lane-long aisle of magazines, from *Sassy* to *Spin*.

Tower opens at 9 a.m. for early risers. You may experience limited hours on Thanksgiving, Christmas, and New Year's Day holidays, when the store closes at 10 p.m. instead of midnight.

Wax'n'Facts

- 432 Moreland Avenue N.E., Atlanta; ✆ (404) 525-2275

Not for the claustrophobic, or the hearing-aid crowd, this funky storefront is great place for used and new CDs and cassettes in jazz, classic rock, soul music, reggae, dance (like hip-hop and techno), indie classic rock, new rock, gothic industrial, free jazz, R& B, and folk. If it's not mentioned here, give them a call, because they probably have it somewhere or can get it for you. Used CDs are priced between $5 and $8, with used cassettes stickered for $3.50 to $5.50. New CDS are $9.50 to $20, and new cassettes are $5.50 to $11.50.

Still into vinyl? They also have a large selection of used LPs, with some collector's items priced at $3.50 and up.

This is also one of the better places in town to try if you're looking to find releases by local bands. If you can wend your way through the crowded aisles to the back corner of the store, you'll find new sampler and full-length CDs by local artists. Mr. C found titles from groups including White Lights, Jennifer Nettles Band, and Oscelot, priced between $5 and $12.

Wax 'n' Facts also sells T-shirts priced between $15 and $20, stickers around $2, and posters (mostly rock but there are some jazz rock posters too) all priced between $6–$10. They're also selling books, mostly biographical rock. And lastly, they've added DVDs and videos priced below list price.

Store hours are 11 a.m. to 8 p.m. Monday through Saturday, and noon to 6 p.m. on Sunday. Since this store is located in Little Five Points, on the same street as Criminal Records, Mr. C recommends you visit them both in one fell swoop.

Wherehouse Music

- 1057 Ponce de Leon, Atlanta; ✆ (404) 898-9441

- 1531 Piedmont Road, Atlanta; ✆ (404) 607-1609

- 2099 Peachtree Road; Atlanta; ✆ (404) 605-7132

- 1496-A Church Street, Decatur; ✆ (404) 371-0981

- 1380 Veterans Memorial Highway S.W., Mableton; ✆ (770) 941-0898

- 4614 Memorial Drive, Decatur; ✆ (404) 294-0129

- 2980 Cobb Parkway South, Atlanta; ✆ (770) 951-8026
- 4800 Briarcliff Road N.E., Atlanta; ✆ (770) 939-9030
- 5480 Peachtree Industrial Boulevard, Chamblee; ✆ (770) 455-6133
- 6235 Roswell Road N.E., Atlanta; ✆ (404) 255-9406
- Perimeter Mall, 4400 Ashford Dunwoody Road, Atlanta; ✆ (770) 395-6228
- 1073 Mount Zion Boulevard, Morrow; ✆ (770) 961-7535
- 4790 Jonesboro Road, Union City; ✆ (770) 969-1360
- 1211 Powder Springs Road, Marietta; ✆ (770) 514-3900
- 150 Banks Crossing, Fayetteville; ✆ (770) 461-4111
- 400 Ernest W Barrett Parkway, Kennesaw; ✆ (770) 423-0365
- 2100 Pleasant Hill Road, Duluth; ✆ (770) 495-0090
- 3625 Satellite Boulevard, Duluth; ✆ (770) 623-0064
- 2471 E Main Street, Snellville; ✆ (770) 972-8393
- 1680 Highway 138 SE, Conyers; ✆ (770) 483-8410
- 1027 Maple Street, Carrollton; ✆ (770) 830-6500
- ✉ www.wherehousemusic.com

Mr. C doesn't care for the trend toward music megastores; they have none of the quirky charms of individual shops. But Wherehouse Music is hard to beat for great buys—especially during a sale. Rock is the language primarily spoken here, but you can also find a good selection of soundtracks, easy listening music, and jazz.

At Wherehouse the top 20 CDs are always on sale and all DVDs are on sale for 20 percent off. Plus, every Tuesday you can trade in five used CDs for a new one.

Store hours are Monday through Friday 10 a.m. to 9 p.m., Saturday 10 a.m. to 10 p.m. and Sunday 11 a.m. to 7 p.m.

Wuxtry Records

- 2096 North Decatur Road, Decatur; ✆ (404) 329-2000
- 197 E. Clayton Street, Athens; ✆ (706) 369-9428
- ✉ www.wuxtryrecords.com

"Wuxtry, wuxtry, wuxtry" cried the old-time newsboys on the corner. They were talking about "extra" editions with hot news, but they could have been talking about the range of offerings at Wuxtry, a venerable music story hereabouts.

Mr. C likes the bunches o'bargains to be had at North Decatur Plaza—Rainbow Foods. Chickibea's consignment clothing, and not to be left out, Wuxtry Records. Specializing in Athens and Atlanta-based bands (such as R.E.M.), CDs, LPs, and collectible vinyl, the shop is crammed with a large selection of new and used LPs and CDs, and carries a wide range of genres, including rock, R& B, jazz, folk, easy listening, classical country, and soundtracks. Used LPs are priced at 50 cents and up and used CDs are $3 and up. New LPs are priced at $7.99 and up and new CDs are $8.99 and up. Plus, you'll find good prices on music by local artists $6.99 and up.

Wuxtry's open from 11 a.m. to 8 p.m. Monday through Saturday and Sundays from noon until 6 p.m.

CAMERAS AND PHOTOGRAPHIC SUPPLIES

Cameras and photographic supplies can present a real shopping challenge for the savvy shopper seeking the absolute best deal on a specific piece of equipment. Not only can the technology itself be complicated, but prices shift constantly due to advances in technology, the relative strength of the dollar against Asian currencies since most cameras come from that part of the world, and a highly competitive market. There's also a very healthy and constantly changing market in quality used equipment. All that makes locking down a "guaranteed best" price very difficult indeed!

Heck, you don't even have to go to an actual camera store anymore to find your dream unit at a great price! Cameras are increasingly available in a wide range of mass merchandisers such as Best Buy and Target, and at major pharmacy chains such as Eckerd and CVS.

The good news is that the many factors affecting the camera and photo-supply market makes it possible for you to find a good deal, especially on high-quality used equipment, at just about any reputable camera store, the best of which Mr. C has included in this section. He's shied away from listing too many specific prices here, since the range of choice and price even from one day to the next can make your head spin! By all means, take any prices listed here as proverbial "snapshots in time," provided only to give you a sense of what's possible.

Word of warning: Atlanta is loaded with places where you can get good deals on photographic equipment. However, some are as far below repute as they are below retail. Since camera and photo supplies are often imported from foreign countries, there is a greater possibility of shady deals, or inferior quality.

One of the best ways to protect yourself, if you have doubts as to any store's reliability, is to ask about their guarantee policy; make sure the item you want carries an American warranty. Since some stores deal directly with manufacturers in the Far East, their merchandise many carry a foreign warranty instead. Even for identical products, a foreign warranty can make repairs a hassle. Remember, you are perfectly within your rights to inquire about this in the store.

Camera Bug

- 1799 Briarcliff Road N.E., Atlanta; ✆ (404) 873-4513

- ✍ www.camerabug.com

This store in the Sage Hill shopping center, on the Atlanta/DeKalb border near Emory University, is a good place to search for new and used cameras and lenses.

Of course, the used photo-supply market is constantly changing, so what's available can change on an hourly or even daily basis. Mr. C has been offered basic SLR cameras priced at $150. If you could find the same camera new, it would cost as much as $250. Meanwhile, the salesman was willing to make the Cheapster a special deal at $125.

At the other end of the tech spectrum, you can save a bundle on film and processing with a range of new digital cameras from Olympus, Canon, and Pentax, available here at competitive prices. During The Cheapster's last spot check he found a 2.1 megapixel model for only $289. These guys are also big into telescopes and telescope accessories, which range in price from $169 to $16,000!

Camera Bug is open Monday through Friday from 9 a.m. to 6 p.m., and Saturday from 10 a.m. to 4 p.m.

Camera Country USA

- 270 Hilderbrand Drive, Sandy Springs; (404) 256-2595

- www.cameracountryusa.com

Just off of Roswell Road, and just north of the Perimeter, Camera Country USA offers solid values on a wide selection of new and used cameras and flashes. The store is not as huge as the name might suggest, but Mr. C found their stock of used cameras particularly impressive.

Camera Country carries Canon, Minolta, Olympus, and Pentax models (no Nikon) as new merchandise, and just about any major brand in their used camera department. They also carry both Bogen (high end) and Velbon tripods, a large selection of frames (including custom framing), darkroom supplies (including paper, chemistry, enlargers, and the like), camera accessories, and books.

The real deals can be found in Camera Country USA's very extensive selection of quality used equipment, which they classify as "Like New," "Excellent," "Good," and "Average." Would you like to own an "excellent" condition Nikon for under $300? You can probably make that deal here, since a wide range of bodies, lenses, and flashes can be had for up to 75 percent off their original retail prices. As Mr. C's piano teacher used to say, "It's all in the timing, honey."

You can better your deal even further by bringing in your older photography gear to sell or trade. Camera Country USA will buy, sell, and trade used equipment, as well as sell used equipment on consignment. For the enterprising photographer looking to upgrade on the cheap, the possibilities are nearly limitless!

Camera Country USA is open from 9:30 a.m. to 6:30 p.m. Monday through Friday, and from 10 a.m. to 5 p.m. on Saturday.

CompUSA Superstore

- 3400 Around Lenox Road NE, Atlanta; (404) 814-0880

- 124 Perimeter Center W, Atlanta; (770) 393-2980

- 3400 Woodale Drive NE, Atlanta; (404) 814-0880

- 3845 Powder Springs Road, Powder Springs; (770) 943-3312

- 380 North Point Circle, Alpharetta; (770) 754-0955

- 2201 Cobb Parkway SE, Smyrna; (770) 952-1042

- 3825 Venture Drive, Duluth; (770) 813-1420

- 1915 Mount Zion Road, Morrow; (770) 960-2660

- www.compusa.com

One doesn't usually think of this computer superstore in regard to cameras, but when it comes to the latest digital models, this is a great resource. In fact, most CompUSA stores feature a great selection of digital cameras and camcorders at competitive prices. Here Mr. Cheap found a Nikon CoolPix 775 2.1 megapixel camera for $399, a Kodak DX 3600 Zoom 2.1 megapixel model for $299, an Olympus D-510 2.1 megapixel unit for $399, and a SiPix SC-1300 1.3 megapixel model for just $80. There are plenty of other models available as well.

The stores are open weekdays and Saturdays from 9 a.m. to 9 p.m., and Sundays 11 a.m. to 6 p.m.

KEH Camera Brokers

- 2310 Marietta Boulevard N.W., Atlanta; (404) 892-5522
- www.keh.com

This is one of America's largest used camera dealers, and while you can't walk into their Midtown location to shop, Mr. C thinks you should know about this underrated mail-order company. They sure do know their stuff, and they carry a truly amazing selection of merchandise, with brands from Bronica to Hasselblad to Mamiya and Pentax represented.

All cameras and lenses sold by KEH are graded by degree of wear. Codes range from "new" and "new demo" on new cameras, to used models tagged as "excellent plus," and "like new," all the way to "bargain" and even "ugly." Mr. C doesn't especially recommend the cameras categorized as "ugly," since these could be damaged enough to affect the quality of your photos; let's face it, there is such a thing as being too cheap.

Some of the better deals found among the astounding selection on their Web site include a Nikon N2020 body in "excellent-plus" condition for $199, a Leica R4S body classified as "bargain," to a Vivitar new camera with a USA warranty priced at $199. KEH offers a 14-day "no hassle" return policy and two-month warranty on all its used equipment. The company also vigorously solicits used equipment and trade-ins, which may be a further way to save yourself some money, and they have a large repair department that will quote you prices 24 hours a day, 7 days a week.

Call KEH or check their Web site for more info.

MR. CHEAP'S PICKS

Cameras

Camera Country USA—This awesome place offers competitive new camera prices and selection, plus a very extensive selection of quality used equipment. Would you like to own an "excellent" condition Nikon for under $300? You can probably make that deal here.

KEH Camera Brokers—Okay, this is a mail-order place, but it *is* based in Atlanta, and it offers an astounding selection of cameras, lenses, and supplies, including used equipment that can't be beat!

Showcase, Incorporated—The exceptionally knowledgeable salespeople here will tailor advice to your abilities and your pocketbook. The store stocks both new and used cameras and lenses in everything from point-and-shoot to advanced SLR styles and digital models.

Showcase, Inc.

- 2323 Cheshire Bridge Road N.E., Atlanta; ✆ (404) 325-7676

- ✍ www.showcaseinc.com

Located near the Tara movie theater, this place is run by exceptionally knowledgeable salespeople who tailor advice to your abilities and your pocketbook. The store stocks both new and used cameras and lenses in everything from point-and-shoot to advanced SLR styles and digital models. They also have lots of books and accessories.

And the place also runs a university of photography classes and rents out professional studios and darkroom facilities.

New cameras and equipment are priced competitively. They carry the full line of Nikon and Canon equipment, as well as some other makers. Showcase also carries the latest digital camera models from Canon, Nikon, and Olympus.

Film prices here rival those at many other discounters. All told, they carry nearly 200 types of film. Hard-to-find photo mailers in a variety of sizes are also for sale.

The darkroom department includes a full line of chemicals from Kodak and other makers.

Showcase is open from 9 a.m. to 6 p.m. Monday through Friday, and from 10 a.m. to 5 p.m. Saturdays. It's closed on Sundays.

Target

- 2400 North Druid Hills Road, Atlanta; ✆ (404) 325-3211

- 3535 Peachtree Road N.E., Atlanta; ✆ (404) 237-9494

- 2201 Cobb Parkway S.E., Smyrna; ✆ (770) 952-2241

- ✍ www.target.com

Yes, this well-known discount department store also carries a full range of cameras and camcorders of both the conventional and digital variety. Mr. C priced a Vivitar 35mm zoom for just $79.99, an Olympus Accura View model for just $148, a FujiFilm FinePix A101 digital model for just $179.99, and a Kodak 3.1 megapixel camera with 3x digital zoom for about $300.

Store hours are 8 a.m. to 10 p.m. seven days a week.

Wolf Camera & Video

- 150 14th Street N.W., Atlanta; ✆ (404) 892-1707

- 231 Peachtree Street, Atlanta; ✆ (404) 614-1766

- 1196 N Point Circle, Alpharetta; ✆ (770) 442-0513

- 8725 Roswell Road, Atlanta; ✆ (404) 252-0893

- 2460 Cumberland Parkway S.E., Atlanta; ✆ (770) 434-9940

- 3333 Buford Drive, Buford; ✆ (678) 482-1749

- 1910 Highway 20 S.E., Conyers; ✆ (770) 785-7291

- 3170 Highway 278 N.W., Covington; ✆ (770) 786-2295

- 2050 Lawrenceville Highway, Decatur; ✆ (404) 325-1034

- 2109 N. Decatur Road, Decatur; ✆ (404) 325-7709

- 805 Glynn Street South, Fayetteville; ✆ (678) 817-6563

- 4850 Sugarloaf Parkway, Lawrenceville; ✆ (770) 822-6990

- 4000 Five Forks Trickum, Lilburn; ✆ (770) 925-9776

- 1000 E. Piedmont Road, Marietta; ✆ (770) 565-7109

- 1325 Johnson Ferry Road, Marietta; ✆ (770) 977-9182

- 2154 Roswell Road, Marietta; ✆ (678) 560-2204
- 663 Holcomb Bridge Road, Roswell; ✆ (770) 587-4318
- 688 Holcomb Bridge Road, Roswell; ✆ (770) 587-0974
- 4002 Highway 78 West, Snellville; ✆ (770) 985-6383
- ⌕ www.wolfcamera.com

Don't be afraid of a big, bad chain like Wolf Camera. (Actually, it's a chain within a chain, now owned by another national company, Ritz Camera.) From serious high-end to everyday point-and-shoot cameras, plus film, developing supplies, photo albums, and processing itself, you can huff and puff your way around town but will have a hard time finding better values than here.

Kodak film, for example, is nice and cheap in general, and we've been offered a "buy three rolls, get one free" deal on 24-exposure rolls of Kodacolor ASA 200 film.

Professional-grade equipment includes Leicas. For consumers there are Canon, Minolta, Nikon, and Pentax film cameras plus cutting-edge digital cameras, camcorders, lenses, binoculars, and telescopes.

On one check by Mr. C, he spied a Pentax ZX-30 with a Quantray 28-89mm zoom for $269.95 and a Canon EOS Rebel 2000 kit for $349.95. He also noticed a Minolta Freedom Zoom 150EX QD camera package, including free film processing for a year, for just $250.

Optical and video equipment are available here at competitive prices: Bushnell 10 × 50 binoculars start at just $44.95, while 7 × 35 binocs start at only $29.95. A Panasonic PV-IQ203 camcorder costs $700, and Sony camcorder packages—complete with filters, three videotapes, a head cleaning tape, and a Sunpak "Readylite 20" video light kit—start at $800.

In the digital department, the photo-Cheapster noticed a Nikon 2.1 megapixel Coolpix 775 Zoom digital model for under $400 and a FujiFilm FinePix A101 digital model for about $180.

Want to produce your own digital home movies? The Canon ZR-25MC mini DV camcorder that La Cheapito spotted could get you off on the right track. A rebate offered that day produced a final, out-of-pocket price of about $750, including free DV tape for a year. What's more, the bargains on DV camcorders will no doubt be even better by the time you read this.

Ritz regularly offers clearance sales on selected cameras, which means you can save even more. Recently their offerings included a Pentax Efina 35mm camera for under $130, a Nikon Lite Touch 110 QD zoom auto-focus for under $150, and a new Ricoh 35mm for under $100.

Wolf Camera stores are open seven days a week. The main location in Midtown (14th Street) is open weekdays from 8:30 a.m. to 6:30 p.m., Saturday from 10 a.m. to 5 p.m., and Sundays from 12:30 p.m. to 5:30 p.m.

CARPETING AND RUGS

If you're talking about carpets—in the Atlanta region or anywhere else in the entire you-nighted states—you've got to talk about Dalton, which calls itself the Carpet Capital of the World.

Whitfield County includes more than 150 carpet factories and about 100 outlet stores for products that range from home and office

SHOPPING: CARPETING AND RUGS

floor coverings to rugs that cover baseball and football fields and more bath mats than you could shake a plunger at.

Although it's not a bad drive to northwest Georgia, you can also get some pretty good deals around Atlanta. Here Mr. C has focused on a select group of lesser-known outlets that day-in and day-out will provide you with exceptionally good deals and service, whether you're looking for Oriental and Persian rugs, commercial-grade carpeting, or a plush, comfy floor covering for your home.

Antique City

- 5180 Peachtree Industrial Boulevard, Atlanta; ✆ (770) 458-7131

This delightful emporium, conveniently located just off I-285, is a 15,000-square-foot space, of which a full 3,000 square feet is dedicated to fine rugs. Mr. C shops here for both rugs and antiques. (See the listing in the *Antiques and Gifts* section.)

Antique City is a great shopping experience, with over 100 dealers selling high-quality Oriental and Persian rugs, as well as jewelry, books, magazines, stained glass, collectibles, home furnishings, and other quality merchandise.

The store holds sales at least twice a year—usually spring and fall—where all the dealers get together to offer their merchandise at discount. You'll also find seasonal and holiday sales here, so get on their mailing list or give them a call.

Overall, you'll find it hard to beat Antique City's wining combo of selection and value. Store hours are 10 a.m. to 6 p.m. Monday through Saturday, and noon to 5 p.m. on Sunday.

Bijar Oriental Rugs

- 1929 Peachtree Road N.E., Atlanta; ✆ (404) 351-0013

This 3,000-square-foot store always seems to be busy, and it's no wonder, since the owner has been building a loyal clientele since 1982 by offering good values on one-of-a-kind handmade rugs from Iran, Turkey, India, Afghanistan, Russia, and elsewhere. Ticketed at $400 and up, we wouldn't call the merchandise here cheap, but it's of rare and unique quality. What's more, Bijar typically hold sales around holidays such as Christmas. Prices are open to negotiation, and you'll most likely be able to get 20 percent off the tag price by just walking in the door. (Mentioning this book wouldn't hurt, either.)

Located across the street from Piedmont Hospital, store hours are 10 a.m. to 6 p.m. Monday through Saturday.

Canco

- 230 Northside Drive S.W.; Atlanta; ✆ (404) 588-0426

How's carpet at about $1 per linear foot sound? Mr. C happened upon this incredible place after his minivan blew a tire across the street on the way back from a game at the Georgia Dome. Since that fateful day he has never shopped for carpeting without stopping here.

Here's a company that takes good advantage of some of the major trade shows that come to Atlanta and other big convention cities. For a few days, thousands of visitors trudge from booth to booth along temporary ribbons of carpet; the major booths themselves are also appointed with rugs.

Canco buys these young carpets from conventions. The carpet is mostly in excellent condition, tends to be in large pieces (up to 12 feet by 50 feet), and can be cut to size.

Here you can pick up a 9' × 10' piece of top-quality plush pile for about $20. Pieces in white and black are the most popular, and are usually a little more expensive, but even they still work out to about $1.25 per linear foot.

These guys also carry ceramics and other floor coverings at cheap prices—and those items are brand-new. You can get a 6' × 9' piece of linoleum for $20, while vinyl wood runs about $35 for a 10' × 10' area.

Canco's hours are easy to remember: They're open from 9 a.m. to 9 p.m. seven days a week.

Carpet Liquidators

- 5168 Georgia Highway 85, Forest Park; ✆ (404) 762-8663
- 3437 Sexton Woods, Drive, Chamblee; ✆ (770) 451-7513

After visiting Carpet Liquidators, you may find yourself sprawled on a plush bed of recycled Coke bottles! Honest!

In business for over 25 years, this owner-operated warehouse and showroom has built a loyal clientele with their personalized service and low prices. Thanks to low overhead, the owners are able to sell you carpets at prices that average 20 to 40 percent off retail, at prices ranging from $2.99 a yard to $20 a yard! And, their large warehouse and substantial on-premises inventory means they can load up the old minivan with just about anything you need—on the spot. On Mr. C's last foray into this fuzzy world, good Berber was going for $3.99 a yard, and room-sized remnants were priced from $69.

Okay, here's the deal on the Coke bottles: Carpet Liquidators sells a high-tech, 70-ounch plush carpet made out of a material called P.E.T., which (you guessed it) is made out of recycled plastic. It looks, wears, and feels as good as any nylon carpet available anywhere, with about 50 colors available, at prices ranging from $4.99 to $11.99 a yard! Makes Mr. C thirsty just thinking about it . . .

Both Carpet Liquidator stores are open Monday through Saturday from 10 a.m. to 5 p.m.

Color Tile and Carpet

- 6204 Roswell Road N.E. #10, Atlanta; ✆ (404) 256-2331
- 2131 Pleasant Hill Road, Duluth; ✆ (770) 495-9222

The massive Color Tile Corporation that used to, uh . . . *cover* the U.S.A. with company stores was dissolved in 1997. In its place are privately owned businesses that carry on the Color Tile name, set their own prices, and have their own sales. Other than the name, the two important things that haven't changed are the thousands of colors and textures available and the abundance of good values on brand-name carpeting. Both Atlanta-area Color Tile stores offer frequent sales throughout the year and like to promote their "everyday low prices."

And the prices are indeed competitive: Saxony carpets, treated with Scotchguard, were seen here at $18 a yard, or at $40 a yard for their softest, most plush version. All prices included padding and installation. Multicolor Berbers were priced in the same range. The Color Tile staff can help you find the right carpet for any room in your home, and there's always an impressively wide selection of designer colors, patterns, and styles. Of course, both local stores also offer factory-authorized flooring sales on all other types of floor coverings.

SHOPPING: CARPETING AND RUGS

The Atlanta store hours are 9 a.m. to 6 p.m. Monday through Friday, 10 a.m. to 5 p.m. on Saturday, and 11 a.m. to 5 p.m. on Sunday. The Duluth store is open from 10 a.m. to 6 p.m. every day except Sunday.

The Consignshop

- 2899-A North Druid Hills Road, Atlanta; ✆ (404) 633-6257
- 4920 Roswell Road Suite 10, Atlanta; ✆ (404) 531-0303

This store looks more like a boutique than a consignment shop, and it has done so well in recent years that they've opened another shop and a children's store too.

Mainly known for its men and women's clothing (see the listing in the *clothing* section), the shops have added a home decorative department, which includes rugs at 20 to 75 percent off retail.

The store openly accepts consignments on a 50/50 split, but only takes items that are in excellent condition.

The Consignshop is open weekdays and Saturdays from 10 a.m. to 6 p.m., staying open until 8 p.m. on Thursday evenings.

Park Avenue Rugs

- 3609 Roswell Road N.E., Atlanta; ✆ (404) 262-0544

Park Avenue imports so many Oriental rugs that they actually wholesale them to other stores. You, meanwhile, can shop here too, at the same wholesale prices. They carry a good variety of sizes from runners to 8 × 11-foot carpets at far from Park Avenue (New York, that is) rates.

All carpets are handmade and are 100 percent pure wool. Persian 8 ×11 carpets start at $900. Imported rugs of the same size from China, India, and Pakistan

MR. CHEAP'S PICKS

Carpeting and Rugs

Carpet Liquidators—Thanks to low overhead, the owners are able to sell you carpets at prices that average 20 to 40 percent off retail, at prices ranging from $2.99 a yard to $20 a yard.

Canco—This great resource offers a large selection of high-quality carpeting that's been used only for a few days at local trade shows. Here you can pick up a 9′ × 10′ piece of top-quality plush pile for about $20.

79th Street Rug Shop—This is the place to go if you're into quality antique and new Persian rugs, with prices 30 percent or more below those you'd find elsewhere.

start at $700, and Tibetan versions start at $600. Park Avenue Rugs does not carry any synthetic fiber rugs.

Park Avenue also sells old and antique rugs, specializing in repair and cleaning.

Store hours are Monday through Saturday 10 a.m. to 6 p.m. and Sunday noon to 5 p.m.

Tuesday Morning

- 3145 Piedmont Road N.E., Atlanta; ✆ (404) 233-6526
- 4502 Chamblee Dunwoody Road, Dunwoody; ✆ (770) 457-3565
- 901 Montreal Road, Tucker,: ✆ (770) 934-3164
- 2790 Cumberland Boulevard S.E., Smyrna; ✆ (770) 435-6678

- 1115 Mount Zion Road, Morrow; ✆ (770) 961-0707
- 736 Johnson Ferry Road, Marietta; ✆ (770) 971-0511
- 6325 Spalding Drive, Norcross; ✆ (770) 447-4692
- 4051 Highway 78, Lilburn; ✆ (770) 978-3573
- 700 Sandy Plains Road, Marietta; ✆ (770) 428-1536
- 1231 Alpharetta Street, Roswell; ✆ (770) 640-8146
- 3500 Satellite Boulevard, Duluth; ✆ (770) 476-0522
- 3600 Dallas Highway N.W., Marietta; ✆ (678) 355-5505
- ✍ www.tuesdaymorning.com

We all know how much better Tuesday mornings are compared to Mondays. TM's bargains will make you feel that much better, since they offer a 50 to 80 percent "everyday" discount on upscale merchandise found in better department stores. Selections range from room and area rugs to luxury linens, fine crystal, china, decorative accessories, lawn and garden accents, gourmet cookware and housewares, luggage, toys, and seasonal decorations or gifts.

Tuesday Morning can save you a lot of money on quality rugs since they buy direct from manufacturers and artisans from all over the world. Whether you're interested in factory-made major brands or colorful and artistic handmade selections, you'll find a wide selection of 100 percent wools, hand-hooked 100 percent cottons, acrylics, and machine-woven polypropylenes.

Store hours are Monday, Tuesday, Wednesday, and Friday from 10 a.m. to 7 p.m., Thursday from 10 a.m. to 8 p.m., Saturday from 10 a.m. to 6 p.m., and Sunday from noon to 6 p.m.

Westbury Carpet One

- 6409 Jimmy Carter Boulevard, Norcross; ✆ (770) 449-0150
- 4361 Roswell Road, Marietta; ✆ (770) 971-1969

It's hard to beat the deals and selection you'll find at this full-service, full-range store. In business for 25 years, these rugmeisters have built a large and loyal customer base of folks who like a one-stop shop for carpets, runs, as well as other floor coverings such as ceramic and vinyl tiles.

Westbury holds sales all year long (they also hit the usual retail holidays such as Labor Day Columbus Day, and Presidents' Day). However, you don't have to rely on an act of Congress in order to find everyday good deals—especially on the in-stock inventory. The last time Mr. C checked, he found in-stock Berber and a cut pile for just $7.49 a yard. They were offering Saxony from $7.99 to $12.99 per yard, and had a very impressive selection of remnants, starting at $29 for a 12 × 8-foot piece.

If you're planning on buying some wall-to-wall for the entire house, you should be aware that Westbury offers frequent financing sales that defers any interest or payments for a year or more. Hey, that's music to C's ears!

Both of Westbury's stores are open Monday and Friday from 9 a.m. to 8 p.m., Tuesday through Saturday from 9 a.m. to 6 p.m., and Sunday from 1 p.m. to 5 p.m.

79th Street Rug Shop

- 2823 Peachtree Road N.E., Atlanta; ✆ (404) 231-2108
- ✍ www.79thstreetrugshop.com

If you're looking for high-quality Persian or oriental rugs, you're going to love this place. For the past 20 years they've specialized in one-of-a-kind antique and semi-antique Persian rugs, as well as handwoven *new* Persian design specimens, from suppliers across several continents. All these are available at great values, often at 30 percent below the prices you'd find for the same kind of rugs elsewhere. Hand-loomed cotton rag rugs begin at $65 for a 3 × 5-foot piece, and run up to $445 for a 9 × 12. Hand-loomed dhurries are priced from $235 to $585. They have even better deals on close-outs, which include discontinued patterns and those with small flaws.

79th Street (the shop, that is) is open from 10 a.m. to 6 p.m. Monday through Friday, and from 10 a.m. to 5 p.m. on Saturday.

CLOTHING—NEW

A Welsh proverb says that clothes are two-thirds of beauty. In Mr. Cheap's case, they may be the whole thing. On Mrs. C, though, handsome clothing enhances her natural beauty. But what really gets Mr. and Mrs. C going, if you know what I mean, are spectacular deals on glad rags.

Clothes, like anything else, are sold at discount for many reasons. Let's quickly go over some basic terms.

With new merchandise, "first-quality" means perfect clothing with no significant flaws, as you would find in any full-price store. Such items may be reduced in price as a sales promotion, because they're left over from a past season, or because too many were made (or too few were sold). Some stores are able to discount first-quality clothing simply through high-volume selling and good connections with wholesalers. "Discontinued" styles are leftovers from past seasons or models that have been superseded by new products; these products are usually new and still perfectly good.

"Second-quality," sometimes called "irregulars," "seconds," or "IRs," are new clothes that have some slight mistakes in their manufacture, or that have been damaged in shipping. Often, these blemishes are hard to find. Still, a reputable store will call your attention to the spot, either with a sign near the items, or a piece of masking tape directly on the problem area.

If you're not sure whether you're looking at a first or a second, go ahead and ask!

The other important secret to clothes shopping is to buy off-season. Look for swimsuits after Labor Day. Atlantans who have discovered the joys of snow skiing should also learn to shop for parkas and boots around Easter.

MEN'S WEAR—GENERAL

Better Menswear

- 4515 Fulton Industrial Boulevard, Atlanta; ✆ (404) 696-1680
- 3435 Writesboro Road, Augusta; ✆ (706) 733-6722
- 2303 John Glenn Drive, Chamblee; ✆ (770) 457-8992
- 2121 Brownbridge Road, Gainesville; ✆ (770) 534-7685
- 1311-A Mount Zion Road, Morrow; ✆ (770) 968-3966
- 4879 Memorial Drive, Stone Mountain; ✆ (770) 296-1401
- ✍ www.bettermenswear.com

This is Mr. C's kind of place, featuring an awesome assortment of quality dress and casual men's clothing at low prices that you're going to be hard-pressed to find at other stores. A family-owned company for four generations, Better Menswear runs its own factories in the United States and Costa Rica, allowing it to sell wholesale to the public, usually under the Barry's label. Here you'll find silk and cotton shirts for as low as $14, and a great assortment of quality suits and tuxes for just $99. Sports coats usually start at about $79 but were on sale for only $39.99 on the day the Cheapster checked in.

Looking for some classy dress shoes to top off your wardrobe? You'll find them here starting at $39.99, with high-end Fatellis at $79 and up. Sweaters are also a bargain starting at $29.99. Also on hand here are tux shirts, hats, belts, jewelry, cufflinks, and other accessories.

Store hours are Monday through Wednesday and Saturday from 9 a.m. to 6 p.m., Thursday from 9 a.m. to 7 p.m., Friday from 9 a.m. to 9 p.m., and Sunday from noon to 5 p.m.

Clayton Big & Tall Men's Clothing

- 5400 Jonesboro Road, Morrow; ✆ (404) 363-3618

Attention all you NFL and NBA players—and other big guys who just sit and watch. Here's a place where you can find a good selection of "big & tall" clothing at lower prices than you'd find in a typical chain store—and the stuff is actually stylish! Clayton carries suits from such brands as Palm Beach and Harmony & Shepherd, and shirts from Cambridge Hall, Arrow, Salmon River, and others. This combination of name brands and great values provides a refreshing alternative to the typical big-guy place, which tends to

---

> **MR. CHEAP'S PICKS**
>
> *Clothing—New Men's Wear—General*
>
> **Better Menswear**—Better Menswear runs its own manufacturing facilities in the United States and Costa Rica, allowing it to sell an awesome assortment of quality dress and casual men's clothing at low prices.
>
> **Freedman Men's Shoe Outlet and Suits**—It's hard to go wrong at this store/warehouse specializing in quality goods at about 70 percent off typical mall prices!
>
> **Men's Wearhouse**—This place features such brands as Yves Saint Laurent, Ralph Lauren, Oscar de la Renta, and Givenchy at 15 to 20 percent off the regular prices.

SHOPPING: CLOTHING—NEW

pump up the price tags along with the sizes.

You won't find sale events here. The owners prefer to focus on offering everyday low prices. There are, though, preferred customer incentives including frequent 20 percent-off sales and $50-off bonuses earned from previous purchases. The staff is small and friendly, lending a personal touch.

Suits run from $249 to $399 and shirts start at $27.

Store hours are Monday through Saturday from 10 a.m. to 8 p.m., and Sunday from noon to 5 p.m.

D & K Discounters

- 1735 Defoor Place N.W., Atlanta; ✆ (404) 355-7675

- 635 George Luther Drive, Decatur; ✆ (404) 508-1445

Here you'll find everyday low prices that amount to 30 to 70 percent of typical retail prices, bolstered by special sales that always keep the shopper's costs down. What more could you want?

See the full description under *Men's and Women's Wear—General.*

Freedman Men's Shoe Outlet and Suits

- 1240 Chattahoochee Avenue N.W., Atlanta; ✆ (404) 355-9009

- 5025 Memorial Drive, Stone Mountain ✆ (404) 297-4309

Freedman is a super shoe and clothing store/warehouse specializing in quality goods at about 70 percent off typical mall prices. Within is 10,000 square feet filled with suits, shirts, leather clothing, hats, ties, and more—just about everything you could possibly need for dress and casual wear.

Here you'll find business suits by Falcone and other major brands starting at just $99. Dress shirts from Stacy Adams and Lucasini can be had for just $14.99 and up. When Mr. C goes for a hip and stylish look, he looks for deals like this one: a quality leather jacket for a measly $79.99.

Freedman also carries a wide assortment of slacks, jeans, leather, sweaters, and pants, as well as a prodigious assortment of fine linen clothing.

So what about the shoes? That's where Freedman really excels, and where the store does a huge amount of business. You'll find Giorgio Brutini dress shoes, as well as exotic varieties (alligator, ostrich, and lizard) in the $150 to $700 range. Keep in mind that the store offers all of these at a substantial discount from what you'd find in a specialty store downtown: a $500 pair of alligators would be priced at around $1,200 at most shoe retailers. Can you imagine Mr. C coming home to Mrs. C wearing $600 on each foot?

The Atlanta store is open Monday through Thursday from 10 a.m. to 6 p.m., Friday and Saturday from 10 a.m. to 7 p.m., and Sunday from noon to 6 p.m. The Stone Mountain outlet is open Monday through Wednesday from 11 a.m. to 7 p.m., Thursday through Saturday from 11 a.m. to 9 p.m., and Sunday from 9 a.m. to 6 p.m.

Men's Wearhouse

- 3255 Peachtree Road N.E., Atlanta; ✆ (404) 264-0421

- 2931 Cobb Parkway, Atlanta; ✆ (770) 956-7297

- Northlake Mall, 1000 Northlake Mall, Atlanta; ✆ (770) 908-1125

- Perimeter Expo, 1121 Hammond Drive N.E., Atlanta; (678) 320-0960

- Southlake Festival, 1510 Southlake Parkway, Morrow; (770) 960-8490

- Fayette Pavilion, 145 Pavilion Parkway, Fayetteville; (770) 719-1662

- Landing at Arbor Place, 9330 The Landing Drive, Douglasville; (678) 838-3145

- Mall Corners, 2131 Pleasant Hill Road, Duluth; (770) 623-6060

- Town Center Plaza, 425 Earnest Barrett Parkway, Kennesaw; (770) 429-8955

- Target Plaza, 6012 North Point Parkway, Alpharetta; (770) 521-1002

- www.menswearhouse.com

As important as clothing is to Mr. C's global image, he's certainly not going to waste any money on the effort. That's why Men's Wearhouse is one of his favorite places. Buying in *big* lots for its 11 stores lets these guys sell top names like Yves Saint Laurent, Ralph Lauren, Oscar de la Renta, and Givenchy at 15 to 20 percent off the regular prices. This place was known as a suit store for the last 25 years, but has in recent years diversified its product line and is offering more selection in the "business casual" category.

Here you'll find first-quality, current fashions at 15 to 20 percent off retail. There's not a heck of a lot here for smaller-sized or really big guys; but it you're an "average size," the stock is plentiful. The suits lean toward conservative, classic styles.

Mr. C found out that the lesser known Vito Rufolo brand sold here, made by the same company that makes Perry Ellis dress shirts, with retail list prices of $55, sold for just $35 here. Shirts from brands like Damon, Adolfo, John Clarendon, and Pattinni were also priced in the $20 to $30 range.

The vast selection of ties is worth a trip all by itself. They're offered in 100 percent silk from County by the Sea starting at $22.99. Lizard-skin belts were about $29, and Kenneth Cole socks are always $5 off retail.

Men's Wearhouse is open Monday through Friday from 10 a.m. to 9 p.m., Saturday from 9:30 a.m. to 6 p.m., and Sunday from noon to 6 p.m.

WOMEN'S WEAR—GENERAL

Arthur's Ladies Sportswear

- 1710 DeFoor Place N.W., Atlanta; (404) 355-2832

Arthur is a real "ladies man," at least when it comes to quality women's clothing at great prices. Don't miss this place if you're looking for something fancy, like the "embellished look" in a two-piece pant or skirt set and related separates. Arthur's sells first-quality designer clothing for women, sizes 8 to 12, at anywhere from 40 to 60 percent off retail. The store doesn't limit itself to a particular set of vendors, so their merchandise is constantly changing. They say they are more concerned with looks than labels.

Arthur's has been around for about a decade-and-a-half and has prospered without print advertising, relying on word-of-mouth for its success. Mr. C says you have to shop this store to see the value, and while you are there ask Arthur him-

SHOPPING: CLOTHING—NEW

self to explain what he calls "legitimate comparables." This is a guy who actually cares about making first-quality clothing affordable.

Store hours are Thursday through Saturday from 10 a.m. to 6 p.m.

Cato

- 7155 Highway 85, Riverdale; ✆ (770) 996-4616

- 5232 Memorial Drive, Stone Mountain; ✆ (404) 297-7020

- 4919 Flat Shoals Parkway, Decatur; ✆ (678) 418-9396

- 5656 Jonesboro Road, Morrow; ✆ (678) 422-6719

- 5590 Mableton Parkway S.E., Mableton; ✆ (770) 739-8001

- 3865 Highway 138 SE., Stockbridge; ✆ (770) 507-8616

- ✍ www.catocorp.com

This is a good place for low-priced, good-quality women's clothing in classic styles and the latest trendy looks. Regular, misses, and plus-sizes are all well stocked.

On the afternoon that Mrs. C dragged hubby out on an expedition, they found chenille sweaters, listed at $32 retail, priced at only $19.99. Cotton jeans were just $29. A fancy pleated rayon dress by Applause, in a floral print, was available for $66. Similar dresses go for over $100 in the malls.

For misses, Cato had Ponte knit skirts and pants, normally $18 to $20 retail, for just $11.99.

On our various visits, the Cato Plus section of the store featured items like a drop waist, long-sleeved dress with a label by Kathie Lee (y'know, Gifford) for Plaza South Plus, for $75.

There is also a footwear section. Doc Marten-lookalike boots, made in the Etc. by Cato label, were just

> ### MR. CHEAP'S PICKS
>
> *Clothing—New*
> *Women's Fashions*
>
> **Midtown Designer's Warehouse**—Here you'll find high-fashion women's clothing at 30 to 60 percent off typical retail prices.
>
> **Natalie's Bridals**—Don't put the father of the bride—or yourself—deep in debt as you go to the altar. Weddings don't have to break the bank—not when you make your arrangements here.

$19.99. Clogs by Gem Collection were $18, and fake leather flats designed by Studio C were just $9.99.

Store hours are 10 a.m. to 9 p.m. Monday through Saturday, and 1 p.m. to 8 p.m. on Sunday.

D & K Discounters

- 1735 Defoor Place N.W., Atlanta; ✆ (404) 355-7675

- 635 George Luther Drive, Decatur ✆ (404) 508-1445

Here you'll find everyday low prices that amount to 30 to 70 percent of typical retail prices, bolstered by special sales that always keep the shopper's costs down.

See the full description under *Men's and Women's Wear—General.*

Dress Barn

- John's Creek Town Center, 3630 Peachtree Parkway, Atlanta; ✆ (770) 814-9870

- Highland Plaza 3605 Sandy Plains Road, Marietta; ✆ (770) 509-1722

- Presidential Commons, 1630 Highway 124, Snellville; (770) 982-7776

- 1757 East West Connector; Austell; (770) 732-1588

- Kings Market, 1425 Market Boulevard, Roswell; (770) 998-6947

- Towne Center Plaza, 425 Ernest W. Barrett Parkway N.W., Kennesaw; (770) 426-8233

- 3999 Austell Road, Austell; (770) 819-0553

- Newnan Pavilion, 1080 Highway 34 E., Newnan; (770) 254-0721

- 112 Pavilion Parkway, Fayetteville; (770) 719-0114

- 2930 Chapel Hill Road, Douglasville; (770) 947-5522

- 1000 Tanger Drive, Locust Grove; (770) 914-1937

- 533 Lakeland Plaza, Cumming; (770) 887-9480

- 1441 Riverstone Parkway, Canton; (770) 345-7880

- www.dressbarn.com

No, you won't look like a farm hand if you shop here; you'll just have more cash in hand to spend at the hootenanny, that's all.

Dress Barn is a well-known retailer of women's career and casual fashion offering a selection of in-season, first-quality merchandise at value prices. This national chain has some name-brand clothing, but the majority of the merchandise carries their own private Dress Barn label, providing customers with substantial cost savings. The first Dress Barn opened in Stamford, Connecticut, in 1962. Now there are over 750 stores nationwide (and 10 new ones in and Around Atlanta since 1994), so they're obviously doing something right.

Mr. Cheap scoped out the place on a hunt for a last-minute Christmas gift for the always-stylish Mrs. C and was pleased to discover that merchandise was discounted 30 to 50 percent off list price. There were also some incredible deals on sweaters and blouses, including a deal to buy one and get the second at 50 percent off. The Cheapster saw a beautiful cable knit acrylic sweater for $34.99, and he could have gone home with two of those sweaters for only $52.49, with "mix and match" definitely permitted! Even better, he was also to pick up a necklace to complete the ensemble.

This national chain is a good place to stock up on basics like T-shirts and jeans. Mr. Cheap saw ribbed long-sleeve tees for half price at $9.99. If you need a pair of jeans try the Gloria Vanderbilt or Westport offerings for only $24.99. For those cool days there are comfortable corduroy pants by Princeton Club for $26.99. Dress Barn has its own label stretch pants in different colors for $29.99, and casual cotton shirts were $21.99, featuring the same promotion as sweaters—buy the second for half price.

There are a great many suits to choose from, with both jackets and skirts. You could furnish your whole wardrobe for work right here and save lots of money in the process. Mr. Cheap found a lovely gold colored pantsuit trimmed with earthtone beading from Collection for Le Suit, which could be dressy or casual, for only $99.99. Dress Barn label suits that are very smart are priced under $100. If you look around you'll find some dressy fashion, too. And C also discovered an Anne Charles royal blue blouse with a black velvet overlay design for $34.99.

You can really stock up on basics here; 60 percent cotton/40 percent polyester turtlenecks were only $9.99 and cotton crew and fashion socks were a bargain at four for $10. Some stores also carry cozy flannel pajamas and slippers.

La Cheaperina found shopping at Dress Barn to be very comfortable, and the service is fantastic.

Most of the stores are open Monday through Saturday from 10 a.m. to 9 p.m. and Sunday noon to 6 p.m., but call ahead because some stores have different hours.

Midtown Designers' Warehouse

- 553-3 Amsterdam Avenue N.E., Atlanta; (404) 873-2581.

The specialty here is unique, dressy, high-fashion women's clothing, including linen and some leather garments, at wholesale prices. The merchandise here is all first quality, straight from the manufacturer, eliminating the middle man. The husband and wife owners of this great place pass those savings directly to their customers, resulting in 30 to 60 percent off on everything! All clothing is current season fashion and MDW dresses several of Atlanta's news anchor celebrities.

In spring and summer MDW carries a huge selection of linen, including Ann Gerlin high-fashion linen suits, dresses, casuals, sun dresses, and sarongs from all over the world. (Sarongs seem to be a particularly popular item here.) Year-round you'll find career, dressy suits and unique casuals with designer names such as Max Studios, Harvé Bernard, John Meyer, Focus 2000, Milano, and Bisou-Bisou.

For those of you who like unique ethnic garb, this is the place for you. Do you know about the Moroccan Magic Dress that can be worn in six different ways? Co-owner Heather will be happy to show you the magic.

MDW also offers a quality selection of handmade ethnic and costume jewelry to go with these fancy outfits, all selling at less than half of their original prices. You'll find unique ethnic jewelry from Africa, Morocco, and India. And there is African and Moroccan artwork, unusual home decors, wall hangings, and artistic painted gourds that include new age themes. Local artists' works on consignment are also represented here.

Located in the Midtown Outlets area, MDW is open Wednesday 10:30 a.m. to 5 p.m., Thursday from 10:30 a.m. to 6 p.m., Friday and Saturday from 10:30 a.m. to 7 p.m., and Sundays from 1:30 p.m. to 6 p.m.

MEN'S AND WOMEN'S WEAR—GENERAL

Best Fashions

- Lindbergh Plaza, Suite B-800, 2581 Piedmont Road N.E., Atlanta; (404) 261-2453

Young hipsters (Mr. C still likes to think of himself in that way; please don't burst his bubble) will look their best after a visit to this emporium of discounted urban clothing and shoes. These are the latest trendy looks, the kind of stuff you'll want for nightclubbing or the gym. For mini-hipsters, there's also some children's clothing here. Everything is discounted at 20 percent off retail prices.

Best Fashions also offers in-house alterations. Store hours are Monday to Saturday 10 a.m. to 8 p.m., and Sunday 1 p.m. to 6 p.m.

> ### MR. CHEAP'S PICKS
>
> #### Men's and Women's Wear—General
>
> **D & K Discounters**—Here you'll find a huge selection of name-brand dress and casual clothing, shoes, and accessories for 30 to 70 percent off typical retail prices.
>
> **Loehmann's**—Loehmann's features upscale designer names for women and men's clothing and shoes for 40 to 80 percent lower than in the department stores.
>
> **One Price and More Clothing Store**—This national chain has off-price fashion in a very clean specialty-store look.

D & K Discounters

- 1735 Defoor Place N.W., Atlanta; (404) 355-7675
- 635 George Luther Drive, Decatur (404) 508-1445

Here's another great place for dress and casual clothing, shoes, and accessories . . . and when Mr. C says "great," he means "large." You'll find a lot of clothes and some big discounts here.

At D&K you'll find everyday low prices that amount to 30 to 70 percent of typical retail prices, bolstered by special sales that always keep the shopper's costs down. All the major brands are represented here, including (but not limited to) Lorenzo Latini, Zanetti, Azione, and Polo for men, and Harvé Bernard, Kasper, and Designs Today for women. In the footwear department they've got David Eden, Phoenix, Brutini, Timberland, Durango, and more. Stylish leatherwear abounds. Here men's suits start at $99, and you can sometimes pick up two for $150. Pure wool suits start in the $100 to $120 range. What's not to love?

Store hours are Thursday through Monday from 10 a.m. to 9 p.m.

K & G Liquidation Center

- 1777 Ellsworth Industrial Boulevard N.W., Atlanta; (404) 352-3527
- 3750 Venture Drive N.W., Duluth; (770) 623-9895

If you don't mind shopping for fancy suits in a supermarket setting, then you certainly won't mind K & G. These stores deal in what the clothing business calls "salvage."

Now, don't let the "salvage" tag scare you off. Here you'll find clothing that manufacturers have to get rid of simply because they made too many, or because department stores ordered more than they could sell, or because they are "past season." (You may like to buy spring clothing in the spring, but major stores are already stocking up for the summer at that point.)

In any event, stores like K & G snap up these clothing deals for both men and women and sell them off at great savings from their big, warehouse-type stores. It's all first-quality merchandise. As one of the store's quirkier clerks told us some time ago, "the only thing that's irregular here is us." Hey, a little personality goes a long way in a crowded, bustling place like this.

Men's suits make up the majority of the stock, from lots of big-name designers in sizes from 36 short to 50 extra long. (The store prefers not to have these big names mentioned in print in order to maintain good relationships with their sources.) Hand-tailored all-wool suits with retail prices of $350 sell here for $120, about as expensive as they get. Wool blend suits, by lesser-known makers, start as low as $90. And there are walls covered with silk print ties to go with the suits, most priced at just $7.90 each. You'll also find lots of the latest tuxedos, too, at around $100. Alterations for all suits are available in the store.

K & G has other looks as well, including casual and sportswear. These include cashmere sweaters reduced from $225 to $99, and full-length leather trench coats for half-price at $199. And, there is a limited but good selection of shoes, dress and casual, at up to 40 percent off.

The selection for women is smaller, and available only at the Atlanta store. This department primarily offers professional outfits, like a classic European wool blazer in bright red (from a very well-known national specialty chain), marked down from $165 to a smarter $50. A rack of flowing rayon print skirts was reduced from $85 each to just $25, below wholesale cost. And our scouting expedition turned up sharp looks for going out, such as a 1960s retro mini dress in purple velvet ($45), or a black sequined vest ($39, down from $80).

There's a lot to see here, with new shipments arriving each week. The stores are open Fridays and Saturdays from 10 a.m. to 7 p.m., and Sundays from noon to 6 p.m.

Loehmann's

- Executive Park, 2480 Briarcliff Road N.E., Atlanta;
  (404) 633-4156

- www.loehmanns.com

Loehmann's means low prices on upscale designer names for women and men's clothing and shoes, plain and simple. Frieda Loehmann practically invented the designer closeout store. She opened the first Loehmann's store in 1921 in Brooklyn, New York. By 2002, there were 44 stores in 17 states.

Upscale designer names can be found here for 40 to 80 percent lower than in the department stores. In addition to fancy clothing, Loehmann's carries career and casual wear, swimwear, sleepwear, purses, shoes, fragrances, gifts such as crystal glasses or Mikasa vases, intimate apparel, and other accessories. You could do all your holiday shopping in this one store.

Loehmann's is best known for its world-famous Back Room, where you will find very fancy evening wear from the top designers like Kay Unger, Adrianna Papell, Tadashi, Tahari, Harvé Bernard, Oleg Cassini, Donna Karen, Jeffrey & Donna, Cachet, and more. Mr. Cheap saw a gorgeous gold 100-percent silk pantsuit by Ice Cube by Michael, originally listed at $278, selling for a mere $99.99. That's music to C's ears!

Talk about holding the line on inflation! C was amazed to find that designer suit prices had hardly changed since the last time we wrote about this place. A beautiful vibrant color jacket and skirt suit by Kasper for A.S.L. and a double-breasted jacket and skirt by Jones New York, originally valued at $230 to $299, were $99.99 each. Long-length wool sweaters by Grace Knitwear listed for $72 were $49.99, and 100 percent cashmere sweaters listed for $140 were marked at $59.99. Finity 95-percent silk blouses were only $19.99.

The list of top designer names is endless—Leon Max, Harlow, Bisou-Bisou, Albert Nipon, Bill Blass, and DKNY to name just a few. Ralph Lauren 100-percent cotton blouses were priced at only $19.99. Moa Moa turtlenecks were listed at $22.99; at that rate, give me more, more.

Loehmann's also features dressy and casual outwear for men and women.

Petites can also do very well for themselves here with plenty of suits, dresses, and pants to choose from. A petite Larry Levine pantsuit that listed for $190 was priced here for $79.99.

In the junior department, Ralph Lauren sweaters listed at $79.90 were marked at $44.99, and corduroy pants by this designer that listed for $59.50 were priced at $29.99. They carry the XOXO brand jeans that juniors love, priced for only $19.99. Mr. Cheap saw a XOXO long tailored black jacket listed for $68, marked down to $26.99. A very pretty lacey pant by Free People that lists for $76.00 was $19.99 here.

Lots of purses by Calvin Klein, Ralph Lauren, Kenneth Cole, and more are sold at Loehmann's. Mr. C found a unique Maxx NY purse listed for $100, priced here at $29.99. Lots of sleepwear here too, luxurious August Silk pajamas priced at $49.99.

Incredible deals on upscale designer clothing can be found here, but you must have patience and persistence—you have to sift through all the merchandise yourself, since there is virtually no sales help.

For further discounts check out Loehmann's Insider Club on the web at www.loehmanns.com or ask them about it when you visit the store. Store hours are Monday through Saturday from 10 a.m. to 9 p.m. and Sunday from noon to 6 p.m.

One Price and More Clothing Store

- 2841 Greenbriar Parkway, Atlanta; (404) 349-5911

- West Ridge Shopping Center, 3050 Martin Luther King Boulevard, Atlanta; (404) 691-5347

- West End Mall, 858 Oak Street S.W., Atlanta; (404) 758-0590

- Northeast Plaza, 3277 Buford Highway, Atlanta; (404) 633-7114

- 1390 Moreland Avenue S.E., Atlanta; (404) 627-8914

- 11 Broad Street Plaza S.W., Atlanta; (404) 521-9911

- 5505 Bells Ferry Road, Acworth; (770) 926-0548

- Covington Gallery, 7143 Turner Lake Road N.W., Covington; (770) 787-1786

- Covington Square, 6118 Covington Highway, Covington; (770) 322-8888

- Avondale Crossing, 1289 Columbia Drive, Decatur; (404) 288-5983

- Suburban Plaza, 2595-D North Decatur Road, Decatur; (404) 373-6624

- Doraville Plaza, 5762 Buford Highway, Doraville; (770) 455-4626

- 2066 Headland Drive, East Point; (404) 209-1955

- Forest Square, 4869 Jonesboro Road, Forest Park; (404) 363-9541

- Lilburn Market Place, 4805 Lawrenceville Highway, Lilburn; (770) 279-7569

- 900 Thornton Road, Lithia Springs; (770) 944-9021

- 6118 Covington Highway, Lithonia; (770) 322-8888

- Village at Mableton; 5590 Mableton Parkway, Mableton; (770) 732-1070

- 125 N. Midland Avenue, Monroe; (770) 267-5057

- 1532 Southlake Parkway, Morrow; ✆ (678) 422-9444
- Belmont Hills Shopping Center, 2468-A Atlanta Road S.E., Smyrna; ✆ (770) 432-0121
- Memorial Bend, 5160 Memorial Drive, Stone Mountain; ✆ (404) 508-2329
- ✍ www.oneprice.com

This store more-or-less stays true to its name; they used to sell everything at one price, just $7. Now they sell in a range from about $5 to $20 or so, which is not quite one price but it is a range Mr. C can ride.

This national chain has off-price fashion in a very clean specialty-store look. Budget-brand casual clothing for misses, juniors, plus-sizes, children, and men are all in good supply here, and everything is first quality; there are never irregulars or seconds.

The Cheapster found that the highest price for an item of women's clothing was $20. Men's shirts, shorts, pants, and sweaters were priced between $8 to $18. Clothing for children was approximately $5 to $10 (and why should you spend more money on children's clothing when it's only six months before they outgrow anything you buy?). You can purchase high-quality school uniforms here for only $10. Accessories from hats to jewelry are priced between $2 and $7.

Some of the things you can get for just a handful of bucks include all-cotton broomstick shirts; Justin Allen plaid cotton walk shorts; and silk tank tops and shorts by names like Manisha, Whistles, and Louise Paris.

Most locations are open Monday through Saturday from 10 a.m. to 9 p.m., and Sunday from noon to 6 p.m., but call ahead to be sure.

BRIDAL AND FORMAL WEAR

New Natalie's Bridals

- 919 Chattahoochee Avenue N.W.; ✆ (404) 352-1616
- ✍ www.newnataliesbridals.com

New Natalie's Bridals is one of the largest bridal stores in the South, drawing customers from five states. This store offers over thirty designer-label wedding gowns, with all the current styles found in the latest bridal magazines, at discounts of 20 to 30 percent off retail. You can even custom order from a selection of 1,400 dresses, with all the service you'd expect at a full-price boutique. Bridal consultants and dressers are ready for action, with ten fitting rooms and alterations available on the premises at reasonable rates. New Natalie's also offers 600 different bridesmaid's lines at 20 to 30 percent off.

Most bridal gowns sell here in the range of $500 to $800. Some can go as high as $2,500, but remember, that same high-priced gown would sell for as much as $5,000 at most other specialty stores. (And remember, too: unless she's into dress-up parties, a bride is likely to wear her gown only once.)

This store has a section called "Bridal Liquidations," which sounds like a Mafia hit on a wedding party. Prices here are slashed in a way any Don would approve. You never know what you may find in this section, but it has to be worth a look; some gowns start as low as $99. Most are priced under $400, and all are sold at 50 to 80 percent off their original prices. The catch? You won't find the latest up-to-the-minute styles, and if something you like isn't within one size above or below your own, it probably can't be fitted to you.

And of course, none of these can be special-ordered; all the actual dresses available at these prices are right there on the racks. Still, for many folks who don't want to spend a lifetime paying off a blowout wedding, these deals present lots of good options.

In addition, there is a good selection of rental tuxedos, again featuring the big designers like Pierre Cardin, Christian Dior, Raffinati, and others (since these are not being sold, Mr. C can tell you the names). Rent six or more tuxes or bridesmaid's gowns and the groom's rental is free. They also have a wedding invitation service, with designs from thirty major catalog books, all at a discount of 20 percent with the purchase of a dress.

Store hours are Wednesday 10 a.m. to 6 p.m., Thursday 10 a.m. to 8 p.m., Friday and Saturday 10 a.m. to 6 p.m., and Sunday 1 p.m. to 5 p.m. The shop is closed Monday and Tuesday.

CHILDREN'S WEAR

The link between love and marriage and the eventual arrival of a baby carriage didn't really occur to Mr. and Mrs. Cheap when they walked down the aisle. But then there they were one day, shopping for diapers and bottle warmers and college scholarships. If you sat down and figured out all the money that you will spend on raising a child . . . you might not want to get back up again.

But there are many ways to save a lot of money on kid stuff, one baby step at a time.

"Baby Depot" at Burlington Coat Factory

- 2841 Greenbriar Parkway S.W., Atlanta; (404) 349-6300
- 3750 Venture Drive, Duluth; (770) 497-0033
- 1255 Roswell Road, Marietta; (770) 971-6540
- 608 Holcomb Bridge Road, Roswell; (770) 518-9800

See the listing under *Discount Department Stores*.

Consignkidz Inc

- Toco Hills Mall, 2205 Lavista Road N.E., Atlanta; (404) 929-0222

See the listing under *Clothing—Used: Consignment/Resale Stores*.

Tiny Tots Consignment

- 100 North Peachtree Parkway, Peachtree City; (770) 487-9100

Some folks think bigger is always better, but the Cheapster firmly believes that "little can be delightful," especially when it comes to low prices for kids clothing. Parents will find a bit of everything at this great store just down the street from Ruby Tuesday's. Tiny Tots has used clothing—in great condition—for infants, babies, and kids up to about 16 years of age, with top brands represented in every category. Pants and shirts for the l'il folks start at the appropriately l'il price of 99 cents and range on up to a painless $6.99 for Gap and Polo merchandise.

Now Mr. C knows that someone out there has just read "used clothing" and said: "Not for my little dear." But wait: we're talking about creatures that are champions at messing things up, but they are generally pretty easy on the clothing. They only wear them a few months. And they could care less if one of the other debutantes-to-be had the same wardrobe.

Tiny Tots also offers similar bargains on maternity clothes, baby

SHOPPING: CLOTHING—NEW

blankets, and strollers (which start at about $25), and you'll usually find selected items on sale for 25 to 50 percent off the regular (already low!) price.

Store hours are 10 a.m. to 6 p.m. on Monday through Thursday, noon to 8 p.m. on Friday, and noon to 6 p.m. on Sunday.

Toddler Outlet

- 2168 Salem Road SE., Conyers; (770) 483-0330

If you need to buy a baby gift, this could be the place. Here you'll find brand-name infant and children's clothing, including OshKosh B'Gosh, Alexis, Mothermaid, Buster Brown, Samora, and Carter's, at a 50 to 75 percent discount off retail. This store carries sweaters, activewear, sleepwear, swimwear, and outerwear. Boys and girls clothing goes up to size 7 and there are some girls' sizes 10 to 12. Infant sizes start at "preemie." Mr. Cheap found a Rare Edition dress for $25 that would have been priced at $75 to $100 in a typical department store.

Toddler Outlet also carries layette match-up sets. These include all bedding: blankets, crib bumpers, and even changing pads for changing tables.

And don't forget the accessories for that extra touch—bibs, socks, baby shoes, or an adorable and unique hat. You can pick up diaper bags here, too.

Toddler Outlet is located at exit 83 off route I-20 in the shopping center with Gold's Gym. Store hours are Monday through Saturday from 10 a.m. to 6 p.m.

Kids 'R' Us

- 3983 Lavista Road, Tucker; (770) 723-0303

- 1960 Day Drive, Duluth; (770) 623-4208

- 7691 N. Point Parkway, Alpharetta; (770) 640-5224

- 2646 George Busbee Parkway N.W., Kennesaw; (770) 426-0725

- 2200 Cedars Road, Lawrenceville; (770) 277-5701

- www.inc.toysrus.com

This national chain has surprisingly good deals and discounts on a wide variety of children's clothing, including items tagged with its own Kids 'R' Us brand, as well those by OshKosh, Healthtex, Levis, Adidas, Nike, and others. You can almost always find a bargain here, often through unadvertised promotions in the store that feature clearance items at 20 to 50 percent off the tagged price. Deals can be especially plentiful during or just after holiday seasons.

Kids R Us also carries numerous accessory items that go with the clothing, including such items as toy bowling sets, umbrellas, backpacks, and purses. And, most locations even have a little Muppet car "ride" and other amusements that tikes can enjoy during the visit.

Store hours are generally Monday through Saturday from 10 a.m. to 9 p.m., and Sunday from 12:30 p.m. to 6 p.m.

OshKosh B'Gosh

- 1000 Tanger Drive, Locust Grove; (770) 914-7423

- www.oshkoshbgosh.com

When you think of OshKosh B'Gosh, classic Americana bib overalls pop to mind. But parents know that this company not only offers bib overalls for children (starting at three months), they also make quality activewear, outerwear, and swimwear clothing for children that is really durable, well-styled, and so popular it is sold in more than 70 countries. And don't forget the footwear and hats, socks, and hair accessories to match outfits—they've got that here too.

In-season clothing is priced at 30 percent off retail and end-of-season clearance is discounted 50 to 70 percent. Clothing sizes start at infant and go up to size 16 for both boys and girls. This OKB store also sells highchairs, swings, baby bassinets, strollers, and car seats.

And Mom and Dad, keep this in mind: OshKosh B'Gosh will replace broken or missing buttons, hooks, and slides free of charge. Contact consumer affairs at (800) 692-4674 or visit the Web site for details.

Store hours are Monday through Saturday from 9 a.m. to 9 p.m., and Sunday from noon to 6 p.m.

Sweet Repeats

- 321 Pharr Road N.E., Atlanta; (404) 261-7519

See the listing under *Clothing—Used: Consignment/Resale Stores.*

ACCESSORIES

Backstreet Boutique

- Tuxedo Festival Shopping Center, 3655 Roswell Road N.E., Buckhead; (404) 262-7783

With a store like this, you can look like a million bucks for a fraction of the original cost. Backstreet Boutique resells well-kept designer fashions and accessories (which includes handbags) from names like Chanel, Gucci, Yves Saint Laurent, Armani, Prada, and Street John's.

See the full description in the *Consignment/Resale Stores* section.

Stone Mountain Handbag Factory Store

- 963 Main Street, Stone Mountain; (770) 498-1316
- www.stonemountainhandbags.com

You've seen them in stores like Rich's and Neiman Marcus for $100 and up. Here, you can get the same first-quality handbags for 20 to 50 percent off the suggested retail prices. The accessories sold in this shop are factory overruns and closeouts.

Stone Mountain's leather handbags are available in tan, navy, black, brown, and burgundy, and trims, all with the company's trademark zipper-closure and multi-compartment style. Other products, such as leather-bound organizers, belts, wallets, eyeglass cases, leather jackets, briefcases, and luggage, are sold here, too, in styles for men and women at the same 20 to 50 percent off retail prices

The store is open Monday through Saturday from 10 a.m. to 6 p.m., and Sunday from noon to 6 p.m.

Stefan's Terrace

- 1160 Euclid Avenue N.E., Atlanta; (404) 688-4929

This well-lit, first-rate shop specializes in cheap vintage clothing, but also features an accessories department with vintage sunglasses from Cat's Eye, Buddy Holly, and Aviator, priced between $10 and $30, plus beaded evening bags, old Mexican silver jewelry, a large selection of rhinestone jewelry, and more!

See the full description under *Vintage Stores.*

Sunglass Hut International

- 3500 Peachtree Road N.E., Atlanta; (404) 364-9522

SHOPPING: CLOTHING—NEW

- Underground Atlanta, 180 Lower Alabama Street, Atlanta; (404) 577-0040
- Lenox Square Shopping Center, 3393 Peachtree Road, Atlanta; (404) 237-0931
- 1378 Cumberland Mall, Atlanta; (770) 432-0432
- 2860 Cobb Parkway, Atlanta; (770) 438-9940
- 6000 N. Terminal Parkway, Atlanta; (404) 762-8746
- 4400 Ashford Dunwoody Road N.E., Atlanta; (770) 671-9026
- 1 CNN Center N.W., Atlanta; (404) 659-7096
- 1000 N. Point Circle, Alpharetta; (770) 740-9146
- 3333 Buford Drive, Buford; (678) 482-7275
- 1430 Arbor Place Mall, Douglasville; (770) 942-9252
- 2100 Pleasant Hill Road, Duluth; (770) 476-9462
- 1285 Washington Street N.W., Gainesville; (770) 535-2746
- Town Center, 400 Ernest W. Barrett Parkway N.W., Kennesaw; (770) 590-0230
- 1801 Highway 155 N., McDonough; (770) 914-4010
- 100 Greenwood Industrial Parkway, McDonough; (678) 432-4114
- 1229 Southlake Mall, Morrow; (770) 968-1786
- Northlake Mall, LaVista/Briarcliff at I-285, Tucker; (770) 934-4895
- www.sunglasshut.com

As part of Mr. C's ongoing quest to burnish his reputation as the coolest guy in both the city and the suburbs (okay, at least the coolest guy in the mall parking lot), he makes sure to always wear some groovy shades.

At the Sunglass Hut he generally finds reduced prices on a large selection of designer label sunglasses for sports and general wear. Lens repair kits, cleaners, and cases are also reasonably priced.

Mr. Cool . . . uh, Cheap, found Code glasses priced at $29.99, Fossil shades priced at $34.99, Stussy at $39.99, and Gargoyle sports eyewear priced at $54.99. Tommy Hilfiger glasses were $49.99, reduced from $69.99. He was also offered Ray-Ban styles priced from $59.99 and up and Ralph Lauren glasses starting at $69.99. There are Armani, Calvin Klein, Guess and, of course, Oakleys. Sunglass Hut also has its own brand of glasses called Sun Gear.

Charlie's Angels' super-glam rimless aviator glasses, as worn by Mr. C's dear friends Drew Barrymore, Cameron Diaz, and Lucy Liu, were priced at $49.99, marked down from $69.99. Must be that the movie has moved out of the current attractions bin.

If you have access to the Internet check out the Web site before you head to the store. Click on "Get the Facts" and that will introduce you to the science behind choosing the right sunglasses. You know about the damage of ultraviolet rays, but do you know the difference between UVA, UVB, and UVC? What about blue, infrared, visible, and polarized light? It's all here.

Customer service can be excellent; the best staff have the knowledge to find the right glasses for the shape of your face, the size of your nose, whether your eyes are wide-set or not, they even take into account the size of your nostrils. If you feel you're not getting the best service, avert your eyes and head elsewhere.

Store hours are usually mall hours: Monday to Friday from 10 a.m. to 10 p.m., Saturday from 9 a.m. to 10 p.m. and Sunday 11 a.m. to 7 p.m.

CLOTHING—USED

Mr. C has already opined on the subject of buying slightly used clothing for babies. Why should they get all the savings? Recycling doesn't just mean bottles and cans, y'know. In these economic times, people are taking this approach to nearly everything, and it makes a lot of sense.

Let's define a few terms: "Consignment' and "resale" shops generally sell what they call "gently used" clothing. Often, these are fancy outfits that some of the beautiful people don't want to be seen in more than once or twice. This is how you can get these high-fashion clothes at super low prices. Since they still look new, your friends will never know the secret (unless, of course, you want to brag about your bargain-hunting prowess).

You can also sell things from your own closets at these shops, if they are recent and in good shape; the store owners will split the cash with you.

"Vintage" clothing is usually older and may show a bit of "character." Sometimes it can cost more than you'd expect for used clothing, depending on which "retro" period is back in style at the moment.

Finally, "thrift shops" sell used clothing that has definitely seen better days. These items have generally been donated to the stores, most of which are run by charity organizations; in such places, you can often find great bargains, and help out a worthy cause at the same time.

CONSIGNMENT AND RESALE STORES

Backstreet Boutique

- Tuxedo Festival Shopping Center, 3655 Roswell Road N.E., Buckhead; ✆ (404) 262-7783

With a store like this, you can look like a million bucks for a fraction of the original cost. Backstreet Boutique has been located in Buckhead, Atlanta's upscale store district, for more than a decade; the owner sometimes also refers to her boutique as "Buckhead's Upscale Resale." The store has everything that women wear or carry that costs a lot of money. Backstreet resells well-kept designer fashions and accessories (which includes handbags) from names like Chanel, Gucci, Yves Saint Laurent, Armani, Prada, and Street John's (which happens to be the store's biggest seller, and according to the owner "the designer choice" of Atlanta women). All merchandise is current and fresh. Women's suits that cost $2,500 retail are sold here between $299 and $399. Chanel suits are 20 percent off the retail price.

Mr. C found a great pair of $600 Blahnik shoes on sale for $99, as well as some Jimmy Choo models that retail for $500-600, also for $99. If you're in the store and contemplating buying a pair of shoes like these, don't hesitate, because they can be gone within a day.

Chanel, Prada, Gucci, Kate Spade, and Louis Vuitton accessories are more than 50 percent off retail prices. Because this merchandise is of such high quality to begin with, some of these items are still priced in the hundreds of dollars. Whatever you purchase, though, you will be saving half off or better compared to the original retail prices.

Backstreet owner Joey told Mr. Cheap that the majority of people we know can't afford these upscale designer names, and she was thrilled when she recently fitted two 85-year-old women in their first Chanel suits.

Backstreet is open Tuesday through Saturday. Hours may vary so call ahead.

Chickibea

- 2130 North Decatur Road, Decatur; (404) 634-6995

Since 1972, Chickibea has been a fixture in Atlanta's designer upscale resale consignment clothing trade. Owner Chicki Lipton will be more than happy to help you find whatever specific items you're looking for among the career wear and evening clothes packed into her store in the North Decatur Plaza.

The items here are generally marked at about 60 percent off the price of similar new items, although you can also find even better deals in the store. Mr. C was offered great bargains like an Ann Taylor linen/rayon two-piece suit, selling for $99 (worth $300, easily), or a never-worn fuchsia silk Casual Corner blouse for just $32. A Liz Claiborne angora cardigan, worth $100, was only $40 here.

Denim lovers can take their pick from Calvin Klein jeans for $59 (these go for over $100 at Neiman Marcus), a Donna Karan New York jean skirt reduced to $49, or a pair of Marithe and Francois Girbaud jeans for just $39.

The shoes at Chickibea are, for the most part, in good shape. Mrs. C has spotted Naturalizer pumps, with real leather uppers, selling for just $24, and a pair of "i.e." Nike Air cushioned suede flats almost half-price at $18.

The eveningwear section of the store featured a black lace gown by Scott McClintock for just $59, a shirred rayon dress from Saks Fifth Avenue for $100, and a velvet evening gown and cape by J. Reynolds Designs for $249.

MR. CHEAP'S PICKS

Clothing—Used

Backstreet Boutique—This is the place for gently worn Chanel and Anne Klein designs at miniscule prices.

The Consignshop—Prices at the Consignshop are marked down as much as 75 percent off retail, all for fashions that are as nearly current as used clothing can be.

Sweet Repeats—For the little ones, clothes from super names like Saks Fifth Avenue and Taffy's sell for a few bucks each at this Buckhead shop.

There are plenty of sequin-decorated dresses to choose from, too.

Accessories like a $39 Gucci bag (really!), a $62 crocodile bag by Saks, and $20 silk scarves should help to complete any of these outfits, without finishing off your budget.

Chickibea is open Tuesday through Saturday from 11 a.m. to 6 p.m.

Circles Unlimited

- 1720 DeFoor Place N.W., Atlanta; ✆ (404) 352-8563

Along this tiny street lined with outlet stores, here's something unusual: Circles Unlimited is the only one on the block selling previously owned designer clothing and samples for women. Yet, in a way, this cozy little frame house-turned-store boasts an even greater variety and better bargains than its neighbors. Okay, so it's not current season stuff. Everything here is close to it, never more than a year or two old, and all in great condition. Relying on what people pull out of their closets, the store's merchandise is always changing, which is part of the fun. Knowing the league she is playing in, owner Faye is every bit as discerning about what she will sell as any retailer. This is certainly an upscale site for resale shoppers.

Store hours are Wednesday through Saturday from 10 a.m. to 6 p.m.

Consignkidz Inc

- Toco Hills Mall, 2205 Lavista Road N.E., Atlanta; ✆ (404) 929-0222

Here you'll find children's clothing (infants to size 14), maternity wear, and baby furniture and equipment at 50 to 70 percent off retail. They have more expensive upscale brand names such as Oilily, Baby LuLu, Lilly Pulitzer, Florence Eiseman, as well as not-so-expensive brands such as Gymboree and Baby Gap. Maternity fashion from casual to special occasion includes designer names such as Mimi, Pea in the Pod, and Maternite.

These folks receive merchandise from several upscale boutiques from across the country that hasn't sold by the end of the season. In fact, when the Cheapster last cruised through, they had just received a thousand pieces of brand-new closeouts from New York and Los Angeles, all still tagged with the retail prices. Consignkidz will turn this stuff around at 40 to 50 percent off retail.

Turnover of the baby furniture here happens so quickly that there's a waiting list! So visit this store ahead of time and put your name on the list for cribs, highchairs, changing tables, baby swings, and strollers. You'll find top-of-the-line furniture by Bellini, as well as cribs and crib mattresses from such brands as Simmons and Jenny Lynn. You can stroll or jog with Peg Perego, Graco, Even-Flo, and Baby Jogger strollers. Everything is in excellent condition and up-to-date. They even have the ever-popular open-top baby swing by Graco.

Stores hours are Monday through Saturday from 10 a.m. to 6 p.m., and Sunday from noon to 6 p.m. Even though this store is in the same mall as the Consignshop (see below) and only four doors away, they have different street addresses. Ours is not to reason why; ours is to shop.

The Consignshop

- 2899-A North Druid Hills Road; ✆ (404) 633-6257

- 4920 Roswell Road Suite 10, ✆ (404) 531-0303

SHOPPING: CLOTHING—USED

This store looks more like a boutique than a consignment shop, and has done so well since Mr. C's first visit in 1993 that they've opened another shop and a children's store too (see above).

Prices at the Consignshop are marked down as much as 75 percent off retail, all for fashions that are as nearly current as used clothing can be. The stock on display is always geared to the season at hand: Unlike some shops, you won't find a floor full of wool suits in the middle of August. Everything is neatly organized in sections such as "career" and "casual," and also by size, too, so you won't waste half the day rummaging. In addition to men and women's clothing, the shops have added a home decorative department with merchandise such as dishes, small furniture, pictures, pillows, and rugs at 20 to 75 percent off retail.

In women's clothes the shop carries designer names like Anne Klein and Dana Buckman. Also you will find the same Alex Garfeld, Womyn, and Mary Jane clothes that you find in upscale specialty stores. Some of the casual designer names represented here are Shu Shu, J. Crew, Banana Republic, and Ann Taylor.

Men too can look dapper for just dimes—in fashion by Banana Republic, Donna Karan, Brooks Brothers, Kenneth Cole, and even some Versace items.

The store also offers a large selection of consigned shoes for men and women in very good condition for 75 percent off retail: Robert Clergerie, Kenneth Cole, Donald Pliner, Donna Karan, Joan Helpern, Via Spiga, Enzo, Nine West, Sacha Too, Joan and David, Nickle, and Ralph Lauren.

Got a special occasion coming up? The Consignshop sells black tuxedo jackets, wool Polo jackets, and dozens of ties made by Geoffrey Beene and other major manufacturers.

The store openly accepts consignments on a 50/50 split, but only takes items that are in excellent condition. It's located in the Toco Hills Shopping Center and is open weekdays and Saturdays from 10 a.m. to 6 p.m., staying open until 8 p.m. on Thursday evenings.

Play It Again

- 273 Buckhead Avenue N.E., Atlanta; ✆ (404) 261-2135

You'll want to shop at this store again and again, with its super prices on better designer brand upscale resale career and casual wear. But, you must remember this: Play It Again only deals in women's clothing. Sorry, Bogey.

Play it Again has been in business for more than two decades and the selection is amazing; you'll find women's designer clothing like Gap, Street John's, Laundry, Ralph Lauren, Ellen Tracy, Talbots, Jones of NY, Armani, Channel, and Ungaro.

They also have a large selection of shoes. Mrs. Cheap was offered a pair of Ferragamos and another pair by Stuart Weitzman. There are hats, scarves, handbags, costume jewelry, sleepware, some lingerie, fur coats, wool coats, and more coats—all for 75 percent off retail. They have leather stuff too, skirts, jackets, shirts, pants, and coats priced between $30 and $70.

For special occasions, Play it Again has both cocktail and ball gown evening wear in velvet, beaded, and sequin designs—knee length and floor length, and strapless too. Prices for evening wear range between $38 to $68.

The store is open weekdays from 10 a.m. to 6 p.m. (Thursdays until 7 p.m.), and Saturdays from 10 a.m. to 5 p.m.

Sweet Repeats

- 321 Pharr Road N.E., Atlanta; (404) 261-7519

Sweet savings on used, consigned maternity, and children's clothing fill this Buckhead store. All the stuff here is in truly exceptional shape, and most of it looks as if it has never been worn at all.

For moms-to-be, we were offered a rayon dress by Mother's Work for just $32, a Saks Fifth Avenue velvet number with puff sleeves at $75, and a Shaker sweater by Motherhood, which would easily cost $60 in the mall, just $32.

For toddlers, Mr. C found a pullover by A Pea in the Pod for $6.50 and a striped rugby pullover by Chesterfield for just $9.50. A girls' knit jacket by Tiny Tots is just $10, while a white fake fur overcoat by Millicents of San Francisco was $18.50.

Moving up to slightly bigger kids, there was a pair of girls' overalls by Imp Originals for $8.50, a cotton dress from the Gap for $14, and a fleece pajama set by Kidding Around for $6. Young boys will enjoy things like Pony soccer cleats (a score for $9.50), OshKosh velcro-close sneakers ($6.50), and a flannel tweed suit by Michael James ($32).

Accessories like crib bumper pads for $15, or an Aprica stroller for $25, are also great values. The shop often gets fun stuff in too, like a tutu for $5, or a pair of Taffy's tap shoes for $8.50. With these, you won't mind so much when your budding ballerina quits after three classes.

Sweet Repeats is easy to find, located right across the street from Oxford Books at Pharr, and is open 10 a.m. to 5 p.m. Mondays to Saturday.

VINTAGE STORES

The Clothing Warehouse

- 420 Moreland Avenue, Atlanta; (404) 524-5070
- 250 Arizona Avenue, Building D, Atlanta; (404) 371-0596
- www.theclothingwarehouse.com

Yes, there are two Clothing Warehouse stores, and they carry similar merchandise. However, while both owners share a friendship, they are not business partners. The two stores Mr. Cheap salutes here focus on wholesale sales through a big warehouse on Arizona Avenue, and a smaller retail store on Moreland.

You'll find a major selection of T-shirts, Hawaiian shirts, '50s and '70s shirts—priced from about $5 to $20 apiece; $30 to $200 for jackets vintage cotton and silk dresses from $15 and up, '60s and '70s party dresses, bell bottoms in both denim and plaid from about $20, halter tops, Izod and Polo shirts priced from $15 to $20, overalls, leather jackets (starting at $30), and vintage belts. You name it and you can probably get it here.

At the warehouse you can get some incredible deals if you're willing to buy in quantity. For example, just recently Mr. C discovered that he could pick up a 100-pound box of Izod and Polo-style shirts for just $125—an average price of 70 cents per shirt! Hey, Mr. C could be set for the next 30 or 40 years, especially for formal occasions.

Store hours are 11 a.m. to 9 p.m. every day of the week.

The Clothing Warehouse

- 2094 N Decatur Road, Decatur; (404) 248-1224

The other Clothing Warehouse specializes in vintage clothing from the

'60s and '70s, and it's jam-packed with bargains.

Here you'll find used Levi jeans dating from 1960s through the '80s, and although they are labeled as menswear, women like to buy 'em too. The same goes for the men's corduroy pants ranging in price from $14.95 to $29.95.

The 1970s, in particular, seem to rule here. A lot of the pants are bellbottoms, harking back to Mr. C's prime. You can also pick up men's and women's '70s-style double-knit slacks! Vintage T-shirts from the '70s are priced at $6.95 to $19.95, and some of these are collectibles. Men's and women's '70s polyester and cotton shirts are tagged at $11.95 to $24.95.

You'll find a good selection of vintage leather jackets, in waist and long lengths for men and women, priced between $25 and $125. Faux fur coats in animal print and solid styles are priced at $25 to $50.

Check out the popular shirts in Hawaiian, Guayabera (they've got four pockets), and bowling styles in the price range of $11.95 to $29.95. And remember those tuck shirts with the ruffles? Here they're back in style. For women they carry tube tops and halters, dresses from the '50s to the '80s from everyday wear to special occasion.

You can also pick up accessories such as foreign military bags, costume jewelry, brand-new cool shades, and wigs (Afros and other '70s hair styles, of course).

And one more thing: If this type of clothing doesn't match your day-to-day style, you could always come back to shop for Halloween.

Store hours are Monday through Saturday from 11 a.m. to 8 p.m., and Sunday from noon to 6 p.m. They're located at the corner of North Decatur and Clairmont, about half a mile from Emory University.

Stefan's Terrace

- 1160 Euclid Avenue N.E., Atlanta; ✆ (404) 688-4929

If you're looking for dressy vintage clothing for men and women, you've got to check out this place: a well-lit, first-rate shop that is colorfully decorated with vintage circus banners and Mexican movie posters.

At Stefan's, vintage clothing is defined as "turn-of-the-century through 1974," and when asked they tell you that they carry "everything from head to toe and in between and underneath." They even have some vintage clothing for children. All clothing is organized by size and color, so it is an easy place to shop. None of Stefan's clothes are shabby looking because the store only accepts items that have been well taken care of.

In men's fashion, El Cheapedo was offered a cashmere sweater for $48, a vintage cashmere overcoat for $160, and a military-issue pea coat for $85. Stefan's has a huge section of 1930s, 1940s, and 1950s vintage ties, including hand-painted neck hangings priced at between $20 and $24. Ties dated from 1960 and beyond are priced at $7 to $18. Stefan's also has some vintage tuxedos (Palm Beach and After Six), made of 60 to 65 percent silk brocade or sharkskin. In the headgear department, The Cheapster found $20 wool felt hats by Wall Street, as well as some very cool fedoras priced at $28 to $38.

Looking for men's embroidered bowling shirts and 1940 Hawaiian shirts? This is the place to find them. And be sure to check out the cufflinks and stud sets dated from 1920 to 1975, ranging in price from $22 to $75.

Women's fashions are represented here, too. This is a great

place to find a basic black evening dress or possibly something embroidered or beaded for a special occasion. Mr. Cheap was told that occassionally you might even find a designer name like Oscar de La Renta.

Mrs. C stopped to admire an aqua-colored satin dress, with cap sleeves, offered for only $20. A gorgeous satin and lace wedding gown that looked like it's never been worn was $95.

Heard enough yet? Stefan's also features discounted prices on a large selection of vintage barcloth fabrics (cotton or cotton blend). There are tablecloths, curtains, and fabric panels ideal for upholstery. What's more, Your Loyal Cheapster spotted fur and beaded trim sweaters; mink, fox, and Persian lamb stoles and wraps. Stefan's also has a large selection of vintage, never-worn women's shoes priced between $30 and $40.

How about some vintage sunglasses? In the accessories department, the store carries vintage top-brand Cat's Eye, Buddy Holly, and Aviator models priced from $10 to $30. Mr. Cheap even found some Ray Bans from the 1950s.

It doesn't stop there! There are beaded evening bags, old Mexican silver jewelry, a large selection of rhinestone jewelry, some designer jewelry like Eisenberg and Weiss, 1970s-style bellbottoms and butterfly collar shirts, old buttons, and a partridge in a pear tree.

Obviously, this is one of Mr. C's favorite places to visit. The staff is very friendly and you just have plain old fun perusing the merchandise. Bring your significant other: It's a cheap date!

The store is open from 11 a.m. to 7 p.m., Mondays through Saturdays, and from noon to 6 p.m. on Sundays.

The Junkman's Daughter

- 1130 Euclid Avenue N.E., Atlanta; ✆ (404) 577-3188

The Junkman's Daughter is not, as you may have expected, full of trash. The looks here are definitely cool-funky, though, with flame-painted and velvet draped walls and prodigious sound system.

The clothing here tends toward retro nightclub styles. Most of it is actually new but designed so that it looks like it was made along time ago. You'll find shirts with butterfly collars and kitschy animal prints in the $20 to $30 range. Used platform shoes are priced at $15 and up, silver heels about $7.50, while a satin baby doll dress was offered for $26. The store also carries vintage lingerie, such as 1940s-ish camisoles for $20, and sleeveless tees for $6.

Guys will find some cool gas station attendant shirts for about $15, and wild paisley button-down cotton shirts at $10. Levi's jeans, available in both men's and women's styles, are usually priced in the $16 range.

The jewelry selection is eclectic to say the least, with everything from mood rings—the ultimate in retro—for $6, to hematite stone earrings for $14.

Junkman's Daughter is open Monday through Friday from 11 a.m. to 9 p.m., Saturday from 1 p.m. to 9 p.m., and Sunday from noon to 8 p.m.

THRIFT STORES

Goodwill Thrift Stores

- 888 Ralph David Abernathy Drive S.W., Atlanta; ✆ (404) 755-6440

- 864 Southway Drive, Jonesboro; ✆ (770) 478-4970

SHOPPING: CLOTHING—USED

- 5279 Highway 29 N.W., Lilburn; (770) 564-1751
- 251 Scenic Highway, Lawrenceville; (770) 963-7793
- 230 Cobb Parkway South, Marietta; (770) 499-2132
- 10885 Alpharetta Highway, Roswell; (770) 649-1994
- Pleasant Hill Road, Duluth; (770) 564-1728

Goodwill is another one of those American institutions that needs little introduction. Here you can get lost in the large selection of clothing in good condition, and at very low prices. The funds raised through Goodwill stores help support this organization's programs, which give job training to people with disabilities.

There is always enough stock on the floor, it seems, to make sure that you never leave empty-handed. Women's two-piece professional outfits start as low as $6.95 and up; men's suits from $9.95; lots and lots of blue jeans from $4.95, dress shirts from $2.95, outerwear from $9.95, and much more. Often, the stores get closeout deals on new clothing as well.

Just about every day brings a different special: Tuesdays are senior citizen days, when appropriately aged shoppers are given 25 percent off their total purchases. On other days, all dresses become half-price, all items with green tags are reduced to $1, sleepwear and jewelry are 25 percent off, shoes go for 25 percent off the tagged price, and so on. Call before you go to find out about current specials.

Stores are generally open Monday through Saturday from 9 a.m. to 8 p.m., and Sunday from 12:30 p.m. to 6 p.m. However, hours may vary by location, so call ahead.

Last Chance Thrift Stores

- 1709 Church Street, Decatur; (404) 296-1711
- 900 Thornton Road, Lithia Springs; (770) 948-4492
- 1241 Mount Zion Road, Morrow; (770) 961-4085
- 1977 S Cobb Drive S.E., Marietta; (770) 433-3322
- 201 Norcross Tucker Road, Norcross; (770) 662-5616

Yet another of Atlanta's many thrift store chains, Last Chance serves the Perimeter suburbs with clothing for men, women, and children. You can find lots of good deals on jeans and sweaters, jackets, dresses, suits, shoes, and more, all in "fair to middling" condition. If you're looking to get a ton of stuff cheap, give this place a chance.

Store hours are 9 a.m. to 8 p.m. Monday through Friday, 9 a.m. to 6:30 p.m. on Saturday, and noon to 6 p.m. on Sunday.

Salvation Army Thrift Store

- 740 Marietta Street N.W., Atlanta; Phone: (404) 523-6214
- 2857 E. College Avenue, Avondale Estates; (404) 299-0703
- 700 Highway 138 S.W., Riverdale; (770) 477-0506
- 1047 Alpharetta Street, Roswell; (770) 992-2241
- 4760 Lawrenceville Highway, Lilburn; (678) 380-9424
- 2471 Austell Road, Marietta; (678) 556-9663
- www.salvationarmy.org

The Salvation Army is more than Santas and men and women in military uniforms shaking the bells in front of stores during the holidays. They not only accept donations from good-hearted folks, but they also pick up more than 50 truckloads of donated furniture, clothing, and household items every week and then use those donations to provide merchandise for the thrift stores scattered about the metropolitan area.

Needless to say, these stores carry a wide variety of nearly every imaginable household and clothing item. Profits from sales support the Adult Rehabilitation Center.

Store hours are Monday to Saturday 10 a.m. to 6 p.m.

St. Vincent de Paul

- 2409 Piedmont Road N.E., Atlanta; (404) 365-8811
- 2050 Chamblee Tucker Road, Chamblee; (770) 458-9607
- 685 N. Central Avenue, Hapeville; (404) 767-5238
- 3256 Buford Highway, Duluth; (770) 622-9533
- 2728 Summer Street, Kennesaw; (770) 919-1458
- Scenic Plaza Shopping Center, Highway 24, Lawrenceville; (770) 339-7997
- 4974 Lawrenceville Highway, Lilburn; (770) 921-7187
- 1171 Powder Springs Road N.W., Marietta; (770) 792-8026
- 4687 Rockbridge Road, Stone Mountain; (404) 292-4102

This international Catholic charity runs numerous thrift shops featuring an assortment of used clothing, household items, furniture, appliances, books, CDs, records, tapes, jewelry, and other items. Ninety-eight percent of the proceeds go to various charitable works, including, among other things, crisis pregnancy centers and emergency rent checks to working folks in a bind.

Store hours are generally 10 a.m. to 3 p.m. Monday through Saturday but vary according to location, so call ahead!

The Thrift House of the Cathedral of St. Philip

- 2581 Piedmont Road N.E., Atlanta; (404) 233-8652
- Lindbergh Plaza Shopping Center, 2581 Piedmont Road, Atlanta; (404) 233-8652

For true thrifty shoppers, this benefit shop for various local charities is a must-see. The small selection of used books and toys isn't that fantastic, but the bargain buys on donated clothing certainly are. Plus, this place also has similar bargains on shoes, draperies, housewares, furniture, and other household items.

Mr. C chased after a Champion sweatshirt for just $2, and Arrow dress shirts for men for $3. Levi jeans will cost you no more than $5.

For $2.50, you can take home a ladies' crocheted wool-angora cardigan, or, for $3.50, a nylon pullover windbreaker. A woman's twill skirt by Dockers was offered for only $3.

The store is very popular with savvy bargain hunters, so you never know what kind of buys you'll find. Leather pocketbooks, Kenya bags, and costume jewelry are hot items that sell almost as fast as the staff can put them on the sales floor.

The Thrift House will gladly accept any clothing items (if in reasonably good condition), and you'll get a tax receipt for any donation. Any items that the store is unable to sell after a certain period of time are ultimately given away at the Union Mission.

The store is open Monday through Friday from 10 a.m. to 6 p.m., and Saturday from 10 a.m. to 4:30 p.m.

Value Village Thrift Store

- 1899 Metropolitan Parkway S.W., Atlanta; (770) 840-7283
- 1320 Moreland Avenue S.E., Atlanta; (770) 840-7283
- 3503 Memorial Drive, Atlanta; (770) 840-7283
- 2555 Bolton Road N.W., Atlanta; (770) 840-7283
- 4298 Old Jonesboro Road, Forest Park; (770) 840-7283
- 119 N. Cobb Parkway, Marietta; (770) 840-7283
- 1023 Alpharetta Street, Roswell; (770) 840-7283
- 3857 Lawrenceville Highway, Tucker; (770) 840-7283
- www.valuevillage.com

Perhaps the biggest and best among Atlanta's thrift shops, this national chain buys used clothing and household items from reputable, nonprofit organizations, and then sells it in bright, clean, well-run outlets that approach the selection, scope, and "look and feel" of full-price department stores. Mr. C found lots of good clothing for women, men, and children: suits for $10 to $20, dresses for $5 to $10, shoes for $3 to $5, and even a few pairs of western boots for $3! Bargain hunters can find name-brand clothes, some with price tags still attached, and on Memorial Day and the Fourth of July, everything goes for half the ticket price!

One of the stores Mr. C checked out had a whole wall of color televisions, most of which were up and running, priced at $80 and $90. These sit behind a protective barrier, but if you're interested, you can ask to see it up close. Value Village also has an especially good stock of toys and games for kids. (Picture a game of "Pictionary" for a buck.)

All branches of the store are open Monday through Thursday from 9 a.m. to 8 p.m., Friday and Saturday from 9 a.m. to 9 p.m., and Sunday from 10 a.m. to 6 p.m.

COSMETICS AND PERFUMES

Take it from The Cheapster: It's a sweet feeling indeed to look pretty and smell beautiful without having to drop a load of bills to do it. Mrs. C feels the same way.

The most popular cosmetics products, like booze, build and maintain their value through savvy branding and marketing by their manufacturers. "In cosmetics, packaging is everything," an ad exec once confided to Mr. C. Indeed, most of the price you pay for top-of-the-line designer brands goes to support all those fancy boxes and bottles, as well as the high-gloss photo shoots with high-strung art directors and pouty international models. If you're willing to forgo the Paul Mitchells and Jheri Rheddings, and you know where to look, you can find some incredible deals on lesser-known (but nearly identical) scents, soaps, rinses, moisturizers, and what have you. Or, if you're one who demands name-brand goods, there are discount places for you, too, specializing in factory-direct and wholesale deals With a little help from the missus, your loyal Cheapness has selected the area's best in each category for your perusal here.

Perfumania

- North Lake Mall, 4800 Briarcliff Road N.E., Atlanta; (770) 723-1404

- 400 Ernest W Barrett Parkway N.W., Kennesaw; (770) 590-9799

- Tanger Factory Outlet Center, 1000 Tanger Drive, Locust Grove; (770) 914-6575

- Northpoint Circle Mall, Alpharetta; (770) 410-9766

- Gwinnett Place Mall, 2100 Pleasant Hill Road, Duluth; (770) 813-0335

- www.perfumania.com

This large national chain's vast buying power enables it to sell top-name designer perfumes at cut-rate prices—20 to 60 percent off retail, and that's a proposition that smells pretty sweet to The Cheapster! Better yet, Perfumania stands by its prices: If you find the same product advertised for less they will refund 110 percent of the difference.

On a recent foray into this aromatic world, Mr. Cheap found a 3.3-ounce bottle of Elizabeth Taylor's "White Diamonds" for $35.99 and 6.8 ounces of "Escada for Women" by Escada for $24.99. Men's colognes by designers Tommy Hilfiger, Gucci, Nautica, and many others were available at similar savings.

Perfumania also has perfumes for children. Baby Blue Jeans for Boys and Baby Rose Jeans for Girls by Gianni Versace were $14.99 a bottle, marked down from $29.00.

You can sample as many of these as you like; the staff is extremely knowledgeable and relaxed. The scents are sprayed onto special papers, which are then labeled for you with the name of the smelly product; this way, you don't walk out of the store wearing ten contrasting fragrances.

The store also specializes in boxed gift sets, again, at up to half off or more. In many cases, you can get a cologne set, with matching lotion, shower gel (or whatever), for the same price as the perfume alone. There are some cosmetic gift sets as well, such as eye shadow color kits. And you should try Nature's Elements aromatherapy oils, discounted here at almost half price!

Store hours are Monday to Saturday 10 a.m. to 9 p.m., and Sunday noon to 6 p.m.

The Perfume Outlet

- 7471 Highway 85, Riverdale; (770) 997-3505

- www.perfumeoutlet.com

This is a retail perfume outlet, not a warehouse, so all the perfumes sold here are in their regular packages, and ready for gift-giving. Some men's colognes and aftershaves are sold here, but the store mainly caters to women.

You'll find more than 4,000 perfumes, including dozens of designer fragrances, including Red, Giorgio Beverly Hills, Elizabeth Taylor's "Passion," Bijan, Chloé, Liz Claiborne, and more. You probably won't find the very latest creations, but plenty of recognizable and classic brand names are kept in stock. Men's aftershaves like Ralph Lauren's "Polo" and Calvin Klein's "Obsession" are in good supply.

They also sell several lines of "rebottled fragrances," which are basically the same name-brand originals available in smaller half an ounce sizes. With this packaging, the savvy and soon-to-be-lovely-smelling shopper can buy several fragrances for the price of one large bottle!

The Perfume Outlet requested that Mr. C not put the actual prices in print, in order to protect their relationships with the manufacturers. But they did say that their perfumes are generally marked 10 to 15 percent (and sometimes more) below department stores like Macy's and Rich's.

The store also sells hair care products from Paul Mitchell, Redken, and Nexxus; but, alas, these are sold at regular retail prices.

Here's an extra bargain-hunting tip: Bring your own empty bottles into the shop, and you'll save even more on some brands. A half-ounce of perfume that may sell for $10 in bulk would be reduced to $8 if they can put it into your own container. Considering the fact that their prices are already lower than other perfumeries, these savings can really add up!

Know the difference between perfume, eau de toilette, and cologne? Check out Perfume Outlet's Web site, which not only lets you search and order that special fragrance, but also provides useful shopping information on fragrance categories and how they're defined and priced.

Store hours are 10 a.m. to 7 p.m. Monday through Saturday, and 1 p.m. to 5:30 p.m. on Sunday.

Sally Beauty Supply

- 590 Cascade Avenue S.W., Atlanta; ✆ (404) 755-0296
- 2973 Headland Drive S.W., Atlanta; ✆ (404) 346-1226
- 2625 Piedmont Road N.E., Atlanta; ✆ (404) 231-4750
- 3728 Roswell Road N.E., Atlanta; ✆ (404) 233-9438
- 5195 Buford Highway N.E., Doraville; ✆ (770) 455-4540
- 3455 Memorial Drive, Decatur; ✆ (404) 288-205
- 2179 Lawrenceville Highway, Decatur; ✆ (404) 633-5144
- 4873 Jonesboro Road, Forest Park; ✆ (404) 366-6379
- 5590 Mableton Parkway S.E., Mableton; ✆ (770) 739-4005
- 3205 S. Cobb Drive S.E., Smyrna; ✆ (770) 436-4969
- 2550 Sandy Plains Road, Marietta; ✆ (770) 578-8210
- 10733 Alpharetta Highway, Roswell; ✆ (770) 992-7714
- ✍ www.sallybeauty.com

A more accurate name for this chain might be "Sally's Hair and Nail Care Supply," but no matter, for on these particular products there are bargains galore. From shampoos to fake nail sets to perming supplies, you'll find it here. And because this is a large national chain with big buying power, their prices are among the best around.

When Mr. C last checked out the store, a 12-pack of Styling-Ese straight perm rods was selling for just 79 cents, and Jheri Rhedding's

"One for All" acid perm kit was offered for $3.99. All Set hair spray in the 20-ounce can cost $1.29, and a pint of Queen Helene Strawberry Shampoo was $2.19. And you could get a whole quart of Tresemmé European Remoisturizing Conditioner for just $2.44.

There is a full selection of quality products geared toward African-American customers here, too. These include such hair care items as Dark & Lovely's Cholesterol Conditioning Treatment, offered for about for $1.99, and the same brand's No Lye Relaxer System for $4.69.

Sally's own brand, Beauty Secrets, will save you even more money. Cotton balls, for example, were just $1.39 for 100 triple-size balls; that's about 75 cents off what you can expect to pay for the same product in a grocery store or regular drug store. Beauty Secrets Nail Glue was offered for just $2.99.

In addition to treatment supplies, Sally also sells pro-grade equipment at salon industry prices. A Conair "Grand Champion" professional styling dryer is $34.99; Helen of Troy's hot curling iron with brush was offered for $8.99, and a Curlmaster Curling Iron for an incredible $2.99.

Store hours are 9 a.m. to 7 p.m. Monday through Saturday, and 11 a.m. to 6 p.m. on Sunday.

Scentsations (at K&G Liquidators)

- 1777 Ellsworth Industrial Boulevard N.W., Atlanta; ✆ (404) 577-3565

This "shop" is actually little more than a counter inside of the women's department at K & G Liquidators (see separate listing under *Clothing—Men's and Women's General Wear*). But it's worth a visit for serious smellers.

Scentsations carries a selection of designer colognes for men and women at discounts of about 10 to 40 percent off retail prices. Most items will save you in the range of $5 to $10 a bottle. On one expedition, though, we were offered a 3-ounce spray bottle of Oscar de la Renta perfume, which lists for $52, for only $36.95. Other women's fragrances include a 2.5-ounce spray of Perry Ellis eau de toilette, reduced from $37.50 to $29.95; a 1.7-ounce Romeo Gigli perfume reduced from $50 to $34.95; and the same size eau de toilette by Paloma Picasso, $7 off at $41.95.

Men could save $5 on longtime favorite Z-14 by Halston, at $19.95 for a 1.9-ounce spray bottle; four ounces of Guess for Men cologne were marked down from $40 to $31.95; and Paco Rabanne saves you about $6 on the 1.7-ounce spray bottle. Scentsations also carries lotions, powders, and other skin care products; they can design custom gift baskets, and they'll ship anywhere in the country.

Scentsations is open Fridays and Saturdays from 10 a.m. to 7 p.m., Sundays from noon to 6 p.m.

Tuesday Morning

- 3145 Piedmont Road N.E., Atlanta; ✆ (404) 233-6526

- 4502 Chamblee Dunwoody Road, Dunwoody; ✆ (770) 457-3565

- 901 Montreal Road, Tucker; ✆ (770) 934-3164

- 2790 Cumberland Boulevard S.E., Smyrna; ✆ (770) 435-6678

- 1115 Mount Zion Road, Morrow; ✆ (770) 961-0707

- 736 Johnson Ferry Road, Marietta; ✆ (770) 971-0511

SHOPPING: DISCOUNT DEPARTMENT STORES

- 6325 Spalding Drive, Norcross; (770) 447-4692
- 4051 Highway 78, Lilburn; (770) 978-3573
- 700 Sandy Plains Road, Marietta; (770) 428-1536
- 1231 Alpharetta Street, Roswell; (770) 640-8146
- 3500 Satellite Boulevard, Duluth; (770) 476-0522
- 3600 Dallas Highway N.W., Marietta; (678) 355-5505
- www.tuesdaymorning.com

Tuesday mornings are indisputably better than early Mondays. So, too, are the prices here on cosmetics and perfumes; we've already discussed this place in other sections of this book.

By the way, if you're worried that these "liquid liquidation" bargains may be a bit old, Mr. C has heard from experts in the business that perfume doesn't begin to lose its potency until after it has been opened. As long as it's sealed, it's fresh.

Tuesday Morning stores are open seven days a week. Store hours are Monday, Tuesday, Wednesday, and Friday from 10 a.m. to 7 p.m., Thursday from 10 a.m. to 8 p.m., Saturday from 10 a.m. to 6 p.m., and Sunday from noon to 6 p.m.

DISCOUNT DEPARTMENT STORES

Sometimes the best places to find super deals are the big discount department stores. These sprawling establishments carry close to the full range of products covered in this book, including appliances, clothing, home furnishings, electronics, photographic supplies, jewelry, and just about everything in between.

Mr. C could have listed each of these places multiple times throughout the book but thought it would be much more convenient for you, Dear Reader, if he put them all in one spot, along with an overview of each of their sales policies and product mixes.

Sure, these places may not have the same atmosphere or personalized service of the independent retailers, but often their prices can't be beat, especially when they offer major seasonal sales. Be sure to compare prices to the smaller stores Mr. C has gathered in these pages.

Best Buy

- 1201 Hammond Drive N.E., Atlanta; (770) 392-0454
- 1568 Bankhead Highway N.W., Atlanta; (404) 792-7856
- 470 Flat Shoals Avenue S.E., Atlanta; (404) 581-0105
- 2035 Martin Luther King, Jr. N.W., Atlanta; (404) 756-9509
- 4145 Lavista Road, Tucker; (770) 939-7660
- 2460 Cobb Parkway S.E., Smyrna; (770) 859-9266

- 1201 Hammond Drive N.E., Atlanta; ✆ (770) 392-0454
- 1576 Southlake Parkway, Morrow; ✆ (770) 968-0884
- 1950 Highway 85, Jonesboro; ✆ (770) 719-9990
- 1450 E Park Place Boulevard, Stone Mountain; ✆ (770) 469-9848
- 5506 Buford Highway, Norcross; ✆ (770) 448-7090
- 1875 Pleasant Hill Road, Duluth; ✆ (770) 381-9494
- 850 Cobb Place Boulevard N.W., Kennesaw; ✆ (770) 424-7868
- 975 N Point Parkway, Alpharetta; ✆ (678) 339-1321
- 2780 Horizon Ridge Court, Suwanee; ✆ (770) 614-6668
- 3379 Buford Drive, Buford; ✆ (770) 614-0533
- 3205 Woodward Crossing Boulevard, Buford; ✆ (770) 614-0533
- ✉ www.bestbuy.com

Sure, this is just another major chain. Still, Mr. C just can't ignore the fact that on many products this store boasts his favorite shopping items: great deals and selection. This is a primo place to shop for computers and peripherals, home audio and video equipment, digital photo and imaging equipment, home office supplies, major appliances, CDs, videos, and more.

Depending on the national financial conditions, Best Buy sometimes offers no-interest financing on major purchases, so there's a way to save even more moola!

Store hours are 10 a.m. to 9 p.m. Monday through Saturday, and 11 a.m. to 6 p.m. on Sunday.

Big Lots

- 7300 Roswell Road N.E.; Atlanta; ✆ (770) 671-1892
- 2685 Stewart Avenue S.W., Atlanta; ✆ (404) 762-5449
- 2581 Piedmont Road N.E., Atlanta; ✆ (404) 237-1919
- 2975 Headland Drive S.W., Atlanta; ✆ (404) 349-1616
- 2557 N. Decatur Road, Decatur; ✆ (404) 373-3220
- 1355 Roswell Road, Marietta; ✆ (770) 578-9030
- 250 S Clayton Street, Lawrenceville; ✆ (770) 995-8914
- 2738 Candler Road, Decatur; ✆ (404) 241-4866
- 680 Powder Springs Street S.W., Marietta; ✆ (770) 422-7565
- 1375 Roswell Road, Marietta; ✆ (770) 565-6208
- 2745 Sandy Plains Road, Marietta; ✆ (770) 973-8947
- 2280 E Main Street, Snellville; ✆ (678) 344-8303
- 5570 Highway 29 N.W., Lilburn; ✆ (770) 279-7107
- 3791 S. Cobb Drive SE #G, Smyrna; ✆ (770) 438-8321
- 6150 Covington Highway, Lithonia; ✆ (678) 418-5464
- 160 Market Square, Cartersville; ✆ (770) 387-2766
- 3142 Proctor Street, Duluth; ✆ (678) 475-1811
- 1111 Bankhead Highway, Carrollton; ✆ (770) 830-6133
- 260 Merchants Drive, Dallas; ✆ (770) 505-8282
- 6017 Memorial Drive, Stone Mountain; ✆ (770) 469-8600

SHOPPING: DISCOUNT DEPARTMENT STORES

- 5200 Glade Road S.E., Acworth; ✆ (770) 529-3344
- 5055 Austell Road, Austell; ✆ (770) 739-5943
- 4200 Wade Green Road N.W.; Kennesaw; ✆ (770) 423-1565
- ✍ www.cnstores.com

Go ahead—call this place cheap. They love it. They have fun with it, in signs all over the store that say "We must be crazy . . ." and so forth. More than forty aisles are packed with closeouts, salvage from other stores, discontinued items, knock-off brands, and every other way to save money. They have a huge selection, as much as the major liquidation places Mr. C has seen in New York and other cities.

You never know what they may have here. As with any store specializing in closeouts, you can't expect them to have exactly the item or brand you want. But you'll probably find something comparable. Or, as many folks do, you can go out and just see what's there—no doubt, a few things you can really use, at rock-bottom prices.

You want toys? They got toys. Need some sneakers? Maybe you'll find Nike running shoes for $15.99. What about hair care? You may be able to buy generic copies of salon brands like Paul Mitchell and Nexus for $1.49 a bottle, or go for the real thing with Jhirmack and Revlon for a buck each.

Not to mention domestics and other home furnishings, hardware and tools, sports equipment, household products, a 15-pound sack of kitty litter for $1.99, greeting cards at 40 percent off the printed price, and several aisles of reduced-price grocery items. BL is also a good place to check out for seasonal items, like Halloween costumes and Christmas decorations—discounted before the holidays, not after.

BL also has furniture departments in most stores, as well as a number of freestanding furniture stores in the Atlanta area, offering living room, dinette and bedroom sets, mattresses, home office furniture, entertainment centers, and more.

All stores are 8 a.m. to 10 p.m. seven days a week. Since merchandise may vary from store to store, call ahead before you make the trek.

Burlington Coat Factory

- 2841 Greenbriar Parkway S.W., Atlanta; ✆ (404) 349-6300
- 3750 Venture Drive, Duluth; ✆ (770) 497-0033
- 1255 Roswell Road, Marietta; ✆ (770) 971-6540
- 608 Holcomb Bridge Road, Roswell; ✆ (770) 518-9800

Don't be deceived by a name! Not content with being a popular clothing discounter for the entire family, Burlington Coat Factory stores have expanded to become something almost like actual department stores. They are quite large, and in each one you'll not only find discounted clothing for the whole family, but also shoes, linens, luggage, cosmetics, and jewelry.

Most folks know of Burlington for its clothing. They carry big names at good prices; some are very good bargains indeed. You can outfit yourself from top to toe here, for inside and out, in conservative or stylish looks. True to its name, you can find all kinds of coats here; Mr. C has seen sights like a Pierre Cardin lambskin bomber jacket, list priced at $300 for just $180, or racks of simulated fur coats for women. How about a *faux* fox, reduced from $200 to $120?

But there's more here than meets the elements. Underneath those coats, guys could be wearing a Harvé Bernard double-breasted suit of 100 percent wool, discounted from $400 to $180. Or creations by Ralph Lauren, Perry Ellis, Nino Cerruti, and Christian Dior at similar savings.

For the gals, a nifty black two-piece Oleg Cassini set, not $270, but $150. A Jones New York turtleneck sweater, reduced from $140 to $90. Or, 100 percent silk blouses for $12.95. Size selection is good here, from petite to plus sizes for women, as well as big and tall sizes for men.

Then, there are all the fashions for children, from tots to teens. Boys' Jordache ski jackets were recently seen reduced from $70 to $40; girls will look smart in a dressy red coat by London Fog, marked down from $110 to $80. Both can save ten bucks or so off Levi's jeans, Guess denim fashions, and others.

You can also stock up on basics and accessories here, like ties, hats, and underwear (particularly Burlington hosiery, at $1 to $2 off all styles). There is also a small but serviceable jewelry counter, selling gold chains, bracelets, watches, and the like at permanent discounts of 40 to 50 percent off retail prices. And don't forget to look for the clearance racks in every clothing department!

But what about the other specialty departments? Here you can also realize savings on all kinds of basic and classy shoes for men, women, and kids. Current styles in dressy shoes and boots are mostly sold at $10–$20 off list prices; for deeper discounts, though, look over on the long self-service racks, arranged by size. These are mainly closeouts and overstocks, all perfectly good. In the women's category, you may find a pair of tailored loafers for $16.99 or Ann Marino pumps from $14.98. On the guy's side, you can ease your dogs into some dressy Dexter tassled loafers that have been marked down from $80 to $59.98, or perhaps some Banker wing tips discounted from $55 to only $24.99. There is a more limited selection of sneakers, like ankle-high tennis shoes by Reebok for $49; plus kids shoes by Sesame Street, Fisher Price, and Hush Puppies.

The "Baby Depot" department sells discounted clothing, furniture, and accessories for newborns and small children. Along with good prices on infant and maternity wear, you can find things like a white crib, reduced from $200 to $144.75, or sheets sets that run from $16.95 to $29.95. There are also plenty of soft and cuddly toys and accessories to put in the crib along with the sheets (and the baby). You'll also find such diverse items as a Little Tykes plastic table and chairs, for toddler tea parties; Glider Lite strollers priced under $80; an Accel DX convertible car seat, reduced from $100 to $79.99; and clothing for both newborns and maternity moms.

Burlington boasts a Christopher Lowell Collection featuring designer linens, rugs, towels, and other accessories for bed and bath, as well as a range of other home furnishings and accessories at very competitive prices. Mr. C found things like California King comforter sets ranging in price from $129 to $289, a Christopher Lowell King sheet set for under $50, towels beginning at $10.99,

SHOPPING: DISCOUNT DEPARTMENT STORES

plus bed pillows (including orthopedic styles), throw pillows, shower curtains, decorative baskets, and more, stacked from floor to ceiling.

Interested in picking up some luggage? How about a Luggage America three-piece set for only $69.99, or a 44" Peabody Brown Suede garment bag, normally retailing for about $100, on sale here for under $60.

Burlington keeps its stores open from 10 a.m. to 9 p.m. Monday through Saturday, and 1 p.m. to 6 p.m. on Sunday. They're usually open a bit later during the holiday season.

Costco Wholesale

- 645 Barrett Parkway, Kennesaw; ✆ (770) 794-1767

- 6350 Peachtree Dunwoody, Atlanta; ✆ (770) 352-8660

- 1700 Mount Zion Road, Morrow; ✆ (678) 201-0003

- ✐ www.costco.com

This is Mr. C's favorite place in the world to stock up on ten-pound jars of pickles; Mrs. C is partial to the bathtubs of mayonnaise.

This membership warehouse club offers such great prices on name-brand merchandise, including appliances, other household accessories, books, DVDs and CDs, computers and other electronics, furniture, hardware, outdoor supplies, health and beauty products, gourmet foods, jewelry, office products, pharmaceuticals, photo supplies, and travel services.

Of course, you have to become a member to shop here, but it's well worth the annual fee, which at press time was $45. From time to time, the store offers short-term "free" memberships and discounts. Call to check.

Costco is open from 10 a.m. to 8:30 p.m. Monday through Friday, from 9 a.m. to 8 p.m. on Saturday, and from 10 a.m. to 6 p.m. on Sunday.

Big Kmart

- 230 Cleveland Avenue S.W., Atlanta; ✆ (404) 766-7543

- 2581 Piedmont Road N.E., Atlanta; ✆ (404) 261-6900

- 2975 Headland Drive S.W., Atlanta; ✆ (404) 349-4810

- 2395 Wesley Chapel Road, Decatur; ✆ (770) 808-0606

- 3205A South Cobb Drive, Smyrna; ✆ (770) 432-0017

- 5590 Mableton Parkway, Mableton; ✆ (770) 745-1133

- 5925 Roswell Road N.E., Sandy Springs; ✆ (404) 255-7330

- 5597 Buford Highway, Doraville; ✆ (770) 458-9506

- 3753 Austell Road S.W., Austell; ✆ (770) 944-8100

- 4975 Jimmy Carter Boulevard, Norcross; ✆ (770) 925-0220

- 7965 Tara Boulevard, Jonesboro; ✆ (770) 477-0521

- 3879 Highway 138 S.E., Stockbridge; ✆ (770) 389-4333

- 1140 Roswell Road S.E., Marietta; ✆ (770) 427-5356

- 4269 Roswell Road, Marietta; ✆ (770) 977-2102

- 606 Holcomb Bridge Road, Roswell; ✆ (770) 992-9525

- 3625 Sweetwater Road, Duluth; ✆ (770) 923-9570

- 1200 Barrett Parkway N.W., Kennesaw; (770) 422-0240
- 3605 Sandy Plains Road, Marietta; (770) 977-7715
- 2229 Atlanta Highway, Hiram; (770) 439-8522
- 2420 Wisteria Drive, Snellville; (770) 972-0553
- 1485 Highway 138 S.E., Conyers; (770) 922-7824
- 9552 Highway 5, Douglasville; (770) 949-0362
- 550 Molly Lane, Woodstock; (770) 517-2920
- 665 Duluth Highway, Lawrenceville; (770) 995-5213
- 400 Crosstown Road, Peachtree City; (770) 487-2295
- 5300 Bartow Road, Acworth; (770) 975-0094
- www.bluelight.com

Bigger is better, and over the years Kmart has tried to battle against the Wal-Marts and the Costcos and other megastores by getting bigger and bigger. The Big Kmart stores are super-sized versions of the familiar discount stores; many include grocery items along with clothing, small appliances, jewelry, and all sorts of other *stuff.* Along the way, it has brought its prices down to interesting levels.

Kmart departments cover household accessories, electronics and CDs, clothes, shoes, hardware, camping gear, pet supplies, groceries and pharmaceuticals, gardening supplies, auto repair and supplies, and more. The great thing about this place is that you can find such a large selection of products—many respected name brands—for far less money than you'll pay in the typical mall-based retailer.

Whether you're picking up a six-pack of large wine goblets for $8.99, socks at 3 for $3.99, or a pair of rugged, brand-name hiking boots for $19.99, you stand an excellent chance of being quite pleased with yourself when you walk out of those big front doors. And if you're careful, you can manage to fill an entire shopping cart with items that do not include the name Martha Stewart!

Most Big Kmart stores are open seven days from 8 a.m. to 11 p.m., with extended hours during the holiday season.

Marshalls

- 3232 Peachtree Road N.E., Atlanta; (404) 365-8155
- 2625 Piedmont Rd N.E., Atlanta; (404) 233-3848
- 6337 Roswell Road N.E., Atlanta; (404) 252-9679
- 1131 Hammond Drive N.E., Atlanta; (770) 396-8623
- 4166 Buford Highway N.E., Atlanta; (404) 329-0200
- 2540 Hargrove Road, Smyrna; (770) 436-6061
- 6011 Memorial Drive, Stone Mountain; (770) 469-4005
- 2300 Miller Road, Decatur; (770) 987-4280
- 1096 Mount Zion Road, Morrow; (770) 961-0612
- 3999 Austell Road, Austell; (770) 948-7276
- 2203 Roswell Road, Marietta; (770) 971-2604
- 5370 Highway 78, Stone Mountain; (770) 413-0945
- 1425 Market Boulevard, Roswell; (770) 641-7949

SHOPPING: DISCOUNT DEPARTMENT STORES

- 109 Pavilion Parkway, Fayetteville; ✆ (770) 719-4699
- 3675 Satellite Boulevard, Duluth; ✆ (770) 497-1052
- 2890 Chapel Hill Road, Douglasville; ✆ (770) 577-9390
- 425 Ernest Barrett Parkway, Kennesaw; ✆ (770) 424-2064
- 6320 N. Point Parkway, Alpharetta; ✆ (770) 667-3495
- 1905 Scenic Highway S.W., Snellville; ✆ (770) 736-9496
- 875 Lawrenceville Suwanee Road, Lawrenceville; ✆ (770) 995-2575
- ✍ www.marshallsonline.com

Mr. C doubts that you need to "discover" this national chain by reading about it in these pages. Still, he could hardly write about discount clothing, shoes, and home furnishings without at least acknowledging the place, right? In the past half-decade or so, Marshalls has almost doubled the number of stores in the Atlanta area, which makes it even easier to find one nearby.

Marshalls has some truly low prices, thanks to its well-executed discount store philosophy of keeping overhead down while buying in very large quantities. Here you'll find top-notch designer brands for women, men and children—names like Liz Claiborne, Calvin Klein, Kasper, Jones of New York, and Polo by Ralph Lauren—almost always at 20 to 60 percent off standard retail prices!

Marshalls has also expanded beyond its clothing store roots to offer a serious selection of bath and body products, cosmetics and fragrances, tool sets, CDs, travel and camping gear, picture frames, candles, and much more. So, what's not to love?

Marshalls is usually open from 9:30 a.m. to 9:30 p.m. Monday through Saturday, and 11 a.m. to 6 p.m. on Sundays. During the holidays, they extend their hours in both the morning and evening.

Sam's Club

- 2901-A Clairmont Road, Atlanta; ✆ (404) 325-4000
- 1940 Mountain Industrial Boulevard, Tucker; ✆ (770) 908-8408
- 7325 Jonesboro Road, Morrow; ✆ (770) 960-8228
- 150 S. Cobb Parkway, Marietta; ✆ (770) 423-7018
- 3450 Steve Reynolds Boulevard, Duluth; ✆ (770) 497-1165
- 10600 Davis Drive, Alpharetta; ✆ (770) 992-4568
- 6995 Concourse Parkway, Douglasville; ✆ (770) 489-6167
- ✍ www.samsclub.com

Sam's Club is another national membership discount chain, where for a mere $35 or so a year you can shop among a prodigious assortment of clothing, appliances, electronics, food, jewelry, office supplies, books, sports merchandise, pet supplies, outdoor gear, and more. What Sam's Club lacks in atmosphere it makes up for in pure choice. Heck, you could almost supply your whole life without ever shopping anywhere else. As with the other discount merchants, Sam's Club is able to offer great prices through volume purchasing, thanks to hundreds of stores in major urban centers across the country, and its 50 million members.

Store hours are 10 a.m. to 8:30 p.m. Monday through Friday, 9:30 a.m. to 8 p.m. on Saturday, and 11 a.m. to 6 p.m. on Sunday.

Target

- 2400 North Druid Hills Road, Atlanta; ✆ (404) 325-3211

- 3535 Peachtree Road N.E., Atlanta; ✆ (404) 237-9494

- 2201 Cobb Parkway SE, Smyrna; ✆ (770) 952-2241

- ⌨ www.target.com

This chain has positioned itself as a slightly upscale discount store, which is a fair definition. In some hip circles, its name is given a faux-French accent, as in, "I bought this at Tar-jhay."

However you pronounce it, you'll find its stores full of good deals on clothes, jewelry and accessories, electronics, music and video, kitchen supplies, sports equipment, luggage, toys, and more. On top of the everyday low prices, they almost always have some kind of departmental clearance sale where you can get merchandise at up to 50 percent off the regular price.

On a recent expedition, Mrs. C picked up a women's wool sweater for a mere $16, and women's pants, jumpers, and tank tops were available for $7.99 to $9.99. In the other departments, a 19" color TV was on sale for $119, a number of just-released music CDs were priced at $12.88, and a range of popular entertainment and productivity software was available for $15 to $30.

Most Target stores are open seven days a week from 8 a.m. to 10 p.m.

Wal-Mart

- 4725 Ashford Dunwoody Road, Atlanta; ✆ (770) 395-0199

- 2496 Wesley Chapel Road, Decatur; ✆ (770) 593-3540

- 6065 Jonesboro Road, Morrow; ✆ (770) 968-0774

- 7050 Highway 85, Riverdale; ✆ (770) 994-1670

- 4375 Lawrenceville Highway, Tucker; ✆ (770) 939-2671

- 1133 East-West Connector, Austell; ✆ (770) 863-9300

- 1785 Cobb Parkway S., Marietta; ✆ (770) 955-2179

- 4700 Jonesboro Road, Union City; ✆ (770) 964-6921

- 5600 N Henry Boulevard, Stockbridge; ✆ (770) 389-1709

- ⌨ www.walmart.com

Talk about American icons! This is another one of those places that needs no description unless you've been living under a rock for the last few decades. (No offense to Stone Mountain residents!) Wal-Mart Stores is the world's largest retailer of general merchandise goods; by the way, they also operate Sam's Clubs, a warehouse club.

Wal-Mart has a fine and bargain-priced selection of electronics, cameras, video games, toys, jewelry, home and garden supplies, movies, books, music, clothes, auto supplies—just about any retail category you can wrap your hands (or arms) around.

Buy a ¼ carat three-stone diamond ring for just $149 (perfect for a wedding at the Elvis Chapel in Vegas). How about a Mr. Coffee Pump Espresso and Cappuccino maker for under $50, a computer desk with pull-out keyboard for under $60, or a Hunter 42" ceiling fan for under $70? In the music department, you can get a wide selection of recently released CDs in the $13 to $15 range. The list goes on and on, of course.

Most Atlanta area Wal-Mart stores are open 24 hours. Call to confirm hours.

ELECTRONICS

AUDIO/VIDEO EQUIPMENT

There are lots of places to save money on appliances and electronics in Atlanta. Some, unfortunately, are as far below repute as they are below retail. You've got to know the products yourself, or find a dealer you can trust.

One of the best ways to protect yourself, if you have doubts as to any store's reliability, is to ask about their guarantee policy. Make sure the item you want carries an American warranty; since some stores deal directly with manufacturers in the Far East, their merchandise may carry a foreign warranty instead. Even for identical products, a foreign warranty can make repairs a hassle—unless you don't mind paying the postage to Japan! Remember, you are perfectly within your rights to inquire about this in the store.

Best Buy

See the listing under *Discount Department Stores*.

Circuit City

- 3393 Peachtree Road N.E., Atlanta; (404) 812-1799
- 2841 Greenbriar Parkway S.W., Atlanta; (404) 349-5422
- 1165 Perimeter Center West, Atlanta; (770) 391-1999
- 2100 Pleasant Hill Road, Duluth; (770) 813-0993
- 1540 Dogwood Drive, Conyers; (770) 483-4712
- 2340 Cobb Parkway S.E., Smyrna; (770) 955-6866
- 9365 The Landing Drive, Douglasville; (770) 947-7197
- 3850 Venture Drive, Duluth; (770) 476-8172
- 3295 Buford Drive, Buford; (770) 831-5489
- 4572 Memorial Drive, Decatur; (404) 299-2001
- 1098 Bullsboro Drive, Newnan; (770) 251-3281
- 6290 North Point Parkway, Alpharetta; (770) 664-0395
- 1165 Perimeter Center West, Atlanta; (770) 391-1999
- www.circuitcity.com

Here's another one of those national chains where you can get just about any consumer electronics item you desire. Computers, cameras, home and car audio systems, wireless phones, and video gear are all here. If you're a savvy shopper and hit Circuit City on the right days, you'll also find some decent deals. This place tends to have regular weekly specials, and they usually offer bonus accessories and manufacturer's rebates with many of their products.

The last time that Mr. C shuffled down these gleaming aisles, he noticed a Sherwood 105-watt stereo receiver for only $79.99, and a Phillips portable CD player for under $50. He could have picked up a 1.1GHz Compaq PC system, complete with a monitor, CD-ROM drive, and printer, for under $600, as well as a 20 pack of AA alkaline batteries for just 99 cents (after a rebate). They also had an Olympus 2.1 megapixel camera available for under $400.

Store hours are 10 a.m. to 9 p.m. on Monday through Saturday, and noon to 6 p.m. on Sunday.

> ### MR. CHEAP'S PICKS
>
> *Electronics*
>
> **Discount Electronics**—This little gem of a store features TVs, VCRs, DVD players, home theater systems, and other consumer electronics products at a fraction of what you would pay at a major electronics retailer.
>
> **Recycle Electronics**—These guys sell used TVs, stereos, VCRs, camcorders, raw speakers, and car stereos at great prices, and with a store warranty.

Discount Electronics

- 4813 Rockbridge Road, Stone Mountain; ✆ (404) 508-4041

This little gem of a store features TVs, VCRs, DVD players, home theater systems, and other consumer electronics products at a fraction of what you would pay at a major electronics retailer. The catch is that all the products on sale here are "open items"—industry slang for floor models and demos. In this case, the owner gets all his slightly used stuff from Best Buy. However, it's all in excellent shape and comes with a six-month store guarantee.

Want to finally own a large-screen television without breaking the bank? Mr. C saw a 35" RCA TV, normally sold for $899, for only $500. A 53" model, usually priced at $1,800, could be had for a sweet $1,200. Bookshelf stereo systems normally on sale for $189 were priced at $130, and similar deals were available on everything in the store.

Discount Electronics is open Tuesday through Saturday from 11:30 a.m. to 8:30 p.m.

Hi-Fi Buys

- 3135 Peachtree Road N.E., Atlanta; ✆ (404) 261-4434
- 2545 Cumberland Parkway S.E., Atlanta; ✆ (770) 436-4242
- Atlanta Industrial Drive N.W., Atlanta; ✆ (404) 699-3800
- 2540-H Hargrove Road, Smyrna; ✆ (770) 436-4242
- 4023 Lavista Road, Tucker; ✆ (770) 938-4434
- 1311 Mount Zion Road, Morrow; ✆ (770) 961-8080
- 5495 Jimmy Carter Boulevard, Norcross; ✆ (770) 449-6223
- 1062 Johnson Ferry Road, Marietta; ✆ (770) 509-2635
- 2021 W. Liddell Road, Duluth; ✆ (770) 622-9133
- 1155 Ernest W. Barrett Parkway N.W., Kennesaw,; ✆ (770) 514-1446
- 10889 Alpharetta Highway, Roswell; ✆ (770) 552-9440
- ✐ www.hifibuys.com

This major chain is not a discount store, but they have plenty of everyday good deals. They specialize in home audio and just about every kind of other consumer electronics product *except* for computers. The product mix here ranges from DVD players to car stereos to digital camcorders to home theaters. The Cheapster would say that Hi-Fi's goods fit just about every price range, from stereo shelf speakers that cost less than $200 to $1,000 home theater systems, from basic VCRs that cost under a $100 to high-end digital camcorders that will set you back $2,000 or more.

The real value proposition here is the regular "open box" and "package" specials that are offered on an everyday basis. "Open box"

SHOPPING: ELECTRONICS

refers to items that were bought and then returned, or were used as demos. These are essentially brand-new, and carry the full manufacturers warranty, yet Hi-Fi Buys will let you have them for 10 to 20 percent off the market price. The folks here will also give you a discount when you create a "package." For example, combining a DVD player with a TV and home theater system. Just tell the salesperson what you want and bargain for your best deal.

Store hours are 10 a.m. to 9 p.m. Monday through Saturday, and noon to 6 p.m. on Sunday.

Radio Shack

- 32 Peachtree Street N.W., Atlanta; (404) 873-6488
- 868 Oak Street S.W., Atlanta; (404) 752-7377
- 3167 Peachtree Road N.E., Atlanta; (404) 237-9665
- 1544 Piedmont Rd N.E., Atlanta; (404) 873-6488
- 2685 Stewart Avenue S.W., Atlanta; (404) 768-5340
- 900 Circle 75 Parkway S.E., Atlanta; (770) 850-9993
- 2581 Piedmont Road N.E., Atlanta; (404) 266-0748
- 1436 Cumberland Mall S.E., Atlanta; (770) 434-1479
- 685 Old National Highway, College Park; (770) 994-3345
- 2907 N. Druid Hills Road N.E., Atlanta; (404) 633-1007
- 2841 Greenbriar Parkway S.W., Atlanta; (404) 349-0751
- 3393 Peachtree Road N.E., Atlanta; (404) 262-7949
- 3695 Cascade Road S.W., Atlanta; (404) 699-9773
- www.radioshack.com

Nerds rule! From transistors and coaxial cable to weather radios, headphones, PCs, home audio, and radio-controlled toy cars, this old, reliable redoubt of the high-water trouser and pocket protector crowd has everything electronic, of course, and always at competitive prices. What's more, Radio Shack always has sales on selected items, allowing you to save 25 percent or more when your need to acquire meets their need to unload. On a recent stealth mission of holiday shopping, Mr. C became intrigued with a cordless phone headset marked down from $49.99 to only $29.99, a long-range, cordless 2.4 GHz phone for only $59.99 (33 percent off their normal price), a full-sized MIDI keyboard for just $149.99, and a nifty non-contact infrared thermometer for $49.99. (Awesome!)

My rule here is: shop when there is a sale. Luckily, that's most of the time, although not everything is reduced at once. Read the flyers, check the online Web site, and make a phone call to track the object of your electronic desire.

Depending upon financial conditions, Radio Shack also offers 12-month, no-interest financing on big-ticket items such as computers.

Store hours are generally 10 a.m. to 9 p.m. Monday through Saturday, and noon to 6 p.m. on Sunday. However, hours may vary by location, so call before you go!

Recycle Electronics

- 6624 Dawson Boulevard #4C, Norcross; (770) 449-1872

Recycle Electronics is part of the Georgia Antique Center and Market, located on the south side of the premises. Recycle buys and sells used TVs, stereos, VCRs, camcorders, speakers, and some car stereos. They have the expertise to repair all these products, and they even accept trade-ins toward a purchase. Because of this, they have an ever-changing selection of recent and not-so-recent (but certainly not antique) models of every kind

Every so often Recycle will have an opportunity to buy a large quantity of a new merchandise, which allows them to offer some especially good deals. Recently Mr. C was offered a 36" television for $499, a 32" model for $399, and a 20" set for only $99. There is a catch, however: to get these low prices you've gotta pay cash. You *can* also purchase these TVs with a check or credit card, but in that case the price goes up just a bit.

When Recycle gets a deal like this the merchandise flies off the shelves, so don't hesitate getting to the store.

Since Recycle is a repair shop too, you can also bring your TV and other electronic products in for lifesaving surgery.

Everything sold here comes with a 30-day in-store warranty, during which the friendly staff will make any necessary repairs for free. They're open five days a week—closed Sunday and Monday. If you get the answering machine, leave a message, and they promise to call you back.

Also worth a look:

A&R Discount Electronics

- 2446 Atlanta Road S.E., Smyrna; ✆ (770) 434-6751

This place specializes in car audio and electronic products for use overseas. Store hours are 10 a.m. to 6 p.m. Monday through Saturday, and noon to 5 p.m. on Sunday.

COMPUTERS

Prices and specifications on computers change daily—almost always in the consumer's favor, with capabilities going up while prices remain the same or drop. What a deal!

The best way to shop for a computer is to know more than the salesperson. Check out the online Web sites, ask your neighborhood weenie, and read the ads in newspapers and specialty magazines. Then walk into a store already knowing what you want to buy and about how much it costs; let the salesperson try to convince you of a better deal than the best you have already found.

Best Buy

See the listing under *Discount Department Stores*.

Circuit City

See the listing under *Electronics—Audio/Video Equipment*.

CompUSA Superstore

- 3400 Around Lenox Road N.E., Atlanta; ✆ (404) 814-0880
- 124 Perimeter Center W, Atlanta; ✆ (770) 393-2980
- 3400 Woodale Drive N.E., Atlanta; ✆ (404) 814-0880
- 3845 Powder Springs Road Powder Springs; ✆ (770) 943-3312
- 380 North Point Circle, Alpharetta; ✆ (770) 754-0955
- 2201 Cobb Parkway S.E., Smyrna; ✆ (770) 952-1042
- 3825 Venture Drive, Duluth; ✆ (770) 813-1420
- 1915 Mount Zion Road, Morrow; ✆ (770) 960-2660
- ✎ www.compusa.com

SHOPPING: ELECTRONICS

Yet another soulless superstore, but, with its huge selection CompUSA is definitely a prime resource when it comes to new computers and accessories, including software packages, printers, scanners, storage options, networking equipment, handhelds, digital cameras, software, computer books, and much more.

Other necessities at good prices include things like scanners, printers, cables, software, books, and more. USB scanners from UMAX and Hewlett Packard are available in the $69 to $79 range. You can buy a 50-pack of Sony CD-R discs for just $29.99, and a Microsoft optical trackball for $39.99. CompUSA's own "house brand" knockoffs are even cheaper.

You can also save big on paper and printers.

A friend of C's, who is a high-tech expert, loves CompUSA because the store puts all of its hardware out on display. Most everything is up and running, from desktops to laptops to digital camcorders, so you can compare models and play with them to your heart's content.

The stores are open weekdays and Saturdays from 9 a.m. to 9 p.m., and Sundays 11 a.m. to 6 p.m.

Delta Computers

- 2633 Beacon Dr, Doraville; ℘ (770) 457-9999
- 2100 Roswell Road Suite 200D, Marietta; ℘ (770) 579-1212
- 7147 Jonesboro Road, Morrow; ℘ (770) 968-8822
- ⌨ www.deltacomputers.com

Born more than 25 years ago, in the infancy of the computer age, this Atlanta tech mainstay can be a great high-value resource for all your computing needs. They custom-build all their computers using key components from Intel and other major companies. Want to create your own cutting-edge PC? You can do it by mixing and matching components, and the staff will help you put together just the system you need.

Preparing for this edition, the Cheapster was offered a loaded current machine for under a thousand bucks and a slower, older, but still wondrous model for less than $600.

These guys also carry a wide range of components and peripherals at great prices: For example, Mr. C saw a wireless networking card for only $8.99, a 56K modem for $15.95, a 17" monitor for only $179, and a 40 GB hard drive for just $139.

They say their hardware is priced about 10 to 15 percent lower than the warehouse stores. What you will not find, though, is software.

They also have a full-service repair and upgrade store.

Delta's a favorite of both small and large businesses. All hardware products are sold with a 30-day money-back store guarantee as well as a one-year manufacturer's warranty.

Store hours are Monday through Saturday 10:30 a.m. to 7 p.m. They are closed Sundays.

MicroSeconds

- 6427 Roswell Rd N.E., Sandy Springs; ℘ (404) 252-7221
- 3505 Gwinnett Place Drive, Duluth; ℘ (770) 232-1011
- ⌨ www.microseconds.net

With the booming growth of the computer business, a new kind of store has evolved—the secondhand computer reseller. Because manufacturers are bringing out newer, fancier models almost every day, you can save lots of money on these big-ticket purchases by going with "slightly used" equipment. After all, a model that's only a year old may be passé to some hackers, but it's still got a lot of life in it.

And there are also "new" models that have been bypassed by the march of new technology.

MicroSeconds is one of the best examples of this kind of business that Mr. C has found in the Atlanta area. It not only carries a great selection of recent-model PCs, but also stocks thousands of other items, including printers, components, and software, and the young, friendly, and knowledgeable staff that really helps its customers get exactly what they need.

Whether you're buying new or used, you can put together your own IBM-compatible, paying only for what you need. All the used equipment has been well-kept, and the in-house repair crew has cleaned and checked every unit, erasing the drives and testing for viruses.

A lot of the PCs that Mr. C found here were either slightly used or "brand-new" models that were never sold. Among these are closeouts from manufacturers priced at 30 to 90 percent off retail. Occasionally MicroSeconds buys in large quantities and gets even a better deal, which allows the store to pass along the savings to you at prices even lower than their everyday stock.

For example, El Cheapster saw an IBM brand model fully equipped at less than $500. Need a monitor to go with that? Name-brand 15" models were going for a dirt-cheap $49 to $69.

How about a printer? For an additional $55 you could own a color ink jet. Several 1.2GB SCSI hard drives were priced $19. He also found popular laptops priced from $299 to $850. You get the idea . . .

If any equipment you buy from MicroSeconds is damaged, you can bring it back and they'll give you a new one. New computers carry a one-year warranty; used items are guaranteed for 30 days, during which they'll patch up any problems they may have missed.

Store hours for Sandy Springs are Monday to Friday 10 a.m. to 7 p.m., and 10 a.m. to 6 p.m. on Saturday. In Duluth you'll find the doors open from 10 a.m. to 8 p.m. Monday through Saturday.

PC Warehouse

- 6760 Jimmy Carter Boulevard, Norcross; ✆ (770) 840-2100
- 7050 Jimmy Carter Boulevard Norcross; ✆ (770) 448-6633

It's not your typical mile-high-ceiling "warehouse," but there's still plenty of selection, plus a

---

MR. CHEAP'S PICKS

Computers

Delta Computers—Everything here is custom-built with name-brand components, so you can get a great system especially tailored to you needs.

MicroSeconds—Great selection of recent-model PCs and peripherals (many slightly used) at rock-bottom prices.

PC Warehouse—Okay, it's a chain store, but if you're looking for prebuilt, new systems, PC Warehouse's combination of great selection and good prices is hard to beat.

knowledgeable staff at this national chain.

They've got a good selection of brand names, including Compaq, Epson, and IBM.

Of course, PC Warehouse has nearly every conceivable PC peripheral and accessory, including PC parts and miscellaneous computing supplies. They even have a selection of digital cameras.

For Macintosh enthusiasts, PC Warehouse offers a dedicated "store within a store" filled with Apple computers, monitors, printers, scanners, and other accessories at current prices.

If you're having a problem with a computer that you already own, you'll be happy to know that Mr. C found PC Warehouse's in-house repair shop to have much better rates than some of its national chain competitors.

The only real drawback with PC Warehouse is that it's not open at night or on weekends: Store hours are 9 a.m. to 5:30 p.m. Monday through Friday.

FACTORY OUTLET CENTERS

Factory outlets are usually good for saving a few hard-earned bucks. Although Mr. C has not been shy about mentioning these types of stores wherever appropriate in the book, he thought you might be able to also save some hard-earned time by focusing in on retail areas or shopping centers boasting several of these stores in one spot. Some of these are a little further from central Atlanta, but they're worth the trip.

But first a word of education: just because it's called a factory outlet doesn't mean it 1) is owned by a factory, 2) offers prices that are better than you'll find in a retail store, or 3) sells the same type and brands of products you might find in a retail store. When you think about it, *every* store is an outlet for a factory—that's what stores do.

As a savvy shopper, you need to know the merchandise. Compare items in factory outlets to those you find elsewhere; don't always assume they are better deals.

Atlanta: Midtown Outlets

- 500 Amsterdam Avenue N.E., Atlanta; (770) 986-0340

This collection of shops is centrally located, making it a convenient place to find great bargains on such items as feather comforters, silk trees, rugs, futons, clothing, shoes, and more.

Adel: Factory Stores at Adel

- 1203 West Fourth Street; next to Exit 39 off Interstate 75, Adel; (912) 896-4545

Stores include: $12 or Less; Bon Worth; Bookworld; Boots 'n Brims; Burger King; Captains D's Seafood; Christmas Factory; Columbo Yogurt; Country Home; Dream Baby; Famous Footwear;

Fieldcrest Cannon; Hush Puppies Factory Direct; Jerzees; King Frog; Kitchen Collection; Pit Row Nascar; Ponderosa; Popeyes; Stuckey's; Van Heusen.

Calhoun: Prime Outlets at Calhoun

- 455 Belwood Road, Interstate 75, Exit 312, about 75 miles northwest of Atlanta. Calhoun; ✆ (706) 602-1300

Stores include: Bass; Big Dog Sportswear; Black & Decker Factory Store; Bon Worth; Bugle Boy; Buster Brown Kidswear; C.J.'s Sock Outlet; Capacity; Carol's Fashions; Carter's; Casual Corner & Co.; Casual Corner Woman; Casual Male Big & Tall; Claire's Accessories; Clifford & Wills; Dress Barn; Factory Brand Shoes; Famous Brand Housewares; Farberware; Gap Outlet; Geoffrey Beene; Izod; J. Crew; Jacob's Well; Jones New York; Leather Loft; L'eggs Hanes Bali Playtex; Liz Claiborne; Lorianna; Maidenform; McDonald's; Mikasa; Naturalizer; Nike Factory Store; Nine West Outlet; Oriental Rug Place; Paper Factory; Perfumania; Petite Sophisticate; Pro Golf; Publishers Warehouse; Regal Factory Outlet; Rocky Mountain Chocolate Factory; Royal Doulton; Rue 21; Samsonite; Springmaid-Wamsutta; Sunglass Source; Tools & More!; Toy Connection; Van Heusen; VF Factory Store; Vitamin World; Welcome Home.

Commerce: Tanger Factory Outlet Center 1

- Route 441, Interstate 85, Exit 149, Commerce; ✆ (706) 335-3354; ✆ (800) 405-9828

Stores include: Adidas; Aeropostale; American Outpost; Banana Republic; Bass Shoe; Bath & Body Works; Bible Factory Outlet; Big Dog Sportwear; Black & Decker; Bon Worth; Britches; Brooks Brothers; Bugle Boy Factory Store; Calvin Klein; Camp Coleman; Capacity; Carters Childrenswear; Casual Corner; Casual Corner Woman; Casual Male Big & Tall; Children's Place; Claire's Accessories; Clothestime; Corning Revere; Cost Cutters; Country Clutter; Croscill Home Fashions; Dexter Shoe; DKNY Jeans; Dress Barn; Duck Head; Easy Spirit; Elisabeth Outlet Store; Etienne Aigner; Factory Brand Shoes; Famous Brands Housewares Outlet; Farberware Inc.; Fieldcrest Cannon; Florsheim; Fossil; Gap; Geoffrey Beene—Women's & Men's; Guess; Haggar Clothing Co.; Harry & David; Hoover; Hush Puppies; Izod; J Crew; Jockey; Jones NY; Kasper; Kirklands; Koret; L'eggs Hanes Bali; Le Gourmet Chef; Leather Loft; Levi's Outlet by Designs; Liz Claiborne Outlet Store; Maidenform; Maternity Works; Mikasa Factory Store; Music for a Song; National Book Warehouse; Naturalizer; Nautica; Nike; Nine West; Old Navy; Oneida Factory Store; OshKosh B'Gosh; Paul Harris; Perfumania; Petite Sophisticate; Pfaltzgraff; Polo Jeans; Publishers Warehouse; Rack Room Shoes; Reebok Factory Direct; Remington; Rockport Factory Direct; Rocky Mountain Chocolate Factory; Rue 21; Samsonite; SAS Shoes; Seiko; Silver Treasures; Socks Galore by Hanes; Springmaid-Wamsutta; Street Nicks; Stride Rite; Sunglass Hut; Timberland; Tommy Jeans; Tools N More; totes/Sunglass World; Toy Liquidators; Ultra Jewelry; Van Heusen; Vans Shoes; VF Factory Outlet; Vitamin World; We're Entertainment; Welcome Home; Wilson's Leather; Woolrich; Zales.

Dalton: Tanger Outlet Center

- Interstate 75 and Walnut Avenue, exit 333, Dalton; ✆ (706) 277-2688; ✆ (800) 409-7029

SHOPPING: FACTORY OUTLET CENTERS 97

Stores include: Bass Company Store; Bon Worth; Book Warehouse; Bugle Boy; Capacity; Carter's Childrenswear; Claire's Accessories; Corning Revere; Dress Barn; Dress Barn Woman; Duck Head; Etienne Aigner; Florsheim; Izod; Jockey; Kitchen Collection; Koret; L'eggs Hanes Bali Playtex; Leather Factory; Malone Outfitters; Oneida; Paper Factory; Rack Room Shoes; Rocky Mountain Chocolate Factory; Rue 21; S & K Menswear; Samsonite; SAS Shoes; Spiegel Outlet; Toy Liquidators; Totes; Van Heusen; Vitamin World; Welcome Home; West Point Pepperell.

Darien: Prime Outlets at Darien

- 1 Magnolia Bluff Way, 50 miles south of Savannah; Interstate 95, Exit 49, Darien; ✆ (912) 437-2700

Stores include: Bass; Big Dogs; Black & Decker Factory Store; Book Warehouse; Boot Emporium; Bose; Bugle Boy; Carter's; Casual Corner & Co.; Casual Corner Woman; Claire's Accessories; Coach; Cosmetics Company Store; Cost Cutters Salon; Dockers Outlet by Designs; Dress Barn; Duck Head Outlet; Esprit; Etienne Aigner; Factory Brand Shoes; Famous Brand Housewares; Farberware; Florsheim; Gap Outlet; Geoffrey Beene; GNC; Johnston & Murphy; K-B Toy Outlet; Kitchen Collection; L'eggs Hanes Bali Playtex; Levi's; Liz Claiborne; Motherhood Maternity; Music for a Song; Nautica; Nike Factory Store; Nine West; Perfumania; Petite Sophisticate; Polo Ralph Lauren; Quiksilver; Rack Room Shoes; Reebok; Robert Scott & David Brooks; Rockport; Rocky Mountain Chocolate Factory; Samsonite; SAS Factory Shoe Store; Springmaid-Wamsutta; Strasburg Children; Sunglass Outlet; The Bean & Leaf; The Jockey Store; The Thomas House Gifts; Tommy Hilfiger; Van Heusen; Welcome Home; Woolrich; Zales.

Dawsonville: North Georgia Premium Outlets

- 800 Highway 400 South, Dawsonville; ✆ (706) 216-3609

Stores include: 1928 Designer Brand Accessories; 2 Day Designs; Adidas; Anne Klein; B & T Factory Outlet; Banana Republic; BCBG; Benetton; Big Dog Sportswear; Black & Decker; Blowout Video; Bombay Outlet; Bon Worth; Bose; Bostonian Clarks; Britches; Brooks Brothers Factory Store; Bugle Boy; Calvin Klein; Carter's for Kids; Casual Corner Outlet; Casual Corner Woman; Charlotte Russe; Claire's Accessories; Coach; Cole Haan; Corning Revere; Cosmetics Company Store; Cost Cutters; Country Clutter; Crate & Barrel Outlet; Dalton Rug; Danskin; Designer Fragrances & Cosmetics; Dockers; Donna Karan; Dress Barn Outlet/Dress Barn Woman; Eddie Bauer; Elizabeth; Factory Brand Shoes; Famous Brands Housewares; Fila; Florsheim; Fossil; Four Seasons Designer Eyewear; Fuzziwig's Candy Factory; GNC Nutrition; G.H. Bass; Gap Outlet; Geoffrey Beene; Guess; Harold's; Harry and David; Harvé Bernard; Home Style; Hoover; Hush Puppies & Family; Izod; Jockey; Johnston & Murphy; Jones New York; Jones New York Country; Jones New York Sport; Jones New York Men; Jos. A. Bank; Kasper A.S.L.; Kenneth Cole; K-B Toy Liquidators; Le Creuset; LEGO Outlet; Le Gourmet Chef; Leather Loft; L'eggs, Hanes, Bali, Playtex; Levi's Outlet; Liz Claiborne; Liz Claiborne Shoes; Maidenform; Mark-Fore & Strike; Maternity Works; Mori Luggage Outlet; Movado; Music For A Song; Naturalizer; Nautica; Nike; Nine West; North Face; Off 5th—

Saks Fifth Avenue Outlet; Olga Warners; OshKosh B'Gosh; Pacific Sunwear; Paper Factory; Perfumania; Perry Ellis; Petite Sophisticates; Pfaltzgraff; Polo Ralph Lauren; Pottery Barn; Quicksilver; Rack Room Shoes; Reebok; Remington; Royal Doulton; Rue 21; S&K Menswear; Samsonite/American Tourister; Sigred Olsen; So Fun! Kids; Springmaid Wamsutta; Stiffel Lamps; Stone Mountain; Strasburg; Stride Rite, Sperry, Topsider, Keds; Sunglass Station; Tahari; Timberland; Time Factory Outlet; Tommy Hilfiger; totes-Isotoner-Sunglass World; Ultra Gold & Diamond Outlet; Unisa; Van Heusen; Vitamin World; Welcome Home; We're Entertainment; WestPoint Stevens; Williams-Sonoma Outlet; Wilson's Leather; Zales

Lake Park: Lake Park Mill Store Plaza

- 5327 Mill Store Road. I-75 Exit 5, Lake Park; ✆ (912) 559-6822; ✆ (888) 746-7333

Stores include: Baby Gap; Bass Outlet; Better Menswear; Bible Factory Outlets; Big Dog Sportswear; Big & Tall Factory Store; Black & Decker; Black & Decker Clearance; Bon Worth; Capacity; Corning Revere; Dockers; Dress Barn/Woman; Duck Head; Famous Footwear; Gap; Gap kids; Garden Cafe; Gift & Gourmet; Kitchen Collection; Le Creuset; L'eggs Hanes Bali; Lenox Factory Outlet; Levi's/Docker's; Lorianna Stores; Oneida; Paper Factory; Pfaltzgraff; Polo-Ralph Lauren; Rack Room Shoes; S&K Menswear; Samsonite; SAS Factory Shoes; totes/Sunglass World; Van Heusen; WestPoint Stevens

Locust Grove: Tanger Factory Outlet Center

- Interstate 75, Exit 212; 35 miles south of Atlanta; Locust Grove; ✆ (770) 957-5310; ✆ (800) 406-0833

Stores include: Bass Company Store; Bible Factory Outlet; Big Dog Sportswear; Bon Worth; Bugle Boy Factory Store; Capacity Clothing; Carter's Childrenswear; Casual Corner Outlet; Casual Corner Woman; Claire's Accessories; Corning Revere; Country Clutter; Dockers; Dress Barn/Dress Barn Woman; Dress for Less; Duck Head; Etienne Aigner; Factory Brand Shoes; Famous Brands Housewares Outlet; Florsheim Shoe Factory Outlet; Haggar Clothing Co.; Heritage Candles; Hush Puppies; Jockey Store, The Kitchen Collection; Koret; Leather Loft; L'eggs Hanes Bali Playtex; Levi's; Liz Claiborne Outlet Store; Mikasa Factory Store; Music for a Song; Naturalizer; Nine West; Old Navy; Olga/Warner's; OshKosh B'Gosh; Paper Factory; Paul Harris; Perfumania; Petite Sophisticate Outlet; Publishers Warehouse; Rack Room Shoes; Reebok Factory Direct; Rockport Factory Direct; Rocky Mountain Chocolate Factory; Rue 21 Company Store; S&K Menswear; SAS Factory Shoe Store; Samsonite; Springmaid-Wamsutta; Tools & More; totes/Sunglass World; Toy Liquidators; Ultra Jewelry; Van Heusen; Welcome Home

Stone Mountain: Stone Mountain Handbag Outlet

- 963 Main Street, Stone Mountain Village, Stone Mountain; ✆ (770) 498-1316

Just like it says: handbags well below retail, along with purses, wallets, briefcases, and more.

FLEA MARKETS AND EMPORIA

Antiques & Beyond

- 1853 Cheshire Bridge Road N.E., Atlanta;
  ℅ (404) 872-4342

Also see the listing under *Antiques and Gifts*.

There are at least 50 vendors that display their wares here. They have used and antique furniture, art deco furniture, mirrors and prints, linens, collectibles, and other decorative items for the home.

Antiques and Beyond is open 7 days a week, from 11 a.m. to 7 p.m.

A Flea An'Tique

- 222 S. Main Street, Alpharetta;
  ℅ (770) 442-8991

Flea market or antique store? This store is a bit of both. More than 30 vendors have banded together to create this wonderfully eclectic shop, filled with antique furniture dating back to the early 1800s.

This is a great place for home decorating needs, and a great place to have some fun treasure hunting.

A Flea An'Tique is open Monday through Saturday 10 a.m. to 6 p.m., and Sunday noon to 6 p.m.

ATZ Salvage

- 1199 Memorial Drive S.E., Atlanta; ℅ (404) 524-2617
- 269 Chester Avenue S.E., Atlanta; ℅ (404) 658-9671
- 24 Moreland Avenue S.E., Atlanta; ℅ (404) 524-5241

Hey, this is Mr. C's kind of place, focusing exclusively on great new and used furniture and . . . uh . . . tires. Apparently, this creative format is pretty popular with other folks, too, since ATZ Salvage has moved and opened two new stores since the last time we looked under the hood.

On a recent perusal of ATZ, the Cheapster found furniture for every room in the house and all around his minivan. Here you can get 30 percent off retail on furniture manufactured by Design Unlimited, Sunrise, Coaster, Acme, IEM, Fine Pine, KOK, Royal Manufactures, Raintree, Jimson, Goldharp, Titan, and Transocean.

There's even a section for what ATZ calls "scratch and dent" used furniture (although you can also find used furniture without scratches and in very good condition). Better yet, ATZ will pay you cold, hard cash for *your* used furniture.

Oh yeah, the tires are in back, and C can vouch for the fact that there's a wide selection of brands, sizes, and tread depth.

ATZ offers a 30-day layaway plan on its furniture, an extra convenience not often found at this kind of establishment.

The store is open Monday through Saturday from 9 a.m. to 9 p.m., and Sunday from 10 a.m. to 7 p.m.

MR. CHEAP'S PICKS

Flea Markets and Emporia

A Flea An'Tique—Lots of good bric-a-brac, from clothing and furniture to records and magazines, representing some 30 dealers under one roof.

Buford Highway Flea Market—More like a Middle Eastern bazaar, with 135 individual vendors selling mainly new merchandise at 30 to 50 percent off retail.

Buford Highway Flea Market

- 5000 Buford Highway, Chamblee; ✆ (770) 452-7140

This is probably not what you think of when you hear the term "flea market." It's more like a Middle Eastern bazaar, with 135 individual vendors set up in booth after booth, selling mainly new merchandise at 30 to 50 percent off retail. They've been around for 20 years in the same location and have become a kind of Atlanta institution, right up there with the Weather Channel and Ted Turner.

The booths—more than 275 of them—are neatly arranged into grids, with the aisles humorously named after the area's major thoroughfares: Lenox Road, Cheshire Bridge Road, and so on. All this, meanwhile, is completely indoors, in a building that clearly began life as a supermarket. This also means plenty of free parking in its huge front lot.

Inside, you'll find tremendous bargains on tons of clothing for men, women, and children, from brightly colored jeans to African dashikis and kufi hats. If you're looking for Western wear, this is the place: They've got it all, including cowboy boots and hats (even Stetsons), belts and belt buckles, and jackets. Yee-haw!

There is one vendor that sells brand-name watches, for example Bulova and Seiko, for 30 percent off retail. (Mr. C traded up from that $30 "Rolex" he bought in Times Square last year.)

You'll also find all kinds of electronics–CD players, speakers, TVs, VCRs, camcorders, and the like—complete with a 30-day warranty. And, there's a gentleman who repairs electronic equipment on site!

Buford Highway Flea Market says that 80 percent of their shoppers are Hispanic and the three restaurants and snack bar serve delicious Hispanic cuisine. You'll also find Hispanic music for sale.

Comforters, linens and curtains, shoes and boots, children's bikes and tricycles, phone cards, videos, Hispanic music, furniture, and more. Even a tattoo parlor. (At a discount? Mr. C did not dare inquire.)

The market is only open on weekends: Fridays and Saturdays from 11 a.m. to 9 p.m., and Sundays from 11 a.m. to 8 p.m.

Great Gatsby's Auction Gallery

- 5070 Peachtree Industrial Boulevard, Chamblee; ✆ (770) 457-1905

This 100,000-square-foot "wholesale to the public" market is one of Atlanta's most fun stores. You can spend hours ogling everything including exquisite antiques, kitschy advertising memorabilia, and huge architectural fragments. Gatsby's supplies hotels worldwide with unusual furnishings; one of John Lennon's guitars was once sold here at auction. Gatsby's is 2 miles inside I-285 on Peachtree Industrial Boulevard.

Lakewood Antique Market

- 2002 Lakewood Way, Atlanta; ✆ (404) 622-4488

See also the listing in the *Antiques and Gifts* section.

Once a month more than 1,500 vendors gather in a massive antique/flea market to sell just about anything under the sun.

This extravaganza is held the second weekend of every month. The hours are 9 a.m. to 6 p.m. Thursday through Saturday, and 10 a.m. to 5 p.m. on Sunday. It will cost you about three bucks to

SHOPPING: FLOWERS AND PLANTS

get in, but you'll probably save that amount many times over, and the fee is good for the entire four days.

Scavenger Hunt

- 3438 Clairmont Road N.E., Atlanta; (404) 634-4948

This name fits perfectly. In true flea market style, twelve collectors have crammed every nook of this shop just off the Buford Highway with a treasure trove of low- to middle-end antiques and collectibles. The store is 4,000 square feet, so you can plan to visit for a whole afternoon of fun.

You'll discover bins and bins of old record albums, books, mirrors, lamps (even Lava Lamps), framed art, sets of china, brass objects, used heaters, fans, air conditioners, and all kinds of new and used furniture including '50s and '60s art deco, any of which can make for an offbeat gift idea.

There are used CDs and videos for $5, but the price drops a buck if you buy five or more. You'll also find used TVs (from 1950 and later), and old-school stereos (some antique), stereo receivers, radios, amps, and speakers—all in working order, of course. Mr. C even found a pair of used speakers for $10, and a new stereo boombox, still in the box, for 50 percent off retail.

There isn't enough space in this book to list all the memorabilia found here, so Mr. C will just mention just a few primo items: How about a $5 special edition Coke bottle, commemorating the University of Georgia, or the Georgia Tech football team's undefeated 1980 season? (The soda, now *really* classic Coke, still sits inside the never-opened bottle, which is imprinted with the score of each game.) You'll also find Harley Davidson and black art memorabilia, 1950s metal tins (emblazoned with the revered images of Elvis, Marilyn, and James Dean), cool classic jukeboxes, and much more.

Scavenger has Atlanta's best selection of neon beer signs, with 25 specimens always on and working.

Looking for some new merchandise? How about box springs, mattresses, and frames at 50 percent off retail? Add to that some cheap (but good quality) sheets and pillowcases (standard $9.35 a pair; queen and king for $15 a pair), and you've got one comfy crib.

Scavenger Hunt is open seven days a week from 10 a.m. to 7 p.m.

FLOWERS AND PLANTS

Nothing warms the heart of Mrs. C more than a pretty display of flowers, especially since she doesn't have to worry about Mr. C frittering away the vacation fund on such frivolities.

Many of the great deals you'll find on flowers are only available for cash-and-carry purchases. If you want your flowers delivered, you'll probably wind up paying at least $10 more than the prices described below, plus an additional delivery charge. Also, be aware that while some florists advertise long-stem roses, they may not always be available in red; or if they are, they may sell out early in the day. Mr. C advises you to call ahead to find out for sure.

Atlanta State Farmer's Market

- 16 Forest Pkwy, Forest Park; ✆ (404) 675-1782

- 🌐 www.agr.state.ga.us

This is the *professional* farmer's market, also known as the "World's Largest Roadside Fruit Stand." Atlanta State Farmer's Market serves a 600-mile radius, so your favorite supermarket or corner store probably gets *its* fruit here. Minivans and 18-wheelers zip around the rows and rows of semi-enclosed stalls, delivering or filling up with fruits, vegetables, and more. So, can you pull up in your clunky old minivan and buy just a pound of tomatoes? Yes you can!

Located at exit 237 off Interstate 75, this massive, state-run complex divides neatly into two sides as soon as you drive in: To your left are the rows of stalls, where farmers stand waiting to sell their wares at a very good value. The warehouses across from the farmers are for stores purchasing in wholesale quantities.

Meanwhile, at the very end of the stalls side, closest to the highway, is the newer Garden Center. Down here, you can get great deals on everything from sod to straw, and a particularly fine selection of locally grown annuals and perennials. Choices (and prices) vary from season to season, but you will find that prices are an exceptional value. Both landscapers and consumers shop here.

These guys have almost every kind of tree that grows, from dogwoods to weeping willows, ranging from $25 to $55.

Don't forget to check up and down the rows of farmers' stalls; there are some florists mixed in here, too, again at exceptional values. For example, you can get 36-count pansies for only $9, and you'll find similar deals for other varieties, depending upon the time of year. Why so cheap here? No fancy packaging (though some dealers will add this for an extra few bucks) and no deliveries. This keeps their costs, and prices, low. To paraphrase Sgt. Joe Friday: Just the flowers, ma'am.

You can cover a lot of ground, literally and figuratively, for little cash by coming to this one place. The Farmer's Market itself is open 24 hours a day, though you're not likely to find much action on the farmers' and garden side after 9 or 10 p.m.; late nights are the truckers' domain. Weekdays, of course, are the quietest and easiest times for regular folks to shop here.

A Blooming Earth Florist and Greenhouse

- 2403 Lawrenceville Highway, Decatur; ✆ (404) 321-4409

- 🌐 www.1800221flowers.com

When Mr. C gets into trouble with the missus, he heads straight to A Blooming Earth. By now they know him well.

All kinds of folks drive miles out of their way to get floral arrangements here, and for good reason. The parking lot is often full, and pulling back out onto Lawrenceville Highway can be a death-defying experience; but when you can buy roses for $12.95 a dozen, who cares? This price is considered a special deal, but it is offered frequently, so call the store first to see if they are running this special These are long stem roses available in pink, yellow, white, and, red. This price is such a bargain, they often sell out quickly.

Sometimes the price for long stem roses is $19.95, and $24.95 is the highest you'll likely pay at this florist. This is the cash and carry

SHOPPING: FLOWERS AND PLANTS

price and it includes baby's breath and ferns, wrapped in paper. You can't get the lower special prices on holidays, such as Valentine's Day or Mother's Day.

Arrangements of long stem roses, with baby's breath and ferns in a vase, are about $49.99. They even offer a delivery service for all special arrangements for an additional fee of $7.50. Still, it makes sense to present them yourself, no?

Other flowers available here include carnations for just $1.25 each ($12.99 a dozen), also with baby's breath and ferns, and snapdragons for $1.75 a stem.

The store is open from 9 a.m. to 6 p.m. weekdays, and from 9 a.m. to 4 p.m. on Saturdays. They're closed Sundays.

Emory Village Flowers and Gifts

- 1573 North Decatur Road N.E., Atlanta; (404) 378-3900

Here's a florist that offers a compelling combination of reasonably priced products and good location. Here you can pick up a dozen plain roses for $39 (cash-and-carry; but delivery costs just $5 to $7) and find other good deals as well. Located across the street from Kroger in Emory Village, this store is very convenient for sending flowers to someone on the Emory or Agnes Scott campuses, or the nearby VA Hospital.

What's more, the shop is not too far from the Virginia-Highland area; if you're on your way to visit someone in ViHi or Morningside, you can stop in at Emory on the way and save some serious cash over the inflated prices of stores in those areas.

Mr. C does want to note that other flower arrangements are not priced as spectacularly low (for example, arranged roses are $57.95

MR. CHEAP'S PICKS

Flowers and Plants

A Blooming Earth Florist and Greenhouse—Great flowers, great prices.

Flora Dora—In the mood to spend about a dozen bucks for a dozen roses? This is the place! Flora Dora makes and sells incredibly lifelike silk flowers, wholesale to you.

Pike Family Nurseries—Best place to put down your green for some greenery.

---

a dozen in a vase). But since you save so much on delivery, the store is sure worth a try for simple arrangements, plain roses, and carnations, and of course, those cash-and-carry bouquets.

They offer delivery service only for orders $35 and above. Store hours are Monday through Friday 8:30 a.m. to 6 p.m., and Saturdays from 9 a.m. to 5 p.m. They're closed on Sundays.

Flora Dora

- 503 Amsterdam Avenue N.E.; Atlanta; (404) 873-6787

At the rear center of the Amsterdam Walk, this large warehouse offers something unique in the world of flower shops, or for that matter, outlets in general. This company makes silk flowers and plants so stunningly lifelike that you can't tell them from the real thing unless you stand right next to them. They create this faux flora for stores, business offices and buildings, movie companies, and other commercial clients; but you can shop here too, and get the same great direct-from-the-source prices. And Flora Dora boasts that they have the best price in town.

The flowers themselves are made of fine Chinese silk, which are assembled here at the factory. Stalks of snapdragons are reduced, for instance, from an original $12 each to just $7.

These guys don't stop at flowers. They "make" over 70 different types of trees, attaching silk leaves to actual wood trunks and branches. This enhances the illusion, yet you never have to water anything!

A seven-foot tall commercial grade ficus tree will cost in the neighborhood of $69. You can even find copies of houseplants, like English ivy bushes and garlands for $8 and up. Again, especially if they're up in a hanging planter, you'd scarcely know they were fake.

Speaking of planters, this store is a great source for all kinds of pots, baskets, and bowls of all sizes and shapes. You can even get things like solid-colored marbles, perfect for filling crystal bowls and glass jars. Plus lots of other glass giftware items, as well as Christmas ornaments and decorations (many of which depict African-American Santas and angels), all at great prices. And don't forget commercial grade Christmas trees, far better than any artificial tree from a department store, starting around $18 for a 3-foot tree.

Service is just as important to the folks at Flora Dora as their carefully crafted copies of Mother Nature. Owner Tony Pernice points out that since the company's main activity is designing displays for corporate clients, good relations are crucial. "We built this place on service," he says proudly, and he means it. Staff will work with you to get exactly the right look for your home or office. And, unlike most of the stores in this outlet complex, Flora Dora is open seven days: weekdays from 10 a.m. to 5 p.m., Saturdays from 10 a.m. to 6 p.m., and Sundays from 1 p.m. to 6 p.m.

Maud Baker Flower Shoppe

- 609 Church Street, Decatur; (404) 373-5791 or (800) 221-3674

- www.maudbaker.com.

Near West Ponce Place and a short walk from the courthouse, Maud Baker, in business since 1947, sells roses and some hardy houseplants at good prices. Boxed, long-stem roses are $49.99 a dozen arranged, which may sound like a lot, but it is cheaper than anyplace in the Peachtree Center or Buckhead areas. And since delivery within the metro Atlanta area is only $9, this becomes a good deal when you want to send a bouquet somewhere downtown. Maud's says that it well deliver anywhere around the world.

Some of the houseplants Mr. C saw include a $35 Christmas cactus, a huge chrysanthemum for $30, and big peace lilies for about $30 to $60. All of these look radiantly healthy, so you probably don't need to have a green thumb to take care of them.

Maud's also has balloon bouquets that can be combined with flowers or gifts like cute teddy bears.

All roses are guaranteed for one week and plants for a month, so if one of your little leafy friends doesn't make it, Maud's will replace it.

Maud's is open six days a week: Monday through Friday 7 a.m. to 6 p.m. and Saturday 8 a.m. to 4 p.m. The're closed on Sundays, but you

SHOPPING: FLOWERS AND PLANTS

can shop 24/7 because Maud's is also online with a Web site.

Pike Family Nurseries

- 1380 South Cobb Drive, Marietta; ✆ (770) 428-4133

- 221 Pounds Road, Tucker; ✆ (770) 381-7355

- 7865 Roswell Road, Atlanta; ✆ (770) 396-0921

- 6100 Lawrenceville Highway, Tucker ✆ (770) 921-8880

- 1983 Highway 78, Snellville; ✆ (770) 972-0400

- 2475 Town Lake Pkwy. Woodstock; ✆ (770) 926-3252

- 1953 Roswell Road, Marietta; ✆ (770) 977-3040

- 4020 Roswell Road, Atlanta ✆ (404) 843-9578

- 2955 Holcomb Bridge Road, Alpharetta; ✆ (770) 641-1217

- 103 Highway 74 South, Peachtree City; ✆ (770) 632-9111

- 2975 Town Center Drive, Kennesaw; ✆ (770) 428-3762

- 2900 Johnson Ferry Road, Marietta; ✆ (770) 640-6468

- 2101 Lavista Road, Atlanta; ✆ (404) 634-8604

- ✍ http://pikenursery.com/home.htm

The folks behind this mega-nursery seem to have taken the garden supply business to a whole new level. Not only do they offer thousands of plants and gardening products at near-wholesale prices, but also sponsor a never-ending plethora of in-store seminars, expert speaker series, and money-saving promotions with other local businesses.

Green thumbs know that Pike is a great place to stock up on all kinds of gardening supplies, perennials, and indoor plants. Wicker baskets for 10" plants are under $5, and potting soil costs as little as $1 for a 20-pound bag. African violets are just $2 each, and tiny angel plants (in 3" pots) are only 97 cents; while medium-sized houseplants like philodendrons, arboricolas, ficus plants, and China dolls are just $7 (on sale, they can be under $4). Ficus trees, rubber plants, and schefflera are around $15 each, but go on sale for as low as $7. Boston ferns in hanging baskets are $6, while Swedish ivy plants are $4.

For the yard, try mums or azaleas (starting at just $1), or potted junipers for $1.75. Bulk tulip or daffodil bulbs are priced at $3 for ten.

Keep your lawn healthy with Sta-Green starter fertilizer, $9.97 per bag, and Atlanta Blend lawn seed is $35 for a 25-pound bag. Regular Kentucky fescue lawn seed by Pennington, though, is considerably cheaper at about $13 for the same size bag.

Pike even offers a "horticultural consulting service," and will send a real live horticulturalist to your home to assess your gardening needs. They'll answer questions relating to your lawn, landscaping, or even insects and diseases affecting your plants. Call ✆ (404) 594-2813 to schedule an appointment. Doctors don't make house calls anymore, but these folks do.

The nurseries are open seven days a week. Hours are from 8 a.m. to 7 p.m. Mondays through Saturdays (depending on the time of year), and from 10 a.m. to 6 p.m. Sundays.

FOOD STORES

Quoting prices on fresh foods, like meat and produce, is about as smart as quoting politicians on their promises. Neither seems to keep very long. The prices mentioned herein, like everything else in this book, are simply examples that should give you some idea of each store's general pricing.

Many of the foods listed under individual categories can also be found at stores in the "General Markets" section.

BAKERIES

Flowers Baking Company Thrift Stores

- 116 Harmony Grove Road, Lilburn; ✆ (770) 638-9399
- 7420 Douglas Boulevard, Douglasville; ✆ (770) 949-4444
- 2879 East Point Street, East Point; ✆ (404) 766-1278
- 4764 Jonesboro Road, Forest Park; ✆ (404) 363-9062
- 605 Indian Trail-Lilburn Road, Lilburn; ✆ (770) 564-1361
- 2601 South Stone Mountain-Lithonia Road, Lithonia; ✆ (770) 482-8451
- 136 Powers Ferry Road S.E., Marietta; ✆ (770) 973-5200
- 6866 Highway 85, Riverdale; ✆ (770) 997-7066

When Mr. C needs to purchase mass quantities of yummy baked goods to restock the house after a visit from the in-laws, he heads over to the nearest Flowers Baking Company outlet. This store features amazingly great prices on name-brand items left over from daily bakery supply runs to area supermarkets. It "clears out" Sunbeam and Roman Meal breads, and Nature's Own Cobblestone Meal, as well as its house brand and several other kinds of packaged foods, at less than half-price.

Usually you can pick up two or three loaves of Flowers' private label bread for just a buck! Snack cakes are about 45 cents each; box cakes run 79 cents to $1.59; dinner rolls are 99 cents, and luscious, freshly baked pies are available around holidays for just $2.69.

Sunbeam thin-sliced white bread is just 99 cents. "Nature's Own" whole wheat bread, which sells in supermarkets for $1.45 a loaf, can be found here for at two for $1.59. You'll find the same price for loaves by Roman Meal, in various flavors.

You may also find foods here such as a six-pack of Jubilee brand apple Danish for $1.89, and they have lots of sugar-free candies, no-salt potato chips, and tons of delicious cookies and chips.

Mondays are "Dollar Day" at Flowers (that's when you can get three loaves of bread for a buck), and senior citizens get 10 percent off on Tuesdays. Store hours vary.

Colonial Bakery Outlet Store/Sara Lee Bakery Group

- 530 Oak Street, Atlanta; ✆ (404) 758-5544
- 545 Edgewood Avenue, Atlanta; ✆ (404) 521-2742
- 5060 Industrial Boulevard, Atlanta; ✆ (404) 691-4094

SHOPPING: FOOD STORES

- 3212 Glenwood Road, Decatur; ✆ (404) 284-7477
- 3310 Pantherville Road, Decatur; ✆ (404) 241-8466
- Old Dixie Highway, Forest Park; ✆ (404) 363-4031
- 167 Millard Farmer Industrial Boulevard Newnan; ✆ (770) 253-2856
- 2102 Browns Bridge Road, Gainsville; ✆ (770) 532-8230
- 2821 South Cobb Drive S.E., Smyrna; ✆ (770) 432-0209

Continuing our luxury tour of bakery factory outlets, we come to the Colonial Bakery Outlet, which is now owned by Sara Lee, with a possible name change in the works.

Colonial sells its bread and pastries at incredible savings here. Buy four "big" (16 ounce) old-fashioned loaves of their white sandwich bread for $2.89, and you could get an extra loaf for free. You can purchase four "Giant" (20 ounce) white loaves for $3.99, and a variety of wheat bread—whole wheat, honey wheat, honey grain wheat, and plain old-fashioned wheat—for the same price.

Who can use that much bread at once? Well, if you're not making lunches for a gaggle of growing teenagers, or preparing for that church picnic, you can probably get comparable deals on just a loaf or two. Remember, though, that most baked goods will freeze nicely and keep for a few weeks or months; just make sure they weren't stale going into the freezer because they won't get any fresher under ice.

On the sweet side, Mr. C recently found things like a package of six cherry-filled Danish pastries sweet rolls selling for $1.99 or a package of three for a buck.

You can also find almost a supermarket's worth of related products, from brown-and-serve dinner rolls to bread crumbs, and from pretzels to candies.

Store hours are Monday through Saturday 9:30 a.m. to 6 p.m., and Sundays 11 a.m. to 5 p.m.

Henri's Bakery

- 6289 Roswell Road, Sandy Springs; ✆ (404) 256-7934
- 61 Irby Avenue NW, Atlanta; ✆ (404) 237-0202

Founding father Henri Fisius hailed from the French province of Alsace-Lorraine, so you know his croissants are to die for. Granddaughter Madeline, who now runs the shop, makes use of all of Henri's culinary secrets and now makes these awesomely delicious morsels available just $1.30 for plain and $1.45 for almond, crème, or chocolate. However, it is Henry's lemon squares ($1.89 each) that have garnered national press. They're almost 350 calories each (ouch!) but that's okay because Mr. C plans to enhance his workout regimen soon . . . honest!

Since Henri's has closed its downtown store, they are no longer offering the breakfast plate (eggs, grits, etc.) but now they have gourmet coffee, so you can certainly have a continental breakfast.

For lunch, Henri's is known as having the best sandwiches around—two favorites are Best Turkey and Po' Boy. You can't beat this value at $4.49, and they're served on Henri's homemade bread.

If you're not in the mood for a salad you can try the garden, pasta, tuna, chicken, or egg salad plates for just $3.29.

Still, it's the bakery items that will really make you say, "C'est magnifique!" Loaves of sourdough rye or herb onion or honey wheat breads are just $3.29; six-grain loaves are the same price. Cheese

> **MR. CHEAP'S PICKS**
>
> ### Bakeries
>
> **Flowers Baking Company Thrift Stores**—Features amazingly great prices on name-brand items left over from daily bakery supply runs to area supermarkets.
>
> **Henri's**—With decadently sweet and delicious French delicacies at reasonable prices, you can't go wrong here. Don't worry about the calories; Mr. C doesn't.

strudel ($1.45) is always a big crowd pleaser. Cream-filled, cinnamon, and chocolate-covered donuts (all yeast raised) are 55 cents each. Don't miss this favorite—the chocolate caramel bomb for $2.19.

No time to cook? No problem. Pick up a dozen of Henri's stupendous chocolate macaroons or chocolate chip cookies for $7.50, or some caramel brownies at 89 cents each. Black Forest cakes, carrot cakes, Swiss mocha, or turtle cakes are priced between $15.95 and $21.99 each. They may not sound exactly cheap, but they are great values.

For the calorie-conscious and those with food allergies, Henri's has a listing of recipe ingredients and nutritional information for many of the breads.

Henri's plans to open stores in north Fulton County, possibly Alpharetta and Gwinnett, so stay alert! In the meantime, Mr. C plans to compensate for all of his recent trips to Henri's by jogging alongside his minivan while the missus tosses those freshly baked and bought lemon squares to him out the window. Hey . . . it sure beats the Navy Seal exercise program C attempted last year!

Henri's hours are Monday to Saturday from 7:30 a.m. to 6 p.m. Sadly, the shops are closed on Sunday.

International Bakery

- 2165 Cheshire Bridge Road #5 N.E., Atlanta;
  ✆ (404) 636-7580

If you're looking for sweet treats cheap, this place will hit the spot. True to its name, the International Bakery whips up not only Greek pastries, nationality of the man in charge, but also pastries from France, Germany, Italy, and other corners of the Western world.

Baklava dripping with honey is certainly the main specialty here, in several different varieties. The basic versions are priced at about just 75 cents for one piece, and they are yummy. Chocolate éclairs are $1.55, with "mini" éclairs (perhaps meant for cheating on your diet?) going for a mere 65 cents. A single serving of tiramisu is $1.55. Or, you can get a good ol' apple turnover for 85 cents.

International also makes cakes to order, in large and small sizes, starting at $12, with a delicious Tiramisu cake available for $20. And they carry fresh and packaged food items, mainly Greek, like feta cheeses (domestic and imported), orzo, crème caramel mixes, and extra virgin olive oil (3 liters were priced at $14.99). Watch carefully for the bakery as you whiz by, tucked into one of the many little shopping centers along Cheshire Bridge Road. International is in the same shopping center as Domino's and Sundown Café Restaurant.

Since International is near Dominos Pizza and the Sundown Café Restaurant, it's a logical stop for dessert.

Store hours are Monday through Saturday 8 a.m. to 7:30 p.m. and Sunday 9 a.m. to 2 p.m.

Palace Bakery

- Toco Hills Shopping Center, 2869 North Druid Hills Rd N.E., Atlanta; ✆ (404) 315-9017

El Cheapster found a place where he could eat his cake while being able to afford another one, too. Breads, cookies, and specialty pastries are cheap, but delicious, at this Palace. Loaves of white, wheat, pumpernickel, and the very popular rye bread cost just $1.99 a piece. Challah bread is $2.49, and on Fridays braided challah is $3.09.

Cream cheese brownies are among the cheapest around—just $1.99 each, while generous slices of apple strudel will only put you back $1.50.

Mountain tops that look like cupcakes are a favorite here. They come in two varieties: chocolate cake dipped in chocolate and yellow cake dipped in caramel. Both are topped with a mound of butter cream.

Mr. C observed (and sampled) lots and lots of cookies here starting at $6.99/lb. Rainbow torte cookies are $8.19/lb., and "black and white" varieties are popular at $1.75 apiece.

Rugelach pastries, which attract shoppers from miles away, are $8.19/lb. (and perfect if you're cooking dinner for someone you need to impress!). They come in cinnamon walnut, raspberry, apricot, and chocolate flavors. Up to 20 pounds of this stuff can sell in an afternoon, so you may want to call ahead to see if it's still available before you hop in the car.

The Palace offers breakfast all day, as well as lunch. It's open every day including holidays, at 6:30 a.m. Weekdays and Saturday they close at 5 p.m., and Sunday at 4 p.m.

CANDY AND NUTS

Maggie Lyon Chocolatiers

- 6000 Peachtree Industrial Boulevard Norcross; ✆ (770) 446-1299

Wallowing in gourmet chocolates is one of Mr. C's favorite sports, and this store, just outside of the perimeter, specializes in just what C needs—and at great prices.

Truffles are $18 a pound and are available in champagne, Grand Marnier, dark chocolate, chocolate chip, caramel, crème brûlée, and tiramisu varieties. Heck, things like that are never going to be cheap, but comparatively speaking, these prices are quite reasonable. Other chocolate specialties, and caramels, are also priced as low as $18 a pound. In fact everything is $18 a pound, including chocolate-covered potato chips, which may sound like a lot; but again, for the amount of chips you get, it's a sweet deal.

The best bargain is their mistakes candy—small mistakes, like candies that have cracks or flaws in decoration. The candies taste exactly like the perfect candies but are sold at half price: $9.00 a pound.

Maggie Lyon's is open from 10 a.m. to 5 p.m. weekdays, and Saturdays from November to Easter from 10 a.m. to 4 p.m. (Call ahead to check, since this changes occasionally.) They are closed Sundays.

Rainbow Natural Foods

- North Decatur Plaza, 2118 North Decatur Road, Decatur; ✆ (404) 636-5553

You never know what you'll find under this Rainbow, but you can bet it'll be a bargain. Carob candies, organic chocolate candy, nutrition bars, and fruit-sweetened treats line the aisles; and the nut prices won't make you nutty, either. A pound of dry roasted peanuts is just $1.39 a pound here.

They have a peanut butter machine so you can make your own peanut butter; you can use one of the store's containers or bring your own. There are other good deals on nuts such as whole cashews, roasted, salted, both, or just plain. You'll find lots of dried fruits: papaya, pineapple, dates, figs, apricots, ginger, mango, and organic raisins (hey kids—a good source of fiber!) will fill you up for just $1.84 a pound. Maybe there really is a pot of gold at the end of the rainbow.

Store hours are 10 a.m. to 8 p.m. Monday through Saturday, and 11 a.m. to 5 p.m. on Sunday.

The Southern Candy Company

- Underground Atlanta, 112 Lower Alabama Street, Atlanta; ✆ (404) 577-3697

You know you're in for a sweet surpnse when you see the 50-pound bags of sugar lined up in the window of this store. Bring the kids—you can watch these folks making pecan rolls and peanut brittle, all while sampling and purchasing classic chocolate concoctions and Georgian specialties. It's an especially good place to try if you're stuck looking for a gift idea—and this is the only candy store in Atlanta to ship worldwide, they say.

A one-pound box of Georgia pralines is $11, and pecan brittle is $6.50 a pound. Fudge comes in plain, vanilla, maple nut, amaretto, chocolate swirl, rocky road, and peanut butter varieties, in prices starting at $8.95 a pound.

Half-pound pecan log rolls are $5.25 (small ones are just 99 cents), and huge peanut butter cups are just $1.25 each. Take that, Reese's! And chewy caramel-packed turtles are just $9 a pound.

Stock up on salt water taffy (at just 5.95 cents a pound), caramel apples ($2 each), and candy apples (just $1.25 each). Yum!

Gift baskets are a specialty here; if you're in a big hurry, you can even phone an order in and have it shipped. A pound and a half of assorted candy, arranged in a basket, starts at $20 and ranges on up to $55.

Store hours are 10 a.m. to 9 p.m. Monday through Saturday, and noon to 6 p.m. on Sunday.

COFFEES AND TEAS

Coffee Plantation

- 2205 Lavista Rd N.E. #F; Atlanta; ✆ (404) 636-1038

Awarded *Creative Loafing's* "Best of Atlanta" three years in a row in the early 1990s for the best neighborhood coffee shop, Plantation Coffee will get you a pound to go without giving you (or your budget) the jitters.

As we went to press, the house blend was just $8.99 a pound, while Columbian Supremo sold for $9.99. The sweet Swiss Chocolate blend was $10.99, as was the Amaretto-flavored roast; getting more exotic, Jamaican Blue Mountain cost $39.99 a pound.

Gourmet teas are also reasonably priced here, sold loose by the pound. "Imperial Gunpowder," is $13.99 per pound, Lapsang Souchong, sells for $11 a pound. and Darjeeling from India is $18.99 a pound. If you enjoy black tea, there is Assam for $14.99 per pound, Chinese Oolong for $11.99 a pound, and Russian Caravan for

$11.99. Another good buy is the mild jasmine tea, at $11.99 per pound. You'll also find boxes of Stash—about 20 different varieties, including herbal flavors and some black teas like English Breakfast.

Coffee Plantation has a Coffee of the Month Club where the coffee (regular, decaf, or flavored) or tea is mailed to your home. You can choose either a 3-month, 6-month, or 12-month plan. Look for the brochure in the store or just call the number listed above.

Store hours are Monday through Friday 8 a.m. to 6:30 p.m., and Saturday 8 a.m. to 6 p.m. They are closed Sundays.

Rainbow Natural Foods

- North Decatur Plaza, 2118 North Decatur Road, Decatur; ✆ (404) 636-5553

Mr. C's friends are beginning to call him "Twitchy" because of his unflagging affection for coffee, fueled by the frequent high-speed runs he makes to this fine establishment.

If you share the Cheapster's affliction . . . er, affection, then you may soon be making some runs of your own. There's only one real problem: There are so many varieties of coffee under Rainbow's roof that it could take you an hour to decide what to get. Among the selection are Kenya AA, Hawaiian Kona, Mocha Java, Columbia Supremo, Columbia Supremo Organic, and organically grown Mexican coffee, with many varieties starting at around $5 per pound.

Teas are also bargain priced. (Remember, this is one of Atlanta's favorite health food stores, and their high volume of sales means low prices for you.) You'll find Celestial Seasonings teas in 24-bag boxes at prices less than what's offered in the supermarkets. You'll also be able to pick up Twinings teas, traditional medicinal, yogi teas, and many other varieties perfectly blended to smooth out twitches of any kind.

Store hours are 10 a.m. to 8 p.m. Monday through Saturday, and 11 a.m. to 5 p.m. on Sunday.

GENERAL MARKETS AND PREPARED FOOD TO GO

Sweet Auburn Curb Market

- 209 Edgewood Avenue S.E., Atlanta; ✆ (404) 659-1665

All of your errands for the week could possibly be accomplished in a day at this Atlanta fixture, which likes to call itself "Downtown Atlanta's greatest shopping alternative." Mr. C would rather go here than to a mall.

Here's the place to save on farm-fresh produce and meats when you're downtown and can't get out to the farm. Since 1918, in what has been declared an historic building, this marketplace has existed in some form or another. Renovation completed in 1997 gave it a new décor that looks as fresh as the food yet maintains the look of a historic building.

Going to this market can be like taking a short trip overseas. Inside this large structure are dozens of individual vendors; a diverse mix of ethnic groups that in several languages. Some sell from wooden tables, others from behind glass refrigeration counters. Everywhere is fresh produce, fresh seafood, meat, and chicken.

You can buy every part of the pig here, from tongue to tail, whether you want slab bacon by the pound, or a 30-pound box of frozen baby back ribs for $45. Fly off with chicken wings at 99 cents a pound, or some chopped chicken liver. Several vendors sell great-looking greens, fruits, and vegetables in season, Georgia peanuts and pecans, and even some homemade jams and preserves.

Sweet Auburn has really expanded since 1994 and now has a variety of snack food bars and at least ten restaurants, including Affrodish, Blimpies, Garden Grill, Kaffe Shopp, Metro Catering & Deli, Pizza Hut, Planet Bombay, Red's Ezpress, Salumeria Taggiasca, and Southcity Cuisine. You'll also find a discount grocery store, an Italian market, a tropical market, and a bakery! These are all located around the perimeter of the market.

Downstairs in a Merchant's Mall you will find jewelry, clothes, electronics, a gift store with balloons, a pharmacy with free delivery, a photography studio, a florist and garden center, and Dollar Store.

Located at Butler and Edgewood, one block east of Auburn Avenue, the Market is open Mondays through Thursdays from 8 a.m. to 6 p.m., and Fridays and Saturdays from 8 a.m. to 7 p.m. Closed on Sundays. Parking is free, and if you're a bus driver or tour guide you even get a free lunch!

Harry's Farmers Market/ Whole Foods Market

- 1180 Upper Hembree Road, Alpharetta; (770)-664-6300
- 2025 Satellite Point Street N.W., Duluth; (770)-416-6900
- 70 Powers Ferry Road N.E., Marietta; (770) 578-4400
- www.hfm.com
- www.wholefoods.com

Wow. Look out, America, This place represents the next generation of supermarket, and it's soon going to get even better.

Decatur has "Your DeKalb," and a wonderful place it is (see listing below); but Harry's, which in late 2001 was bought by the national Whole Foods Market chain, has always blown the roof off of just about any supermarket you've ever seen. This is a cutting-edge supermarket, and it is gorgeous. In many areas, it is even cheap!

You see, besides making a quantum leap in quantity purchasing, which keeps prices low, Harry's is a gleaming, glistening, brightly lit, white-walled palace. It's a massive place, selling not only the freshest looking produce you've ever seen, but everything else you'd find at any other supermarket—again, beautifully presented, quality stuff, often at warehouse prices. Plus hot foods, liquors, glassware, cut flowers, plants, firewood . . . it's the "superstore" approach to supermarkets.

By early 2003 Harry's will be fully converted to Whole Foods' signature mix of top-of-the-line natural boxed and canned products, incredibly fresh and delicious "gourmet" deli offerings, pristine and tasty fish, and beautiful produce (see the Whole Foods entry below), actually not too different from what Harry's has been offering all along!

It's futile to print exact prices on the foods that Harry's has always offered, since they fluctuate all the time. Suffice it to say, you can do very well here if you spend carefully—and especially if you, like Harry, can purchase in bulk. In the coffee bean section, Mr. C did find a 3-pound bag of in-store ground Columbian roast for $7.99, as well as two or three gourmet flavors at weekly special prices of $2.99 and $3.99 a pound. He also noted heads of iceberg lettuce being sold in pairs, for the price most other stores charge for one. You get the idea. It's quantity and quality.

Even the layout of this store is revolutionary. Instead of the usual grid of aisles, there is one, winding path that takes you through the entire place, like a giant game board. In fact, that's exactly what the printed map, handed out to you upon entering, looks like. As one of Mr. C's friends pointed out, this is all very shrewd on Harry's part—it's hard to just run in for one item and head for the register. Suddenly, you're saying, "Hey, we do need some Belgian endive at home—and just look at the price!" Well, maybe.

Even more cunning is the placement of the bakery/hot coffee/juice bar as the first station you come to on the long and winding road. There didn't seem to be one kid in the whole place who wasn't nibbling something sweet. For that matter, there are little stands in many sections where friendly folks have bites of food for you to sample. This store is such a production that official tours for foreign businessmen are frequently seen winding along with the shoppers.

All locations are open 9 a.m. to 8 p.m. Monday through Friday, 9 a.m. to 8 p.m. on Saturday, and 10 a.m. to 7 p.m. on Sunday. Various stores open or close later on some days.

Harry's In A Hurry

- 1875 Peachtree Road N.E., Atlanta; (404) 352-7800
- 3804 Roswell Road, Atlanta; (404) 266-0800)
- 2939 Cobb Pkwy. S.E., Atlanta; (770) 541-9316
- 1418 Dunwoody Village Pkwy., Dunwoody; (770) 238-1400
- 1061 Ponce de Leon Avenue, Atlanta; (404) 439-1100
- 258 City Circle, Peachtree City; (678) 364-9100
- 1180 Upper Hembree Road, Alpheretta; (770) 664-6300
- www.hfm.com

More than a yuppie grocery store, Harry's In A Hurry is the answer to all your eating-on-the-run dilemmas. Meals are prepared using fresh ingredients from Harry's Farmers' Market, and packaged—much of it in microwaveable form—for those of you who just don't have the time to cook.

Did you ever think you could have a sushi dinner for $3.29? It's possible here, though the same dishes aren't necessarily available every day. Pasta dishes like spaghetti and meatballs or macaroni and cheese start at $3 each. Roast turkey and vegetarian lasagna dinners can be had for under $5. Goat cheese pesto pizzas have been available for as little as $4.99, too.

"Briefcase" lunches, like the 28-ounce fruit plate ($3.99) or brie cheese and fruit ($4.49) are good buys. If you're shopping for basics such as bread, fruit, and vegetables: A loaf of foccaccia bread costs just $1.39, and seedless grapes are pre-washed and ready to go for $1.59 a pound. Two pounds of organic carrots sell for just $1.29.

Having a party, but no time to cook? Wow your guests with a two-pound marble cheesecake (for $9.99), or a custard pie (for only $6.99). Dark chocolate and banana cream pies are under $8, too.

Oh, and to really win points, you can even pick up a dozen roses on your way out, for just $8.99. Beat that, A & P!

Store hours are generally 9 a.m. to 9 p.m. Monday through Saturday, and 10 a.m. to 9 p.m. on Sunday, though this can vary by location.

International Farmer's Market

- 5193 Peachtree Industrial Boulevard, Chamblee; (770) 455-1777

- 5380 Jonesboro Road, Lake City; (404) 361-7522

This awesome farmer's market lives up to its "international" moniker with food stands representing forty-plus countries. Situated in a no-frills, 80,000 square-foot warehouse setting, it boasts a huge selection not only of fresh produce, but of everything else you'd find at any supermarket—much of it at terrific prices. Weekly sale items are even better bargains. During Mr. C's visit, these included chicken at 49 cents a pound, small shrimp for only $3.99 a pound, French bread for 99 cents, and 30-pound watermelons for $5.99. Many of the aisles have central tables laden with more unadvertised deals. Also, in the meat and produce departments, you way inquire about wholesale price deals if you're purchasing in large quantities.

And, these guys sell 180,000 to 200,000 pounds of rice per month in 10-, 25-, 50-, and 100-pound bags. Amazing!

The IFM goes beyond these foods to sell liquor, flowers (buy your sweetheart a dozen roses for just $3.99), live seafood, freshly baked breads, and more.

If you're a coffee aficionado, you'll find this a good place to buy gourmet beans, with many varieties priced at a low $3.45 per pound. (There is a hot coffee and pastry counter toward the rear, where you can get a small cappuccino, just 75 cents!) IMF also has a large inventory of international drinks, including Havana Cola (made in Miami) and Swedish Malta—a consistent big seller.

The market is open seven days a week, from midmorning into the early evening; it's a popular stop on Sundays after church, when families stream in to stock up for the week.

Market Grocery at the Atlanta State Farmer's Market

- 16 Forest Pkwy., Forest Park; (404) 361-7980

Hidden inside the Atlanta State Farmer's Market, which is completely open to the public, is the real hidden treasure of the whole place: The Market Grocery. It's a true warehouse for supermarkets, but you can shop here too. In this cavernous space, there are package deals on just about every kind of grocery item, making this a particularly great place to shop for large families. There are all kinds of sodas and juices; get a case of Coke—24 12-ounce cans—for just $5.99, or a quarter apiece. Mr. C noticed a case of Van Camp's pork and beans, again 24 cans, for $9.90.

In the meat and dairy section, you may find slab bacon at $1.19 per pound—or just 79 cents a pound if you can manage a 30-pound case (maybe you've got a big freezer, or a company cookout coming up). Extra-lean ground chuck may sell as low as $1.59 a pound, and locally grown baby lima beans—in frozen, five-pound bags—as low as $5.

Plus bulk household supplies, such as laundry detergent and toilet paper; pet foods, like a 25-pound bag of Purina Dog Chow for $9.90; even a case of Quaker State motor oil, twelve quarts for $15.40. Many items are packaged for resale, like a box of 36 2-ounce packs of Famous Amos cookies for ten bucks, or six-pack "bricks" of Tylenol or Band-Aids.

SHOPPING: FOOD STORES

The whole marketplace runs 24 hours a day, but the grocery itself is open from 8 a.m. to 5 p.m. daily. Weekdays, of course, are the quietest, easiest times to shop here. After you've driven into the main Farmer's Market entrance, take the first right; go all the way down this central drive to building "K", and turn right again for the southern end of the building.

Preferred To-Go

- 2221 Peachtree Road N.E., Atlanta; (404) 352-8099

If you're short on time but hankering for a healthy gourmet lunch, make a quick trip to this Buckhead "emporium." It's not the cheapest, but the value is high since it's all top-quality eats. You can choose from a selection of tasty "container meals" (catering to orders from area offices), including a chef's salad with a roll and cookies ($8.75) to a grilled Chicken Roma salad ($10.75) and a big, overstuffed focaccia sandwich ($8.95).

Hot and cold entrees change daily, featuring elaborate dishes (complete with salad, side dish, rolls, and desert) such as pasta shells Florentine with marinara sauce ($13.75), pork tenderloin with cranberry Dijon relish ($16.50), seafood cakes with remoulade sauce ($18.50), grilled salmon with roasted red pepper coulis, or cucumber dill sauce ($17.50) and southwestern grilled chicken breast topped with jack cheese and salsa with saffron rice ($15.50).

You can save a few bucks with such a la carte savory delights as stuffed mini croissants ($2.50 each), chicken satay with Thai Peanut sauce ($2 each), and a petit focaccia with assorted fillings ($2.50).

> **MR. CHEAP'S PICKS**
>
> *General Markets*
>
> **Harry's Farmer's Market/Whole Foods Market**—These two, which recently merged, take the "superstore" approach to supermarkets, with dazzling selection and surroundings.
>
> **International Farmers Market**—A huge place (80,000 square feet) with just about any kind of quality food you can image, and at hard-to-beat prices.
>
> **Market Grocery at Atlanta State Farmer's Market**—Buy where the grocery stores buy, and at their prices.
>
> **Your DeKalb Farmer's Market**—A legend in Decatur, this world-beater supermarket has warehouse prices in an appropriate setting.

Deserts include a selection of delicious cakes and cobblers.

The store is open Monday through Friday from 7:30 a.m. to 4:30 p.m.

Your DeKalb Farmer's Market

- 3000 East Ponce de Leon Avenue, Decatur; (404) 377-6400

- www.dekalbfarmersmarket.com

Your Dekalb Farmers Market was founded in 1977 as a small open produce market. Get ready to be overwhelmed—by great values, that is. Today, Your DeKalb Farmer's Market is as big as two (yup—two!) football fields, filled with terrific values along.

The deli will delight you, with especially good deals on seafood.

Fresh shrimp is available for at little as 99 cents a pound, ranging on up to $14.99 a pound for not-so-shrimpy jumbos. Mr. C sniffed out whitefish fillets for $2.99, and live blue crab is an incredible dollar a pound. Even delicacies like frog legs are here.

The dairy department is equally impressive, with treats like German brie for $6.39 a pound, along with more basic staples. Older cheeses are marked down from their already-low prices. Some of the cheeses can be sliced, cut, or shredded to order, too.

And what could be better to put some of that cheese on than the Market's pasta—like their soft, fresh spinach linguini ($1.15 a pound), wheat noodles ($1.30), and ready-to-cook lasagna, (just $1.15 a pound).

The produce selection is simply astounding, with selections flown in from all over the world, and varying by season. From organic sweet potatoes to bok choy, apples to endive, everything is farm-priced. You can even buy in bulk quantities; a 14-pound bag of broccoli is just $11, and you can get 14 pounds of broccoli crowns for just $13.50. A 25-pound bag of carrots—either organic or "conventional"—is yours for as little as $7.50! Of course, most customers who don't own rabbits, a restaurant, or both, prefer the five-pound bag, at around $2.29.

The Market's bakery is simply out of this world, too, with muffins available at $1.99 for five, or a three-pack of croissants for $1.99. A six-pack of bagels, available in many varieties, will cost you $1.99.

The Market's extensive (and Mr. C means it when he says extensive) wine and beer selections include Newcastle Brown Ale in the big 18.6-ounce bottle for just $2.09, and China Five Star beer for $7 a six pack. Champagnes, too, like Freixenet's Cordon Negro, which goes for up to $10 in some liquor stores, was offered for $6.79 here. Wines from as far away as Greece, Lebanon, Spain, Portugal, Argentina, and Chile are here for the choosing. Some of the recently spotted special deals included $8.99 bottles of Raymond Napa Valley chardonnay and cabernet sauvignon (seen elsewhere for $14), $5.29 bottles of Caliterra cabernet sauvignon from Chile, and Weibel Black Muscat red dessert wine for $9.

And speaking of dessert, sweets are also sweetly priced, with scrumptious pies—banana, pecan, and key lime were on sale the day Mr. C checked—available for only $1.29. You'll also find such sweets as Danish butter cookies, Lindt caramel, chocolate-covered almonds, and much more.

They also have a restaurant for weary shoppers, or anyone who seeks out the truly international flavor of this unique kind of store (see "Market Cafe" listing under *Restaurants*).

The market's open seven days a week from 9 a.m. to 9 p.m. They're closed on Christmas and Thanksgiving.

Whole Foods Market

- 2111 Briarcliff Road, Atlanta; (404) 634-7800

- 5930 Roswell Road, Sandy Springs; (404) 236-0810

- www.wholefoods.com

Also see Harry's Farmers Market locations above.

The amazing and incredible Whole Foods Market is at the cutting edge of the food shopping experience today, and one of those places where it's hard *not* to spend a lot of time.

Whole Foods specializes in organic food products—those pro-

SHOPPING: FOOD STORES

duced without the use of artificial fertilizer or pesticides. Yet Whole Foods is no funky, neo-hippie co-op. Indeed, it's an increasingly successful national chain of gleaming supermarkets, fully stocked with top-of-the-line natural boxed and canned products, incredibly fresh and delicious "gourmet" deli offerings, pristine and tasty fish, a high-end meat counter, a bakery, an in-store salad bar, and, of course, beautiful produce.

When you first walk in the door your senses are seduced by the sight and fragrance of a wall of fresh-cut flowers, flanked by extended stands of fresh produce, most (but not all) of which is organic. (All produce is labeled as "organic" or "conventional.")

The rest of the store is made up of row upon row of high-quality organically produced food—everything you'd find in any supermarket—only not the mainstream national brands you're used to seeing. Instead of Post Raisin Bran, for example, you'll find the same cereal by a major organic foods manufacturer, or packaged under the Whole Foods Market *house* brand.

At the end of most rows, and along the extended deli counter at one end of the store, you'll find free samples of many of the delightfully fresh and tasty delicacies on sale in the store. On more than one occasion, The Cheapster has had lunch while grazing these free sample stations. Would you like some herb and tomato-flavored gourmet potato chips? Check them out! How about a taste of that imported Brie on a sourdough crisp—or perhaps a few bites of one of the store's scrumptious veggie quesadillas? Top everything off with a taste of a chocolate mousse layer cake. It's on the house!

Samples or no, everything in this store looks so great, you'll end up spending more time than planned feasting your eyes on what's displayed on the shelves.

Whole Foods is not by any means a discount store. In fact, you could spend a bundle here if for no other reason than the seductiveness of the food. Yet there are always deals to be had, and Whole Foods always offers weekly specials. On a recent trip to the store Mr. C noticed six pieces of freshly made sushi for as little as $3.99. Honeydew melons were $1.98 each. Whole or cut-up chickens were only $1.49 a pound, and you could get a completely cooked whole bird for $3.99. White trout fillets were on sale for $5.99 a pound, and you could pick up thick-cut sirloin steaks for $5.99 a pound.

With Whole Foods Market, the savings is really in the value of the merchandise. The quality for the price is a good deal.

Whole Foods Market is open 8 a.m. to 10 p.m. Monday through Saturday, and 8 a.m. to 9 p.m. on Sunday.

LOCAL FARMERS MARKETS

An extra note from Mr. C: Don't forget your local farmer's market when it comes to saving big bucks on fresh fruit, veggies, and even plants! Some locations are only open on a seasonal basis—call ahead to make sure they're open. Here are some good ones to check out, along with their specialties:

For a complete listing of the state's farmer's markets, call or write the Georgia Farm Bureau Federation, 1620 Bass Road, Macon, GA 31298; ✆ (478) 474-8411 or check out the Web site at ✉ www.gfb.org.

Adams Farms

- 1486 Highway 54 West, Fayetteville; ✆ (770) 461-9395

Vegetables, fruits, pecans.

Berry Patch Farms

- 786 Arnold Mill Road, Woodstock; ✆ (770) 926-0561

- ⌘ www.berrypatchfarms.net

Blueberries, pumpkins, cut-your-own and precut Christmas trees.

Flintwood Farms

- 516 McDonough Road, Fayetteville; ✆ (770) 461-4643

Bedding plants at wholesale.

Gardner Farms

- U.S. 23/Georgia 42, Locust Grove; ✆ (770) 957-4912

Peaches, blueberries, blackberries.

Harp's Farm Market

- 1692 Highway 92 South, Fayetteville; ✆ (770) 461-1821

Herbs, berries, peaches, pumpkins, Christmas trees.

Pete's Little Idaho Tater Farm

- 1060 Old Hog Mountain Road, Auburn; ✆ (770) 867-8096

Potatoes, beans, okra, peppers.

Yule Forest Christmas Tree Farm

- 1220 Millers Mill Road, Stockbridge; ✆ (770) 957-3165

- ⌘ www.yuleforeStreetcom

Mr. C loves "cutting his own" during Yule's annual Christmas tree season. When you first show up you're provided with a saw and cart (or plastic sheet) to cut down your tree of choice—Leyland Cyprus, White Pine, Diodara Cedar, or Carolina Sapphire. All trees are reasonably priced. When you bring your tree back, you will be treated to hot cider and Christmas music and an occasional airplane "toy drop." This was the Cheapster's first experience of a toy drop and you don't want to miss it. You can call ahead for toy dropping days.

The farm is open everyday, beginning at Thanksgiving and through the holiday season from 10 a.m. to dark. They have tours for school, church, and scout groups with hayrides.

Yule Forest Highway 155

- 3565 Highway 155N, Stockbridge ✆ (770) 954-9356

Landscape trees, pumpkins. Yes, these two Yule Forests are related—father and son—at two different locations. The pumpkin patch opens October 1 until the end of Oct—Monday through Friday 3 p.m. to 6 p.m., Saturday 9 a.m. to 6 pm and Sunday 10 a.m. to 6 p.m. There provide hay rides, a petting zoo, a science center, and birthday parties. The Web site for both is ⌘ www.aboutyule.com

---

HEALTH FOOD AND VITAMINS

Bill Stanton's Health Food Market

- Lindbergh Plaza, 2581 Piedmont Ave N.E., Atlanta; ✆ (404) 814-9935

Health food stores often have surprisingly good buys on staple items such as cooking and baking ingredients—and Bill Stanton's Health Food Market is no exception.

Mr. C found turbinado (unbleached) sugar for $1.29 a pound, navy beans for $1.49 a

SHOPPING: FOOD STORES

pound, and jumbo prunes on the cheap at $3.69 a pound. Poppy seeds, $1.59 for four ounces, and sunflower seeds, $2.39 a pound, are also good (and healthy) buys.

Bulk spices are real bargains, like poultry and seafood seasoning mixtures, going for $4.69 a package. Jasmine tea is only $3.49 for a four-ounce package, while UniTea Herb's herbal teas from Boulder, Colorado, are $7 for each four-ounce bulk purchase. You can even find health-conscious cosmetics here. Many high-end organic products are reasonably priced here, as compared to the prices found in general grocery stores and drug stores. Kiss My Face olive and aloe moisturizer, for instance, is $6.60 for a one-pint bottle, but it could easily be more expensive elsewhere.

The Market is open seven days a week.

Nuts 'N Berries

- 4274 Peachtree Road N.E., Atlanta; ✆ (404)-237-6829

See also the listing under *Restaurants: Decatur and Northeast Atlanta*.

Within walking distance of the Brookhaven MARTA stop, Nuts 'N Berries will keep you from going nutty from other stores' ridiculously high prices on health food.

As you'd expect, they do sell nuts and dried fruits in bulk, including pumpkin seeds ($6.19 a pound), soybeans (2.01 a pound), shelled walnuts ($6.79 a pound), sliced almonds ($6.79 a pound), and more. Freshly made peanut butter is just $1.99 a pound—cheaper than what you'd pay for most of that that preservative-laden stuff in the supermarket!

Other unusual and well-priced items include Annie's Raspberry Vinaigrette salad dressing for $2.99 a bottle, Eddie's organic durum wheat spaghetti ($3.19 per pound), and bulk Basmati rice ($1.65 a pound). And for you health nuts (pun intended), a quart of Natural High brand aloe vera gel is $6.39.

You can forage in Nuts 'N Berries from 9 a.m. to 8 p.m. Monday through Friday, 10 a.m. to 7 p.m. on Saturday, and 11 a.m. to 6 p.m. on Sunday.

Rainbow Natural Foods

- North Decatur Plaza, 2118 North Decatur Road, Decatur; ✆ (404) 636-5553

Organic and health-food lovers take note: You never know what you'll find under this Rainbow, but you can bet that it's a bargain.

Mr. C found many organic grains, whole spelt, cereals (New Morning Fruit-E-O's), and Mori Silken tofu (tofu's got to be the benchmark for any health food store, right?), as well as turbinado sugar for your baking needs.

Rainbow does it's own baking and their muffins are delicious: Specialties include cranberry apple, banana nut, pumpkin, and blueberry. But their most popular item is their Cowboy Cookies—Mr. C doesn't have the recipe but he's pretty certain that most of the ingredients are chocolate.

Harvest all your fresh veggies at Rainbow, where you can find lots of organic items. However, if you feel like going on a "junk" food binge, Garden of Eatin' (love that name!) blue corn chips are a natural way to do it.

Cosmetics, like Aubrey Organics, Avalon, and Desert Essence, are also reasonably priced. Maybe there is gold at the end of the Rainbow, as the legend goes. You'll certainly have more change in your pocket after shopping here, at any rate!

Store hours are 10 a.m. to 8 p.m. Monday through Saturday, and 11 a.m. to 5 p.m. on Sunday.

Return to Eden

- 2335 Cheshire Bridge Road N.E., Atlanta; ✆ (404) 320-3336

- ⌨ www.return2eden.com

There's so much more than just apples in this Eden! It's hard to find organic and vegetarian foods (you won't find any animal products here) much cheaper than this. Mr. C noted Boca Burgers for $2.79 that sell for $3.69 to $3.99 in grocery stores, Fantastic Foods Soup Cup for 89 cents ($1.19 to $1.49 in the big stores). Tofutti sour cream is sold every day for $1.59 (it's usually $1.79 to $2.19 elsewhere).

They also carry organic produce, fruit, dried fruit, frozen food, dairy, canned products, and other grocery store products.

Nuts are also super-cheap, like whole raw organic cashews for $10.99 a pound, almonds for $11.39, sunflower seeds for $1.99, and Valencia peanuts for 3.29. And R2E has a machine to make your own peanut butter for $3.49 a pound!

Other good buys include Barbara's Puffins cereal for $2.39 a box, one liter of Edensoy Soy Drink for $1.79, and Lightlife tempeh for $1.39 to $1.69 a package.

Coffees by Cafe Tierra and Frontier Coffee sells for just $9.99 a pound in over 32 different blends, including Dutch Bavarian chocolate, French roast, and Irish cream. Decaf coffee is $11.99 a pound, and Celestial Teas are 30 percent off the price in other supermarkets.

You'll find excellent prices on Solgar and Country Life vitamins, Megafoods and New Chapter food supplements, and health and beauty aids.

Return to Eden is open Monday through Friday 9 a.m. to 8 p.m., Saturdays 10 a.m. to 8 p.m., and Sunday 10 a.m. to 6 p.m.

Sevananda Community Owned Natural Foods Market

- 467 Moreland Avenue N.E., Atlanta; ✆ (404) 681-2831

- ⌨ www.sevananda.com

As the name implies, Sevananda is actually a food co-op, which means you can save extra cash if you choose to join. Membership is $100 and you can choose to pay that over five years if need be ($20 a year). But you don't have to be a member to shop here. Sevananda is the largest consumer-owned cooperative in the Southeast, and it's been in business for 25 years.

Prices are already reasonable; but, if you choose to work as few as three hours a week, you will get an extra 20 percent discount every day on store purchases. Sevananda carries everything you'd find in a regular grocery store, and then some. You can find anything here from bread to shampoo to vegetarian dog and cat food. Sevananda carries all organic fruits and vegetables and some are locally grown.

What makes this market unique is their bulk food section—the largest of its kind in Atlanta.

And when you can buy in bulk you save money. Some of the products sold in bulk quantities are beans, grains, pasta, candy, oils, honey, nuts, trail mix, and all kinds of dried fruit including mango and pineapple. You can also purchase liquid soaps in bulk quantities.

Medical and culinary herbs and spices are also a smart buy here, and the selection is extraordinary—they even have Galangal root—for those of us who never heard of this root, it is used in Asian and Indonesian recipes. You can purchase herbs and spices by the ounce or the pound.

There's a whole aisle of regular and herbal teas at reasonable prices, brands like Celestial Seasonings, Stash, Traditional Medicinals, Alvita, Choice, Tazo, and more. Plus plenty of homeopathic health products, vitamins, and cosmetics. Some of the health and beauty brands carried here are Nature's Gate, Solgar, Solaray, Now, and Country Life.

And, we can't forget that he kitchen serves fresh and nutritious baked goods, soups, sandwiches, and salads. Heck, they even have ongoing health, cooking, and nutrition classes! Some of these classes are free, and it doesn't get much cheaper than that.

Sevananda is open Mondays through Saturdays from 9 a.m. to 10 p.m., and Sundays from noon to 9 p.m. There's plenty of free parking and the market is located in the heart of Little Five Points, one block south of Freedom Parkway.

FURNITURE

NEW FURNITURE

Antique City

- 5180 Peachtree Industrial Boulevard, Atlanta; ✆ (770) 458-7131

Why in the world is Mr. C opening the new furniture section with mention of an antique store? No, Mr. C hasn't lost his discounted marbles: It's just that a number of this store's hundred or so dealers augment their stocks of old jewelry, books, magazines, stained glass, collectibles, home furnishings, and other quality merchandise with some interesting *brand-new* reproductions of classic antique furniture.

The place organizes a sale at least twice a year—usually spring and fall—where all of the dealers get together to offer their merchandise at discount. You'll also find seasonal and holiday sales here, so get on their mailing list or give them a call. Overall, you'll find it hard to beat Antique City's wining combo of selection and value.

Store hours are 10 a.m. to 6 p.m. Monday through Saturday, and noon to 5 p.m. on Sunday. (See the full store description under *Antiques and Gifts*.)

Brownlee's Furniture

- 309 Maltbie Street, Lawrenceville; ✆ (770) 963-6435

You wouldn't think that a sprawling ten-acre complex and two-acre showroom would be hard to find, but it is. Once you get there, though, you'll be glad you stayed with the hunt.

In business for 35 years, this humble little store has expanded a bit since Mr. Cheap's first visit nearly a decade ago, and it now boasts an inventory of more than six million pieces. There are at least a thousand sofas and loveseats in stock at this mammoth place; more than 150 bedroom and dining room sets, too. More, you say? How about more than 100 brand-name recliners? Do you like Karastan and Kapel rugs? They've all been added to the inventory.

The remote, low-overhead location and lack of amenities (like no carpeting on the floor) allow Brownlee's to sell their merchandise every day at 50 to 60 percent off retail prices. In a major concession to modern necessities, Brownlee's now has air-conditioning.

Names like Lane, Sealy, Pennsylvania House, Hooker, Broyhill, Craftmaster, Huntington House, and Fairfield are all here, and all at great discounts. There is a charge for delivery (they are out in the boonies, after all), but after you save hundreds of dollars on the furniture itself, you'll still come out way ahead on the deal. It's a lot better than driving all the way to North Carolina for furniture.

One way to save money on delivery: rent or borrow a truck for the shopping trip.

Brownlee's is open weekdays from 10 a.m. to 8 p.m., Saturday from 10 a.m. to 6 p.m., and Sunday from 1 p.m. to 6 p.m. Look for their ad in the Saturday *Gwinnett Daily Post* or call for directions.

Castleberry's Treasures for Your Home

- 3614 Chamblee Dunwoody Boulevard, Chamblee; (770) 457-0216
- 1808 Lower Roswell Road, Marietta; (770) 973-6121
- 3635 Highway 78 West, Snellville; (770) 972-4343
- 305 Bradford Street North, Gainesville; (770) 536-6851
- www.castleberrysfurniture.com

If you can't find a bargain here, Mr. C has to doubt whether you can find one anywhere. These shops are literally jam-packed with dinettes, sofas, tables, bedroom sets, and accessories, many of them from fine brand-name makers, and all at discounted prices. The sales volume is high, the overhead is low, and many items are special purchases—usually marked down for clearance or because they've been discontinued. All of these factors help you save money!

Every Castleberry's store is a little different in its mix of brands and sets, since each store manager buys for his or her own location. Overall, you'll find approximately forty of the top brands in the business, including Clayton Marcus and Broyhill. On one visit, a Hooker mahogany chest, listed at $423, was seen at one of the stores for just $264. A Tempo ceramic

---

MR. CHEAP'S PICKS

Furniture

Brownlee's Furniture—Huge inventory and 50 to 60 percent off retail prices make this warehouse store a winner in Mr. C's book.

Designer Furniture Source—A 100,000-square-foot showroom where you can buy new, first-quality furniture of major name brands at prices below wholesale.

Rhodes Furniture—This place is jam-packed with great value furniture for every room in the house, including the home office.

Storehouse—Here you can save 25 to 80 percent off retail on floor samples, overstocks, furniture used for the company's photo shoots, and other leftovers for every room.

lamp, listed at $120, was reduced to $75. In the showroom downstairs, Mr. C found a plant stand by Lane, originally $300, reduced to just $160 for a special closeout. A Berkshire daybed frame, meant to sell for over $300, was an unbelievable $80, and a mahogany finish Fairfield chair was cut by $150 down to $267.

Sofa sales will save you big bucks, like a Clayton Marcus model (reduced by half to $700), and a Broyhill club chair (cut from $437 to $273), or the Delft love seat (originally $813, reduced to $513). Even a Taylorsville sofa, valued at $1,313, was reduced by over a third to $814.

Castleberry's stores generally are open Monday and Thursday from 9:30 a.m. to 9 p.m.; Tuesday, Wednesday, Friday, and Saturday from 9:30 a.m. to 6 p.m.; and Sunday from 12:30 p.m. to 5 p.m.

Casual Image Furniture

- 10895 Alpharetta Highway, Roswell; (770) 518-4003
- 1893 Piedmont Road N.E., Marietta (770) 971-5605
- www.casualimage.com

Just writing about this place makes Mr. C want to stop working on this book and take a little therapeutic nap in the ol' backyard hammock. This family business started in 1984 and has always placed an emphasis on personal service, selling more than 120 high-quality brands at prices significantly below typical retail. Their image is "leisure," and they carry furniture and accessories for every leisure space.

This includes furniture for family rooms, sunroom, screen porches, decks, gardens, pool-side, bar stools. CIF also has associated leisure "accessories" such as grills, hammocks, lamps, and fireplace items.

Store hours are Monday to Friday 10 a.m. to 8 p.m., Friday from 10 a.m. to 6 p.m., and Sunday noon to 5 p.m.

Designer Furniture Source

- 3455 Peachtree Industrial Boulevard, Duluth; (770) 623-1788
- 2505 Chastain Meadows Parkway, Kennesaw; (770) 973-7100

Even Mr. Cheap would ordinarily have trouble getting overly excited about a furniture store, but this place is so exceptional that he starts to giggle to himself just thinking about it.

The Designer Furniture Source is the third incarnation of what many locals might remember as the Carriage House Consignment Gallery, which began as an antique shop and then developed into a used furniture store. David Herckis, the past and present owner, has now transformed the Carriage House into a showroom (100,000 square feet) that sells only new, first-quality furniture of major name brands at prices below wholesale. Yes, *below wholesale* prices. How is he able to do this? DFS receives phenomenal discounts from manufacturers on discontinued models, showroom and photo samples, and excess inventory. There is furniture here for every room, formal to informal, contemporary to modern.

In addition to the showroom, DFS has a large warehouse on site. If you buy furniture and your home isn't ready, you can store it here for no charge, then delivery is free.

Mr. C was asked not to print specific names and prices in order to protect these relationships; but he saw some real knockout deals that can save you hundreds of dollars. (Psst! The Cheapster will tell you that he found a sofa, priced originally $3,000, reduced to $100!)

DFS also offers *additional* price cuts on already discounted furniture if you pay cash or pay within 90 days. Depending on economic conditions, the store often offers a 12-month interest-free payment plan, and they honor all major credit cards.

Designer Furniture Source has been so successful that they are looking to open showrooms in other locations in Georgia and possibly in other states. Store hours are Monday, Tuesday, and Wednesday from 10 a.m. to 6 p.m., Thursday from 10 a.m. to 8 p.m., and Sunday 1 p.m. to 5 p.m.

Gateway IV Real Solid Oak Furniture

- I-85 Northeast Expressway Access Road at Dawson Boulevard, Norcross; (770) 441-1739

Another store found in the Georgia Antique and Design Center, Gateway manufactures its own line of real solid oak furniture in antique reproductions and old-fashioned styles.

These pieces would never fool an antique collector—they're made with sturdy modern components and engineering—but if you like period dining tables, rolltop desks, and such, you'll enjoy an expedition through their showroom. And you can save money, because you're buying at "direct from the factory" prices. The proprietor, Mr. Ghering, is a fourth-generation woodworker, hence the Roman numeral IV; he takes great pride in his work and says that his furniture will last for generations.

Among the pieces Mr. C was offered were a Windsor oak rocker, high-backed with arms, selling for $199; a 42" round drop-leaf kitchen table for $325; and a 44" × 24" secretary's writing desk for $395. Another incredible deal was a 48" round table with a 19" leaf (with space for eight people) made of an inch and a quarter thick oak for $435. This table might sell for $670 in other furniture stores, if you could find it.

At Gateway, you'll find real solid oak furniture for every room—12 families of desks, 39 styles of chairs, dozens of tables, and bookshelves, and over 100 pieces of bedroom furniture on display in the showroom and hundreds of pieces of furniture one mile away in to the store's warehouse. There are china cabinets, hutches, benches, coat trees, planters, and many other kinds of items. Many of these have handles, knobs, and other details in solid brass. The sides of every drawer and shelf are made of real solid oak—the way the tree grew it. Every room includes office centers, entertainment centers custom-made for yachts, and tables for church vestibules—and you know how careful most churches are about spending.

The packed showroom, which is accessible from inside the market or from the parking lot, actually spills over into several smaller rooms as well, giving you plenty to look at. And if you don't see exactly what you want, ask—chances are, they can custom-build it at well below other furniture store prices.

The owner told Mr. Cheap the 1996 Olympic Italian Tae Kwan Do team ordered a 12-foot-long table with chairs for camaraderie during meals while they were in Atlanta training. After the Olympics they had the table shipped to Italy.

Gateway is located one mile south of Jimmy Carter Boulevard, and a mile-and-a-half north of Spaghetti Junction. Store hours are Monday from noon to 6 p.m., Thursday and Friday noon to 7 p.m., Saturday noon to 8 p.m., and Sunday noon to 7 p.m. They are closed Tuesday and Wednesday. From Thanksgiving to the end of December, they are open every day noon to 7 p.m.

Haverty's Fine Furniture

- Warehouse Clearance Center, 5600 Buford Highway, Doraville; ✆ (770) 454-3450

- 6731 N. Point Parkway, Alpharetta; ✆ (770) 442-2810

- 2079 Cobb Parkway S.W., Smyrna; ✆ (770) 953-2160

- 2297 Highway 78 East, Snellville; ✆ (770) 972-0564

- 4013 Lavista Road, Tucker; ✆ (770) 491-0536

- 724 Home Center Drive N.W., Kennesaw; ✆ (770) 423-0266

- 1230 Morrow Industrial Boulevard, Morrow; ✆ (770) 961-7476

- 132 Perimeter Center West, Atlanta; ✆ (770) 352-0901

- 5849 Peachtree Road, Chamblee; ✆ (770) 454-3450

- 2055 Atlas Circle, Gainesville; ✆ (770) 538-6021

- 3333 Buford Drive, Buford, ✆ (770) 831-6110

- ✐ www.havertys.com

The clearance center at the top of the list above supports all of the Haverty's furniture stores in the Atlanta metro area, with cool deals on furniture for every room in the house, including the home office. (Haverty's tells Mr. C that the clearance center will be moving sometime in the near future, so call to get the new location.)

At the clearance center you'll find the same name brands that are sold in all Haverty's stores, including Thomasville, Broyhill, Clayton Marcus, Bernhardt, and others. They have every kind of style, contemporary to traditional. Furniture in the clearance center is 25 to 70 percent off retail, and you may spot some imperfections, but you can't beat the deals. As with most clearance centers, there is a "no return" policy.

Mr. C recommends that you also check out some of the other Haverty's stores because they're always having great sales. The Cheapster found some of the best prices in town on Thomasville furniture, and these guys guarantee their low prices: If you purchase furniture and find it in another store for less within 30 days, Haverty's will refund you the difference.

Haverty's is open Monday through Saturday from 10 a.m. to 9 p.m., and Sunday from noon to 6 p.m.

La-Z-Boy Furniture Galleries

- Clearance Center, 6478 Dawson Boulevard, Norcross; ✆ (770) 242-7313

- 2176 Henderson Mill Road NE, Atlanta; ✆ (770) 938-0890

- 1610 Mount Zion Road, Morrow; ✆ (770) 960-0042

- 1320 Pleasant Hill Road, Lawrenceville; ✆ (770) 935-0080

- 835 Ernest Barrett Parkway NW, Kennesaw; ✆ (770) 499-9819

- 11060 Alpharetta Highway, Roswell; ✆ (770) 594-9914

- ✐ www.lazboy.com

Mr. C has been called a "lazy boy" at various times in his life and career, but in truth he's a mere pretender. During special sales, La-Z-Boy's factory-direct showrooms sell these famous implements of relaxation for as low as two for $599. "Classic Series" chairs, with styles like Chippendale and Queen Anne, also go for $599 a pair. You can also talk to the folks here about buying individual chairs at comparable prices. Sofas are also value-priced, starting at $599, with reclining sofas from $799, and La-Z-Boy leather sofas from $1,499.

The factory stores are open Mondays through Saturdays from 10 a.m. to 8 p.m., and Sundays from noon to 6 p.m.

The Clearance Center in Norcross has sofas, chairs, and accessories such as end tables and lamps, all at a discount of 30 to 70 percent off the manufacturer's list prices. The clearance center is open Thursday, Friday, and Saturday from 10 a.m. to 8 p.m., and Sunday noon to 6 p.m.

Mattress Liquidators

- 3106 Buford Highway Duluth; ✆ (770) 813-0504

This place is a great find for anyone looking for bed products or furniture. In business for eight years, Mattress Liquidators has built a reputation based on personalized service and great deals. Even through they're a small store, they have an amazingly full range of offerings.

In addition to mattresses and futons, this relatively small store is also packed with floor displays of new, tasteful furniture. To save room and keep prices down, they might display one piece of a bedroom group, along with a color photo of the entire set. They pick up merchandise from local distributors, so you don't have to wait weeks for your order. All the furniture is brand-new, in the package, much of it ready-to-assemble. The furniture ranges from the "promotional" variety (made of lower-quality particleboard, tubular steel, imitation brass, etc.) to $10,000 bedroom groups that are available for half price!

Store hours are 10 a.m. to 7 p.m. Monday through Friday, and 10 a.m. to 6 p.m. on Saturday. They're closed on Sunday.

Norcross Furniture Outlet

- 5500 Jimmy Carter Boulevard, Norcross; ✆ (770) 368-0000

- ✍ www.norcrossfurniture.com

Located directly across the street from Cub Foods Grocery Store (just east of Interstate 85), this full-line furniture outlet discounts "better quality" furniture by 30 to 70 percent off retail. NFO is a store for every room, with an especially large selection of living room furniture. They also carry mattresses. The goods here are not necessarily name brands, but they are good stuff, made from solid wood. Mr. C liked a cherry wood four-poster bed frame, reduced from $699 to $398, and other matching pieces were available if you care to add a mirror or a dresser.

Another good deal was a kitchen table and four chairs, made from solid ash in a natural finish. The table was topped with white ceramic tiles, and the set was marked down from its retail price of $559 to just $298.

NFO is open Mondays through Saturdays from 10 a.m. to 7 p.m., and Sundays from noon to 6 p.m.

Rhodes Furniture

- 4370 Peachtree Road N.E. # 100 (corporate office), Atlanta; ✆ (404) 264-4600

- 3655 Memorial Drive, Decatur; ✆ (404) 289-2136

- 2540 Hargrove Road, Smyrna; ✆ (770) 434-8911

- 4715 Ashford Dunwoody Road, Atlanta; ✆ (770) 395-1812

SHOPPING: FURNITURE

- 4363 Northeast Expressway, Doraville; ✆ (770) 934-9350
- 1972 Mount Zion Road, Morrow; ✆ (770) 471-2200
- 114 Pavilion Parkway, Fayetteville; ✆ (770) 719-0856
- 2340 Pleasant Hill Road, Duluth; ✆ (770) 476-1890
- 870 Cobb Place Boulevard NW, Kennesaw; ✆ (770) 425-4275
- 6050 North Point Parkway, Alpharetta; ✆ (770) 475-1656
- 1416 Dogwood Drive SW, Conyers; ✆ (770) 922-9971
- 5955 Stewart Parkway, Douglasville; ✆ (770) 489-5300
- 2338 Henry Clower Boulevard, Snellville; ✆ (770) 972-8289
- ⌨ www.rhodesfurniture.com

Hit the Rhodes for great values on furniture for every room in the house, including the home office. You'll find furniture in contemporary, traditional, Mission, and transitional styles.

Queen-sized sleeper sofas are priced right, as low as $699 complete. (Mr. C has seen similar-quality pieces for up to twice that price.) A queen-size contemporary, solid wood construction bed with a rich dark finish was seen for $499. A contemporary dark finish dining room group in solid wood, including china cabinet, a 44" × 66" table with 22" leaf that extends to 88", *and* four side chairs was only $1,999. Another great deal was a breakfront 12-drawer dresser in solid wood construction and beveled glass oval mirror for $899.

Rhodes backs up their prices with a good satisfaction guarantee, the sort of thing that makes the very careful Mr. C a bit more ready to part with some of his cash: If you're not happy with your purchase, return it within seven days for a full refund or exchange. If within 30 days of the purchase you find the identical item with the same service and finance terms advertised for less, Rhodes will refund the difference.

Rhodes is open from 10 a.m. to 9 p.m. Mondays through Saturdays, and from noon to 6 p.m. on Sundays.

Rich's Furniture Clearance

- Cobb Center, 2144 South Cobb Drive, Smyrna; ✆ (770) 433-4790
- ⌨ www.richsonline.com

This clearance center sells closeouts, samples, and floor models from its many stores around the Atlanta area. Major brands of indoor and outdoor furniture, as well as bedding, rugs, lamps, and accessories are sold here at reductions of 30 to 50 percent off original retail. To keep things moving, an additional 10 percent is knocked off the price every 45 days until the item sells.

Some of these pieces are slightly damaged and are sold "as is," but if you're not too fussy, you can find incredible deals on furniture for every room in the house, and even patio furniture for outdoors.

You will find well-known brand names such a Henredon, Bernhardt, Pulaski, Natuzzi, Karastan, Nourison, and many more. Rich's carries diverse styles from traditional to contemporary, and formal or casual.

Mattresses are sold in sets only and are rated in overall firmness and quality as "good," "better," "best," and "top of the line." In full size, these range from $199 for a good set, to $369 for better, $449 for best, and $599 for top-of-the-line. Delivery on any item is available for a fee. The store will not hold an item for you, nor does it offer layaway plans.

This clearance center is open the same hours as Rich's Furniture stores: Monday through Saturday from 10 a.m. to 9 p.m. and Sundays noon to 7 p.m.

Storehouse

- Clearance Center, 3106 Early Street N.W., Atlanta; (404) 233-4111

- Clearance Center, 6368 Dawson Boulevard (I-85 & J. Carter Boulevard), Norcross; (770) 446-2646

- 3393 Peachtree Road, N.E., Atlanta; (404) 261-3482

- Sandy Springs Plaza, 6277 Roswell Road, Atlanta; (404) 256-3844

- 440 Barrett Parkway at Town Center, Kennesaw; (770) 424-1422

- Northpoint Mall, Kennesaw; (770) 754-5590

- 4475 Roswell Road, Marietta; (770) 971-5861

- www.storehouse.com

You probably know Storehouse, the regional chain of contemporary and traditional furniture stores based in Atlanta. You may not know about their clearance centers, where you can save money on floor samples, overstocks, furniture used for the company's photo shoots, and other leftovers for every room. Furniture is discounted 25 to 80 percent off retail prices. The stock always varies, but you can find a pretty good selection of one-of-a-kind pieces, and there is furniture for every room of the house.

It's a bit of mix-and-match here, and when there's a lot of stuff, everything is crammed in rather tightly. Some of these items are slightly damaged. But, if you're willing to poke around, you may come up with a good bargain.

You might also want to visit any one of the retail stores in the Atlanta area (listed above) when they are having sales. Mr. C found dining room tables discounted $100, buffets $75, hutches $75, and $25 off dining chair and barstools. Rugs are also discounted during sales. Give them a call to find out what's on sale or visit their Web site.

Clearance Centers are open Monday to Saturday 10 a.m. to 7 p.m. and Sunday 12:30 p.m. to 6 p.m.

Retail store hours are Monday to Saturday 10 a.m. to 9 p.m. and Sunday noon to 6 p.m.

USED FURNITURE

Ballard's Thrift Store

- 2065 Main Street, Atlanta; (404) 799-5064

This cool little place, located on the corner of Bolton and main near I-285, could be your Main source for furnishing a house on a shoestring budget. They carry a wide variety of good- to excellent-condition furniture and accessories for living rooms, bedrooms, dining rooms, family rooms—you name it. They even have a smattering of nice antiques. All of this stuff comes from individuals who are moving, estates, and so forth. Bedroom sets are available from $295 and up. Sofas and chairs are priced from $195. Dinette sets are $95 and up, while lamps start at $25! Table sets for nearly every room in the house are tagged in the $100 to $300 range.

Great prices, eh? Even better, the staff here is friendly and helpful, making Ballard's a pleasant (and economical) shopping experience.

Store hours are Monday through Friday from 9 a.m. to 5 p.m. and Saturday from 9 a.m. to 4 p.m.

DHS Sell-Out Center

- 1374 Moreland Avenue S.E., Atlanta; ✆ (404) 622-1800

Part of the Moreland Center shopping plaza, this vast store buys up furniture and furnishings from hotels when they renovate their rooms. Then, they turn around and "sell out" the stock at incredibly low prices. Sure, these items have seen better days; some pieces are in good condition, some are not. But if you doubt there's a market for this stuff, guess again. The place gets a steady stream of shoppers. And, twice a year, when DHS holds its half-price sale on everything in the store, it becomes a mob scene.

So, think about your average hotel or motel room. Whatever you'd find there will be on sale here: bedding, tables, chairs, lamps, the pictures on the walls, the carpeting under your feet. Get a king-size Sealy mattress and box spring for $95 per set. Plush side chairs in every color and shape imaginable (so it seems) from $20 and up. Circular glass tables with lamps built into the center for $25. Framed prints from $15. A huge piece of rolled-up carpeting for $45. You get the idea.

Occasionally, DHS also gets deals on new items too; on Mr. C's most recent investigation, there was a special on mahogany veneer nightstands, with drawers, for $39 each. These were still in their original boxes, and there were tons of them. Plus lots of other unusual items, including a bit of a sideline business in vintage clothing and collectibles. It's a fascinating place, run by friendly folks.

Check them out; they're open Monday through Saturday from 10 a.m. to 6 p.m. and Sunday from noon to 5 p.m.

Treasure Mart

- 3641 Pierce Drive N.E., Chamblee; ✆ (770) 458-1200

If you like older furniture—the way it looks and the memories it evokes, you'll love coming here and just wandering around. Mr. C could easily spend an afternoon wandering this quaint and friendly purveyor of used furniture and household items.

Everything in here—not only used furniture, but also lamps, pictures, copper and brass items, and collectibles (even the occasional bona fide antique)—is on consignment, and it's all priced according to a system that can really save you money: When a piece first enters the store, the store manager agrees on a price with the consigner. That is always a good bargain to begin with. Then, every 30 days the piece is marked down another 10 percent. That makes for good bargains, of course, and also causes the nicer pieces to move. (The store manager reports that some customers stop by at least once a week for fear that they will miss something!)

During the Cheapster's last stroll through these burnished aisles, he spotted a 1960s Drexel dining set (china cabinet, server, table, and chairs) for $1,500. Sofas were priced at $100 to $300, a lot of table and chairs were ticketed starting at $75 and up, and a beautiful wood chest of drawers—great for a bedroom—was priced at $120.

Store hours are 10 a.m. to 5 p.m. Monday through Saturday, and 1 p.m. to 5 p.m. on Sunday.

My Favorite Place

- 5596 Peachtree Industrial Boulevard, Chamblee; ✆ (770) 452-8397

Mr. Cheap didn't give this place its name; they took it all by themselves. But it's not far from the truth: This place could become anyone's favorite place to shop for furniture and household items because it has a winning combination of quality and low prices.

My Favorite Place is one of the largest used furniture and antique store in northeast Atlanta. A large percentage of this shop's customers are antique dealers and interior decorators, who snatch up some of the fine old furniture here and then resell it (at a markup, of course) to their own clients. This is not a consignment shop: The numerous dealers who work here buy goods directly from the usual sources—people who are moving, downsizing, or upgrading, and estate sales. My Favorite Place rents space to these dealers, who take shifts as on-site managers during store hours.

Here you'll find just about anything you need at a range of prices, starting at the very cheap and ranging into the big (yet good value) bucks. Entire bedroom suites start at $175. Couches can be had for $50 and up. Lamps from a measly $5 to Tiffany jobs ticketed at $1,000 or more. While the selection is mind-boggling, the shopping is fun and rewarding.

My Favorite Place is open seven days a week from 10 a.m. to 5:30 p.m.

OFFICE FURNITURE

Alpha Business Interiors

- 2133 Mountain Industrial Boulevard, Tucker; (770) 934-2229

- www.alphabusinessinteiors.com

This ten-year-old warehouse/showroom store encompassing 26,000 square feet is small-business heaven. They sell new and used famous-brand office furniture, from desks to electric filing systems, at fractions of their original prices.

Alpha's prices on new furniture are good, but the real story is its deals on used items. Some of the highest-quality brands are found here: Desks and chairs by Steelcase and Herman Miller sell for 70 percent off retail. A five-year old Steelcase file cabinet, for example, which sold for $1,000 when it was new, may go for just $250 here. And if you know office furniture, you know these babies last forever—five years is a drop in the bucket! Bookshelves, data racks, freestanding cubicle panels, and work stations also sell here at true bargain prices.

Among the best deals are the floor samples that well-known companies use in their catalog photo shoots. These floor samples get shipped straight to Alpha, and you can get incredible discounts on brand-new office furniture.

The store is open Monday to Friday from 9 a.m. to 5 p.m.

Atlantic Office Furniture

- 4194 Jimmy Carter Boulevard, Norcross; (770) 729-0655

This place is an ocean of new and used office furniture, awash in desks, credenza, hutches, bookshelves, more than 300 chairs, cubicles, and much more.

Everyday low prices will save you at least 10 percent on what you'll pay for office furniture most other places, and the savings compared to new furniture are huge.

If you had tagged along with The Cheapster on his last cruise through here, you would have been able to purchase a pure oak desk, three inches thick, with an eight-foot credenza on the back, for $799 (as opposed to the $7,000 it would have cost new). Also spotted was a mahogany desk and credenza, tagged at $999, and table and two chairs for $279. According to the manager, that whole set would cost you about $4,400 new.

Herman Miller desk chairs that normally sell for $450 were priced at $89.99; a steel bookcase, normally priced at $450 new, was available for just over $100; and Kimball side chairs were going for $119.

Located less than half a mile from Peachtree Industrial Parkway, the store is open for business Monday, Tuesday, and Wednesday from 9 a.m. to 5 p.m.; Thursday and Friday from 9 a.m. to 4:30 p.m.; and Saturday from 10 a.m. to 2 p.m.

Business Furniture Liquidators

- 890 Chattahoochee Avenue N.W., Atlanta; (404) 355-9493

This gigantic store is divided into two sections. The front room displays new and practically new office furniture of very high quality, at discount. Here, you may find such items as a Hooker credenza in rich walnut, with brass trim, selling at $500 off its retail price, or $999; handsome Paoli side chairs, in cherry wood with teal upholstery, reduced from $540 to $280; or a mahogany executive's desk, with just a nick or two, marked down from an original $1,240 to $795. You can get a fine wood desk and credenza for around $800 ($400 for a laminate model); the desk alone goes for about $300 and up ($195 and up for laminate).

Walk through to the much larger back warehouse area and it's as though you've entered another world. In a storeroom as big as the proverbial football field, older furniture is stacked as far and as high as the eye can see. Much of it is still in good, useable condition, even if it wouldn't win any beauty contests. Many other pieces have undoubtedly seen their last coffee break. Still, for starting up an office on a dime, this place is likely to have whatever you need!

How much do these items cost? Who knows? Nothing is marked. Presumably, this gives you an opportunity to sharpen your negotiating skills. Generally, chairs are priced around $35 and up; file cabinets start at $60 or thereabouts; and so on. In any event, you'll have a good time just poking around back there.

BFL is open Monday through Friday from 9 a.m. to 5 p.m., and Saturday from 11 a.m. to 2 p.m.

Corporate Office Furniture

- 135 Bucknell Court S.W., Atlanta; (404) 344-0340
- 11060 Alpharetta Highway, Roswell; (770) 645-2131

Each of these stores boasts a large selection of mostly used furniture and great deals. At either place you'll find scads of perfectly good, high-quality used furniture that the company picked up from businesses that have moved or downsized. Desk credenza sets priced here at $300 to $1,000 would cost you $1,000 to $5,000 new. Hayworth mahogany groups with overheads,

> **MR. CHEAP'S PICKS**
>
> ### Office Furniture
>
> **Alpha Business Interiors**—This is small-business heaven, with new and used famous-brand office furniture for sale at fractions of their original prices.
>
> **Wholesale Office Furniture**—This establishment boasts a good selection of used office furniture, as well as new furniture from major catalogs, all at reduced prices.

tagged at just $1,500, would set you back $3,000 to $5,000 if you were to buy them factory-fresh. These folks also have 5,000 chairs priced from $20 to $1,000, so why not shop around and save big bucks?

The Atlanta store has that traditional warehouse feel and is open Monday through Friday from 8:30 a.m. to 4:30 p.m. The Roswell location, located in a shopping center with carpet and low ceiling, is open Monday through Friday from 9 a.m. to 5 p.m., and Saturday from 10 a.m. to 3 p.m.

Wholesale Office Furniture

- 4295 Northeast Expressway, Atlanta; (770) 414-8220; (404) 873-5491

- www.wholesaleofficefurn.com

This establishment boasts a good selection of used office furniture, as well as new furniture from major catalogues, all at reduced prices. "We don't sell junk that eventually falls apart," says owner Laura Kamenitsa. Indeed, the WOF offers lots of good deals on a variety of furniture: Ergonomic chairs are priced at $30 and up. Desks are available from $50 (for the basic, black metal sort). Used executive office sets, like a three-piece desk, credenza and bookcase, sell for $800, which is $2,000 below its original level.

Here you'll find everything from little accessories like letter trays and wastebaskets to big workstations, like a Herman Miller setup for two people (originally $6,000, here $1,000). There's a lot to see.

WOF also carries brand-new lines from over 250 national manufacturers, from budget to high-end brands. You can get discounts on desks by Jasper and OFS, upholstered chairs by Hickory and Fairfield; plus products from Carolina, DMI, HON, Thomasville, and many others.

Located on the northbound I-85 access road between Northcrest and Pleasantvale (near the Econo Lodge), the store is open Monday through Friday from 9:30 a.m. to 5 p.m., and Saturdays from 11 a.m. to 4 p.m.

Also worth checking out:

Eastside Office Furniture

- 2125 Mountain Industrial Boulevard, Tucker; (770) 908-9311

This busy place features new and used office furniture, with plenty of good deals. Store hours are Monday through Friday from 9 a.m. to 5 p.m., and Saturday from 10 a.m. to 3 p.m.

HOME FURNISHINGS

DECORATIVE ITEMS, KITCHENWARE, LIGHTING, LINENS, PAINT, WALLPAPER

The Container Store

- 3255 Peachtree Road N.E., Atlanta; (404) 261-4776

- 120 Perimeter Center, Atlanta; (770) 351-0065

- www.containerstore.com

Hallelujah! A store for both the organizationally impaired and the budget-impaired, with items for home and office. Containers, shelving, hooks, racks, and creative holders in every shape and size are on sale here.

Here you'll find tie racks by Xtendables, priced at $14.99 each, or, for the kitchen, a stainless steel (it won't rust) recipe box for $16.99, or graceful grape decanters made from 100 percent recycled material for $2.99 to $4.99. And how have you managed all these years without an acrylic toothpick dispenser for $12.99, or a suction paper towel holder for $14, tray dividers that divide the vertical space of your kitchen cabinets to more efficiently store baking sheets, cake pans, and muffin tins for only $8.99.

For work, pick up a mouse pad calculator for $12.99 and a turf monitor board for messages that you can mount at the top of your computer for $19.99. If you want to splurge—or if you were "born to be wild"—buy the dragonfly or critter pushpins.

At the Container Store you can be creative with your wastebasket choices—Mr. C recommends the innovative designer Karim Rashad sway can, for only $7.99.

Furniture for home and office is bargain-priced to help you get your act together. Mr. C likes their exclusive tchotchke shelf that's simple and elegant, available in a choice of three lengths and three finishes $16.99 to $22.99. Build your own bookcases with Nordic birch wood cubes, or perhaps with chestnut stackable folding shelves to make any storage area super-efficient.

There are lots of bath and laundry organizing items, too, including clothes hangers and garment bags. A canvas L.L. Bean lookalike tote bag was tagged at just $9.99, and Mr. C also spotted an iron and board holder that hangs on the wall or closet. It lets you put a warm iron in the heat-resistant plastic holder immediately after ironing, and it's only $8.49. They even have lipstick and makeup organizers starting at $4.99!

They also have basics like wrapping paper or creative packaging and cardboard shipping boxes, too. Now that you've gotten your life so organized, you can pack up all the junk and ship it off to Kalamazoo.

Store hours are Monday to Saturday 9 a.m. to 9 p.m. and Sunday 11 a.m. to 6 p.m.

Georgia Lighting Clearance Center

- 1510 Ellsworth Industrial Drive, Atlanta; ✆ (404) 875-7637

No doubt you've heard of Georgia Lighting (a divisions of Home Depot), but, you may not be aware of this clearance center where they sell factory closeouts, discontinued, one-of-a-kind, and scratch-and-dent items that have been taken off the floors of their regular retail showrooms. These sell at reductions of 30 to 70 percent below retail prices. The Atlanta store has that genuine warehouse ambiance; it's like an airplane hangar, inexplicably strung with gorgeous lights.

Most of GL's lines are traditional in style, though there are some contemporary models here and there. Flush-mount lanterns in polished brass, for your front door, start as low as $19.95; a five-lamp brass chandelier was seen for $59.95. Plus, they have ceiling fan/lights from $39.95, table lamps, floor lamps, strip lights for bathroom mirrors, and lots of bulbs, globes, and shades to go with them.

The clearance centers also get deals on other home furnishings, like framed paintings and mirrors, as well as some accent furniture pieces like plant stands, end tables, and coat trees. The knowledgeable staff is ready to answer all your questions, technical and esthetic; amazingly, they seem to know every single item in this vast store by name and number.

Clearance Center hours are Tuesday to Saturday from 10 a.m. to 4 p.m.

> ### MR. CHEAP'S PICKS
>
> *Home Furnishings*
>
> **The Container Store**—Everything you need to help store all the stuff you've bought with this book!
>
> **Georgia Lighting Clearance Center**—Fantastic closeout deals on all kinds of indoor and outdoor lighting.
>
> **Tuesday Morning**—Closeout bargains on cookware, linens, and doodads.

Hill Street Warehouse

- 2050 Hills Avenue, N.E., Atlanta; (404) 352-5001

This down 'n dirty, open-raftered warehouse located in the Chattahoochee industrial district west of midtown has by most opinions the largest selection of decorative home accessories and overall best values you're likely to find in the Atlanta area.

Sometime ugly can be beautiful, however, and The Cheapster was basking in that glory as he perused Hill Street's impressive selection of lamps, pictures, mirrors, rugs, candles, Italian ceramics, and terra cotta, crystal, lampshades, and more. These guys are directly linked with Merchandise Market downtown, and do most of their business with retailers. Consequently, they sell a lot of floor samples as well as factory closeouts, and large quantities of Italian imported items, resulting in huge savings (up to 70 percent off retail) to regular folks looking for a good deal.

They get new stuff in every day, which only adds to the attraction of the place. And, the dust is free!

Warehouse hours are 10 a.m. to 5 p.m. Monday through Saturday. They're closed on Sunday.

"Luxury Linens" at Burlington Coat Factory

- 2841 Greenbriar Parkway S.W., Atlanta; (404) 349-6300

- 3750 Venture Drive, Duluth; (770) 497-0033

- 1255 Roswell Road N.E., Marietta; (770) 971-6540

- 608 Holcomb Bridge Road, Roswell; (770) 518-9800

See the Burlington Coat Factory listing under *Discount Department Stores*.

Tuesday Morning

- 3145 Piedmont Road N.E., Atlanta; (404) 233-6526

- 4502 Chamblee Dunwoody Road, Dunwoody; (770) 457-3565

- 901 Montreal Road, Tucker; (770) 934-3164

- 2790 Cumberland Boulevard S.E., Smyrna; (770) 435-6678

- 1115 Mount Zion Road, Morrow; (770) 961-0707

- 736 Johnson Ferry Road, Marietta; (770) 971-0511

- 6325 Spalding Drive, Norcross; (770) 447-4692

- 4051 Highway 78, Lilburn; (770) 978-3573

- 700 Sandy Plains Road, Marietta; (770) 428-1536

- 1231 Alpharetta Street, Roswell; (770) 640-8146

- 3500 Satellite Boulevard, Duluth; (770) 476-0522

SHOPPING: HOME FURNISHINGS

- 3600 Dallas Highway N.W., Marietta; (678) 355-5505
- www.tuesdaymorning.com

Every day of the week, the bargains at Tuesday Morning will make you feel glad you got out of bed; they offer a 50 to 80 percent "everyday" discount on upscale merchandise found in better department stores. Selections range from room and area rugs to luxury linens, fine crystal, china, decorative accessories, lawn and garden accents, gourmet cookware and housewares, luggage, toys, and seasonal decorations or gifts.

Tuesday Morning can save you a lot of money on quality runs since they buy direct from manufacturers and artisans from all over the world. Whether you're interested in factory-made major brands or colorful and artistic handmade selections, you'll find a wide selection of 100 percent wools, hand-hooked 100 percent cottons, acrylics, and machine woven polypropylenes.

For the home, you may find a queen-sized quilted comforter by Impressions reduced from $200 to $90; and an Eileen West king-size sheet set, marked down from $165 to $60. Low-priced doodads for around the house include a Chantal omelet pan, on sale at half-price at $30, as well as a Vigaro teapot, normally listed at $35, selling for $15. Porcelain by Rosenthal of Germany is just $9 per dinner plate (down from $21), and only $30 for a server (regularly $88). Linen damask tablecloths are half-price at $30, and cloth place mats are just $13 (about half their going retail price).

The Cheapster has never been averse to going the "disposable" route on occasion, and he was offered a package of 42 plastic utensils or a dozen 12-ounce tumblers, each priced at $1.99.

Occasionally, Tuesday Morning gets special deals on larger items for the home, like a recent special on Weider home workout gyms, which were priced at just $49. These can sell out quickly, though, sometimes within one day; if you see or hear an advertisement for a great bargain like this at TM, you may want to head right on over.

Store hours are Monday, Tuesday, Wednesday, and Friday from 10 a.m. to 7 p.m.; Thursday from 10 a.m. to 8 p.m.; Saturday from 10 a.m. to 6 p.m.; and Sunday from noon to 6 p.m.

Wallpaper Atlanta/Dwoskins

- 3512 Satellite Boulevard, Duluth; (770) 623-1937

Wallpaper Atlanta? These guys probably could! Volume purchasing allows this former chain (now an independent business) to offer some great discounts on plain and fancy designs. Discontinued closeouts and overstock items make for even better bargains.

This store claims to represent every major wallpaper manufacturer in the country. All in-stock wallpaper is 45 to 65 percent off retail list prices and special-ordered paper is discounted up to 50 percent.

In addition to wallpaper, this store represents all major custom blind manufacturers, and all of that stuff is discounted up to 82 percent off the retail list price.

Store hours are Monday to Friday 10:30 a.m. to 6 p.m., and Saturday 11 a.m. to 5 p.m.

Wallpaper Plus

- 4145 Roswell Road N.E., Atlanta; (404) 252-1329

This shop's run by an interior designer who knows his stuff, and he knows how to price it well enough to rival any of the city's mega-chain wallpaper stores.

Designer wallpaper orders from the store's books are always discounted. Patterns by Strobeim & Roman, and Schumacher, are 30 percent off list price; Waverly is 35 percent off. Any special order from other sources will automatically be slashed 35 percent off retail.

Prepackaged wallpaper and border paper is priced low everyday, too. A double roll pack of a Waverly floral print may go for just $11.99 (that's down from $25.99 retail), and 56 square feet of Linden Street Gallery wallpaper is priced $10 off retail, at $18.99. Bright striped paper by Village is also $10 off, selling for $11 per roll. A willow print by Eisenhart, $25.99 elsewhere, is $10 for two rolls, and water-resistant prints by Rosedale, normally selling for $15.99 or more, are just $4.99 a pack. The popular Waverly American Classics line, regularly selling at a hefty $23.99 for a double roll, is just $11 here. Add five yards rolls of border prints for $9.99 each.

Wallpaper Plus! also pledges to match any advertised prices listed by mail-order companies, too. Unfortunately, however, they were unable to locate the "Infinite Elvis" pattern that The Cheapster had heard about.

Store hours are Monday to Friday 10 a.m. to 5 p.m. and Saturday 10 a.m. to 4 p.m.

Not satisfied yet? Then you may also want to check out:

The Hill Street Warehouse Sample Store

- 1345 Collier Road N.W., Atlanta; (404) 352-5001

Outrageous Bargains

- 1355 Roswell Road, Marietta; (770) 578-6944
- 5952 Peachtree Industrial Boulevard, Duluth: (770) 497-9577

JEWELRY AND CRAFTS

Shop for gold and gems very carefully! Diamonds vary greatly in quality, especially clarity and color; there is a very intricate set of official ratings, far more detailed than the A, B, and C grades some stores use. Be sure to have the jeweler explain any diamond's rating to you before you decide to buy, and don't hesitate to seek a second opinion. There are similar ratings for other gemstones, too.

If you're buying something very expensive—even if it seems to be a fabulous deal—the Cheapster recommends you protect yourself by hiring an independent appraiser to check the quality and price.

Buckhead Jewelry

- 935-B Chattahoochee Avenue N.W., Atlanta; (404) 352-9001

In spite of the name, this store is not in Buckhead but rather the Atlanta Outlet district. It's an interesting shop. Here, you can find 14- and 18-carat gold, platinum, and even diamond jewelry and watches at about 50 to 70 percent below retail values.

Now, these can be very tricky items when it comes to such price comparisons, but hear Mr. C out. Jack, the owner, is a goldsmith by

SHOPPING: JEWELRY AND CRAFTS

trade; he makes his own designs right in the shop, which helps keep the overhead costs low. And he's a real master of the art, as one look at his creations will tell you. His particular expertise is in gold rings—wide bands with ornate designs and inlays, for men or women. Have something in mind? He'll design it for you. Seen something you like in a magazine or catalog? Bring it in to him—and in a week's time, Jack should be able to produce a replica that is nearly indistinguishable from the picture, with the same materials (even diamonds, thanks to a family contact in the New York gem trade) for hundreds of dollars less than it might have cost elsewhere. A few years ago, Jack showed Mr. C one such ring, an intricate pattern set with tiny diamonds, first in a pricey catalog where it was listed for $3,125. Then he brought out his version, which might just as well have been the real McCoy; His price was $750.

The store also sells basic gold chains and silver rings, from $15 up into the thousands; plus bracelets, necklaces, and earrings; and Pulsar watches at discount. And they offer expert repairs, often while you wait.

This gem of a store is open Friday and Saturday from 11 a.m. to 6 p.m.

Cumberland Diamond Exchange

- Cumberland Crossing Shopping Center, 2800 Cumberland Boulevard S.E., Smyrna; ✆ (770) 434-4367

The Cumberland Diamond Exchange has been busily importing diamonds for over 12 years. They say they can offer low prices for two reasons: no middlemen and volume purchasing.

MR. CHEAP'S PICKS

Jewelry

Buckhead Jewelry—Here, you can find 14- and 18-carat gold, platinum, watches, and even diamond jewelry at about 50 to 70 percent below retail values.

Great Western Emporium—More than just a lovely jewelry and gift shop, this cool little store features a reasonably priced assortment of Western and Southwestern home décor, jewelry, sand paintings, pottery, and Southwestern-style furniture.

Solomon Brothers Diamonds—It's hard to go wrong here. Solomon Brothers offers one of Atlanta's largest selections of diamonds and jewelry at affordable prices.

Worthmore Discount Jewelers—Purveyors of rings, watches, bracelets, earrings, silver, gold, platinum, loose stones, custom pieces, and more, these friendly folks carry about 40 percent liquidation items, and get great wholesale prices on the rest, resulting in everyday low prices.

Tennis bracelets start at $399 for a one-carat total weight bracelet, up to $1,599 for a four-carat total weight style. Diamond earrings start as low as $119 for 1/5-carat stones, $179 for 1/3-carat stones, and $799 for one-carat diamonds. And engagement rings start at a modest $199 for a 1/4-carat style, $249 for a 1/3-carat, $349 for a 1/2-carat, and $599 for a 3/4-carat stone.

Even more dramatic savings can be found on their rings of one carat or more. A 1 1/4-carat ring is $1,299;

a 1½-carat is $1,899; a two-carat is $2,299, and a hefty three-carat ring is $2,999. Heavy as those prices sound, they could well be much higher at many other stores.

CDE offers delayed payments and 90-day financing.

The store is open Mondays, Wednesdays, and Fridays from 10 a.m. to 6 p.m.; Tuesdays and Thursdays from 10 a.m. to 8 p.m.; and Saturdays from 10 a.m. to 5 p.m.

It's About Time

- 1149 Cumberland Mall S.E., Atlanta; (770) 435-8463
- 3393 Peachtree Road N.E., Atlanta; (404) 233-0357
- 4400 Ashford Dunwoody Road N.E., Atlanta; (770) 399-6958
- 4800 Briarcliff Road N.E., Atlanta; (770) 493-8404
- 2420 Southlake Mall, Morrow; (770) 968-1191
- 3250 Peachtree Corners Circle, Norcross; (770) 441-9088
- 2100 Pleasant Hill Road, Duluth; (770) 476-8368
- 400 Ernest W. Barrett Parkway, Kennesaw; (770) 423-1441
- 1156 N. Point Circle, Alpharetta; (770) 442-9854

It's about time that someone started selling watches at half-decent prices, and doggone it, this store did it. Seiko, Citizen, and Bulova are the major brands stocked here. You'll also find stylish clocks for the home and office, as well as accessories such as cigarette lighters.

A Rolex-style watch made by Timex is just $64.95. Mr. Cheap spotted a Rolex-style Seiko watch for $120, and with an additional 25 percent off special, the watch sold for $90. Men's and ladies' Pulsar watches sell between $70 and $150 and come with three-year warranties. Seiko and Bulova also have a three-year warranty; Citizen promises five years. Mr. C, always on the go himself, liked the travel clocks that were priced $12.95 and up. Most normal-sized kitchen and living room clocks range between $24 and $100. Yes, if you've got the time, this store has, er . . . got the time.

Store hours are Monday through Saturday from 10 a.m. to 9 p.m., and Sunday from noon to 6 p.m.

Friedman's Jewelers

- 1165 Cumberland Mall S.E., Atlanta; (770) 438-7816
- 2801 Candler Road, Decatur; (404) 241-2909
- 2050 Lawrenceville Highway, Decatur; (404) 248-0324
- 1128 Southlake Mall, Morrow; (770) 960-8690
- 553 Shannon Mall, Union City; (770) 969-0909
- 8003 Tara Boulevard, Jonesboro; (770) 210-3799
- 105 Pavilion Parkway, Fayetteville; (770) 460-4862
- 2100 Pleasant Hill Road, Duluth; (770) 476-7455
- 400 Ernest W Barrett Parkway, N.W., Kennesaw; (770) 428-1581
- 2016 N Point Circle, Alpharetta; (770) 667-8770
- 1105 Woodstock Road, Roswell; (770) 552-4819
- 2400 Arbor Place Mall, Douglasville; (770) 920-8420

SHOPPING: JEWELRY AND CRAFTS

- 4215 Jimmy Lee Smith Parkway, Hiram; ☎ (770) 222-2898

- 2135 E. Main Street, Snellville; ☎ (770) 979-5200

- 10029 Highway 92, Woodstock; ☎ (770) 592-7441

- 455 Grayson Highway, Lawrenceville; ☎ (770) 338-9105

Not to be confused with the equally bargain-laden Friedman's Shoe stores (see the listing under *Shoes and Sneakers*), this chain is equally focused on value and exceptional customer service.

The deals at Friedman's are plentiful: Here you can get 50 percent off the ticket price for most gold pieces, 40 percent off colored gemstones, 40 percent off diamonds, and 30 percent off bridal and anniversary rings, which start at $99 and up. Mr. C found a great looking ½ carat solitaire engagement ring for $499. Most of the gold jewelry in the store is of 10- or 14-carat quality. A ruby ring, set in 14-carat gold, was seen for $119 (the retail value was estimated at $149), and an 18" flat chain of 14-carat gold was $224 (valued at $320). A braided rope chain of 14-carat gold is $595 (list price, $850). And gold-plated hoop earrings we priced as low as $15.

Bulova, Citizen, and Seiko watches, as well as diamond tennis bracelets, are available at similar discounts. The Cheapster spotted total weight double rope tennis bracelet for $799 (retail $999), and a similar two-carat bracelet worth $1,750 reduced to only $975.

A 1/2-carat total weight triple-row ladies wedding band, intended for a thirtieth anniversary, was recently selling for $100 off the retail price, at just $399. A marquis-cut ¼-carat solitaire ring is only $299 (about $75 off retail).

Store hours are Monday through Saturday from 10 a.m. to 9 p.m., and Sunday from 1 p.m. to 6 p.m.

Gold and Diamond Gallery

- 3835 N. Druid Hills Road, Decatur; ☎ (404) 636-5690

This family-owned shop has been around for more than 30 years, and there's a reason for that! Here you'll find great prices on more than just the baubles in its name. And, if a particular item is just a bit over your budget, you may find these folks willing to make a deal with you.

The savings here are the result of direct importing, cutting out middleman markups. Thus, a truly gigantic diamond ring, with a total weight of five carats—which would retail for $9,650—costs $3,299 here. Similar savings can be found on a three-carat ring, which retails for over $5,000 but sells for a lighter $2,000, and a ½-carat diamond ring for $1,300, Don't worry if these prices are still out of your range: Ruby rings start at $69 (with most designs running between $100 and $200), emerald rings are priced from $139 to $1,200, with amethysts starting at $79.

Looking for something more unusual? Show your Braves spirit with a tomahawk charm for $39, in 14 carat gold; or a pair of 10-carat tomahawk earrings for $24. You can also find a pair of emerald-and-gold earrings for just $79, or classic cameo pins for $119.

Items for guys: Gold tie tacks, priced from $30 and up, onyx and gold rings from $99 and up, and a hefty Claddagh ring in 14-carat gold for $229.

Store hours are Monday through Saturday from 10 a.m. to 6 p.m.

Great Western Emporium

- 6875-F Douglas Boulevard, Douglasville;
  ✆ (770) 489-9494

More than just a lovely jewelry and gift shop, this beautiful little store, formerly known as the Oglewanagi Gallery, features a mixed assortment of Western and Southwestern home decor, jewelry, sand paintings, pottery, and Southwestern-style furniture, including Pendleton Blankets.

Here you'll gaze upon beautiful jewelry in sterling silver and turquoise, made by members of tribes like the Navajo, Hopi, and Zuni. Some of these items are more expensive than others, but all are of great value given the incredible skill and handcraft that go into making them. You may want to stop in to check out their cases of rings and earrings, which start as low as $6 and run up to $150, or perhaps their bracelets, priced at $10 to 350. Great Western also features wonderfully creative crafts, ceramic pottery, wall hangings, and furniture. Coffee tables are priced from $150 to $350, while lamps go from $28 to more than $200.

Located in the strip mall next to Best Buy and I-20, and near Arbor Place Mall, store hours here are Monday through Thursday from 10 a.m. to 6 p.m.; Friday and Saturday from 10 a.m. to 9 p.m.; and Sunday from noon to 6 p.m.

Kaminski Jewelry

- 2116 Post Oak Tritt Road, Marietta; ✆ (770) 971-4653
- 🖳 www.kaminskijewelry.com

Starfleet Command to Captain Kirk: Kaminski Jewelry claims to have 40,000 pieces of jewelry and "the lowest prices in the universe," and they operate from a renovated single-family home in Marietta. Proceed at warp speed to acquire and return artifacts!

In fact, founder and owner, Carol Kaminski, started the business with a card table set up in her driveway in 1980, and it steadily grew. Now she and her staff offer watches, earrings, rings, bracelets, charms, and a variety of gift items made from gemstones, sterling silver, gold, and platinum.

It's hard to believe until you come here, but they really do have around 40,000 pieces of jewelry here, and at great deals.

During a recent "close pass" of this gleaming world, Captain Cheap observed 14-carat, solid-gold post earrings for $10 and up, diamond earrings for $80 and up, and 14-carat gold and diamond tennis bracelets starting at around $399. A 14-carat gold pearl pendant was on sale for $200, and 1/3 carat solitaire diamond engagement rings start at $399.

Take special note of this: If you buy something here and hang on to your sales receipt, you can upgrade whenever you want and get full credit for the original purchase price, whether it's next week, next month, next year, or next millennium! (And what's a millennium when you're traveling at Warp 8?)

Kaminski's is open Monday through Friday from 10 a.m. to 7 p.m., and Saturday from 10 a.m. to 7 p.m.

Midtown Designer's Warehouse

- 553 Amsterdam Avenue N.E., Atlanta; ✆ (404) 873-2581

The specialty here is dressy, high-fashion women's clothing, including leather garments, at wholesale prices or nearly so. On the leather clothing in particular, this store can save you $200 or more over department or specialty store prices.

In addition, MDW offers a quality selection of costume jewelry

SHOPPING: JEWELRY AND CRAFTS

to go with these fancy outfits, much of which was selling at around $25. Mr. C was shown a three-piece, gold-plated necklace and earring set—solidly made, not the flimsy junk often sold as an afterthought with clothing—selling for $23, down from its retail price of $60. Some of the jewelry is made with semiprecious stones, such as a handsome necklace of green malachite chips. Long enough to be worn at full or doubled-over length, it was reduced from $40 to $12.99.

Located in the Midtown Outlets area, MDW is open Thursdays through Saturdays from 10 a.m. to 7 p.m., and Sundays from 1 to 6 p.m.

Solomon Brothers Diamonds

- Tower Place Buckhead, 3340 Peachtree Road NE, Suite 1700, Atlanta; (404) 266-0266

- www.solomonbrothers.com

Solomon Brothers touts itself as offering Atlanta's largest selection of diamonds at the most affordable prices. They certainly have a lot to see, and since they are diamond cutters, Solomon lets you buy direct and save big. They carry many of the major jewelry brands, including Scott Kay, Nova, Charles Krypell, Jeff Cooper, and Tacori.

Better-quality emerald cut diamond rings start around $495 for a half-carat stone. A 1½-carat emerald-cut ring is $3,850. Princess-cut diamond rings (round-shaped) sell at $495 for a half-carat, while one-carat rings are priced at $1,950 and up. Two-carat rings can be had for $5,400 and up.

There are lots of tennis bracelets, in a variety of settings. A one-carat total weight bracelet is just $249, a three-carat total weight goes for $900, a seven carat set in 14-carot gold commands $2,499 while a whopping ten-carat total weight bracelet is yours for a mere $6,000. But. . . it could cost a lot more!

Pearls are also available here in 6mm to 8mm sizes, almost half off their suggested retail prices.

Solomon Brothers also carries quality watches from such manufacturers as Ebel, Hamilton, Longine, Concorde, and others.

The store is open Mondays and Wednesday from 10 a.m. to 6 p.m.; Tuesdays and Thursdays from 10 a.m. to 8 p.m.; and Friday and Saturday from 10 a.m. to 5 p.m. Parking is free.

Tuesday Morning

- 3145 Piedmont Road N.E., Atlanta; (404) 233-6526

- 4502 Chamblee Dunwoody Road, Dunwoody; (770) 457-3565

- 901 Montreal Road, Tucker,: (770) 934-3164

- 2790 Cumberland Boulevard S.E., Smyrna; (770) 435-6678

- 1115 Mount Zion Road, Morrow; (770) 961-0707

- 736 Johnson Ferry Road, Marietta; (770) 971-0511

- 6325 Spalding Drive, Norcross; (770) 447-4692

- 4051 Highway 78, Lilburn; (770) 978-3573

- 700 Sandy Plains Road, Marietta; (770) 428-1536

- 1231 Alpharetta Street, Roswell; (770) 640-8146

- 3500 Satellite Boulevard, Duluth; (770) 476-0522

- 3600 Dallas Highway N.W., Marietta; (678) 355-5505

- www.tuesdaymorning.com

This place sells a lot of stuff—including jewelry—every day, not just Tuesday, and we know why.

One sale, for example, offered stylishly sculpted rings in 10-carat gold, set with pearls or semi-precious stones. The retail values of these rings ranged from about $200 to $500, but here they were all selling for prices under $100.

Another style, the narrow "stack" ring, meant to be worn in groups, was on sale for $29.99 each. There were several versions to choose from, decorated with rows of tiny emeralds, sapphires, gannets, amethyst, and more; they had originally retailed for as much as $89 each.

Of course, Tuesday Morning sells closeouts on discontinued styles, though the selection can be limited, with not all sizes be available in all designs. Should you decide to gamble on something here as a gift, and it does not fit, TM does have a 30-day return policy; just remember to keep your receipt!

Store hours are Monday, Tuesday, Wednesday, and Friday from 10 a.m. to 7 p.m.; Thursday from 10 a.m. to 8 p.m.; Saturday from 10 a.m. to 6 p.m.; and Sunday from noon to 6 p.m.

Walter R. Thomas Wholesale Jewelers

- 400 Barrett Parkway, Kennesaw; (770) 426-5651

- 6700 Douglas Boulevard, Douglasville; (678) 838-1352

Walter Thomas is another direct importer, bringing in much of its jewelry from Antwerp. Eliminating the middleman allows them to offer you super buys on diamonds and other precious stones.

A tennis bracelet, decorated with three carats' worth of diamonds, sells for $660 during a sale. A 14-carat gold ring with sapphire, carrying a retail price of $600, costs $300 here, and a seven-carat emerald studded with over four carats' worth of diamonds is $5,600, about half its retail price tag of $10,500. And a large opal, set in 14-carat gold with two diamond baguettes, was $210, but worth $900.

Loose diamonds are also dramatically reduced, like a .60-carat brilliant round stone, internally flawless for $5,300 (again, half of retail value). A diamond valued at $21,300 (it's a big 1.11 carat rated E VVS2) was reduced to $10,650 here. (If you don't know what the ratings mean, don't buy the gem without hiring your own independent appraiser, please!)

Layaway and financing are available.

Store hours are 10 a.m. to 9 p.m. on Monday to Saturday, 12:30 p.m. to 6 p.m. on Sunday.

Worthmore Discount Jewelers

- 500 Amsterdam Avenue, Atlanta; (404) 892-8294

- www.worthmorejewelers.com

This is a gem of a store, with a friendly, knowable staff and great values. Purveyors of fine jewelry, Swiss watches, sterling silver, platinum, and handmade jewelry, as well as loose stones, they also offer complete jewelry and watch repair, and they will fill special orders.

When Worthmore opened in the early 1990s, about 80 percent of what they sold was liquidation stock. Now a lot of customers want designer pieces, so their liquidation merchandise is down to about 40 percent. For the rest of their jewelry, they find great deals by paying cash to wholesalers and then pass those savings on to the customers. Their low overhead helps, too.

Here earrings start at $18 for 14-carat gold hoops and go up from there, while Sterling silver rings start at $8. Tag Heuer watches that retail for $1,295 are on sale here for $900. One-carat diamond stud earrings that command $2,200 most places are available for $1,250 here. Worthmore also features a wedding band line that ranges from $30 up to $2,500. You can pick up a one-carat engagement ring, worth $5,500 elsewhere, for only $3,500 here. Handmade jewelry ranges from $15 to $1,800.

Overall, this is a great place, with a relaxed atmosphere, no high pressure, and everyday discounts. The staff is trained by the Gemological Institute of America, and they'll sit down with every customer, examine each stone through a microscope, and tell you just about anything you'd like to know to help inform your purchase.

Store hours are Thursday from 11 a.m. to 5 p.m., Friday and Saturday from 10 a.m. to 6 p.m., and Sunday from noon to 5:30 p.m., with extended hours during holiday seasons.

Worth the Weight

- 231 Peachtree Street N.E., Atlanta; (404) 681-4653

This tiny counter-top shop in the Peachtree Center Mall is worth a trip downtown for bargains on 14-carat gold rope chain necklaces, bracelets, and the like.

There are a variety of thicknesses and cuts available: diamond cuts from smooth to brilliant, braided ropes, and more. Prices start at $11.95 per gram, depending on thickness. A man's thick rope-style gold necklace, weighing about 21 grams, costs $349 here. A comparable-length necklace would cost over $600 in fancy department stores.

Sterling silver chains start at $9.95 a gram, although there's not as large variety of cuts as compared to the gold chains. Other goodies seen here include gold nugget rings, with a retail value of $40, selling for $19.95.

Worth the Weight is open Monday through Saturday from 9 a.m. to 6 p.m.

LIQUOR AND BEVERAGES

Whether your taste runs from Thunderbird to Tanqueray, from Cuervo to Chivas Regal, it usually doesn't take long to find a halfway decent price on your favorite beverage. Heck, let's face it folks, there are literally hundreds of liquor and beverage stores around Atlanta, and most of them are very competitive in the prices they can offer. Most have regular specials on selected wines and liquors, and nearly all them will offer customers a 10 percent discount on purchases of wine by the case. Where these stores differ most is in the size of their selection, and the personal knowledge their managers bring to their offerings (especially when it comes to wine). Here Mr. C showcases a few of the biggest, best, and most unique of the many shopping options available to the savvy but cheap connoisseur.

The prices listed here are just examples; they are likely to change based on foreign currency exchange rates, taxes and tariffs, and sales.

All-American Package Store

- 1238-A Pryor Road S.W., Atlanta; ✆ (404) 627-6752
- 4465-A Roswell Road, Atlanta; ✆ (404) 255-6826

High prices for liquor? Why, that would be positively un-American! This chain gives you many ways to save. They offer a 5 percent discount on half-cases of wine, and 10 percent reductions when you buy a whole case. You could find French Merlot wines for about $5.99 a bottle, and Robert Mondavi Sauvignon Blanc California wine was about $8.99 for 1.5 liters. A large bottle of Moet & Chandon champagne was $26.99. And good ol' Sutter Home Chardonnay or Cabernet is $9.99 for a 1.5 liter size.

Liquor bargains may include Taylor Golden Sherry for $4.99 a bottle, Dekuyper Amaretto at $9.89 for a 750ml bottle, Peachtree schnapps by the same maker for $8.99 a bottle, and Bacardi Light rum at $11.99 for a 750ml bottle. Again, hard liquor in quantities of three or more may entitle you to a further price break; just ask the sales staff.

Mr. C spotted many good deals on beer, like a 12-pack of Rolling Rock for $7.99, a suitcase of Bud Light for $13.99, and a six-pack of Miller Genuine Draft bottles for $4.59. The specials are ever-changing, but you're always sure to find something good on sale.

Store hours are 8 a.m. to 11:40 p.m. Monday through Saturday.

Cheers Beer & Wine

- Loehmann's Executive Plaza, 2490 Briarcliff Road N.E., Atlanta; ✆ (404) 321-7777

Cheers is sure to brighten you up with its great prices. The selection isn't as extensive as some of the other liquor stores Mr. C visited, but the values found here are sure worth a special trip. Speaking of Cheers, these are prices even ol'Normie could love.

A big 1.75 liter bottle of Smirnoff vodka recently was seen for $19, while you can go wild with a liter of Wild Turkey Bourbon at $28.

Buy a case of wine and you save 10 percent. If you pay in cash, the manager will even give you the 10 percent discount on a half case!

Beer is similarly discounted, with 12-packs ranging from $5.99 (for a brand like Bulldog) to $13.99 (for Heineken). Six-packs of Sam Adams were priced at $6.99, and a 12-pack of Fosters Lager was spotted for $8.99.

Cheers is open Monday through Wednesday from 10 a.m. to 11

MR. CHEAP'S PICKS

Liquor

All-American Package Store—This chain gives you many ways to save, with a great wine selection and ever-changing specials.

Green's Beverage Store—Green's features an excellent selection and great prices for all beverages, but their wine deals are really something special. Recently, they had 25 quality wines from France and Italy priced at less than $10

Habersham Vineyards and Winery—Here you can save money by buying quality, Georgia-produced Cabernet, Merlot, Chardonnay, and other varieties direct from the company, and this is the only place in the city where you can buy bottled alcohol on Sunday!

p.m., and Thursday through Saturday from 10 a.m. to 11:45 p.m.

Green's Beverage Stores

- 739 Ponce de Leon Avenue N.E., Atlanta; ✆ (404) 872-1109

- 2612 Buford Highway N.E., Atlanta; ✆ (404) 321-6232

- 🖰 www.greensbeverages.com

A local leader in liquor sales. Green's can save you lots of green on all kinds of beverages. They must be doing something right, since they seem to be constantly packed; on a recent weeknight, people were pulling up to the Ponce store in everything from BMWs to bicycles. Inside, the store was bustling with shoppers mopping up bargains like twelve-pack of Heineken beer for $13, and six-packs of Pabst Blue Ribbon 16-ounce bottles for $3.39, 750ml bottles of Cuervo tequila for $17, and more.

Green's has a large wine section as well, with quite a variety of well-known names and their own "discoveries." You can pick up a newsletter, 'Green's Grapevine,' devoted to their latest acquisitions. Money-savers recently included lesser-known domestics from Washington State, a variety of good Cabernets and Merlots for $7.99 a bottle, as well as some great vintages from France and Italy (25 wines in all) for under $10 a bottle!

The wine buyer here really knows his stuff and will be happy to advise you on some great values. Inquire in the store about their excellent discounts on beer and wine by the case.

Store hours Monday through Wednesday from 8 a.m. to 9:30 p.m., and Thursday through Saturday from 8 a.m. to 11:30 p.m.

Habersham Vineyards and Winery

- Underground Atlanta, 122 Lower Alabama Street, Atlanta; ✆ (404) 522-9463

Habersham specializes in wines produced at its own vineyards in nearby Habersham County, Georgia. At their store, you can save money by buying direct from the company; so you can afford these wines (many with special labeling for gift-giving purposes) more easily.

Perhaps most important, this is the only place in the city where you can buy bottled alcohol on Sunday!

And the wines here, all from Georgia-grown grapes, are pretty good. Take your pick from Chardonnay, Cabernet, Merlot, Rose, Reisling, Georgia Muscadine (a wild grape), and Habersham's famous peach wine. Everything is priced at a very reasonable $9 to $15 a bottle.

If you're interested in how they create these delightful beverages, you can visit Habersham's Vineyards in Helen, Georgia, about 80 miles north of Atlanta. There you can view the whole operation, as well as check out the working grist mill, ride white water or on horses, or try fly-fishing. Make a weekend of it! This tiny village is not far from Commerce, where you'll probably want to stop for more bargain hunting!

Store hours are Monday through Saturday from 10 a.m. to 9 p.m., and Sunday from noon until 7 p.m.

Harry's Farmers Market/ Whole Foods Market

- 1180 Upper Hembree Road, Alpharetta; ✆ (770)-664-6300

- 2025 Satellite Point Street N.W., Duluth; ✆ (770)-416-6900

- 70 Powers Ferry Road N.E., Marietta; (770) 578-4400
- www.hfm.com or www.wholefoods.com

See the listing under *Food Stores—General Markets*.

International Farmer's Market

- 5193 Peachtree Industrial Boulevard, Chamblee; (770) 455-1777
- 5380 Jonesboro Road, Lake City; (404) 361-7522

See the listing under *Food Stores—General Markets*.

Jax Beer & Wine

- 5901 Roswell Road N.E., Sandy Springs; (404) 252-1443
- 928 Market Place Boulevard, Cumming; (770) 888-8036

Here are the facts, Jax: This store will certainly surprise you with its excellent wine selection, and its liquor and beer prices are also hard to beat, with specials available all of the time.

Among the scores of different wines here, recent deals included Corvo red wine from Sicily, regularly $9.99, selling for $6.99, and Valdivieso cabernet sauvignon from Chile, same deal. Clos du Bois cabernet sauvignons or the Australian Black Opal brand were $8.99 each.

Carlo Rossi California Burgundy was only $9.48 for the jumbo four-liter bottle. And for real bargain prices, consider wines from less likely parts of the world. Avia Chardonnay, imported from Slovenia, is only $2.99 a bottle.

Sake lovers will adore the $7.99 price tag on Gekkeikan; and you'll be toasting up a storm when you bring home Bollinger Special Cuvee Brut champagne for just $25.99, or Korbel Brut for $9.99.

Buying hard liquor here won't be hard on your budget, either. Grand Marnier is $28.99 for a 750ml bottle, Cointreau is $27.99, and Emmets Irish Cream Liqueur is $9.99 for that same size. Absolutely, you can pick up a bottle of Absolut vodka for $27.98 in the big 1.75 liter bottle. And, if you're having a big bash, don't forget Jose Cuervo margarita mix, only $4.99.

Jax has a mind-boggling beer selection, from six-packs of Bud Lite for $4.49 to $11.98 for a twelve-pack of Heineken in cans. Other good prices were found on brands like Telluride beer from Colorado, Lone Star from Texas, and many others.

Jax is open at 8:30 a.m. every day except Sunday, when they're closed. The store closes at 10 p.m. on Monday and Tuesday, at 11 p.m. on Wednesday and Thursday, and at 11:45 p.m. on Saturday.

Peachtree Road Liquor Store

- 1895 Peachtree Road (at Collier Road), Atlanta; (404) 355-4990

This South Buckhead package store, located near Harry's In A Hurry, offers a wide selection of wine and liquor at good value prices.

A good selection of California Chardonnays, Cabernets, and Merlots start at $9.99, and, for those of you living rough, a three-liter jug of Gallo Chablis Blanc wine, was recently seen for just $7.99.

Seagram's wine coolers in several flavors are just $3.99 for a 4-pack. On a more celebratory note, a 750ml bottle of Korbel Brut Champagne was a decent $9.99.

Mr. C also found plenty of other liquor on the cheap, like a liter of

Bombay Dry Sapphire gin for $19.99; Jack Daniel's in the 375 ml size for $11.99 and the same size of Cuervo Gold tequila for $18.99.

Beer bargains included a twelve pack of Molson Golden or Molson Light for $9.99, and a twelve-pack suitcase of Rolling Rock in bottles for $8.99.

Peachtree Road is open from 8 a.m. to 11:30 p.m. every day except Sunday.

Toco Hills Giant Package Store

- 2941 N. Druid Hills Road NE, Atlanta; ✆ (404) 320-1903

- 223 Moreland Avenue S.E., Atlanta; ✆ (404) 688-2744

- 3196 Bankhead Highway N.W., Atlanta; ✆ (404) 799-8685

Giant store, giant savings, what more could you ask for? Head for the hills—Toco Hills, that is—for super buys on beer, wine, and liquor. The beer selection from around the world is impressive, and volume discounts are available; just ask.

Mr. C saw a six-pack of Newcastle Brown Ale in bottles for just $6.99, George Killian's Red for just $4.69 a six-pack, and a 34-ounce "mini-keg" of Kronenbourg for just $2.99. Steinlager from New Zealand is only $2.49 for 25 ounces. Here's to the Kiwis!

For wine drinkers, Beringer white zinfandel is $6.99 a bottle, and a 1991 Pouilly-Fuisse white burgundy is just $9.99. Geikkeikan sake from Japan is $7.99 for a 750ml bottle.

Good heavens! Heaven Hill Kentucky bourbon is $8.49 for a liter, Crown Royal Canadian Whiskey is $22.99 for a 750ml bottle, and Southern Comfort 80 proof is $11.99 for the same size. Liqueurs like Bailey's Irish Cream and Kahlua are reasonably priced, too.

For the big party, basics like Daily's margarita mix ($5.99), and two-liter bottles of Canada Dry Ginger Ale ($1.29 each) will also save you big bucks.

Store hours are 10 a.m. to 11:45 p.m. Monday through Thursday, and 10 a.m. to 11:45 p.m. on Friday and Saturday.

Tower Beer & Wine Stores

- 223 Moreland Avenue S.E., Atlanta; ✆ (404) 688-2744

- 3196 Bankhead Highway N.W., Atlanta; ✆ (404) 799-8685

You won't find any towering prices here, that's for sure. These stores sell a stupendous variety of wines, from California to France, Germany, and Australia, along with an incredible selection of beers and hard liquors—all at warehouse prices but without the warehouse feel.

In addition to its regular prices, Tower has a quantity discount policy on wines an extra 5 percent off if you buy six bottles, and 10 percent off if you buy twelve or more bottles. That means you can do very well on Riunite Blush Bianco, priced at $4.79 for 750ml; a bottle of Black Silk from Australia for $6.99; or a bottle of Veuve du Venay Blanc de Blancs French sparkling wine, just $5.49. The four-liter jug of Carlo Rossi California Chablis is $9.98 and not subject to this volume-purchasing offer, but is a bargain enough in itself.

Beer drinkers will be impressed with the $8.69 price on a twelve-pack suitcase of Bud Lite or Bud Dry in bottles. Even fancier specialty brands are reasonably priced, like Sam Adams Double Bock at $6.29 for a six-pack.

For mixed drinks, how about a 375ml bottle of Chambord for

$19.99? A one-liter bottle of Appleton Jamaican rum is just $16.49, so hey mon, why not stock up on some for your next party?

Other deals scoped out by El Cheapster include a 1.75 liter bottle of Finlandia vodka for $15.29, and the same size bottle of Jack Daniel's for $18.29.

Tower will welcome you from 8 a.m. to 11 p.m. Monday through Thursday, and 8 a.m. to 11:45 p.m. on Friday and Saturday.

Your DeKalb Farmer's Market

- 3000 East Ponce de Leon Avenue, Decatur; (404)-377-6400

- www.dekalbfarmersmarket.com

This huge farmer's market carries extensive (and Mr. C know big and sprawling when he sees it) wine and beer selections, including Newcastle Brown Ale in the big 18.6 ounce bottle for just $2.09, and China Five Star beer for $7 a six-pack. Champagnes, too: Freixenet's Cordon Negro, which goes for up to $10 in some liquor stores, was $6.79 here. Wines from as far away as Greece, Lebanon, Spain, Portugal, Argentina, and Chile are here for the choosing. Some of the recently spotted special deals included $8.99 bottles of Raymond Napa Valley Chardonnay and Cabernet Sauvignon (seen elsewhere for $14), $5.29 bottles of Caliterra Cabernet Sauvignon from Chile, and Weibel Black Muscat red dessert wine for $9.

The market's open seven days a week from 9 a.m. to 9 p.m. They're closed on Christmas and Thanksgiving.

See also the listing under *Food Stores—General Markets*.

LUGGAGE

Bentley's Luggage & Gifts

- Phipps Plaza, 3500 Peachtree Road N.E., Atlanta; (404) 841-6247

- Perimeter Mall, 4400 Ashford Dunwoody Road N.E., Atlanta; (770) 671-1071

- 517 Shannon Mall, Union City; (770) 969-0970

- 4475 Roswell Road, Marietta; (770) 321-2408

- 2100 Pleasant Hill Road, Duluth; (770) 497-8447

- 400 Ernest W Barrett Parkway N.W., Kennesaw; (770) 422-9406

- North Point Mall, 1000 N. Point Circle, Alpharetta; (770) 667-0678

- 3333 Buford Drive, Buford; (678) 482-6404

- www.bentleys.com

You sure don't have to drive a Bentley to afford luggage here, where you'll find good discounts on fine bands like Samsonite, Scully, Hartmann, Jansport, Kenneth Cole, Razor, and many others. Many of Bentley's items are on sale for 50 percent off the ticketed price.

A bit of an old-fashioned emporium, Bentley's is definitely male-oriented, and geared toward the corporate customer. A man's leather briefcase with combination lock, made by Mark Phillip, was recently seen discounted from $200 to $159. The Cheapster also spotted a Andiamo 19" Pullman, usually priced at $495, for only $220.

A Lewis N. Clark overnighter was marked down to $32 from its usual $65, while a Ricardo Beverly Hills 22" Expandable Wheelaboard Suiter was discounted from $300 to only $150. A Samsonite hybrid carry on suiter was tagged at $99, down from its usual $335.

On the soft side, you can pick up a Bill Blass 29" wheeled duffle, usually priced at $70, for a meager $19.99, and an El Portal extra-large duffle was only $37.50 (discounted from $75). You get the idea.

There are some items for the ladies, such as a feminine-styled briefcase with three big inner compartments and a top zipper. List priced at $225, it sells here for $140. You'll also find luggage suitable for the whole family here, like a Hartmann leather-trim suitcase marked down from $350 to $210, and a Hartmann garment bag, selling for $198 (retail price, $330).

As these places tend to do, Bentley's also stocks fine-maker pens by Parker, Cross, and the like; as well as other travel necessities such as clock radios, hair dryers, voltage converters, toiletries, organizers, backpacks, and travel guides, all at competitive prices.

Bentley's stores are generally open from 10 a.m. to 9 p.m. from Monday through Saturday, and noon to 6 p.m. on Sundays, though hours may vary slightly by location.

Leather & Luggage Depot

- 1151 Chattahoochee Avenue N.W., Atlanta;
  (404) 351-7410

Like Rick Nelson, Mr. C is a "Travelin' Man," though he likes to do his roaming as inexpensively as possible. That's why he likes Leather & Luggage Depot. This shop is filled with a wide variety of inexpensive luggage. The store does carry some big names, but mostly focuses on budget brands, which are good values, if not likely to become heirlooms. Hey, you gotta have a niche, y'know?

What they do have, they sell at about half the retail prices—the same prices, in fact as you'd get at the Apparel Mart, if you could shop in that wholesale-only center. You can get an entire five-piece ensemble of suitcases, overnighter, and garment bag for as little as $65. Most sets, though, are in the $100 to $185 range and are made of more durable materials, although some higher-end brands, such as Briggs and Rilley, are priced upwards of $300 or more. Speaking of which, have you seen those brightly colored, hard-plastic suitcases by Echolac? They're here, ergonomically designed to roll easily, even through Hartsfield, and reduced from a list price of $180 to just $99. Get 'em in eye-catching blue, yellow, and red.

You'll find some knapsacks and duffle bags here too, starting at a most-reasonable $14.90. And L&L has a good selection of leather and synthetic briefcases. These range in price—from $19.90 to $300, with most under $100.

The other part of the store's name refers to its limited, but funky, collection of bomber jackets.

Store hours are Monday through Saturday from 10 a.m. to 6 p.m., and Sunday from 12:30 p.m. to 5 p.m.

> **MR. CHEAP'S PICKS**
>
> *Luggage*
>
> **Bentley's Luggage & Gifts**—Even the Buckhead branch of this local chain offers special bargains on travel bags and briefcases.
>
> **Leather & Luggage Depot**—Here you'll find a good selection of luggage at about half the retail prices—the same prices, in fact as you'd get at the Apparel Mart, if you could shop in that wholesale-only center.

Mori Luggage & Gifts

- 4400 Ashford Dunwoody Road N.E., Atlanta;
  ✆ (770) 394-3235
- 2385 Peachtree Road N.E., Atlanta; ✆ (404) 231-0300
- 3393 Peachtree Road N.E., Atlanta; ✆ (404) 231-2146
- 1201 Cumberland Mall S.E., Atlanta; ✆ (770) 436-6112
- 4800 Briarcliff Rd N.E., Atlanta; ✆ (770) 934-8221
- 31000 Southlake Mall, Morrow; ✆ (770) 961-7322
- 3492 Satellite Boulevard, Duluth; ✆ (770) 813-9910
- 1000 N Point Circle, Alpharetta; ✆ (770) 667-9177
- 3333 Buford Drive, Buford; ✆ (678) 482-7742
- ✎ www.moriluggage.com

Mori offers a wide selection of luggage and briefcases by Atlantic, Briggs & Rilley, Bosca, Harttmann, Kenneth Cole, London Fog, Samsonite, Scully, and many other major manufacturers. Like most other luggage stores, they also carry travel accessories, leather goods, pens, and gifts, with selected luggage items on sale throughout the year.

There are always bargains to be found here, with one special or another just about every day of the year. The day Mr. C stopped by recently, Mori was having a 25 percent-off sale of Hartmann luggage, and Swiss Army pieces were also on sale for 20 to 30 percent off retail. However, the best deals of all were on some Metro Dakota pieces, which were being discontinued by the company and were available for over half off!

Mori also carries a wide assortment of gifts starting at just $2 and ranging up to $1,000, with many items under $25. There aren't just travel accessories, either. In addition to the ubiquitous pens, they also offer games, jewelry boxes, picnic baskets, those Chicago collectible cows (okay, they've also been ubiquitous of late), music CDs, keychains, high-design flashlights, and numerous other items.

Store hours are 10 a.m. to 9 p.m. on Saturday, and noon to 6 p.m. on Sunday.

Terrell Mill Shoe & Luggage

- 1475 Terrell Mill Road S.E., Marietta; ✆ (770) 956-1168

This shop specializes in luggage and shoe repair but also has a small modest selection of new luggage for sale at prices ranging from $50 to $200. The store is open from Monday through Friday from 8 a.m. to 6:30 p.m., and Saturday from 9 a.m. to 5 p.m.

Tuesday Morning

- 3145 Piedmont Road N.E., Atlanta; (404) 233-6526
- 4502 Chamblee Dunwoody Road, Dunwoody; (770) 457-3565
- 901 Montreal Road, Tucker,: (770) 934-3164
- 2790 Cumberland Boulevard S.E., Smyrna; (770) 435-6678
- 1115 Mount Zion Road, Morrow; (770) 961-0707
- 736 Johnson Ferry Road, Marietta; (770) 971-0511
- 6325 Spalding Drive, Norcross; (770) 447-4692
- 4051 Highway 78, Lilburn; (770) 978-3573
- 700 Sandy Plains Road, Marietta; (770) 428-1536
- 1231 Alpharetta Street, Roswell; (770) 640-8146
- 3500 Satellite Boulevard, Duluth; (770) 476-0522
- 3600 Dallas Highway N.W., Marietta; (678) 355-5505
- www.tuesdaymorning.com

Tuesday Morning's bargains include a 50 to 80 percent "everyday" discount on upscale merchandise found in better department stores, and that includes luggage.

Among the well-priced travel gear Mr. C found on a recent visit were Samsonite duffel bags-available in an assortment of neutral colors—reduced from $90 to $40. A Samsonite soft-sider suitcase was reduced from $220 to $80, while a smaller, wheeled suitcase was marked down from $150 to $70.

Leisure Luggage brand carry-on tote bags, listed at $90 retail, were just $30 here; and a Pierre Cardin carry bag sells for $90—half its original retail price. Garment bags are also well stocked, with brands like Ascot and Samsonite, starting as low as $40. All sell for at least half of their retail prices.

Store hours are Monday, Tuesday, Wednesday, and Friday from 10 a.m. to 7 p.m., Thursday from 10 a.m. to 8 p.m., Saturday from 10 a.m. to 6 p.m., and Sunday from noon to 6 p.m.

See also the full description under *Carpeting and Rugs.*

MUSICAL INSTRUMENTS

Mr. Cheap loves the way that car dealers dress up their used car lots with a fancy sign that reads: "Previously Owned." He feels the same way about musical instruments. If you can find one in good shape, it should have many years of useful life in it. Often, a top-quality used instrument that can be repaired is a better investment than a cheaper, newer version. It will sound better and last longer. And many instruments actually *increase* in value as they age.

Cooper Music Superstore

- 1610 N.E. Expressway Access Road N.E., Atlanta; (404) 329-1663
- www.cooperpiano.com

In business since 1906, this is *the* place for pianos, and it's hard to miss—just look for the huge store with the big piano sticking up into the air. These guys sell everything from upright acoustic pianos to digital keyboards. Area churches often come here to purchase budget-priced organs, and Cooper Music has the largest collection in the area of vintage Hammond B3 organs.

Some of the Steinways here are of vintage or heirloom quality (yep, way out of Mr. C's budget), but new and restored pianos, from brands like Kawai, Mason & Hamlin, Yamaha, Baldwin, Knabe, Bechstein, Petrof, Chickering, Wurlitzer, Young Chang, and Pramberger (a high-end Asian piano), are on sale at reductions that will be music to your ears. New baby grands start at $5,988 (cheap, actually!), and you can get a used upright for as little as $588! The more expensive pianos here are discounted thousands of dollars—just check out the prices on their Web site.

If you've got an instrument to trade in, or if you're looking to buy, you can call them for a price quote.

Cooper Music also operates music and wellness centers, teaching seniors how to enjoy the health benefits of music making. If you're interested in reducing stress, give 'em a call for more information.

Store hours are Monday through Thursday from 10 a.m. to 8 p.m., Friday and Saturday from 10 a.m. to 6 p.m., and Sunday from 1 p.m. to 5 p.m.

Emile Baran Instruments, Inc.

- 117 Clairemont Avenue, Decatur; (404) 377-3419
- www.emilebaran.com

School children from more than fifty school systems in the area buy and trade in their instruments here; that means smaller sizes along with smaller prices. There are lots of half-size and three-quarter-size violins, with the appropriate bows; plus violas, basses, cellos, and lutes; and almost any other common instrument, too. As owner Emile Baran told Mr. C, they sell "just about anything a high school band or orchestra uses." The stock goes on to include piccolos, flutes, French horns, tubas, clarinets, drums, and trombones, plus tuning instruments.

Parents shop here when they don't want to buy their growing children a brand-new instrument, only to need a new one the next season. Since about 50 percent of this store's business is done in the month of September, you'll probably find good specials during the off months, when business is a bit slower.

Baran's sells about 750 string instruments a year. Suzuki violins are available in 1/10 to full size, Germans from 1/4 to full, and cellos from 1/4 and up.

On one of the Cheapster's trips, he learned that a child's used German violin or viola would go for $475 or so, and a high-quality Gibson acoustic guitar is just $269. Instruments are obtained from all over the country, and vary in quality and price; but they must all match the company's standards before being taken in. You can also rent instruments here, or have them repaired. The store staff includes former band and orchestra directors who know their stuff and really care about the kids.

Emile Baran's is open from 9:30 a.m. to 5:30 p.m. Monday through Friday, and from 10 a.m. to 5 p.m. Saturdays.

England Piano & Organ Warehouse Showrooms

- 1660 Northeast Expressway, Atlanta; (404) 633-7378
- 1873 Cobb Parkway South, Marietta; (770) 9841124
- 359 Pike Street, GA 120, Gwinnett; (770) 963-5159

These stores are making noise (pun intended) in the Atlanta area for offering some of the lowest prices on new pianos around, including those from Yamaha, Samick, PianoDisc, Kawai, Wurlitzer, Roland, Baldwin, and Young Chang. They also have a good inventory of organs, digital pianos, player pianos, and midi keyboards. Samick grand pianos start at $5,995, and Yamaha models are priced from $6,000 or so to $8,000. In recent years, sales have included grand pianos priced under $5,000, digitals under $700, and console pianos under $2,300.

England also offers used and display models; these seem to fly out of the store.

The stores are open seven days a week: Monday through Saturday from 10 a.m. to 6 p.m., and Sunday from 1 p.m. to 5 p.m.

Famous Bargain Music

- 5944 Roswell Road N.E., Atlanta; (404) 252-1427

- www.famousbargain.com

This is where Dunwoody's own Black Crowes used to shop—before they got rich and famous. This store carries mostly used instruments, as well as some new, and they have expanded quite a bit since Mr. Cheap's first visit. In addition to electric and acoustic guitars, banjos, amplifiers, and speakers they now stock almost every orchestral instrument. We're talking violins, cellos, mandolins, ukuleles, keyboards, percussion, woodwinds, and brass instruments. For those looking for vintage, they've got guitars, drums, and amps.

The professional staff gives honest information about what instruments and equipment would be best for you. Parents of budding rock guitar gods can feel welcome shopping here, even if they know little about these instruments themselves.

When you call or visit, be sure to ask about closeout and sale items. They also will do repairs on some instruments, so you need to ask them for the specifics.

Get a famous bargain for yourself anytime from 10 a.m. to 7 p.m. Monday through Friday, and from 10 a.m. to 6 p.m. on Saturday. They're closed on Sunday.

Galaxy Music Center

- 5236 Highway 78, Stone Mountain; (770) 879-8381; (800) 653-4327

- www.galaxymusicusa.com

Galaxy lays claim to being the largest used music equipment dealer in the Southeast, and Mr. C would be hard-pressed to debate the point. About half of their business is selling new instruments, and the other half is buying, selling, and trading old instruments. They specialize in finding really good-quality instruments and gear, and some are only slightly used and still the latest trends. A large volume of sales activity enables this place to sell new musical instruments at a 30 to 40 percent discount off the list price. On his last visit Mr. Cheap found a brand new Takamine acoustic guitar for $179, and a Ludwig drum set for $329.

Galaxy also carries bargain-priced band instruments, like flutes and clarinets, and the occasional French horn; plus string instruments from violins to mandolins to banjos. In fact, they always have 400 plus guitars in stock alone. There are keyboards and MIDI, amplifiers and recording gear. They also give music lessons, and they have a good selection of music books.

Galaxy really does seem to have everything under at least our sun here. As an employee told Mr. C,

"We carry every imaginable instrument known to man."

Check out their awesome Web site. If you're looking to buy an instrument and they don't have it in stock, you can submit your name and when your coveted item arrives they will call you. They also list the used instruments they're looking to buy.

Store hours are Monday through Friday from 10 a.m. to 7 p.m., and Sunday from 10 a.m. to 6 p.m.

Midtown Music

- 3326 North Druid Hills Road, Decatur; (404) 325-0515
- www.midtownmusic.com

Lots of local bands trust Midtown for their acoustic and electric guitar needs, as well as for amps and synthesizers. The occasional used drum set shows up from time to time, but guitars are the real name of the game here. Midtown's inventory is 80 percent used or vintage instruments, and 20 percent is new high-end amps. If you're looking for something unique, this is the place to find it. Midtown Music's clients may not all be professionals, but they're all serious.

The store's low overhead helps keep prices low too (it's in a tiny house-like building along a residential stretch of North Druid Hills Road). The staff knows what's up, too. They can recommend just the right used Gibson, Martin, Fender, or Gretsch acoustic or electric guitar for your needs. All guitars in this store are made in America. Vintage guitars, like a Fender Stratocaster from the '60s, can be found here, too, but they ain't gonna be cheap.

All synthesizers in this store are vintage quality with names like Moog, Arp, and Wurlitzer. The amps are not necessarily vintage, and they carry Marshall, Fender, Vox, and more.

Midtown is open Mondays through Saturdays from 10 a.m. to 6 p.m.

The Music Trader

- 3964 Lawrenceville Highway, Tucker; (770) 934-7919

The Music Trader deals only in used instruments and equipment, from sound systems to keyboards, basses, electric and acoustic guitars, and drum sets. The stock is ever changing and always worth a look.

The store is open from 10 a.m. to 6 p.m. Mondays through Saturdays.

MR. CHEAP'S PICKS

Musical Instruments

Cooper Music Superstore—In business since 1906, this is *the* place for pianos, with major savings available on all manner of pianos, organs, and digital keyboards.

Emile Baran—From big-band brass instruments to the house specialty—violins—you can save with previously owned music makers here.

Guitar Center—Good discounts on a wide range of guitars, keyboards, and the electronics to wail on them with.

Galaxy Music Center—Laying claim to being the largest used music equipment dealer in the Southeast, Galaxy offers new musical instruments at a 30 percent to 40 percent discount off list price, and the used items are even cheaper!

Guitar Center

- 1-485 Northeast Expressway N.E., Atlanta; ✆ (404) 320-7253
- 1901 Terrell Mill Road S.E., Marietta; ✆ (770) 980-9222
- 🖱 www.guitarcenter.com

Do you remember Rhythm City? Well, now it's Guitar Center, although they sell lots more than guitars. This vast store just off I-85 almost seems to be too successful for its own good. Even though Mr. C dropped in late in the afternoon on a weekday, the place was packed; shoppers were waiting for any of a dozen salesmen to become available, and the phone never stopped ringing.

In other words, if it's this hard to shop here, it must be good. And it is. In fact, Guitar Center has become the nation's largest retailer of musical instruments. The store's inventory is 85 percent new and 15 percent used and vintage. Besides guitars, you'll find keyboards, synthesizers, MIDI peripherals, music software, pro audio and recording equipment, DJ and lighting gear, percussion instruments, and amplifiers. About the only thing in short supply here are band instruments, since it's really more of a rock 'n' roll store.

They guarantee the lowest prices in the nation, and their blemished instruments—those with small cosmetic flaws, can be had at up to 60 percent off the list price! For example, a Fender Stratocaster electric guitar normally listed at nearly $1,200 was available for just $714, and a Guild acoustic/electric bass with a list price of $1,500 was on sale for $892! There are literally hundreds of other similar deals here. Also check out their sales that sometimes are 50 percent off *on top of* reduced prices. Mr. Cheap found a Yamaha Pacifica 112 electric guitar for $129.97.

They have private acoustic rooms where you can try out dozens of instruments—even a room where rock bands can test out entire packages of instruments, amps, and related concert gear. The staff is top-notch here, and each department has product specialists.

Guitar Center also guarantees total satisfaction: You can return your instrument within 45 days for as full refund.

Mr. Cheap loves their Web site, so check it out. And stop in the store for a free buyer's guide that lists the hottest deals in the industry at the lowest guaranteed prices in the country.

Store hours are Monday to Friday from 10 a.m. to 9 p.m., Saturday 10 a.m. to 8 p.m., and Sunday from noon to 6 p.m.

PARTY SUPPLIES

Mr. C's social lifestyle demands several reliable sources of plentiful party materials—especially those made of high-quality paper and plastic. (Hey, if the Queen of England wants to bring her own china, that's her business.) The establishments listed below have all passed The Cheapster's rigorous standards for selection, quality, and value. However, these aren't the only places carrying good deals on party supplies. Also check out the liquidation stores listed in the "Discount Department Stores" section: Costco, Target, Wal-Mart, and the like, as well as just about any "dollar" store you come across.

Dan-Dee Sales

- 839 Beecher Street S.W., Atlanta; ✆ (404) 753-7815

- ⌘ www.dandeesales.com

This party store sells party decorations, party favors, and invitations, as well as plastic, solid color, or patterned tableware, for every soiree imaginable, even a St. Patty's Day celebration. And, everything is priced at 25 to 50 percent off retail. In fact, Dan-Dee ships cases of supplies at wholesale prices to smaller stores and rental shops all over the Southeast. As an individual consumer, if you want to buy in bulk, you too would be given the wholesale prices.

You can also buy discounted school supplies here, including bulletin boards, fund-raising supplies, prize items, and more.

Store hours are Monday through Friday from 10 a.m. to 5 p.m. Call for weekend hours.

In Any Event . . .

- Roswell-Wieuca Shopping Center, 4413 Roswell Road, N.E., Atlanta; ✆ (404) 256-4033

This paper and party supply shop is tiny, compared to other stores Mr. C found, but it's jam-packed with bargains.

Here The Cheapster found Contempo brand plastic plates, in bold colors and pastels, at $2.39 for a pack of ten. Rectangle plastic table covers were priced to sell at $1.95, and round ones going for $2.95. Sturdy 10-ounce tumblers by Beverage Ware were $1.89 each; a dozen plastic utensils by Oak Hill, available in bright colors, were $1.00; and fifty dinner napkins were tagged at $3.89.

A package of ten plates, decorated with the University of Georgia Bulldog, was priced at $2.99, and plastic bowls were 30 cents each.

To liven up the house, try 500 feet of crepe paper streamers, which were available in a wide assortment of colors for $4.25.

In the gift-wrapping section, a 5-foot roll of wrapping paper was $1.79, and 250 yards of colored ribbon carried a price of $3.75.

In Any Event . . . will keep you well supplied for any kids' bash, with tons of cute party favors by Unique. Most sell under $2, like a four-pack of big chalk sticks, or a six-pack of plastic bracelets. Those noisemakers used on New Year's Eve are a measly 39 cents each, as are metal horns decorated with fun confetti patterns.

Hey, don't miss the store's gag and joke section. Some of the tricks Mr. C found were salt water taffy, with an emphasis on the salt, for $1.49; plus fake beer, sneezing powder, and trick candies that turn your mouth blue—all available for under two bucks.

This store is open Monday through Saturday from 9 a.m. to 6 p.m.

Paper Parlour

- 3363 Buford Highway N.E., Atlanta; ✆ (404) 728-0100

- ⌘ www.paperparlour.com

Paper Parlour is one of those one-stop party stop stores, whether the special event is a birthday, retirement, graduation, Mardi Gras celebration, or any other excuse you have in mind. The store is good-sized (15,000 square feet), but PP considers itself more of a specialty boutique with personalized service. The owner told Mr. Cheap that they carry a wider selection of items than other party store, and prices are competitive.

Here's one example of said personalized service: If you're interested in printed invitations and you want to do something original, they have graphic designers on site here to assist you. (Now that's what you call service!) The price per invitation could range from $1 to $40.

Mr. Cheap found a package of 50 solid color triple-ply paper luncheon napkins for $2.79 and a package of 24 paper dinner plates for $4.99. The same size plates in plastic (a package of 20) sold for $5.99 and a 24-piece of plastic forks was $1.49. A plastic 54" × 108" rectangle tablecloth sold for $1.69, with a 84" round was $2.69.

Or, you might be interested in patterned tableware. The store carries at least 25 patterns, from Isabelle's Peony (Mrs. Cheap's favorite) to South of the Boarder, to Animal Prints. Peony's package of eight dinner plates cost $4.99 and 20 triple ply napkins were priced at $5.39. An "Animal Prints" 54" × 102" tablecloth will cost you $5.69. Other party ware Mr. Cheap came across: a 10" cake plate for $5.99, a set of five elegant looking 50-ounce pitchers was $12.99, and a 8-quart punch bowl with ladle for $8.99 (the punch cups are priced at 89 cents each). And if you are throwing a children's party, there are party crafts like glitter and poster paints, and sand art bracelets. You can make eight pipe cleaner flowers for $4.39, and lots of different bubble sets—dinosaur, flower and more—priced at $1.99 to $2.89. There are also tons of children's party favors, and you can't beat the prices.

Is it inconvenient to make a trip to the store right now? Then you may want to check out PP's superb Web site (see the address above). It makes shopping a breeze for almost every item they sell, since you can view a picture and price, and your online purchases are discounted 10 percent with free shipping. (All leftover seasonal products are discounted 75 percent, and often you'll find other items priced at 25 to 50 percent off retail.)

So go on, plan a party, and don't forget those guest towels that feel like cloth but are disposable. Store hours are Monday through Friday from 10 a.m. to 8 p.m., Saturday from 10 a.m. to 6 p.m., and Sunday from 12:30 p.m. to 5 p.m.

Party City

- 2100 Henderson Mill Road N.E., Atlanta; (770) 414-9900
- 3101 Towercreek Parkway S.E., Atlanta; (770) 933-3983
- Sandy Springs Crossing Shopping Center, 6690 Roswell Road; Sandy Springs; (404) 303-8100
- 3655 Roswell Road N.E., Buckhead; (404) 233-3600
- 2400 Cobb Parkway S.E., Smyrna; (770) 937-9300
- 6690 Roswell Road N.E., Sandy Springs; (404) 303-8100
- 1958 Mount Zion Road, Morrow; (770) 478-4500
- 4101 Roswell Road, Marietta; (770) 509-3422
- 126 Pavilion Parkway, Fayetteville; (770) 460-0322
- 2910 Chapel Hill Road, Douglasville; (770) 947-1722
- 1630 Pleasant Hill Road, Duluth; (770) 931-9300
- 50 Barrett Parkway, Marietta; (770) 419-1300
- 635 W Crossville Road, Roswell; (770) 641-8100
- 5900 States Bridge Road, Duluth; (770) 814-7422
- 1390 Dogwood Drive S.E., Conyers; (770) 483-0023
- 1708 Highway 124 N., Snellville; (770) 982-6809

Wherever your city may be, Party City is worth the trip when you're getting ready for a big bash. This metropolis-sized store is set up warehouse style, with floor-to-ceiling displays, but without the cold warehouse feel. And, its prices are amazing.

Be sure to pick up a shopping checklist when you first walk in—a very cool and useful idea. There are checklists for wedding receptions and showers, children's birthday parties, retirement parties, and seasonal events; the lists are arranged by aisle, making shopping here a breeze.

Newlyweds can put more money toward their honeymoon by shopping here for wedding decorations and accessories. Champagne glasses start at $8.99 for a package of 100, and wedding cake toppers start at $14.99; a "Wedding Treasure Masters" set gives you glasses, a cake server and plate, garter belt, and guest book, all for $42.99.

Basic party supplies are incredibly well stocked here. A box of a dozen thank-you notes was $1.99. A pack of eight shower invitations, listed at $2.95, sells for $1.50. A 9-foot "Happy Birthday" banner, covered with metallic glitter, was $4.99. You can get fancy napkins and a matching tablecloth at good prices, or save even more with the store's own brand, available in an impressive array of brights, darks, and pastel shades.

Need some gift wrapping? One hundred square feet of the stuff from the Gift Wrap Company was $7.99. Taper candles were $6.90 each, and scented votive candles were $5.90. To make sure your party packs a punch, you might to also consider getting an 8-quart plastic punch bowl with server—just $5.99 at the City.

Bargains on kid stuff include a Big Bird-shaped cake pan for $9.77, two-foot balloons for $9.99, an eight-pack of party blowouts for $3.29 (list $3.85), and an eight-pack of "Party Loot" bags for $1.49. A tissue paper clown, to be used as a table centerpiece, was $1.88. Napkins and paper plates come decorated with a variety of characters, like Thomas the Tank Engine, the Little Mermaid, Beauty and the Beast, Snow White, 101 Dalmatians, and Cinderella. Most are priced at $1.59 for a set of 16.

Super-embarrassing cardboard placards ("Look Who's Forty!" (Fifty!, Sixty!, etc.) are just $8.80, while a huge "Look Who's 30!" button was $2.97. And an "Over The Hill" talking doormat was $9.99. Better hope your guest of honor has a good sense of humor.

Party City keeps on partying Monday through Friday from 9:30 a.m. to 9 p.m., Saturday from 9:30 a.m. to 8 p.m., and Sunday from 11 a.m. to 6 p.m.

Winn Dixie

- Locations throughout Atlanta
- ✍ www.winndixie.com

Unless you already shop at one of the South's biggest supermarket chains, you may not be aware that Winn Dixie sells greeting cards at 40 percent off the printed price—every day. The size of the card aisle varies from one store to another, but there's always at least a decent selection of cards for all occasions—birthdays, holidays, thank yous, etc.

The store actually carries only one line, the Gibson brand (a division of American Greetings), but they make as much of a variety as any other company, whether you want your message to be silly, sentimental, or just plain straight.

There are also cards with famous figures on the front, from Mickey Mouse and the Little Mermaid to characters from television shows. Since Winn Dixies are everywhere, this is a great little tip to store away for that time when you're late for the party and need to grab a card on the way.

PET SUPPLIES

These are some of the best places to buy pet foods and supplies around the metro area. Mr. C also suggests that you check out some of the "dollar" stores (see the listings under "Discount Department Stores'), since many of them sell reduced-price canned food, and sometimes even leashes, collars, and doggie and kitty toys.

Investigating pet stores this time around, the C-Man learned that there are actually three categories of pet food. The first includes foods that are considered "natural" (which does not mean organic), with no fillers and preservatives. The second includes the "premium" dog foods, which have fewer fillers and additives than the third category, the "standard" brands.

Mr. C also learned that some pet food filler could even be sawdust, and that the holistic and the premium manufacturers profess that *more* of their nutritious food is absorbed, meaning you can feed your pet less, and the "cost per feeding," costs you no more than the "other foods." (Hmmm. Ohh-kay . . .) But don't listen to Dr. Cheap when it comes to this kind of advice. (After all, he may have been feeding Jackson the Shetland sheepdog little bowser kibbles and sawdust until relatively recently. Maybe that's why he was always nosing around the linseed oil under the sink.) What you buy for your furry (or feathery) loved one is ultimately your decision, so research the ingredients of various products and talk to your vet about the best choices for your pet.

The Aviarium

- 3500 Gwinnett Place Drive, Duluth; ✆ (770) 495-0540

The Aviarium, as its pedigreed name hints, specializes in birds and fish, plus everything you'll need for their care. Here you'll find exotic birds such as parrots that talk, finches, and cockatiels at prices that range from under $20 to hundreds of dollars.

In the pet accessory department, a chrome birdcage by Hoei, with a retail price of $53.99, was on sale for $42.99. A two-pound bag of L&M safflower seed for hook bill birds was $2.98. Perfect-A-Scene, the plastic-coated photography that presumably tricks pet fish into thinking that they're back in the ocean, starts at $1 a foot, while Tetra-Min fish food costs $2.49 for the 12-gram canister.

Store hours are Monday through Friday from 11 a.m. to 9 p.m., Saturday from 11 a.m. to 7 p.m., and Sunday from noon to 6 p.m.

Market Grocery at the Atlanta State Farmer's Market

- 16 Forest Parkway, Forest Park; ✆ (404) 361-7980

Hidden inside the Atlanta State Farmer's Market, which is completely open to the public, is the real hidden treasure of the whole place: The Market Grocery. It's a true warehouse for supermarkets, and yes, they also offer good values on a range of pet supplies!

See also the listing under *Food Stores—General Markets.*

The Pet Set

- Loehmann's Executive Plaza, 2480 Briarcliff Road N.E., Atlanta; (404) 633-8755
- 3313 Highway 5, Douglasville; (770) 949-0579
- www.thepetset.net

Talk about "a dog's life"! Featured on CNN and in the *New York Times*, this upscale store, complete with plush décor and track lighting, is where wealthy Atlantans come for costumes to dress their dogs and cats for nights on the town—really. They even have a pet Jacuzzi! Mr. C isn't kidding, although he almost wishes he were.

Despite all this luxurious decadence, Pet Set's prices for basics like cat litter and pet food aren't as outrageous as you might expect. A 4-pound bag of Iams kitten food is just $7.50. The store also offers regular patrons a discount program: When you buy ten bags, you'll get one free.

Twelve pounds of EverClean cat litter are just $9.99, and Science Diet dog food in the "small bite" variety is $20.92 for a 20-pound bag. For all those gourmet pets, a special deli section offers freeze-dried chicken.

Since this store is as much for the elite set as the pet set, they offer a wealth of grooming services as well, from whirlpool baths to hot oil coat treatments to "complete makeovers."

The Atlanta store is open Monday through Friday from 7:30 a.m. to 7 p.m., Saturday from 7:30 a.m. to 6 p.m., and Sunday from noon to 5 p.m. The Douglasville location is open Monday through Saturday from 8:30 a.m. to 5 p.m.

Pets Etc.

- 2131 Pleasant Hill Road, Duluth; (770) 476-4749

This is another pet store that is concerned about the food we feed our little furry and feathery darlings. The owner believes only in "natural" pet food, with no byproducts, fillers, preservatives, or allergens. The Cheapster has had a cat and a dog (and a teenaged son and daughter) for some time, but readily admits that he was a tad surprised to learn that pets can have allergies to corn, soy, and wheat. Hey, you can't be a scholar in everything.

Pets Etc.'s prices are competitive, even with the PetsMart stores, and they provide specialized service. If you give them a call, they will happily quote prices over the phone. The most popular food brand here is Solid Gold, and they also carry Innova, Wellness, Canidae for dogs, and Felidae for cats. Here's a real treat for your pet—a local woman whips up her own natural biscuits with names like banana apple, pumpkin tater pie, liver chews, salmon surprise, and cheesy chips. Sounds like Mr. Cheap's last dinner party.

If you are looking for a pet bird, this is the place. Pets Etc. brings in baby birds, as young as two weeks old, and hand feeds them until they are ready to be weaned, at which point they are offered for sale. These birds think that a person is their mama and make lovely sweet pets. There are big and small parrots, cockatoos, and cockatiels. Other birds, sold here but not hand-fed, are parakeets and finches. The birds are also fed vitamin-enriched and natural foods that contain dried fruits and vegetables, such as the Sunseed, Supreme, and Volkman brand names.

SHOPPING: PET SUPPLIES

You'll also find some smaller pets, such as guinea pigs, ferrets, and tropical fish. The reptile family is represented here by the iguanas and bearded dragons. These reptiles are vegetarians, so Pets Etc. cuts up fruit and veggies for these guys. The ferrets get the high-quality Marshall-brand food.

The store has food and habitats for all these pets, and a lot more—even grooming for dogs and cats.

Store hours are Monday through Friday from 10 a.m. to 8 p.m., Saturday from 10 a.m. to 7 p.m., and Sunday from noon to 6 p.m.

PetsMart

- 650 Ponce de Leon Avenue N.E., Atlanta; ✆ (404) 872-2363
- 3221 Peachtree Road N.E., Atlanta; ✆ (404) 266-0402
- 128 Perimeter Center W., Atlanta; ✆ (770) 481-0043
- 4023 Lavista Road, Tucker; ✆ (770) 414-5126
- 2540 Hargrove Road, Smyrna; ✆ (770) 432-8250
- 1986 Mount Zion Road, Morrow; ✆ (770) 478-0860
- 1285 Johnson Ferry Road, Marietta; ✆ (770) 971-3010
- 2150 Paxton Drive S.W., Lilburn; ✆ (770) 985-0469
- 101 Pavilion Parkway, Fayetteville; ✆ (770) 719-4444
- 2940 Chapel Hill Road, Douglasville; ✆ (770) 942-3326
- 3803 Venture Drive, Duluth; ✆ (770) 813-8400
- 860 Cobb Place Boulevard N.W., Kennesaw; ✆ (770) 424-5226
- 6370 N Point Parkway, Alpharetta; ✆ (770) 343-8511
- 625 W Crossville Road, Roswell; ✆ (404) 352-9766
- 1370 Dogwood Drive, S.E., Conyers; ✆ (770) 922-1772
- 875 Lawrenceville Suwanee Road, Lawrenceville; ✆ (770) 995-2449
- ✍ www.petsmart.com

Just about everyone who owns a pet is familiar with the national pet "superstore" chain called PetsMart. The big savings available here have made it a very popular place to shop, indeed. In fact, since Mr. Cheap's last visit in 1994, an additional 12 stores have sprouted in Atlanta and the surrounding suburbs. PetsMart has everything you could need, and more, whether your pet is a dog or cat, bird or wild bird, reptile or fish, chinchilla or ferret, mouse or a rat (and these animals are sold at the store). You might cringe at the thought of a pet rat, but you probably haven't seen *fancy* rats, which are intelligent, fuzzy, and quite cute.

MR. CHEAP'S PICKS

Pet Supplies

The Pet Set—This upscale store is where wealthy Atlantans come for costumes to dress their dogs and cats for nights on the town. Yet despite all of the luxurious decadence, they have decent prices on basics like cat litter and pet food

PetsMart—The superstore approach to animals, their care, and feeding. The big savings available here have made it a very popular place to shop

Many of the PetsMart stores have adoption centers for cats and dogs. If you're looking for a new dog or puppy, go to the store on Saturdays, when breeders and pet parents are often there with their furry charges, looking to make a deal. Call ahead to make sure the store has an adoption center, and to verify hours.

You'll find at least ten different premium brands of cat and dog food here. On The Cheapster's last visit, a 20-pound bag of Eukanuba dog food was priced at $20.99. Iams was $17.29, and Pro Plan $17.49. An 8-pound bag of Iams cat food was $13.99, while Pro Plan's product was $12.49. Pets-Mart's own "house brand" 30-pound bag of dog food was $22.99, and that's a saver! There are lots of bird foods to choose from too, like Kaytee, ZuPreem Avian, and others. A 3-pound bag of the house food for cockatiels was $4.19, while the Kaytee version was $9.19.

Food for just about every other little creature is sold here—even for blue tongue skink lizards. They also stock pet habitats, food, medication, vitamin supplements, cleaning, odor control supplies, dental care, and lots more.

PetsMart also offers grooming, as well as obedience training at reasonable prices, and they will trim your pet's nails for a cheap $8. (You just need to make an appointment.)

All stores are open Mondays through Saturdays from 9 a.m. to 9 p.m., and Sundays from 9 a.m. to 6 p.m.

Pet Supermarket

- 2508 N Decatur Road, Decatur; (404) 634-3808

- 4498 Chamblee Dunwoody Road, Dunwoody; (770) 234-9905

- 5025 Floyd Road S.W., Mableton; (770) 732-6161

- 50 Powers Ferry Road, Marietta; (770) 321-3959

- 6010 Singleton Road, Norcross; (770) 248-9020

- 10502 A. Alpharetta Highway, Roswell; (678) 352-9733

- 6690 Roswell Road, Sandy Springs; (404) 531-9938

- 1977 Scenic Highway, Snellvillle; (678) 344-7009

- 9425 Highway 92, Woodstock; (770) 517-7355

- www.petsupermarket.com

Pet Supermarket is one of those big national chains, loaded with premium food, vitamins, minerals, and amino acids to keep your animal healthy. Some of the food sold here is even designed for pets with allergies. The staffers know their foods, and will help you choose the right one for your pet.

You'll find the usual—birds, fish, cats, reptiles, and adorable small animals like rabbits, ferrets, hamsters, gerbils, guinea pigs, mice, and rats. Call before you visit to make sure the pet you want is available. Mr. Cheap found rabbits for $19.99 each and hamsters for $3.99. Goldfish were $5.99 each.

Their Web site features a number of printable coupons that can save you money. Mr. Cheap printed a "20 percent off" dog apparel coupon and a "$10 off" coupon for a Doskocil travel kennel for his cat. The site also includes some great information regarding how to select a pet, a habitat, and the proper food and toys. It's also informative regarding how to keep your pet healthy, including grooming.

SHOPPING: PET SUPPLIES

Store hours are Monday through Saturday from 9 a.m. to 9 p.m., and Sunday from 10 a.m. to 6 p.m.

Petco

- 2468 Southlake Mall, Morrow; (770) 961-7799
- 2080 Henderson Mill Road, N.E., Atlanta; (678) 937-0137
- 2340 Holcomb Bridge Road, Roswell; (770) 649-6360
- 2131 Pleasant Hill Road, Duluth; (678) 475-1925
- 10980 State Bridge Road, Alpharetta; (678) 297-0673
- 1630 Scenic Highway 124, Snellville; (770) 972-9995
- 2160 Riverside Parkway, Lawrenceville; (770) 995-9394
- 9559 Highway 5, Douglasville; (770) 942-5442
- 3264 Buford Drive, Buford; (678) 714-8048
- www.petco.com

PetsMart and Petco are direct competitors, and they're neck-and-neck in the race to add new stores *and* offer customers the best prices. Of course, Petco is loaded with all manner of food and accessories for dogs, cats, birds, rabbits, ferrets, gerbils, guinea pigs, hamsters, reptiles, and fish.

In the chow department, Petco carries some of the same brand-name food as you'll find in the other pet "supermarkets" (for example, Iams, Eukanuba, Pro Plan, Bil Jac and Science)—about 18 name-brand pet foods in all. Meanwhile, the prices here are about the same as those you'll find at PetsMart (see above). For example, a 20-pound bag of Iams dog food was priced at $17.99 here, while the same size from ProPlan was $16.99. A 24-can case of Nutro Max cat food could be had for $13.99, and a 25-pound bag of EverClean clumping kitty litter was marked down from $15.99 to $12.99.

Petco offers full-service grooming salons, as well as obedience courses, veterinary services, adoption service, and pet photography. They actually sell pets here: fish and other small aquatic animals, reptiles, birds, and small, cuddly mammals such as mice, "fancy rats," hamsters, guinea pigs, and the like.

Petco's Web site features a deal called "Bottomless Bowl & More," where you buy food and supplies at a discount and they are delivered right to your door.

Store hours are Monday through Saturday from 10 a.m. to 9 p.m., and Sunday from noon to 6 p.m.

Wildside Pet and Aquarium Connection

- 2855 North Druid Hills Road N.E., Atlanta; (404) 325-4945

This shop's manager told Mr. Cheap "if you wouldn't feed it to your family, you shouldn't feed it to your pet, because they are family too." So here you will only find organic (no preservatives) food without any unwanted fillers.

The organic food brands sold here for both cat and dog are Solid Gold, California Natural, and Innova. Mr. C found a 40-pound bag of Solid Gold dog food for $38.99, and a 20-pound bag of cat food for $23.99. Birds are part of our family too, so you can pick up a 5-pound bag of organic Forti-Diet for only $3.99.

Your own grinning tabby will love climbing five-foot beautiful wooden trees that are priced at $199. (The six-footer goes for $299.)

You'll probably spot a Spot or two while shopping here, since pets are always welcome with their owners. In fact, Mr. C saw no less than three cats and a golden retriever while visiting. The only animals sold here are small mammals, like gerbils, hamsters, guinea pigs, rats, mice, ferrets, and chinchillas. You can also buy fresh and salt-water fish, plus food, accessories and domiciles for all these little creatures.

The store is open Monday to Friday 10 a.m. to 8 p.m., Saturday 10 a.m. to 6 p.m., and Sunday 12:30 to 4:00 p.m.

SEWING AND FABRICS

Mr. Cheap is a man of many talents, but he's totally inept when it comes to the art and science of sewing. Maybe that's because he hasn't touched a needle and thread since he was forced to hand-repair a particularly unfortunate rent in the seat of his yellow-and-blue bell-bottom trousers on morning three of the Woodstock Music and Arts Festival back in 1969. (Ahhh, those groovy memories.) Thank goodness that Mrs. C, while no Martha Stewart (a blessing to all involved), does know a bit about the craft and was able to help him stitch together this section on sewing and fabric stores worth a close look. Remember, these outfits are specialists, with great selections of fabric and accessories. If you're just looking for the basics, you would do well to visit your local pharmacy, or any of the establishments listed under "Discount Department Stores."

Ashby Discount Sewing Center

- 2990 Canton Highway, Marietta; ✆ (770) 427-9947

This family-operated store has been in the Atlanta area for about 60 years. Expect to find great bargains on used brands like White, Viking, Pfaff, Singer, and Baby Lock, as well as new machines from Pfaff and Brother. All of the used models are obtained through trade-ins, which have been carefully checked out before being accepted.

According to the experts here, machines manufactured in Japan are better made than those from Thailand, two of the main suppliers of equipment; Mr. C suggests that you keep this in mind when you shop, and if you're interested in a particular machine, don't be afraid to inquire.

Ashby keeps about 150 machines in stock at any given time, so you'll always have a good selection from which to choose, including regular pedal-controlled machines and even backstitch machines. The used Singer sewing machines generally start as low as $75 and go up from there, depending on their quality and degree of wear and tear.

You can get good deals on new machines here as well; Ashby makes purchases in high volume, allowing them to offer discounts of up to 25 percent off suggested retail prices, with the Pfaff and Brother models ranging in price from $149 to $6,000. Guess you

SHOPPING: SEWING AND FABRICS

could say that they've got bargains all sewn up!

These folks also run sewing classes and clubs, so check them out. Store hours are 10 a.m. to 6 p.m. Monday through Friday, and 10 a.m. to 5 p.m. on Saturday.

Forsyth Fabrics

- 1190 Foster Street, NW, Atlanta; ✆ (404) 351-6050

This store is excellent for designer drapery and upholstery fabrics, with an inventory of 10,000 (count 'em) bolts of fabric. You'll find prints, stripes, solids, tapestry, silks, canvas, imitation suede, velvets, denims, and designer names like Waverly, P. Kaufman, Richloom, and many, many more. During sales, which are fairly often, fabric is marked down 50 percent. And there is also the Forsyth Closeout section, featuring remnants and anything five yards and under is 50 percent off. Waverly prices start at $8.95 and go up to $19.95.

Store hours are Monday through Saturday from 9 a.m. to 6 p.m., and Sunday from noon to 5 p.m.

Hancock Fabrics

- 2625 Piedmont Road, Atlanta; ✆ (404) 266-0517
- 2655 N Decatur Road, Decatur; ✆ (404) 378-8220
- 5512 Peachtree Industrial Boulevard, Chamblee; ✆ (770) 451-4600
- 6332 Roswell Road N.E., Sandy Springs; ✆ (404) 256-5768
- 1602 Lake Harbin Road, Morrow; ✆ (770) 961-0803
- 2570 S Cobb Drive S.E., Smyrna; ✆ (770) 435-2349
- 1481 Roswell Road, Marietta; ✆ (770) 578-8159
- 4400 Roswell Road, Marietta; ✆ (770) 971-1257
- 2131 Pleasant Hill Road, Duluth; ✆ (770) 923-2850
- 3000 Canton Highway, Marietta; ✆ (770) 428-1578
- 9559 Highway 5, Douglasville; ✆ (770) 920-0109
- 10945 State Bridge Road, Alpharetta; ✆ (770) 740-8502
- 1997 Scenic Highway S.W., Snellville; ✆ (770) 979-0855
- 665 W Pike Street, Lawrenceville; ✆ (770) 962-4775
- ✐ www.hancockfabrics.com

Serious seamstresses go to Hancock for its guaranteed low prices on everything from decorator fabrics to gabardine to gingham prints, and the store guarantees 100 percent satisfaction. You can return material as long as you return it exactly as it was cut in the store, for cash or store credit. That's certainly a deal. They carry Vogue, Simplicity, McCalls, and Butterick patterns at 50 percent off.

Hancock Fabrics has a huge selection of decorator fabrics in designer patterns (over 350) including their own Lauren Hancock Fabric Collection by Waverly that's priced at $12.47 a yard.

Thinking about creating a new drapery look? How about a toile drapery print like Jamestown Black or American Cottage Red for just $9.99 a yard? Maybe you're in the mood for a new bedspread? Try their 100 percent cotton chenille for $14.99 a yard. And, keep your eye out for sales, when fabric is marked down 20 percent from its already low prices.

Mr. Cheap located an all-polyester gabardine fabric for just $6.49 a yard, and a cotton broadcloth—

for spiffy-looking dress shirts—was a mere $1.99 per yard. Solid color fleece was $6.99 a yard, and if you want a soccer fleece material the unit price is $9.99. White sheer drapery was $3.97 a yard and lace was $4.17 a yard. Other craft-making necessities, like felt ($3.97 per yard), and felt squares (25 per package), were $5.

You'll also find decorating accessories, home accents, quilter's materials, yarns, sewing machines and sewing accessories, as well as White, New Home, and Singer sewing machines priced at $199 and up.

Hancock stores are open Monday through Friday from 9:30 a.m. to 9 p.m., and Saturday from 9:30 a.m. to 6 p.m.

Jo-Ann Fabrics & Crafts

- 1355 Roswell Road, Marietta; (770) 973-3220
- 1341 Mount Zion Road, Morrow; (770) 968-6692
- 8562 Tara Boulevard, Jonesboro; (770) 719 5257
- 4760 Highway 29 N.W., Lilburn; (770) 923-2101
- 608 Holcomb Bridge Road, Roswell; (770) 992-7575
- 1283 Iris Drive S.E., Conyers; (770) 760-7515
- 9439 Highway 5, Douglasville; (770) 947-4195
- 2500 Cobb Place Lane N.W., Kennesaw; (770) 428-9986
- 2302 Main Street E., Snellville; (770) 972-9656
- www.joannfabrics.com

Get into vogue at Jo-Ann Fabrics (as in Vogue patterns, that is) as well as those by New Look, McCall's, Simplicity, Burda, and Butterick, which are always sold at 50 percent off retail here, and keep your eye out for specials that provide even greater savings.

Other bargains may include flannel material, selling for just $4.99 a yard, while similar deals can be found on solid-color fleece for $7.99 a yard, Waverly drapery prints starting at $15.99 a yard, and calicos recently on sale for $3.00 a yard. Chenille (wave cut), great for making blankets or bedspreads, regularly sells for a low $7.25 per yard. The Daisy Baby Kingdom cuddly chenille for baby quilts was recently on sale for $4.49. For children's bedroom pillows or window treatments, have some fun with Disney's Mickey Mouse or the Peanuts gang, or the new popular guy on the block, Harry Potter, all priced at $6.99 a yard.

If you're in the mood for crafts, Jo-Ann's has lots of fun projects for you, from rubber-stamping and "scrap booking" to jewelry and candle making. Materials for needle arts, such as cross stitch, crocheting, knitting, and quilting, are also available.

You'll also like Jo-Ann's low prices on notions like the Clover Double Needle Threader for just $3.99, and high-quality Fiskars scissors ($26.99 a pair—seen for up to $37.99 elsewhere). Mostly White sewing machines are sold here, and Mr. Cheap found your basic beginner's model (number 1418) priced at $129, as well as a Rowenta Sew 'n Press Iron priced at $49.99 (retail price $69.99)

The stores are open from 9 a.m. to 9 p.m. Monday through Saturday, and from 10 a.m. to 6 p.m. on Sunday.

Lewis & Sheron Textile Company

- 912 Huff Road N.W., Atlanta; (404) 351-4833; (800) 835-4833

- 🖳 www.lewis-sheron-textiles.com

Located in a real warehouse (30,000 square feet), this place is like a discount outlet for gorgeous fabrics. The majority of the material here is decorator fabric for upholstery and drapery. L&S carries a full line of silks and solids, and their most popular designers are Waverly, P. Kaufman, and Richloom. Right next door to the warehouse is their outlet store where all fabric is discounted 50 percent. L&S also offers decorative trim and custom furniture.

Store hours are Monday to Saturday from 9 a.m. to 5 p.m.

Outrageous Bargains

- New London Square Shopping Center, 1355 Roswell Road, Marietta; ✆ (770) 578-6944
- 3455 Peachtree Industrial Boulevard, Duluth; ✆ (770) 497-9577

These folks sell designer fabrics wholesale and retail, specializing in such brand names as Waverly, P. Kaufman, and Braemore 200. Remnants in solids and prints, and in natural and synthetic fibers, are marked down 30 percent. What's more, they even have furniture from Hooker, Pulaski, Universal, Lane, Lexington 300, and others available for 20 to 35 percent off.

Store hours are Monday through Friday from 10 a.m. to 7 p.m., Saturday from 10 a.m. to 6 p.m., and Sunday from noon to 5 p.m.

Textile Warehouse

- 4230 Lawrenceville Highway N.W., Lilburn; ✆ (770) 381-1199

Textile Warehouse has been in business for over 40 years and their inventory is huge, composed of both "in stock" and made-to-order first-quality fabrics for upholstery, drapery, and bedding. Some of their popular name brands are Waverly, P. Kaufman, Covington, Braemore, Bloomcraft, and Richloom. The owner did not want Mr. Cheap to list prices, but they are competitive and offer good deals. In addition to fabric, you'll find trim, drapery hardware, rugs, framed pictures, and occasional furniture. Woven fabrics in the store are organized by colors, and prints by designer names. Remnants of two yards and under are 50 percent off.

Sometimes the store gets crowded and you need to take a number, but the wait is worth it, since staffers are very helpful and friendly.

Store hours are Monday through Saturday from 9:30 a.m. to 6:00 p.m., except for Thursday when they're open until 7 p.m.

SHOES AND SNEAKERS

With all the shopping he does, Mr. Cheap gives careful consideration to his footwear, and part of that equation is price, of course. Following are a number of totally superb shoe stores were you can also save some significant bucks. Not listed here are the Wal-Marts and Kmarts of the world, which also carry a number of reliable name brands at low, low prices. See the descriptions for those establishments under *Discount Department Stores*.

Abbadabba's

- 421-B Moreland Avenue N.E., Atlanta; (404) 581-0072
- 322 East Paces Ferry Road N.E., Atlanta; (404) 262-3356
- 1580 Holcomb Bridge Road, Roswell; (770) 998-2222
- 3360 Satellite Boulevard, Duluth; (770) 623-0033
- www.coolshoes.com

The savings you'll find here might leave you at a loss for words. Maybe that's how they named the place, after their delirious, happily babbling customers. Or, possibly, they just like the Flintstones.

Abbadabba's caters to the young, flavor-of-the-month crowd, offering decent prices on high-end casual shoes. Brands found here include Clarke's, Birkenstock, Rockport, and others. They also carry the trendy, industrial Doc Martens, as well as platform shoes and wilder creations for nights out on the town. The store's high-volume purchasing translates into discounts passed on to you.

Store hours are Monday through Saturday from 10:30 a.m. to 7:30 p.m., and Sunday from 1 p.m. to 6 p.m.

Army Surplus Sales

- 342 Peachtree Street N.E., Atlanta; (404) 521-2227
- www.armysurplussalesinc.com

Alas, the phrase "army surplus" doesn't automatically mean the kind of bargain shop it once did. Still, there are some deals to be found in a traditional store like this one, especially in footwear. Whether you're the outdoor type, or perhaps looking to get into the "downtown-urban" look with a pair of military boots, you'll be sure to find something here at a good discount.

Work boots in brown-brushed leather, with rugged cut soles by Georgia Boot, sell here for $65 a pair. The same boots may go for as much as $115 to $140 in department stores. Shiny black patent leather uniform shoes can be found here for $69.99, along with a range of inexpensive alternatives to Doc Martens and the like. Army jungle boots, great for hiking, outdoor activities, and just looking cool, go for $69.99.

Of course, there are lots of other items to be seen here too, including military uniforms, camping equipment, knives, flags, tarps, sleeping bags, police gear, duffle bags, footlockers, clothing, and more. Here you'll find good prices on pea coats, which start from just $115, as well as on field jackets, priced at $75. Those cool fatigue pants (the original "cargo pants") are a reasonable, $29.99, and you'll find plenty of other bargains if you take the time to scout around.

Store hours are Monday through Friday from 9 a.m. to 5:30 p.m., and Saturday from 9 a.m. to 5 p.m. The parking is free, a nice money-saving bonus at a downtown store!

The Athlete's Foot

- 2385 Peachtree Road N.E. Atlanta; (404) 233-9161
- 2685 Metropolitan Parkway Atlanta; (404) 768-2850
- 1978 Candler Road, Decatur; (404) 534-6637
- 3393 Peachtree Road N.E., Atlanta; (404) 812-0220
- 3553 Memorial Drive, Decatur; (404) 284-7989
- 2050 Lawrenceville Hwy, Decatur; (404) 633-0185

SHOPPING: SHOES AND SNEAKERS

- 2044 Northlake Mall N.E., Atlanta; ✆ (770) 414-8040

- 1230 S Hairston Road, Stone Mountain; ✆ (404) 508-4355

- 6690 Roswell Road N.E., Atlanta; ✆ (404) 257-0322

- 8079 Tara Boulevard, Jonesboro; ✆ (770) 4 78-4388

- ✍ www.theathletesfoot.com

Scratch where it itches, C always says, so when you feel the urge to put your paws on a large, well-priced selection of name-brand athletic and recreational shoes—Nike, Puma, Adidas, and the like—it pays to check out The Athlete's Foot. The Cheapster won't spend a lot of space here describing this ubiquitous national chain, so suffice it to say that it always boasts some good clearance deals on footwear for men, women, and kids, while also offering a range of pro and college sports jerseys, apparel, and accessories. On the day Mr. C decided to soothe his rash desire for new running shoes, he stopped in at the closest AF and discovered a "Value Wall" filled with the things (with a few basketball shoes thrown in). Grouped by price at $19.99, $39.99, and $59.99, most of these deals represented a 20 percent to 40 percent discount off list prices. Ahhh . . . relief!

Store hours here vary by location. The stand-alone and strip stores are usually open Monday through Thursday from 10 a.m. to 8 p.m., Friday and Saturday from 10 a.m. to 7 p.m., and Sunday from noon to 6 p.m. The mall stores routinely do business Monday through Saturday from 10 a.m. to around 9 p.m., and Sunday from noon to 6 p.m. Remember, if you're planning a visit early or late, it pays to call ahead to verify opening and closing times!

Bennie's Discount Shoes

- Lindbergh Plaza, 2581 Piedmont Road N.E., Atlanta; ✆ (404) 262-1966

- Cumberland Square North, 2441 Cobb Parkway, Smyrna; ✆ (770) 955-1972

- Brook Hollow Center, 5192 Brook Hollow Parkway, Norcross; ✆ (770) 447-1577

- ✍ www.benniesshoes.com

Attention gentlemen: Looking for fine imported dress shoes by brands like Cole-Haan of Switzerland, or casuals from Bass and Timberland? Search no further. Bennie's means bargains.

The store is bursting with great brand names. Many are sold at the normal list price, but a number of styles are available cheap! In fact you can save up to 70 percent on closeout and blemished footwear from Bass, Bostonian, Florsheim, Foot-Joy, Merrell, Rockport, Sebago, Timberland, Cole Haan, and many other famous manufacturers. The big bonus here is that big sizes are always stocked; Mr. C saw a size 15C pair of Foot-Joy leather loafers, with tassels, list priced at $190, but selling here for just $79.95.

Other styles seen recently included a $24.95 pair of Dockers lace-up casuals, a $45 pair of New Balance running shoes, and Brooks hi-tops for $35 (listed at $85). Sebago marked Sperry Classic Double Sole Tripsiders from $80 down to $50, while $39 was the price on a pair of deck shoes.

More dress shoe deals: a pair of Giorgio Brutini tassels, listed at $75, for $60. Same price for lace-up "jazz shoes" by Florsheim. Wing tips by Steeple Gate, listed at $120 retail, were reduced to $100. And Italian Wets by Bruno Magli,

> ### MR. CHEAP'S PICKS
>
> *Shoes and Sneakers*
>
> **Bennie's Discount Shoes**—This store is bursting with great brand names available cheap! In fact, you can save up to 70 percent on closeout and blemished footwear from Bass, Bostonian, Florsheim, FootJoy, Merrell, Rockport, and other famous manufacturers.
>
> **Florsheim Factory Outlet Store**—Put some glide in your stride without tripping over your budget. Here you can routinely save as much as $20 to $100 on a typical pair of classy Florsheim shoes.
>
> **Friedman's Shoes**—Great buys on brands from Bacco Bucci, Marteens, Dunham, Fratelli, Mezlan, Vaneli, Palizzio, J. Renee, Paul Melian, Timothy Hitsman, and others.
>
> **Payless Shoe Source**—The lowest prices on shoes you'll probably find anywhere around Atlanta.
>
> **Shoemakers' Warehouse**—More designer bargains for men and women, in the Midtown Outlets.

retailing for a fortissimo $205, were only $119.

Mr. C reminds you that the best finds in all shoe stores are often hidden in the back—Bennie's is no exception. Don't miss their bargain-laden table, piled high with deals like a $20 pair of Bally sneakers, and a $40 pair of Rockport walkers (which were ever-so-slightly scuffed). Some of these shoes have obviously been worn once or twice and returned; check them carefully for blemishes. You may well decide that a scratch here or there, which (let's face it) is gonna happen anyway, is worth it at these prices.

The Lindbergh Plaza location is open Mondays through Saturdays from 8 a.m. to 6 p.m. Monday through Saturday, and noon to 5 p.m. on Sunday. In Norcross, the doors are open from 9 a.m. to 6 p.m. Monday through Saturday, and noon to 5 p.m. on Sunday. The Piedmont Road location is open from 9 a.m. to 6 p.m. Monday through Saturday, and closed on Sunday.

En Vogue Shoe Warehouse

- 935-C Chattahoochee Avenue N.W., Atlanta; ✆ (404) 352-4333

If you're looking for style and savings in women's footwear, you may have to look no further than En Vogue. These folks manufacture their own European-styled shoes and sell them to other stores around the U.S. And of course, they sell them right at this warehouse—for about 15 percent above wholesale (as compared to the 50 percent to 80 percent markup you'll pay most shoe retailers).

About 90 percent of what's here is made up of En Vogue's own brands: Monique, Simo Jourdan, Xavier Roberto, and Yannick. The rest is composed of a few European names that you probably won't find elsewhere. Everything is made of first-grade leathers, in many colors, heights, and sizes.

What this all means is that you can buy the latest European looks for far less than what you'd pay for the big brands, even when they're on sale elsewhere. In fact the *Atlanta Constitution* named this store "Best European Style Shoes."

SHOPPING: SHOES AND SNEAKERS

Sandals, pumps, sling backs, boots, and more—they're all here, in sizes 5 to 11, including wide widths. Everything is clearly identified, with all the boxes stacked along the floor.

A flashy pair of silver lame sandals, for instance, decorated with fake colored stones, is available for a mere $39.

In February 2002, En Vogue expanded its hours in response to customer demand and is now open Thursday from 10 a.m., to 6 p.m., Friday and Saturday from 10 a.m. to 7 p.m., and Sunday from 1 p.m. to 6 p.m.

Famous Footwear/Factory Brand Shoes

- 2152 Henderson Mill Road N.E., Atlanta; (770) 908-2144
- 1757 East West Connector, Austell; (678) 945-9454
- 3999 Austell Road, Austell; (770) 944-1774
- 4101 Roswell Road, Marietta; (770) 565-7429
- 3200 Holcomb Bridge Road, Norcross; (770) 368-9009
- 1425 Market Boulevard, Roswell; (770) 552-8548
- 5370 Highway 78, Stone Mountain; (770) 498-4011
- 113 Pavilion Parkway, Fayetteville; (770) 719-1512
- 3675 Satellite Boulevard, Duluth; (770) 623-1960
- 425 Ernest W Barrett Parkway, Kennesaw; (770 423-2236
- 1125 Woodstock Road, Roswell; (678) 352-1093
- 7003 Concourse Parkway, Douglasville; (770) 577-7950
- 7561 Northpoint Parkway, Alpharetta; (770) 998-6814
- 4272 Jimmy Lee Smith Parkway, Hiram; (770) 439-2931
- 1596 Dogwood Drive, Conyers; (770) 929-3600
- 126 Woodstock Square Avenue, Woodstock; (770) 591-2651
- 116 Peachtree East Shopping Center, Peachtree City; (770) 631-3144
- 2100 Riverside Parkway, Lawrenceville; (770) 682-9815
- www.famousfootwear.com

You may not have Imelda Marcos' shopping budget, but with the money you can save here on shoes, you may be able to hire away her chauffeur.

These folks boast that they're America's number-one retailer of discounted brand-name shoes. Also operating as Factory Brand Shoes in the Atlanta area, they offer a huge selection of footwear at 10 percent to 50 percent off manufacturers suggested retail prices.

All shoes are first quality, with savings provided to customers by cost cutting within the company on shipping, billing, and such. Recent bargains found at Famous Footwear include women's tailor-made Aerosoles, regularly $49.99, for $29.99; Reebok women's Accolade sneakers for $29.99 (listed at $58.99); Anne Marion high-heeled sandals reduced from $50 to $29.99; and London Fog women's cold-weather boots discounted from $39.99 to $29.99.

Buster Brown Kids' Kaylee high-topped boots, normally priced at $39.99, were on sale here for just $14.99, while girls' Tretorn tennis shoes scored an ace at 20 percent off retail, only $30.

Men can jog out of the store having saved big on Adidas athletic shoes, a range of which were available for 15 bucks off at $39.98 to $59.99, and famous-brand hightops, regularly $85, selling for $75. For more dressy occasions, men's Dexter tasseled loafers, usually listed at $80 a pair, were marked down to $44.99 here.

There's plenty of stuff for your famous child here as well. Playskool sneakers for toddlers, for example, sell for $20, which is almost $10 off the list price.

Almost as impressive as the savings was the fact that the sales floor was extremely neat and organized, despite the massive sales event that happened to be taking place during Mr. C's visit.

Most Famous Footwear stores keep their doors open Monday through Saturday from 10 a.m. to 9 p.m., and Sunday noon to 6 p.m.

Florsheim Factory Outlet Store

- 201 Peachtree Street N.E., Atlanta; (404) 523-6221

Hey gents, want to put some classy glide in your stride without breaking the bank? Just check out this unique factory outlet. A Florsheim retail store for decades, this location became a clearance outlet for the famous manufacturer in 1993. Since then they've featured incredible prices on the same highquality Florsheim shoes available elsewhere, along with similar bargains on other brands. (Sorry, ladies: Women's styles are no longer available here.) Boasting a prodigious 10,000 pairs of shoes under one roof, this awesome retail resource features deals mixed around throughout two floors, combining first-quality closeouts with irregulars.

Here you can routinely save as much as $20 to $100 on a typical pair of shoes. For example, The Cheapster discovered that Florsheim's "Royal Imperial" Dress shoes, a rock-solid black leather slip-on with tassels for a European look, were available from $49.90 to $129.90. He also noticed 50 percent discounts on pairs of Florsheim and Timberland hiking boots, as well as some brown suede lace-ups for $59.90 (representing about a 40 percent discount on the usual retail price).

Downstairs, the bargains get even better. For a real cheap thrill, check out the clearance racks there, which feature discounts of up to 70 percent off retail prices; the last time Mr. Cheap checked it out, nothing was priced higher than $40. Many of these are lines from past seasons, which have gone out of date. Still, they include the full range of Florsheim fashions, plus some other brands.

In case you're still not impressed, consider that this outstanding outlet allows you to save even more hard-earned moola by running additional special promotions throughout the year. Typically, these allow you to buy one pair and get half price on a second, or buy selected pairs for $59.90, or two for $100! All sales are final; though you may return shoes for an exchange.

Florsheim Factory Outlet also stocks a full line of accessories, including belts, hosiery, etc.

Clearly the bargains here are terrific—and you don't have to trek out to the outlet malls to find them. The store is located right across from the Westin Hotel in downtown Atlanta.

Store hours are 10 a.m. to 6 p.m. Monday through Saturday; and noon to 5 p.m. on Sunday.

Foot Locker/Lady Foot Locker

- 1 Broad Street S.W., Atlanta; (404) 658-0055

SHOPPING: SHOES AND SNEAKERS

- 78 Lower Alabama Street S.W., Atlanta; ✆ (404) 659-8479
- 829 Ralph David Abernathy Boulevard, Atlanta; ✆ (404) 753-0806
- 1544 Piedmont Road N.E., Atlanta; ✆ (404) 685-3151
- 3393 Peachtree Road N.E., Atlanta; ✆ (404) 364-9726; **Lady:** ✆ (404) 266-0107
- 3588 Memorial Drive, Decatur; ✆ (404) 288-2705
- 2841 Greenbriar Parkway S.W., Atlanta; ✆ (404) 629-1002; **Lady:** ✆ (404) 629-0087
- 2801 Candler Road, Decatur; ✆ (404) 241-8960; **Lady:** ✆ (404) 241-6114
- 2050 Lawrenceville Highway, Decatur; ✆ (404) 636-6229
- 4607 Memorial Drive, Decatur; ✆ (404) 297-7963
- 1124 Cumberland Mall S.E., Atlanta; ✆ (770) 434-8710
- 4800 Briarcliff Road N.E., Atlanta; ✆ (770) 491-8660
- 4400 Ashford Dunwoody Road N.E., Atlanta; ✆ (770) 393-4447
- 1222 Southlake Mall, Morrow; ✆ (770) 961-8827; **Lady:** ✆ (770) 968-5807
- 6777 Highway 85 Riverdale; ✆ (770) 994-9292
- 157 Shannon Mall, Union City; ✆ (770) 969-1034; **Lady:** ✆ (770) 969-7514
- 2100 Pleasant Hill Road, Duluth; ✆ (770) 476-7422
- 400 Ernest W Barrett Parkway N.W., Kennesaw; ✆ (770) 425-0904; **Lady:** ✆ (770) 426-9076
- 1036 N Point Circle, Alpharetta; ✆ (770) 667-8555; **Lady:** ✆ (770) 667-8006
- ✉ www.footlocker.com

A thumping hip-hop beat pulsated through Mr. C's sinewy body as he swaggered through the front door of Foot Locker, his head and shoulders moving ever so slightly to the funky groove blaring from the store's sound system. Hey, C stands for *cool*, my man, and Crown Prince of Cheap is definitely *down* with this streetwise establishment. Decked out in purples, blues, and reds, with track lighting and that urban soundtrack permeating the air, Foot Locker is simply where it's at for checking out a hip selection of name-brand athletic and recreational shoes at discount prices.

These cats regularly offer 30 percent to 50 percent off a wide range of brands and styles, and there are plenty of unique deals scattered around the premises. As the C-Man cruised the aisles one evening, he noticed some Nike men's Air Max, regularly priced at $139.99, just $89.99, and Nike men's Air 40-40s, normally priced at $79.99, for just $29.99. He also spotted a clearance table offering sneakers for $19.99 and up. Women's running shoes were priced at up to 50 percent off list prices, with a good selection of Nike and Reebok running shoes for both genders available from $49.99 on up to $115—and those included styles that normally carry list prices up to the $150 mark!

Did Mr. C mention boots? Colorado-brand hiking boots were available in one of those "Buy one and get one free" deals, with one pair discounted from $84.99 to 69.99, and another slashed from $119.99 to $79.99.

And that's not all, man. Foot Locker also carries outdoor-type clothing, also at discount. For example transition jackets normally costing $60 were priced at $29.99, and college T-shirts were tagged at just $9.99.

The same company, of course, runs Lady Foot Locker with stores generally located next door to the original establishment. It offers similar selection and deals, as C-Man found out when the missus interrupted his funkadelic reverie with a persuasive "request" to assist her in shopping there. Well, C's gotta say that the atmosphere on the distaff side was a bit more, uh . . . sedate, with a scene more along the lines of that at The Gap: Think florescent lighting, tasteful Earth-toned décor, and hushed conversation. Here they had a table of boots, sandals, and sneakers that were all priced under $20, as well as Nike running shoes reduced from $89.99 to $59.99. Actra suede boots, normally $59.99, were reduced to a most-groovy $19.99. Athletic socks ("buy one and get one at half off") and other accessories were also available.

Store hours are Monday through Saturday from 10 a.m. to 9 p.m., and Sundays from noon to 6 p.m.

Friedman's Shoes

- 209 Mitchell Street S.W. (men's only), Atlanta; ✆ (404) 524-1311

- 223 Mitchell Street S.W. (women's only), Atlanta; ✆ (404) 523-1134

- ✍ www.largefeet.com

Open since 1929, Friedman's claims the title of Atlanta's first discount shoe store, and is in fact an Atlanta institution, with the photos of professional athletes and other famous customers gracing the walls. The management has always specialized in customer service, along with good prices. Although Mr. C wouldn't put most of their current offerings under the "discount" label, they still offer good values on top-brand footwear, and always have a number of closeout specials that will allow the savvy shopper to strike a great deal.

These days Friedman's stocks high-quality designer and name-brand shoes, mostly in larger sizes: 7½ to 14 for ladies, 7 to 22 for men, and does so in separate stores serving each gender. The inventory is ever changing, so if you see something you really like, grab it; who knows if it'll be there on your next trip?

The men's store carries Bacco Bucci, Marteens, Dunham, Fratelli, Kenneth Cole, Marco, Stacy Adams, Timberland, and many other top brands, and good deals are definitely available. Mr. C found some Paolo de Marco dress shoes for just $99, and they'd normally go for much more. A Fratelli Lizard men's dress shoe was just $79 on closeout, and a Nike Air International athletic shoe could be had for $90, and a Lugz Tie hiking book could be had for a mere $45. A Lugz leather sandal was just $35, while a Hush Puppy loafer was just $45. The store also features a closeout wall where you can pick up four pair for $100.

Ladies will love the dress and casual styles from Mezlan, Vaneli, Palizzio, J. Renee, Paul Melian, Timothy Hitsman, and others, offered at 20 percent to 30 percent off on selected styles. Alligator loafers and pumps from Meslen, usually $625, were priced at $325 the day The Cheapster checked them out. Halston dress shoes were available at 50 percent off. And, the women's closeout wall featured two pair for $70. Imelda Marcos would be in heaven!

Friedman's opens at 9 a.m. Monday through Saturday. The ladies store closes at 5 p.m. on those days; the men's store closes at 5:30 p.m.

Galyan's

- Lenox Courtyard, 3535 Peachtree Road, Atlanta; ✆ (404) 267-0200

- Town Center Commons, 691 Ernest W Barrett Parkway NW, Kennesaw; ✆ (770) 281-0200

- 3333 Buford Drive, Buford; ✆ (678) 482-1200

- ✍ www.galyans.com

This chain carries just about every major brand of sporting equipment, as well as clothing and footwear. See the complete listing under *Sporting Goods*.

The Junkman's Daughter

- 1130 Euclid Avenue N.E., Atlanta; ✆ (404) 577-3188

The Junkman's Daughter is not, as you may have expected, full of trash. The looks here are definitely cool-funky, with flame-painted and velvet-draped walls, and a prodigious sound system.

The clothing here tends toward retro nightclub styles, and they also have footwear: Used platform shoes are priced at $15 and up, silver heels are $7.50, and there's much more along those lines for the enterprising hipster who wants to make a statement with his or her feet!

See the full description under *Clothing—Used: Vintage Clothing*.

Loehmann's

- Executive Park, 2480 Briarcliff Road N.E., Atlanta; ✆ (404) 633-4156

- ✍ www.loehmanns.com

Loehmann's means low prices on fancy women's clothing and shoes, plain and simple. These folks practically invented the designer closeout store years ago in New York, and suave Manhattanites still schlep out to Brooklyn for their famous deals. Heck, everything in the store is priced from 30 percent to 50 percent off standard list prices, and they hold special clearance sales in January and July.

Loehmann's also has great deals on footwear. Funky shoes, boots, and high heels are reduced, like DKNY platform heels (listed at $158, selling for $70), and you'll find plenty of bargains on shoes by big names like Steve Madden, Nine West, Franko Sarto, and others. Other accessories include colognes and jewelry.

See the full description under *Clothing: Women's Wear—General*.

Men's Wearhouse

- 3255 Peachtree Road N.E., Atlanta; ✆ (404) 264-0421

- 2931 Cobb Parkway, Atlanta; ✆ (770) 956-7297

- Northlake Mall, 1000 Northlake Mall, Atlanta; ✆ (770) 908-1125

- Perimeter Expo, 1121 Hammond Drive N.E., Atlanta; ✆ (678) 320-0960

- Southlake Festival, 1510 Southlake Parkway, Morrow; ✆ (770) 960-8490

- Fayette Pavilion, 145 Pavilion Parkway, Fayetteville; ✆ (770) 719-1662

- Landing at Arbor Drive, 9330 The Landing Drive, Douglasville; ✆ (678) 838-3145

- Mall Corners, 2131 Pleasant Hill Road, Duluth; ✆ (770) 623-6060

- Town Center Plaza, 425 Earnest Barrett Parkway, Kennesaw; ✆ (770) 429-8955
- Target Plaza, 6012 North Point Parkway, Alpharetta; ✆ (770) 521-1002
- ✍ www.menswearhouse.com

See the description under *Clothing—New: Men's Wear—General*.

Rack Room

- 1205 Johnson Ferry Road, Marietta; ✆ (770) 977-3223
- 2207 Roswell Road, Marietta; ✆ (770) 971-1273
- 5370 Highway 78, Stone Mountain; ✆ (770) 498-6426
- 2550 Sandy Plains Road, Marietta; ✆ (770) 565-4668
- 120 Pavilion Parkway, Fayetteville; ✆ (770) 716-8320
- ✍ www.rackroomshoes.com

The whole family can find footwear at Rack Room Shoes. From tots to moms and pops, everyone will save big on popular lines of casual and dress shoes, since they sell the major brands routinely at 20 percent to 30 percent off the manufacturer's suggested retail price, and up to 50 percent or more during semiannual sales. Let's start small and work our way up:

On Mr. C's last investigation, kids' boots were 20 percent to 30 percent off, with Sammy high leather boots for girls discounted from $39.99 to only $27.99. Nike sneakers were just $39.99, and cute, multicolored slippers could be picked up for $14.99.

Rack Room's entire stock of women's boots from such brands as Mia, Pesaro, Capezio, and Nine West was also marked at up to 70 percent off the suggested retail price! Madeline black leather boots were on sale for only $29.99 (down from $39.99) and Capezio tall leather boots were slashed from a $90 retail price to only $47.99. Etienne Aigner heels are $58, down from $70, while Upland canvas sneakers, seen for $55 in department stores, are $44.99 here. Men—you don't have to walk to Maine to save big on Rockport walking shoes. Styles retailing for $70 and more sell around $55 here. Dexter shoes are also reduced, to $57 for the normally $67 pair, while Stacy Adams dress shoes, normally $62.99, were on sale for $49.99 And men's Reebok sneakers, retailing for $63, are $53 at the Rack Room.

Rack Room stores are generally open from 10 a.m. to 9 p.m. Monday through Saturday, and from noon to 6 p.m. on Sunday. However, it's always a good idea to call ahead to check the hours for a particular location.

Payless Shoe Source

- 55 Peachtree Street S.W., Atlanta; ✆ (404) 659-5200
- 619 Boulevard N.E., Atlanta; ✆ (404) 872-1599
- 861 Ralph David Abernathy Blvd. S.W., Atlanta; ✆ (404) 753-1225
- 527 Moreland Avenue S.E. Atlanta; ✆ (404) 622-5010
- 1899 Metropolitan Parkway S.W., Atlanta; ✆ (404) 755-4385
- 3024 M L King Jr. S.W., Atlanta; ✆ (404) 696-7779
- 2685 Bankhead Highway N.W., Atlanta; ✆ (404) 794-5277
- 2625 Piedmont Road N.E., Atlanta; ✆ (404) 816-6200
- 1446 Cumberland Mall S.E., Atlanta; ✆ (678) 309-5858

- 2841 Greenbriar Parkway S.W., Atlanta; (404) 349-6919
- 3268 Buford Highway N.E., Atlanta; (404) 634-1825
- 2839 Paces Ferry Road N.W., Atlanta; (770) 436-7121
- 5038 Buford Highway, Chamblee; (770) 452-1300
- 4800 Briarcliff Road N.E., Atlanta; (770) 934-4135
- 5120 Old National Highway, Atlanta; (404) 765-9052
- www.payless.com

Pay less indeed! The prices at this ubiquitous, no-frills chain are super-low, and although the brands aren't world-renowned, the aisles are stacked high with stylish, good-quality footwear. When Mr. C last strolled through these doors, selected styles were being offered at 50 percent off the everyday prices, which already are laughably cheap, even by Mr. C's standards. However, any licensed psychologist will tell you that humor is a good thing . . . a *very* good thing.

So get a load of this: Women's sneakers were priced at $9.99 (ha!) to $15.99; stylish leather boots were $14.99 to $24.99; and C spotted some high-heeled pumps for $9.99 (giggle) and sandals for (choke . . . someone help the Cheapster!) $7. Kids' sneakers were tagged at $9.99 and up, and there was even a wall of children's shoes priced at $3.99 and up.

And what's in store for the guys? How about sneakers priced at $10.99 to $16.99 (titter), or a pair of rugged State Street outdoor hiking boots for $24.99? (Now that's what C calls conservation!)

You definitely don't want to shell out more for your socks than you paid for the shoes, so you might as well get the former here, too. Men's dress socks were priced at three for $10, and you could pick up two six-pair packs of athletic socks for the same price! (snicker!) Women's panty hose was on sale for $1! (lone guffaw!)

Frugally priced accessories, notably leather purses ($6.99) and sunglasses ($3), are also available, so what are you waiting for? Strike up the band and get the heck over there!

Store hours are generally 9:30 a.m. to 6 p.m. Monday through Saturday, except in the malls, where Payless is usually open 10 a.m. to 9 p.m. Monday through Saturday, and noon to 6 p.m. on Sunday.

Outback Bikes

- 1125 Euclid Avenue N.E., Atlanta; (404) 688-4878

Located in Little Five Points, this store sells a superb selection of bikes and biking gear, including shoes, at prices that are definitely down-to-earth. See the complete listing under *Sporting Goods*.

Phidippides

- Amsley Mall, 1544 Piedmont Road N.E., Atlanta; (404) 875-4268
- 220 Sandy Springs Circle, Atlanta; (404) 255-6149

This store is filled with running shoes and related apparel from Nike, Adidas, Sporthill, Hind, New Balance, Asics, and other major brands. See the complete listing under *Sporting Goods*.

S & H Shoes

- Loehmann's Plaza, 2840 Briarcliff Road N.E., Atlanta; (404) 633-7774

It's moved around a bit over the last 15 years, but S & H is one of Atlanta's very first shoe discounters. In fact, the business—with a handful of stores up and down the East Coast—began where all outlet shopping began: Reading, Pennsylvania. And the family that started S & H is still running the stores today.

The stores sell some 80 name brands of women's shoes, all at discounts of 20 percent to 70 percent off retail. Here you'll find nearly every kind of women's shoe in such brands as Life Stride, Unisa, White Mountain, J. Renee, Timothy Hitsman, Caressa, Vaneli, and others—positively priced to sell at prices ranging from $10 to $150. In fact, S&H has over 500 pairs at $29.90 or less, covering the most popular sizes! S & H carries sizes up to 12, and there's always something on sale.

So go ahead, save some big bucks, say . . . on a pair of Victorian-style high-heeled ankle boots, in black suede, reduced from $178 to just $99, or just pick up some basic white canvas sneakers for $15.

S&H also carries a decent selection of handbags and socks in a variety of styles. And some of you shoe addicts may want to join the "Frequent Buyers Club": After you buy any ten pairs of shoes, you get the eleventh pair free—valued at the price of the *most expensive* of the other ten! Hey . . . that's what Mr. C likes to hear!

S & H is open Monday and Friday from 10 a.m. to 8 p.m.; Wednesday and Thursday from 10 a.m. to 9 p.m.; Saturday from 10 a.m. to 6:30 p.m.; and Sunday from 12:30 p.m. to 5:30 p.m.

Shoe Depot Warehouse

- 1708 Defoor Place N.W., Atlanta; (404) 609-9904

Another part of the Chattahoochee outlet trail, Shoe Depot Warehouse offers dress and casual women's shoes in sizes from 6 1/2 to 12. They carry the latest lines from brands like Paul Melian, J. Renee, Coup de' Tat, Pazzo, and Timothy Hitsman and others, and usually offer about 30 percent off of retail on just about every brand!

On the afternoon the missus dragged . . . er, accompanied . . . Mr. C to the store, women's boots were available for $29 to $99. Athletic shoes, including Sketchers and other brands, were priced at $29 to $59, while sandals ranged from a super-cheap (and you know C means that in a *good* way) $9.90 all the way up to $69 for the Hitsman brand.

Alas, Mrs. C gravitated toward the pumps, which, thankfully, were priced at a quite reasonable $19 to $79.

Shoe Depot also has a large "sale wall" area, where all of the very same brands are offered for an additional 40 percent off!

Shoe Depot is open Wednesday from noon to 5 p.m., Thursday through Saturday from 10 a.m. to 6 p.m., and Sunday from 1 p.m. to 5 p.m.

Shoemakers' Warehouse

- 500-A Amsterdam Avenue N.E., Atlanta; (404) 881-9301

- www.shoemakerswarehouse.com

Part of the Amsterdam Walk (formerly known as Midtown Outlets) complex, Shoemakers' Warehouse is one of the city's largest and best-laid-out shoe discounters, (13,000+ square feet), with a big selection of hot fashions for men and women. Here the savvy cheapskate (and you know that Mr. C uses that phrase with utmost respect) can save a serious 30 percent to 60 percent off top designer shoes for men and women!

This is good stuff! Brands include Kenneth Cole, Charles David, Aerosoles, Nine West, G.H. Bass, Steve Madden, Mia, and many others. The Warehouse's owner is a former buyer for Macy's and Rich's, giving her some fantastic insider connections. The stock, in boxes lined up along the floor like low building-block walls, is all first quality. It divides into current season styles from well-known manufacturers, and past-season leftovers priced at a discount of 30 percent to 60 percent off almost every big designer label you could think of. From dressy to casual, athletic to sandals, boots, belts, and handbags, you'll find it here.

There are clearance racks in both the men's and women's sections, with everything cut down to $29.95, as well as a special sizes area with narrow and wide sizes. Every stack of shoes is clearly identified with a sign noting the maker, the list and sale prices, and sizes available. For a no-frills store, Shoemakers' Warehouse is about as civilized as bargain hunting gets.

Here's a bonus: You can save an extra five bucks if you visit the Shoemakers' Warehouse Web site (see above), print out the coupon there, and use it when you spend $50 or more at the store.

Store hours are Fridays and Saturdays from 10 a.m. to 7 p.m., and Sundays from 1 p.m. to 6 p.m.

The Sports Authority

- 3221 Peachtree Road, N.E., Atlanta; ✆ (404) 814-9873
- Akers Mill Square, 2963 Cobb Parkway N.W., Atlanta; ✆ (770) 955-6662
- 3200 Northlake Parkway N.E., Atlanta; ✆ (770) 270-1644
- 6690 Roswell Rd N.E., Sandy Springs; ✆ (678) 560-7299
- 1987 Mount Zion Road, Morrow; ✆ (770) 478-1590
- 50 Powers Ferry Road S.E., Marietta; ✆ (770) 509-5700
- 4235 Stone Mountain Highway, Lilburn; ✆ (770) 979-7020
- 121 Pavilion Pkwy, Fayetteville; ✆ (770) 719-8883
- 3450 Steve Reynolds Boulevard, Duluth; ✆ (770) 418-9354
- 850 Cobb Place Boulevard N.W., Kennesaw; ✆ (770) 426-1444
- 130 Greenwood Industrial Parkway, McDonough; ✆ (770) 898-4444
- 7461 N Point Parkway, Alpharetta; ✆ (770) 518-3303

This national chain is truly jock heaven—a place where you can score just about any kind of sports paraphernalia under the sun (or dome), including all manner of equipment and clothing. The everyday prices here are nothing special, but there's almost always some kind of sale taking place, with specially priced merchandise placed in aisles all around the store.

On the day El Cheap jogged into his nearest location, SA was offering 20 percent to 50 percent off a wide range of its inventory, including footwear. In fact, all of the footwear on the premises was offered as a "buy one and get one at 50 percent off" deal. And the prices were good: Nike Cross Trainers were marked down from $84.99 to $69.99; women's Nike's were offered at $39.99 and up; Nike running shoes were priced from $44.99; and a range of hiking boots (including the Hi-Tec and Timberland brands) were discounted from the $130 range at $70 to $90. The Cheapster pulled out his solar calculator and determined that combining special deal and discounted prices meant that he could grab two pairs of high-end athletic shoes for as low as $30 a pair. Not bad!

See the full description under *Sporting Goods*.

SPORTING GOODS

Mr. Cheap is not a jock, but he has played one in his dreams—especially when he's decked out in his internationally branded sports duds that he bought at discount. (In fact, Mrs. C has taken to calling him "L'il Nike.") Getting super deals on sports equipment and clothing is not difficult around Atlanta. Shopping choices range from mega-chains such as The Sports Authority to used equipment outlets like Play It Again Sports, to scores of specialty shops that dot the retail playing field around these parts. Here El Cheap has listed the big boys, as well as several mom-and-pop nuggets that will offer you good deals on the big brands along with personalized service.

Galyan's

- Lenox Courtyard, 3535 Peachtree Road, Atlanta; (404) 267-0200

- Town Center Commons, 691 Ernest W Barrett Parkway NW, Kennesaw; (770) 281-0200

- 3333 Buford Drive, Buford; (678) 482-1200

- www.galyans.com

Whether you're into running, hiking, skating, rock-climbing, hunting, skiing and snowboarding, camping, bicycling, fishing, or golf—or whether you just want to look like a real outdoors person with some cool duds—the large and lovely Galyan's Trading Company will most likely have what you need, and at competitive prices.

In 1946 Albert and Naomi Galyan opened the first store—a small grocery and hardware outlet—in Indianapolis, Indiana. Now the chain carries just about every major brand of sporting equipment, as well as clothing and footwear, and covers the country from Utah to Virginia, including three locations in greater Atlanta.

Not a discount store per se, Galyan's always has a clearance section where you can get top-name gear made by all the usual suspects, at prices that range from 97 cents on up to thousands of dollars.

If browsing all of the super-cool equipment and clothes isn't exciting enough for you, you may want to take a turn on Galyan's popular rock-climbing wall, or—heck, just get your stuff and head for the great outdoors!

Store hours are Monday through Saturday from 9:30 or 10 a.m. (depending on the location) to 9 p.m., and Sunday from 11 a.m. to 6 p.m.

Golf Discount

- 9451 Highway 5, Douglasville; (770) 577-4202

If the dues at Augusta National were a little less pricey, The Cheapster just might consider thrilling its membership committee with an unsolicited application. And, if they invited him up for a look-see, he would first make a stop at Golf Discount to pick up the latest top-line equipment and accessories. This place is packed with golf clubs. Probably 200 different sets of irons from such major brands as Callaway, Adams, and TaylorMade adorn one of the walls. In fact, they may have the largest selection of golf shoes, gloves, coats, and bags within a 100-mile radius. And there are some good

SHOPPING: SPORTING GOODS

deals here, since the manager always keeps an eye on the competition in order to make sure the shop lives up to its name. You can usually find golf balls and clothing at 20 to 30 percent off, and the last time Mr. C checked out the store they were offering a great selection of drivers at 25 to 30 percent discount from the list prices.

While you're shopping, check out one of the store's three golf simulators. They're a good way to have some fun while getting the feel of the equipment. And, if for some reason you don't actually make it to Augusta, you can at least play those fabled holes virtually.

Golf Discount is open from 10 a.m. to 7 p.m. Monday through Saturday. In season they're also open on Sundays from 1 p.m. to 5 p.m.

Outback Bikes

- 1125 Euclid Avenue N.E., Atlanta; ✆ (404) 688-4878

Located in Little Five Points, this store sells a superb selection of bikes and biking gear at prices that are definitely down-to-earth.

Here you'll find international-brand bikes from such manufacturers as Gary Fisher, K2, Redline, Eastern, Bianchi, Gunner, and Waterford, starting as low as $229 and going on up to $3,300 for the really high-end models.

Mr. C also priced some quality men's and women's bike shoes by Shiamano, Fidi, and Diadora, ranging from $70 and $170. Novelty silkscreen shirts, some with humorous bicyclist scenarios, designed by Louis Gameau, were $20 each, and biking jerseys were going for about $50.

Outback's seasonal sales generally offer 15 percent off bikes and 40 percent off clothing. Be sure to check out their sale racks and discount tables, too. There you'll gen-

> **MR. CHEAP'S PICKS**
>
> ### Sporting Goods
>
> **Galyan's**—Probably Atlanta's premiere sporting goods store. Though not a discount store, you can always find sales here on selected items.
>
> **Play It Again Sports**—New and used gear, all at incredible prices; save even more by trading your old stuff in.
>
> **The Sports Authority**—National mega-store prices on equipment, clothing, and team memorabilia.

erally find lots of athletic shorts and tops, made by Nike and other big brand names, for as little as $10 each. In fact, some stuff is discounted up to 60 percent off. Le Cheap checked out a pair of Vasque hiking boots, originally priced at $200, on sale for just $120.

Outback has a friendly, knowledgeable staff and even has a bulletin board where you can post or peruse ads for used goods, bike events, trip companions, and just about any kind of outdoor activity.

Outback is open Mondays through Friday from 11 a.m. to 7 p.m., Saturdays from 10 a.m. to 6 p.m., and from noon to 5 p.m. Sundays.

Phidippides

- Ansley Mall, 1544 Piedmont Road N.E., Atlanta; ✆ (404) 875-4268

- 220 Sandy Springs Circle, Atlanta; ✆ (404) 255-6149

This moderately sized store, named for the legendary Athenian messenger who ran 260 miles in two days, is huge in the minds of runners around Atlanta.

Filled with running shoes and related apparel from Nike, Adidas, Sporthill, Hind, New Balance, Asics, and other major brands, Phidippides will always give you 10 percent off if you pay by cash or check. Aside from that, they always have sale items, usually at 25 to 45 percent off the regular list price. On the day The Cheapster checked out the store, they had a women's Sugoi vest, normally priced at $60, on sale for $40. A pair of women's Nike running shoes was discounted from $80 to $55, and men's Adidas were reduced from $90 to $55.

The apparel here includes vests, shirts, base layer and outer layer garments, hats, gloves, underwear—anything you need to stay comfortable while putting those feet to the pavement.

An added value here is the service. For example, if you come in to buy some shoes, the staff just might ask to watch you run so that they can best evaluate what kind of shoe will work the best for your style.

Store hours are Monday through Saturday from 10 a.m. to 6 p.m.

Play It Again Sports

- 2050 Lawrenceville Highway, Decatur; (404) 329-2005
- Chastain Square, 4279 Roswell Road, Atlanta; (404) 257-0229
- 4279 Roswell Road N.E., Atlanta; (404) 257-0229
- 2080 Henderson Mill Road N.E., Atlanta; (770) 493-8299
- 1775 Georgia Highway 85, Riverdale; (770) 907-1338
- 1851 Mount Zion Road, Morrow; (678) 422-7454
- 3675 Satellite Boulevard, Duluth; (678) 584-9788
- 10800 Alpharetta Highway, Roswell; (770) 642-4880
- 800 Barrett Parkway, Kennesaw; (770) 429-8636
- 1543 Highway 138 S.E., Conyers; (770) 918-1001
- 1630 Scenic Highway N., Snellville; (770) 338-9444
- 2100 Riverside Parkway, Lawrenceville; (770) 338-9444
- www.playitagainsports.com

From its humble beginnings in Minneapolis, this company has grown into a national chain of independently owned stores—all buying, selling, and trading new and used sports equipment. The merchandise gets swapped around between stores, insuring a large, balanced selection in every store. About 60 percent of the stock is used, and the rest is composed of good deals on new items that have been discontinued.

Revisiting a Play It Again Sports store for this new edition of the book, Mr. C perused a $1,000 Horizon treadmill available for $699, and a used Weider gym machine reduced from $599 retail to $250. A pair of Ultra Wheels in-line skates was $50 off at $150, and a Mizuno baseball mitt, worth over $100, was selling here for $59.

A boy's mountain bike could be picked up for as little as $75 (down from the retail list price of $300), football helmets were reduced from $89.99 new to the $35 to $50 range. In the golf department, a Callaway ERC driver, valued at $500, was selling for $300. Plus, they also carry hockey sticks, basketballs, baseball bats, footballs, shoulder pads for linebackers of all ages, tennis racquets, and lots more. Best of all, you can trade in your old stuff toward anything in the store—even new items.

Since there's a different owner for each store, business hours can vary by location, so call ahead. Generally, store hours are Monday through Friday from about 10 a.m. to 8 p.m., Saturday from 10 a.m. to 7 p.m., and Sunday from noon to 6 p.m.

Pro Golf

- 168 Peachtree E. Shopping Center, Peachtree City; (770) 632-5911

- www.progolf-discount.com

Offering a full range of discounted golf equipment ranging from clubs to cleats, and with salespeople who are clearly players themselves, this is the place to swing for some high-value deals. Pro Golf sells nearly all of its merchandise at 10 to 30 percent off, including equipment from major brands such as Titleist, Champion, Callaway, Adams, TaylorMade, Spalding, and many others. During a recent round of comparative shopping, Mr. Cheap priced an Orlimar bag at 50 percent off its $179 list price. A ladies' EP Pro Adidas shirt was discounted 40 percent, and Mizuno and Adidas shoes were marked down 50 percent. A Unique VFS men's iron, normally priced at $750, could be acquired for as low as $399; Excalibur drivers were marked down from over $400 to $269; and Dunlop Double Titanium balls were marked down from $19 to $14.99.

Store hours are Monday through Friday from 10 a.m. to 7 p.m., Saturday from 9 a.m. to 6 p.m., and Sunday from noon to 5 p.m.

Soccer Alley

- 3265 Roswell Road N.E., Atlanta; (404) 266-0762

- 890 Atlanta Street, Roswell; (770) 992-1010

- 14295 Birmingham Highway, Alpharetta; (678) 366-9111

- 1825 Rockbridge Road, Stone Mountain; (770) 413-6660

- www.socceralley.com

The prices here on sportswear, uniforms, and shoes by big names like Umbro and Puma should be right up your alley. The merchandise is geared to all ages, including sizes for children and young teens.

Bounding through these aisles, Mr. C saw shorts by Umbro, which sell for over $25 in department stores, available for just $18.99; reversible shorts by Lotto for $22.99; and T-shirts imprinted with "World Cup" designs, for just $5 to $10. Adidas, Nike, and Kappa shirts were priced at $18 to $26.

The soccer shoe collection is good, with Diadora turf and indoor shoes selling for $69.99 and 79.99. Hats were on sale for $2.50 each, and you could get two pairs of playing shorts for $3. (In fact there was an entire rack with shorts and shirts priced at $5 to $10.)

Store hours vary according to location but are generally Monday through Friday from 10 a.m. to 6 p.m., Saturday from 9 a.m. to 6 p.m., and Sunday from 1 p.m. to 5 p.m.

Soccer & Sports Warehouse

- 278 Laredo Drive, Decatur; (404) 373-9944

Located across from the Farmers Market, this is the place to find excellent deals on equipment, apparel and shoes for soccer, baseball, basketball, and football. The main business here is selling uniforms to local amateur sports teams, but SSW has plenty of other sports clothing, balls, and equipment that it will sell at discount to anyone who walks in the door.

Probably the best deals here are on soccer balls and equipment. That's because SSW manufacturers and imports its own under the Krown brand name, resulting in wholesale prices for individuals like you and The Cheapster. The management here offers 15 percent off list on everyday retail purchases, and off-season sales push the prices down even further. Shoes from Adidas and Umbro were priced at $25 (cheap!) to $90. Soccer turf shoes started at just $30.

You can also find good deals on trophies, embroidered shirts and jackets, sweat clothing, and more.

Store hours are Monday through Friday from 10 a.m. to 7 p.m., Saturday from 10 a.m. to 5 p.m., and Sunday from 1 p.m. to 4 p.m.

The Sports Authority

- 3221 Peachtree Road N.E., Atlanta; (404) 814-9873
- Akers Mill Square, 2963 Cobb Parkway N.W., Atlanta; (770) 955-6662
- 3200 Northlake Parkway N.E., Atlanta; (770) 270-1644
- 6690 Roswell Road N.E., Sandy Springs; (678) 560-7299
- 1987 Mount Zion Road, Morrow; (770) 478-1590
- 50 Powers Ferry Road S.E., Marietta; (770) 509-5700
- 4235 Stone Mountain Highway, Lilburn; (770) 979-7020
- 121 Pavilion Pkwy, Fayetteville; (770) 719-8883
- 3450 Steve Reynolds Boulevard, Duluth; (770) 418-9354
- 850 Cobb Place Boulevard N.W., Kennesaw; (770) 426-1444
- 130 Greenwood Industrial Parkway, McDonough; (770) 898-4444
- 7461 N Point Parkway, Alpharetta; (770) 518-3303

This national chain is truly jock heaven—a place where you can score just about any kind of sports paraphernalia under the sun (or dome), including all manner of brand-name sports equipment and clothing from makers like Champion, Lamar, Nautilus, MacGregor, Spalding, and literally hundreds of others. The mere sight of this megamarket can bring a tear of joy to the eye of any sports fan.

The everyday prices here are nothing special, but there's almost always some kind of sale taking place, with specially priced merchandise placed in aisles all around the store.

On the day El Cheapedo jogged into his nearest location, SA was offering 20 percent to 50 percent off a wide range of its inventory. Athletic clothing for women, including tanks, tops, and running outfits, were being offered at 20 percent to 30 percent off. Other clothing was discounted up to 50 percent.

More bargains: Basketballs were available for $19.99 to $29.99; Royce Union mountain bikes were priced at 30 percent off; inline skates were available for $49.99 to $199; and sleeping bags with a comfort rating of 32 degrees could be acquired for an unbelievable $14.99! (The Cheapster feels warmer already.)

How about tearing down the slopes on a cutting-edge snowboard? You could save about 50 percent or more by picking up your implement of transportation here. Static brand snowboards were marked down from $200 to just

$79; Karam models were priced at $249, down from $350; and a Viper (normally $200) could have been yours for under $145!

If you'd rather get your exercise indoors, be aware that Sports Authority regularly knocks $100 to $500 or more off the suggested retail prices for treadmills. A Healthrider S150, normally $1,199, was tagged at $799, and a Weslo Cadence 985, listed at around $500, was discounted to $399.

Of course, Sports Authority is also the place to get the official clothing of your favorite pro or college sports team. Baseball caps feature several Braves designs, as well as those for every other major league team in baseball, football, basketball, and hockey; these start at around $16, higher in all-wool. You can also get an official Braves Cooperstown pennant jacket for $79.99. A Falcons jersey was $69.99, with a logo-emblazoned fleece priced at just $29.99

All of the footwear on the premises was offered as a "buy one and get one at 50 percent off" deal. And the prices were good: Nike Cross Trainers were marked down from $84.99 to $69.99; women's Nike's were offered at $39.99 and up; Nike running shoes were priced from $44.99; and a range of hiking boots (including the Hi-Tec and Timberland brands) were discounted from the $130 range at $70 to $90. The Cheapster pulled out his solar calculator and determined that combining special deal and discounted prices meant that he could grab two pairs of high-end athletic shoes for as low as $30 a pair. Not bad!

The stores are open Mondays through Saturdays from 10 a.m. to 9:30 p.m., and Sundays from 11 a.m. to 6 p.m.

STATIONERY, OFFICE, AND ART SUPPLIES

Whether you're a left-brained *artiste* or a nose-to-the grindstone, right-brained business dweeb, you've still gotta find good deals on the tools of your trade. The stores listed here—mostly of the large, multiple department variety—offer large, name-brand selections and plenty of bargains.

Artlite Office Supply

- 1851 Piedmont Road N.E., Atlanta; (404) 875-7271
- www.artlite.net

Since 1964, Artlite has been one of the city's great resources for office supplies, fine-quality mechanical pens, and gifts. Even though it's an independent store, they do enough high-volume sales to offer good discounts—often 20 to 30 percent off retail. You'll save money here whether you're buying a single elegant Cross pen or a whole batch of Bics.

Those classy pens are perhaps Artlite's prime calling card, with so many brands and models to choose from that they get their own room—Mont Blanc, Sheaffer, Waterman. Krone, Parker, Montegrappa, ballpoints, fountain pens, mechanical pencils, in men's and women's styles—they're all here, at discount. A Parker "Sonnet" fountain pen, for instance, with a sterling silver cross-hatch design, was recently seen on sale for

$165, down from its regular price of $215.

Cross pens start as low as $15.95 in chrome (and are usually discounted 20 percent off retail), but if you really want to improve your writing style, perhaps the quickest method would be to get yourself a 14-karat solid gold ballpoint. It retails for $500, but sells here for around $369. And for gift giving, the folks at Artlite can engrave these right in the store.

Other essentials for the exec-on-the-go include Filofax organizers; the handsome leather "Westminster" model is discounted from $195 to $156, and lower-priced brands are here, too.

Meanwhile, Artlite has every kind of old-fashioned office need from paper clips to manila folders. Buying in quantity will keep the boss extra happy (especially if you're self-employed); get a dozen legal pads for $6.60, or a dozen Bic stick pens for 89 cents. "Post-it" pads are as low as 33 cents for the 3"-square size. And you can save about a dollar off the retail price on packages of smart-looking Southworth watermark writing paper.

Artlite also offers personalized stationery and invitations, custom rubber stamps, custom mailing labels, desk sets, and much more. The store is open Monday through Friday from 8 a.m. to 6 p.m., and Saturday from 9 a.m. to 5 p.m.

Binders Art Center

- Lindbergh Plaza, 2581 Piedmont Road N.E., Atlanta; ✆ (404) 233-5423

- ✍ www.bindersart.com

Binders can definitely help keep your budget from falling apart. Good as their rates are, they are always focused on staying competitive, so feel free to challenge them with advertisements from other art stores. These guys also win points for their own sense of organization—there's plenty of room between aisles, and the merchandise is arranged meticulously, unlike some supply stores.

For the serious artist, watercolor easels are available for 20 percent off at around $300. A Nielsen & Bainbridge ready frame, in the 18" × 24" size, was marked down over 40 percent. Forty-sheet packages of Strathmore colored art paper were marked down 25 percent to around $5. Plus, faux marble contact paper, spray mount, and lots more is offered at discount.

For your kids (or the kid in you), a 64-pack of Crayola crayons is $6.82. Rich Art Fresco powder tempera paints, a good nontoxic choice for children's art projects, is just $3.35 a pound (retailing for $5). Binders also sells its own brands, for additional savings on many items.

There are plenty of other creative ways to keep the kiddies busy, like jewelry-making kits and an Origami paper-folding kit by

---

MR. CHEAP'S PICKS

Stationery, Art and Office Supplies

Binders—This store features a great selection of arts and craft supplies, with some of the best deals you'll find anywhere in the area.

Pearl Artist and Craft Supply—A true gem of a shop for all—and they mean all—your art needs.

Office Depot, Office Max, Staples—These office superstores have vast selections of business supplies, furniture, books, and tech gear, with plenty of store sales and manufacturers' rebates.

Altoh, listing at $6, which sells for about $4.50. A cartoon drawing kit, appropriate for older children, teens, and adults, was marked down from $12.95 to $9.

If you want to save a few bucks on supplies for a class, you can get 10 percent knocked off your bill by presenting your class supply list at the store along with a student or teacher I.D., although that discount doesn't apply to items that are already on sale.

Store hours are Monday through Thursday from 9 a.m. to 8 p.m., Friday from 9 a.m. to 6 p.m., Saturday from 10 a.m. to 6 p.m., and Sunday from noon to 6 p.m.

Michael's Arts & Crafts

- 2625 Piedmont Road N.E., Atlanta; (404) 266-8711
- 4073 Lavista Road, Tucker; (770) 939-3774
- 2540 Hargrove Road, Smyrna; (770) 4 33-1700
- 1155 Mount Vernon Highway, Dunwoody; (770) 394-4988
- 1355 East West Connector, Austell; (770) 941-0652
- 1968 Mount Zion Road, Morrow; (770) 477-1178
- 4281 Roswell Road, Marietta; (770) 565-0872
- 9365 The Landing Drive, Douglasville; (770) 947-7004
- 7361 N Point Parkway, Alpharetta; (770) 587-1397
- 2131 Pleasant Hill Road, Duluth; (770) 813-8328
- 425 Barrett Parkway, Kennesaw; (770) 424-2344
- 27 Hudson Plaza, Fayetteville; (770) 461-6300
- 1977 Scenic Highway, Snellville; (770) 979-5667

Michael's is a bright and cheery national arts and crafts chain at which you'll find a seriously fine selection of supplies, posters, frames, books, wedding accessories, and more. Mr. C perused some Creative Edge Gallerywrap canvas starting as low as $10.99; a 12-color set of Reeves Acrylic paints for $6.99, and a huge assortment of brushes, pastels, pencils, paper and board media, and much, much more at competitive prices.

Posters and prints are also sold here, both framed and unframed, at prices as low as $13.99. In the book department, you can shop among a large selection of design topics and how-to tomes covering various art and crafts techniques.

Check the Sunday paper for regular sales at Michael's, usually involving coupons that you can take to the store to get as much as 40 percent off list prices.

Michael's store hours are 9 a.m. to 9 p.m. Monday through Saturday, and 10 a.m. to 7 p.m. on Sunday.

Office Depot

- 151 14th Street N.E., Atlanta; (404) 724-0584
- 2851 Piedmont Road N.E., Atlanta; (404) 261-4111
- 4505 Fulton Industrial Boulevard S.W., Atlanta; (404) 505-9033
- 5064 Memorial Drive, Stone Mountain; (404) 297-4841
- 2126 Henderson Mill Road N.E., Atlanta; (770) 493-6060
- 5300 Peachtree Industrial Boulevard, Chamblee; (770) 452-0187
- 2449 Cobb Parkway S.E., Smyrna; (770) 952-9922

- 5925 Roswell Road N.E., Atlanta; ✆ (404) 257-0123
- 6443 Tara Boulevard, Jonesboro; ✆ (770) 473-1333
- 1155 Mount Vernon Highway, Dunwoody; ✆ (770) 396-8898
- 5495 Jimmy Carter Boulevard, Norcross; ✆ (770) 446-6646
- 6050 Oakbrook Parkway, Norcross; ✆ (770) 734-9219
- 119 Cobb Parkway N., Marietta; ✆ (770) 499-2001
- 4295 Stone Mountain Highway; Lilburn; ✆ (770) 972-7554
- 1580 Holcomb Bridge Road, Roswell; ✆ (770) 642-6886
- 1529 Highway 85 N., Fayetteville; ✆ (770) 460-7305
- 1630 Pleasant Hill Road, Duluth; ✆ (770) 921-8147
- 845 Ernest W Barrett Parkway N.W., Kennesaw; ✆ (770) 422-0763
- 1295 Iris Drive S.E., Conyers; ✆ (770) 860-8993
- 9559 Highway 5, Douglasville; ✆ (770) 942-6969
- 2750 Breckinridge Boulevard, Duluth; ✆ (770) 931-2204
- 1905 Scenic Highway N., Snellville; ✆ (770) 736-3553
- 299 Molly Lane, Woodstock; ✆ (678) 445-7000
- 900 Raco Drive, Lawrenceville; ✆ (770) 995-5280
- 915 Parkside Walk Lane, Lawrenceville; ✆ (678) 442-8342
- ✎ www.officedepot.com

Office Depot, along with Office Max and Staples, fits into that category of retail chains that need no introduction from the likes of Mr. Cheap. After all, they not only cover the American landscape from sea to shining sea (including scores of stores in and around Atlanta), but also have nearly identical business models: They all offer a selection of nearly every conceivable office supply item, including paper, folders, labels, planners and the like, plus office furniture, technology products (computers, printers, fax machines, software, cell phones, etc.), and even books. They also provide copying, printing, and binding services.

All of the office stores regularly offer manufacturers' rebates (usually the mail-in variety) that can save you $30 to $40 a pop, and hundreds of dollars during a typical shopping spree. These stores advertise heavily in the daily and Sunday papers, and that's where you'll learn about their current deals. During one such promotion, Microsoft Money financial software was available at $29.99, which was $30 off the suggested retail price; Smead colored file folders were $9.99 for a pack of 100; an Iris four-drawer storage system was discounted from $29.99 to $19.99; and you could pick up 500 sheets of the house-brand copy paper for just $2.99. A 50-pack of Verbatim CD-R discs was just $14.99 after a $12 mail-in rebate; and Epson black ink printer cartridges were on sale for as little as $27 each.

In the market for a high-backed leather executive chair? You can pick one up at one of these stores for as little as $59.99, and several other models are in the $200 range.

The list of good deals on business-based merchandise goes on and on, and as a guy who as worked out of the old homestead for more than 20 years, Mr. C can assure you that one of these office superstores should be a required stop on any shopping spree.

Store hours at Office Depot are generally Monday though Friday from 7 a.m. to 9 p.m., Saturday from 9 a.m. to 9 p.m., and Sunday from 11 a.m. to 6 p.m. The in-town locations usually keep shorter hours, so call ahead!

Office Max

- 3183 Peachtree Road N.E., Atlanta; (404) 266-2552

- 2963 Cobb Parkway, Atlanta; (770) 859-0130

- 3983 Lavista Road, Tucker; (770) 270-1144

- 1181 Hammond Drive, N.E., Atlanta; (770) 396-8250

- 5600 Buford Highway, N.E., Doraville; (770) 455-7626

- 1344 Mount Zion Road, Morrow; (770) 961-6048

- 1757 East West Connector, Austell; (770) 739-5000

- 1287 Johnson Ferry Road, Marietta; (770) 971-6993

- 4484 Jimmy Lee Smith Parkway, Powder Springs; (770) 943-2600

- 4235 Stone Mountain Highway, Lilburn; (770) 736-3479

- 123 Pavilion Parkway, Fayetteville; (770) 716-8966

- 2900 Chapel Hill Road, Douglasville; (770) 920-7900

- 7531 N Point Parkway, Alpharetta; (770) 998-8800

- 2300 Pleasant Hill Road, Duluth; (770) 476-0823

- 860 Cobb Place Boulevard N.W., Kennesaw; (770) 590-9944

- 645 W Crossville Road, Roswell; (770) 518-7305

- 170 Woodstock Square, Woodstock; (678) 445-1714

- www.officemax.com

Office Max, Office Depot, and Staples are almost identical in their offering and services, which Mr. C has described in the Office Depot section above.

Office Max store hours are typically Monday though Friday from 8 a.m. to 9 p.m., Saturday from 9 a.m. to 9 p.m., and Sunday from 11 a.m. to 6 p.m. The in-town locations usually keep shorter hours, so call ahead!

Pearl Artist and Craft Supply

- 3756 Roswell Road N.E., Atlanta; (404) 233-9400

- www.pearlpaint.com

Pearl is one of the country's leading art supply houses (known in some other locations as Pearl Paint). Mr. C thinks of it as an art supply department store. They seem to sell everything under the sun, all at around a 20 percent discount from manufacturer's list prices. Whether you want to decorate your office, a blank canvas, or a cake, you're sure to find whatever you need for the job.

"Art Markers," by Design usually retail for $3 each but sell for $2 at Pearl. Fifty-sheet newsprint sketchpads by Beinfang, in the 24" × 36" size, are $11.10, while sheets of "marbleized" paper, perfect for gift wrapping or construction, are $3.50 each.

A sixty-piece Rembrandt soft pastel set was recently on sale for $70, half its retail price; you'll also find paints, brushes, airbrush kits, the works.

Finish off your masterpiece with a wooden picture frame, which are priced at $5 and above. An 11" × 14" gold frame with a linen liner, usually priced at around $40 elsewhere, was only $28 here.

Jazz up your walls with decorative stencils from $2.80 and up. A 16.9 ounce jar of Winsor & Newton acrylic paint to use with it is $3.50 and up per tube. Sea sponges, about a dollar off at $1.75 and up, are great to use instead of paintbrushes to give walls a textured look, without the expense of wallpaper.

Getting into crafts? Boxes of tiny Pearl-brand beads, perfect for jewelry making and other projects, are tagged at $3.50 and up.

Pearl also has an extensive collection of art guidebooks and manuals. The comprehensive *Artist Handbook*, full of information about the latest techniques and technologies in the art world, sells here for about 30 percent off its cover price. And then there are the furniture—easels, looms, drafting boards, storage systems, and more. It's all contained in an attractive catalog; the store does an extensive (but not expensive) mail-order business here and around the world.

Pearl is open Monday through Saturday from 10 a.m. to 7 p.m., and Sunday from 1 p.m. to 6 p.m.

Suburban Picture Frames

- 2573 North Decatur Road, Decatur; (404) 373-3544
- www.suburbanframes.com

This interesting shop offers both ready-to-use and custom frames, and also combines two other businesses under the same roof: It's also an art gallery with over three dozen regional and national works of art (including limited edition prints) *and* a trophy retailer offering corporate or sports awards for as little as $3.93 each. (Suburban also offers a CD containing images of 40,000 prints and posters that you can order.)

Frames, from sedate to ornate, are well stocked here and range in price from $15 to $220. A 9" × 12" wooden frame with a liner was $19, and Mr. C also saw an 8" × 10" plain wood frame for $15. (Occasionally, you can pick up miscellaneous specimens for even less.) Suburban also carries oval frames, which aren't that easy to find elsewhere!

Custom framing starts at around $17 for an 11" × 16" model.

The store is open from 9:30 a.m. to 5:30 p.m. Monday through Friday, and from 10 a.m. to 4 p.m. on Saturday.

Staples: The Office Superstore

- 650 Ponce De Leon Ave N.E., Atlanta; (404) 881-0354
- 6650 Roswell Rd N.E., Atlanta; (404) 255-9635
- 1865 Mount Zion Rd, Morrow; (770) 961-0518
- 5370 Highway 7, Stone Mountain; (770) 413-0722
- 2535 Dallas Hwy S.W., Marietta; (678) 354-1415
- 2255 Pleasant Hill Rd, Duluth; (678) 474-4761
- 1125 Woodstock Rd, Roswell; (770) 992-9781
- 945 N Point Pkwy, Alpharetta; (678) 366-0245
- 2059 Scenic Hwy N, Snellville; (678) 344-7141
- 1550 Dogwood Dr S.E., Conyers; (770) 761-3636
- 225 Market Place Blvd, Peachtree City; (770) 486-9767
- www.staples.com

Staples, Office Max, and Office Depot are almost identical in their offering and services, which Mr. C has described in the Office Depot section above.

Staples store hours are typically Monday though Friday from 7 a.m. to 9 p.m., Saturday from 9 a.m. to 8 p.m., and Sunday from noon to 6 p.m.

Tuesday Morning

- 3145 Piedmont Road N.E., Atlanta; ✆ (404) 233-6526
- 4502 Chamblee Dunwoody Road, Dunwoody; ✆ (770) 457-3565
- 901 Montreal Road, Tucker; ✆ (770) 934-3164
- 2790 Cumberland Boulevard S.E., Smyrna; ✆ (770) 435-6678
- 1115 Mount Zion Road, Morrow; ✆ (770) 961-0707
- 736 Johnson Ferry Road, Marietta; ✆ (770) 971-0511
- 6325 Spalding Drive, Norcross; ✆ (770) 447-4692
- 4051 Highway 78, Lilburn; ✆ (770) 978-3573
- 700 Sandy Plains Road, Marietta; ✆ (770) 428-1536
- 1231 Alpharetta Street, Roswell; ✆ (770) 640-8146
- 3500 Satellite Boulevard, Duluth; ✆ (770) 476-0522
- 3600 Dallas Highway N.W., Marietta; ✆ (678) 355-5505
- ✎ www.tuesdaymorning.com

TM offers a 50 to 80 percent "everyday" discount on upscale merchandise found in better department stores. Check out the aisles and aisles of flashy closeout bargains for which Tuesday Morning is so popular. There are also great buys on plain and fancy office supplies. You can find incredible deals on fine-maker pens and pencils, fountain pens, and roller ball pens. They also have lots to see in quality stationery sets; there are generally a good variety of colors and thicknesses. Packages of seasonal greeting cards are also priced right.

Cross writing instruments are usually about half price, while some Sheaffer sets were recently marked down from $35 to a mere $15. Both ladies' and men's styles, sold singly and in sets, tend to be well-stocked; but remember, when this store advertises a special in the paper, you can expect them to sell out fast.

Store hours are Monday, Tuesday, Wednesday, and Friday from 10 a.m. to 7 p.m.; Thursday from 10 a.m. to 8 p.m.; Saturday from 10 a.m. to 6 p.m.; and Sunday from noon to 6 p.m. Got all that?

TOYS AND GAMES

There days, good deals on toys and games are mostly limited to the large toy department stores such as Toys 'R' Us and K-B Toys (which, not coincidentally, are the main entries in this section). However, the savvy cheapster should also check out the offerings at the businesses listed in the "Discount Department Stores" section: Costco, Target, Wal-Mart, and the like, as well as just about any "dollar" store you come across. And, of course, remember that you'll likely find the best deals during post-holiday clearance sales.

K-B Toys

- 1000 Cumberland Mall S.E., Atlanta; ✆ (770) 434-1805
- 4400 Ashford Dunwoody Road N.E., Atlanta; ✆ (770) 396-9776
- 4800 Briarcliff Road N.E., Atlanta; ✆ (770) 938-1224
- 🖱 www.kbtoys.com

When The Cheapster and the missus set out on a grueling toy-search mission for their extended brood of nieces and nephews, they head directly to one of the big toy department stores, which in these parts means either Toys 'R' Us or K-B Toys. With a large selection and competitive prices, it's hard to go wrong at either of these outfits. K-B is generally not quite as large as the 'R' store, but nevertheless has plenty from which to choose.

The last time Mr. C darkened these doors, K-B was offering up to 75 percent off retail on a number of playthings, including Toy Story figures, marked down from $12.99 each to just $4.99 each; a Generation Girl Barbie or friends, regularly $9.99, on sale for $7.99 each; and an Ask Me More Eeyore (ask your kids: they'll know), slashed from $34.99 to a magnificently cheap $9.99! Also on sale were a Tonka "Mighty Backhoe" construction vehicle, discounted from $27.99 to just $14.99! For budding pop stars, you could pick up a Dance Diva home recording studio, regularly $89.99, for just $49.99.

In fact, K-B often has $9.99 sales, where you can pick up Barbie Dolls, $17 board games, and many other items super cheap. Post-season clearance sales and special promotions can save you even more.

The deals on toys go on and on, but that's not all. You can also get good prices on a range of video game systems, software, collectible action figures, sports equipment, dolls, videos and DVDs, kids furniture, models, board games, and more.

With a selection like that, and with K-B's good prices, what's not to like?

K-B's store hours are generally Monday through Saturday from 10 a.m. to 9 p.m., and Sunday from noon to 6 p.m.

Kiddie City

- 4750 Alabama Road N.E., Roswell; ✆ (770) 645-1945

This independent store offers toys, gifts, used clothing for children—mostly new (though some used) and mostly for the younger age ranges. They have a collection of stuffed animals, as well as a good selection of popular TV icons and Beanie Babies. They also sell yo-yos, Legos, toy cars, dart games, laser swords, Teletubbies, Chutes and Ladders, puzzles, and books, as well as gifts such as candles, music boxes, porcelain picture fame sets, and vases

On the day Mr. C checked them out, Kiddie City was holding a 50 percent-off sale, so there were plenty of Cheap-worthy bargains.

Store hours are Monday through Saturday from 10 a.m. to 6 p.m.

Richard's Variety Store

- 2347 Peachtree Road N.E., Atlanta; ✆ (404) 237-1412

All toy hunters should head over to Richard's, where prices are competitive with Toys 'R' Us, and the service is fantastic. Richard's was founded in 1951 by Richard (of course), his brother-in-law Max, and Richard's father, Frank. Now Richard's nephew, Robert, is managing the store. Since its founding, Richard's has been honored by the

Atlanta Constitution's Buyer's Guide for being one of the best stores for hard to find items. It has also been recognized *by Atlanta Magazine* as the "Best Variety Store." Indeed, Richard's boasts over 20,000 items in the store's 8,000 square fee, with 35 percent of that devoted to toys.

Richard's has one of the best selections in Atlanta for toys made by Fisher Price and Hasbro. They have a huge selection of Thomas the Train and Tin Wind Ups toys, as well as games and books. If you're looking for a specific Beanie Baby and any other TV item, you'll probably find it here. They also have novelty toys for adults and party favors. (Richard's prides itself on selling traditional toy items; the last time the Cheapster checked they turned up their noses at computer games.)

Other merchandise available here includes open stock glassware, blue and white porcelain, frames, back-to-school and home office supplies, kitchen gadgets, and the best greeting cards on the planet, with prices that will allow you to walk out of the store with cash still in your wallet, making you feel . . . uh . . . richer.

Richard's will welcome you Monday through Friday from 9 a.m. to 7 p.m., Saturday from 9 a.m. to 6 p.m., and Sunday from 12:30 p.m. to 5:30 p.m.

Toys 'R' US

- 1 Buckhead Loop N.E., Atlanta; (404) 467-8697
- 2842 Whites Mill Road E., Decatur; (404) 243-4333
- 2997 Cobb Parkway Atlanta; (770) 951-8052
- 4033 Lavista Road, Tucker; (770) 938-4321
- 1496 Mount Zion Road, Morrow; (770) 961-1331
- 9365 The Landing Drive, Douglasville; (770) 577-5755
- 132 Pavilion Parkway, Fayetteville; (678) 817-0359
- 2205 Pleasant Hill Road, Duluth; (770) 476-4646
- 501 Roberts Court N.W., Kennesaw; (770) 424-9100
- www.toysrus.com

Mr. Cheap doesn't have to tell Atlanta parents about Toys 'R' Us, and you must know it's hard to beat their prices, which can range anywhere from 10 to 60 percent off list. Whether you're looking for action figures, building sets, dolls, games, puzzles, stuffed animals, educational toys, computer games, and even bikes and sports equipment—really anything you could possibly think of for kids—you will find it all here.

On a recent toy search, Mr. C noticed a G.I. Joe doll by Hasbro and a Barbie Glam Tour Bus, both

---

MR. CHEAP'S PICKS

Toys and Games

K-B Toys—This alternative to the Toys 'R' Us juggernaut offers pretty much the same selection, with mucho bargain opportunities every day of the year.

Richard's Variety Store—Competitive prices, great selection, and super service make this family-owned store a sure-winner.

Tuesday Morning—Tons of toys for girls and boys are bargain priced at TM, whether your child wants dolls or darts.

$19.99. A nifty toy monorail set, normally listed at $119, was marked down to $80, and a Harry Potter "Troll On the Loose" was only $10.99.

Mr. Cheap looked around for his favorite games and found Monopoly: The dot.com Edition for $14.98; a Lord of the Rings Board Game priced at $29.98 (list price $44); and Who Wants to be a Millionaire and Men Are from Mars, Women Are from Venus, both priced at $19.98. (Bring on the party!)

Most Toys 'R' Us locations are open every day from 10 a.m. to 9 p.m.

Tuesday Morning

- 3145 Piedmont Road N.E., Atlanta; ✆ (404) 233-6526
- 4502 Chamblee Dunwoody Road, Dunwoody; ✆ (770) 457-3565
- 901 Montreal Road, Tucker; ✆ (770) 934-3164
- 2790 Cumberland Boulevard S.E., Smyrna; ✆ (770) 435-6678
- 1115 Mount Zion Road, Morrow; ✆ (770) 961-0707
- 736 Johnson Ferry Road, Marietta; ✆ (770) 971-0511
- 6325 Spalding Drive, Norcross; ✆ (770) 447-4692
- 4051 Highway 78, Lilburn; ✆ (770) 978-3573
- 700 Sandy Plains Road, Marietta; ✆ (770) 428-1536
- 1231 Alpharetta Street, Roswell; ✆ (770) 640-8146
- 3500 Satellite Boulevard, Duluth; ✆ (770) 476-0522
- 3600 Dallas Highway N.W., Marietta; ✆ (678) 355-5505
- ✍ www.tuesdaymorning.com

We all know how much better Tuesday mornings are compared to Mondays. TM's bargains will make you feel that much better any day with 50 to 80 percent discounts on everything from rugs to china to cookware to toys to luggage.

Tons of toys for girls and boys are bargain priced at TM, whether your child wants dolls or darts. Famous European collectible dolls, sold elsewhere for $15 to $90 will cost you between $6.99 and $39.99. Barbie's play sets like Light Up Kitchen and a Fun Family Room cost only $9.99. Mr. C saw action figures for $11.99 and that included characters like Batman and Robin and some evildoers. Gund plush stuffed animals are sold here for half their retail price. You'll find interactive games here, too. Galaxy Hunt was selling for $10.99 and Road Relay was $19.99. There are infant and toddler toys, water/swim toys, books, puzzles, building blocks, and educational toys for all ages.

Store hours are Monday, Tuesday, Wednesday and Friday from 10 a.m. to 7 p.m.; Thursday from 10 a.m. to 8 p.m.; Saturday from 10 a.m. to 6 p.m.; and Sunday from noon to 6 p.m. Got all that?

UNUSUAL GIFTS

This is Mr. C's "catch-all" chapter, in which he's put some of the stores that just don't fit anywhere else in the book. Many of the stores below are places to find truly nice gifts, while others fall more into the realm of the fun and decidedly offbeat.

Boomerang

- 1145 Euclid Avenue N.E., Atlanta; ✆ (404) 577-8158

Once you visit Boomerang, you'll definitely want to return again and again (ha ha) to check out their eclectic collection of handmade jewelry and funky decorative items. This is the place to try if you've looked everywhere for a gift and just can't find something that Aunt Betsy would like.

Admittedly, the furniture also sold in the shop is not what you'd call cheap—uniquely hand-painted, hand-carved wooden dressers and tables, for example—but the artsy vases, frames, and accessories are worth a trip.

Mr. C saw a good-sized wall mirror, trimmed with fancy stained glass, for just $12, and a hand-blown colored glass vase for $20. Multicolored glass candlestick holders are $11, and dainty glass perfume bottles with swirled-glass stoppers are $15.

Cloisonné earrings shaped like cats are $14, while a painted oak double picture frame made to hold two 3" × 5" pictures, is only $12. Teach the kids geography by buying plastic placemats with globe designs for just $3.50. And you would be crazy to pass up a real cuckoo clock for just $16, wouldn't you?

Store hours tend to be irregular, so call ahead. The doors are usually open seven days a week from around noon to 5 p.m.

China Cabinet

- Northeast Plaza, 3363 Buford Highway N.E., Atlanta; ✆ (404) 634-8091

For nearly 30 years, designer Judy Appel has been filling her Cabinet with the most beautiful objects she could find—and selling them at well below retail prices. Her business has grown and grown. Judy won't say exactly how she does it, but she discounts only brand-new, top-quality accessories and decorative pieces suitable for every room in your house. In fact, she is the sole Atlanta retailer for many of these items.

The selection here is always changing, with new pieces arriving every day. A William Wayne antique brass sheep, costing $45 in New York, is sold here for $15.99; a Wilton Armetel small chip and dip server that sells elsewhere for $75 is only $49.99; and mouth-blown hand-cut lead Hurricanes are priced at $79, reduced from $125.

Porcelain from Limoges, France, as well as silver from Godinger, Towle, International, and many other top crafters are all represented here. You'll also find decorative items large and small, from hand-painted Italian armoires to silver pate knives. European oil paintings with hardwood frames, lithographs, copper plate engravings, and fine-quality prints were available at 25 to 30 percent savings. Looking for wooden birdcages, Mr. Cheap spotted a small bamboo specimen from the Shanxi province of China, suitable for finch and lovebirds, priced at $22.99. Also from Shanxi were some lovely rural primitive found pieces (1860) such as trays, platters, and chests.

You can also find interesting small gifts, such as a triple-heavy silver tomato server, gift wrapped and ready to go for $4.99. China Cabinet also offers a full design service for your home. By appointment you may consult with Judy and her staff, free of charge.

Store hours are Monday to Friday from 10 a.m. to 6 p.m., and Saturday 10 a.m. to 5 p.m.

Coyote Trading Company

- 419 Moreland Avenue, Atlanta; ✆ (404) 221-1512

This Native-American art shop, right in the heart of Little Five Points, is chock full of beautiful yet relatively inexpensive jewelry. Most pieces are made with sterling silver and turquoise, and some of them are fashioned into intricate beaded patterns.

Mr. C saw triangular-shaped turquoise earrings on hanging sterling posts for $15. One of the more interesting items in the shop is a Navajo ghost bead necklace, which is traditionally used to keep away bad spirits. At just $6, it will certainly keep the creditors away from your door.

You'll find dream catchers, starting at $9 Kachinas at $35, and beautiful Indian pottery. The Cheapster bought a beautiful pottery vase for $45, and when he and the missus go to their next wedding this will make a lovely gift (though he might be tempted to keep it for himself). Navajo sand paintings were priced at $28 to $50, and hand-woven Zapotec tapestry rugs were $120 to $295.

Coyote also sells belt buckles, bolo ties, bracelets, and rings, most of which are quite moderately priced. Incense was two bucks a package, a sage bundle was $8, and Native-American tapes were $10 and CDs $18.

Coyote is open from Monday through Saturday from 11 a.m. to 7:30 p.m., and Sunday 1 p.m. to 7 p.m.

Crystal Blue

- 1168 Euclid Avenue N.E., Atlanta; ✆ (404) 522-4605

Mr. C sees savings in your future if you shop at Crystal Blue, yet another artsy store in Little Five Points. This shop caters to the New Age crowd, featuring crystal balls, incense, candles, figurines, tapes, books, and funky jewelry, mostly sterling or beaded, and wind chimes a plenty.

A whole wall is devoted to incense, and if you want to try a new scent you can buy a small package of 10 sticks for 79 cents or buy a 100-gram box of your favorite scent for $6.50. You can't beat the price of their scented candles—seven-day sticks in glass jars are $3.25 and smaller 2-day candles are only $1.50. If you're looking for a talisman charm necklace, they've got a good selection here, Celtic to Egyptian, priced between $11 and $16. What a deal!

Chunks of amethyst crystals are $3 each, while the always-fun glass prisms are only $5. Make beautiful music with a medium-sized metal wind chime for $17, or bamboo chimes for $15. Mr. Cheap found some exquisite bookends in both natural and colored agate for only $15 a pair.

Store hours are Monday through Saturday from 11 a.m. to 7 p.m., and Sunday from noon to 7 p.m.

If you like these kinds of gifts, Mr. Cheap recommends that you also check out the additional new age shops listed at the end of this section.

Identified Flying Objects

- 1164 Euclid Avenue N.E., Atlanta; ✆ (404) 524-4628

Don't go throwing good money out the window when you're trying to find unique gifts! IFO in Little Five Points is a great place to try when you want something inexpensive for a hard-to-please kid or a space-case adult who's still young at heart.

A Grateful Dead Head, lending a laid-back, pressure-free atmosphere to the shop, appropriately enough, runs IFO. Mr. C found lots of fun stuff, like those way-cool, glow-in-the dark stars that stick to your ceiling. They're just $5 a package—a neat way to get your kids into astronomy! Miniature frisbees, perhaps the original IFO, are just $1 each; a real live boomerang is $12, and you'll spy a lot of kites available in a variety of sizes, colors and patterns. Mr. C saw a 4½-foot delta kite for $16, perfect for a breezy afternoon in Piedmont Park. You must be from Mars if you don't love these prices.

But wait, there's more, including darts and juggling kits, including both pins and balls. Whether you are looking for smooth and slick, suede, hollow nonbouncing, and solid bouncing juggling balls, you find them all here. And naturally, any store owned by a Dead Head, you've got the tie-died shirts, patches, and stickers. IFO has some other nonflying object toys too.

You can zoom in here from Monday through Saturday from 11 a.m. to 6 p.m., and Sunday from noon to 6 p.m.

Junkman's Daughter

- 1141 Euclid Avenue N.E., Atlanta; (404) 222-9514
- www.junkmansdaughter.com

Formerly known as Princess Pamela's Palace, this store is definitely not for older folks—it's loud, campy, and more than a bit irreverent; but, as a gift resource for surly, hard-to-shop-for teenagers, it's a pleasure palace.

Rock concert T-shirts, featuring bands like U2 and 10,000 Maniacs, are $15 to $20, depending on how long ago the tour actually took place. Mr. C saw all sorts of unique action figure dolls such as Pee Wee Herman, Jerry Garcia, Rob Zombie, Marilyn Manson, Eddie from Iron Maiden, and Jesus. They also carry spooky character dolls from the movie *Nightmare Before Christmas,* priced somewhere between $20 and $30.

What else? Big racks of celebrity postcards, from James Dean to Madonna, are fun to flip through, and you'll see lots of books here—from cooking collections, to tattoo tomes, rock star road diaries, and children's stories.

Pop culture is the reigning force in this palace, so you can expect to find lots of paraphernalia from TV shows like *Speed Racer,* the *Brady Bunch,* the *Simpsons,* and whatever else happens to be the trend of the day. These images adorn shirts to clocks to standup placards, all at good, cheap prices.

Store hours are Monday through Friday from 11 a.m. to 7 p.m., Saturday from 11 a.m. to 8 p.m., and Sunday from noon to 7 p.m.

Also Worth Checking out: More New Age Shops

Those of you with crystal and incense leanings should also investigate these New Age shops, where you're always find unusual gifts—metaphysical videos, music, herbs, jewelry, gifts, incense, books, tapes, Tarot cards, candles, and more—in a range of cheap and not-so-cheap prices. Call the individual shops for more information.

Inner Space & Hoot Owl Attic

- 185 Allen Road, N.E., Atlanta; (404) 303-1030

Store hours are Monday through Friday from 10 a.m. to 10 p.m., Saturday from 10 a.m. to 8 p.m., and Sunday from 11 a.m. to 8 p.m.

Phoenix and Dragon

- 5531 Roswell Road, Sandy Springs; (404) 255-5207

Features New Age books. Store hours are Monday through Saturday from 10 a.m. to 8 p.m., and Sunday from noon to 6 p.m.

Sensua Gallery

- 660 Irwin Street N.E., Atlanta; (404) 584-0237
- www.sensuagallery.com

Specializes in minerals, fossils, meteorites, spheres, jewelry, and woodcarvings from around the world, and also holds spiritual workshops. Hours are Tuesday through Saturday from 11 a.m. to 7 p.m.

Entertainment

Atlanta has so much to see and do—and if you do it right, there's so little to spend.

Movies, concerts, theater, museums, nightclubs . . . you name it, there's a way to experience it on the cheap. Nearly everything in this section of the book is free or inexpensive; Mr. C has also found some great deals that knock down the prices of some more expensive entertainment.

To find out the latest information about goings-on, Mr. C suggests you call the Atlanta Arts Hotline at ✆ (404) 853-3278. With a touch-tone phone, you can hear the current offerings from dance troupes, theater companies, art galleries, and much more. And here's why Mr. C really likes this service—it's FREE! Hey, there is no reason why a limited budget should keep anyone from enjoying the arts.

ARTS CENTERS

These centers are great places for a variety of fun and inexpensive activities, whether you're just viewing, or actually participating. Many of the programs and classes are designed for adults, children, or both.

AtlanTIX

- Underground Atlanta Visitor's Center, Corner of Upper Alabama and Pryor Streets, Atlanta; (770) 772-5572

- www.atlantatheatres.org

Walk right up to the window—the only way you can deal with these good folk—and purchase same-day, half-price tickets to greater Atlanta theatre, dance, music, cultural attractions, and more. The window, located in the Atlanta Convention & Visitors Bureau's Underground Atlanta Visitors Center, is open Tuesday from 11 a.m. to 3 p.m., Wednesday through Saturday from 11 a.m. to 6 p.m., and Sunday from noon to 3 p.m.

Join the AtlanTIX e-mail group and receive free notices of what's on sale for half-price the following day; there's a link to the e-mail service on the AtlanTIX Web site.

Callanwolde Fine Arts Center

- 980 Briarcliff Road N.E., Atlanta (404) 872-5338

- www.callanwolde.org

Callanwolde Fine Arts Center, a magnificent Tudor-style mansion, is home to a number of fun and inexpensive activities for young and old alike. Callanwolde offers classes in the performing arts—including theater, dance, and music—as well as in the visual and literary arts like painting, pottery, photography, textiles, and writing. It also boasts a good selection of exercise and fitness classes such as karate and yoga. Classes usually meet once a week for 8 to 10 weeks. The session fee for most classes is $100, which works out to a modest $10 to $12 a class. Course offerings do change from time to time, so call Callanwolde at (404) 872-5338 to request information about the upcoming quarter.

If you and your children are more interested in enjoying other people's work, Callanwolde has something for you, too. Regular programs include poetry readings, held on the second Wednesday of each month at 8:15 p.m., and storytelling on the first or second Friday of each month at 7 p.m. Admission to these events is just $3. Callanwolde also offers regular theater performances and recitals, featuring young students from the performing arts classes, and others from around the country and the world. Mr. C loves their classical and jazz piano concert series. These events cost $12 for members and students, and $15 for nonmembers.

Callanwolde also has an art gallery, which is free and open to the public. Each year, the gallery presents seven solo exhibits by local artists and hosts opening night receptions approximately every six weeks. The gallery is open Monday through Friday from 10 a.m. to 8 p.m., and Saturday from 10 a.m. to 3 p.m.

If you're in town December 1 to December 17, check out Christmas at Callanwolde, which is magnificent.

ENTERTAINMENT: ARTS CENTERS

Admission for that is $10 for adults and $6 for children 4 through 12.

For more information about any of Callanwolde's programs, or to get on their mailing list, call them at the number above or go to the Web site. Administrative offices are open Monday to Friday 9 a.m. to 5 p.m.

Chastain Arts Center

- 135 West Wieuca Road N.W., Atlanta; (404) 252-2927
- www.bcaatlanta.org

Operated by the City of Atlanta Bureau of Cultural Affairs (BCA), Chastain Arts Center was established in 1975 and is the oldest city-operated arts facility in Atlanta, offering more than 100 classes in each eight-week session. Class topics include pottery, ceramics, jewelry making, glasswork, drawing and painting, plus special workshops taught by regionally and nationally renowned artists. There are classes for children too, such as "Classical Mud Pie" for ages 2 to 4 (parents join in on this class)—children explore painting, clay sculpture, papier-mâché, and more. This class runs for ten weeks and costs $99.

Formerly a poorhouse offering custodial care for the indigent elderly, disabled, and unemployable, the site was renovated in the early 1970s and is now in the National Register of Historic Places.

Chastain is generally open Monday through Thursday from 8:30 a.m. to 10 p.m., Friday from 8:30 a.m. to 5 p.m., and Saturday from 10:30 a.m. to 5 p.m.

There is also the **City Gallery at Chastain**, same location, but a different phone number ((404) 257-1804), which displays innovative exhibitions of local, regional, and national contemporary artists that portray social and political themes. The gallery also hosts symposiums and lectures. Gallery hours are Tuesday through Saturday 1 p.m. to 5 p.m.

The Gilbert House

- 2238 Perkerson Road S.W., Atlanta; (404) 766-9049

Listed on the National Register of Historic Places, The Gilbert House, built in 1865, was renovated in 1984 and opened as a cultural arts center. It boasts a small gallery that exhibits works ranging from fine art to historic memorabilia. The facility is also available for meetings, workshops, training, and retreats. Admission to the home, including a tour, is free!

Southeast Arts Center

- 215 Lakewood-Way S.E., Atlanta; (404) 658-6036

Southeast Arts Center offers more than 30 classes per quarter for adults and children in jewelry making, framing, sewing, printmaking, children's multimedia, mask making, pottery, silk-screening, and beginning and advanced photography. Classes meet once a week for eight weeks

---

MR. CHEAP'S PICKS

Arts Centers

Callanwolde Fine Arts Center—This magnificent Tudor-style mansion is home to a number of fun and inexpensive activities for young and old alike.

Chastain Arts Center, The Gilbert House, and Southeast Arts Center—Three city-run arts centers offer arts classes at prices that make Mr. C most happy.

and the cost is $75, and that's less than $10 a class. SAC hours are Monday to Thursday 9 a.m. to 9 p.m., Friday 9 a.m. to 6 p.m., and Saturday 10:30 a.m. to 12:30 p.m.

Thanks to funding from the city and county, all three arts centers above are able to keep their prices low. Thank goodness someone still thinks of the arts as essential, not a luxury. To get more information on these programs, or to get on their mailing lists, call the respective numbers above and visit the Web site at ✍ www.bcaatlanta.org.

Spruill Center for the Arts

- 5339 Chamblee Dunwoody Road, Dunwoody;
  ✆ (770) 394-3447

- ✍ www.spruillarts.org

Here at the Spruill Center for the Arts you won't have to spend a lot of money to pick up a new hobby or have fun learning to express yourself through various art forms. Spruill has classes in the performing, literary, and visual arts. Learn how to write a novel, learn how to redecorate your home. Take a class in belly dancing or directing the stage.

Spruill has classes in painting, photography, landscape design, jewelry making, woodcarving, and much more. Class sessions are usually eight to ten weeks, (although some classes are just one session) and on average cost $150 a session. Some classes can be expensive, like glassblowing, which is $300 for four weeks. But with more than 100 courses to choose from, you shouldn't have much trouble finding something both interesting and affordable.

The Spruill Arts Center also has its own art gallery, mounting four new exhibits every year, some of which are geared for children. For further information call Monday to Saturday 10 a.m. to 5 p.m. or check the Web site.

But wait, we're not through yet! You can also visit the **Spruill Center Gallery and Historic Home**, at 4681 Ashford Dunwoody Road in Dunwoody. There are four exhibits a year at this gallery that feature local works and artists from around the world. The Spruill Historic Home also includes a gift shop. All exhibits are free and open to the public. You can reach the gallery at ✆ (770) 394-4019 between 11 a.m. and 5 p.m. Wednesday to Saturday. The exhibits here are also listed on ✍ www.spruillarts.org.

ART GALLERIES

Most city dwellers know that browsing through art galleries is one of the truly enlightening and (best of all) free cultural activities around. For no more than the price of an espresso at a nearby cafe—you have to do that, right?—you can while away an afternoon or early evening in fine style.

Mr. C doesn't know much about art, but he knows what he likes . . . even if he limits himself to looking rather than buying.

Some galleries may require you to buzz in, only for security purposes. Don't fear that you're being kept out because of an annual income below that of, say, Bill Gates; go on in! After all, the richer people are, the less they have to care about their appearances—for all the gallery owners know, someone in torn jeans could be an eccentric millionaire. Be sure to sneer at one or two paintings, as though you could buy one if you wanted to.

Buckhead, naturally, is the heart of Atlanta's high-priced fine art scene, but there are lots of other interesting galleries all over town. Some are tucked away in unlikely places. With the development of the "Arts Corridor" currently gathering steam in the northwest part of Atlanta, more will certainly follow.

Ann Jacobs Gallery

- 3261 Roswell Road N.E., Atlanta; ✆ (404) 262-3399
- ✍ www.annjacob.com

Since 1968, the Ann Jacobs Gallery has been showing a variety of contemporary artwork and sculptures. Regional, national, and international artists are represented here with a significant amount of Southern artists. Its exhibits include the work of John Boatright, Gary Bukovnik, and Ben Smith.

Located in the heart of Buckhead, Ann Jacobs is open Tuesday through Saturday from 10 a.m. to 5 p.m.

Artists' Atelier

- 800 Miami Circle N.W., Atlanta; ✆ (404) 231-5999

Artists' Atelier is an artists' working gallery. The French word "atelier" means studio, and it derives from the phrase "in process," which seems appropriate not only to these artworks but to the very place itself. As you wander around through the studios and the gallery area, you'll see as many as 21 artists at work on watercolors, oil and acrylic paintings, sculptures, photography, and collage. You may purchase art at direct-from-the-artists' prices, and that will save you money.

Meanwhile, looks are free. You can easily spend a delightful hour or two browsing through the studios and perhaps chatting with the artists. The art on the gallery wall changes every two months, and about three times a year there are gallery exhibit openings (check the local papers for announcements). So come and rub elbows with Atlanta's art crowd.

The Artists' Atelier is open weekdays from 10 a.m. to 5 p.m., and on Saturday from noon to 4 p.m.

Atlanta Contemporary Art Center (The Contemporary)

- 535 Means Street N.W., Atlanta; ✆ (404) 688-1970
- ✍ www.thecontemporary.org

Celebrating its 30th anniversary in 2003, The Contemporary (formerly Nexus) began as a small but dedicated group of photography artists who opened a small storefront gallery in Virginia-Highland. Three decades and two locations later, they have become one of Atlanta's leading forces for cutting-edge art in all media. Their newer, larger home presents not only major exhibitions of photography, painting, and sculpture, but also live music, performance art, video, and all kinds of classes for adults and kids. Next door, the award-winning Nexus Press publishes books of both national and international artists from every continent.

The gallery itself, a former body shop (the words "Truck Repair" can still be seen over the door) has been gloriously renovated with skylights, glass brick windows, and interiors of white walls and exposed brick. It's large enough to display artworks created on a grand scale. The Contemporary provides studio space for twelve artists and many of them open their doors to visitors. A sign inside the gallery directs you to the particular studios, which you can visit on any given day.

When you stop in, you can check the bulletin boards and pick up flyers and newsletters about all the different happenings at The Contemporary. They are many and varied indeed, and always exciting.

Gallery hours are Tuesday through Saturday from 11 a.m. to 5 p.m., closed Sunday and Monday. Admission is free to members, $3 for nonmembers, and $1 for students, seniors, and children.

Atlanta International Museum of Art and Design

- 285 Peachtree Center Avenue N.E., Lobby and Garden Levels, Atlanta; (404) 688-2467

- www.atlantainternational museum.org

Hidden inside the Marriott Marquis Hotel, up the escalators of Tower Two, you'll find this elegant and serious gallery focusing on arts and crafts from around the world. An affiliate of the Washington-based Smithsonian Institution, its mission is to promote better understanding among different peoples by displaying their art. But in a Marriott? Only the steady stream of international tourists and conventioneers staying at this and other glitzy downtown hotels makes the location seem appropriate.

Among the recent exhibits has been *Treasures from the Smithsonian, a First Look,* featuring terra-cotta sculptures of the Tamil Nadu artists from southern India; and *At Home with Our Neighbors to the North,* including two artists, Danielle Carignan and Andre St-Cyr, who have designed expertly crafted, unique, and imaginative furniture sculptures.

The museum is open Monday through Friday from 11 a.m. to 5 p.m. Admission is free for members and children under age 10; otherwise it is $3, except on Wednesday, when admission is free for everyone.

Atlanta Photography Gallery

- 660 9th Street N.W., Atlanta (404) 877-1144

- www.atlantaphotography group.org

The Atlanta Photography Group (APG) promotes the photographic arts through education, exhibitions, programming, and support groups. At its gallery, you can see the work of its members, many of whom are winners of prizes and grants from around the country and the world.

Serious photographers can submit their work to be considered for any of the eight exhibits a year (entry fee per exhibit is $25 for members and $50 nonmembers). Some exhibits are limited to Georgia photographers or regional artists of the Southeast.

The APG gallery is open Wednesday through Saturday from noon to 4 p.m. and of course, admission if free. Exhibits and monthly meetings are listed on their Web site.

Fay Gold Gallery

- 764 Miami Circle, Atlanta (404) 233-3843

- www.faygoldgallery.com

Described by one of Mr. C's experts as "the blue-chip gallery in town," Fay Gold is indeed a place to see some of the finest quality exhibitions by contemporary and other 20th-century artists, sculptors, and photographers. If you're looking to buy, it ain't gonna be cheap. If you're just plain looking, it won't cost you a cent.

There are several rooms in this large gallery, offering two or three different exhibits on any given visit. The Fay Gold Gallery represents the estates of Robert Mapplethorpe, Louise Nevelson, and Milton Avery, just to mention a few. Recently Mr. C got lucky and caught a Picasso exhibit.

The gallery offers two solo exhibits a month and is open Tuesday through Saturday from 9:30 a.m. to 5:30 p.m.

Hammonds House

- 503 Peeples Street, S.W., Atlanta; (404) 752-8730
- www.hammondshouse.org

Somewhere around 1984, the late Dr. Otis Thrash Hammonds, an African-American physician and collector of art, purchased a vacant house on a quiet street in the West End. Believed to have been built around 1857, rundown and somewhat "Addams Family" in style, it was often referred to as "the ghost house." Hammonds set about restoring it to its former beauty, but, alas, he did not live to enjoy it; it was later acquired by the Fulton County Arts Council and turned into a gallery specializing in the works of African-American and Haitian artists.

Today, Hammonds House is not only one of the city's leading galleries, but it sits in a part of town that is poised for an urban renaissance. The West End, always a proud and historic neighborhood, is fast becoming recognized as one of Atlanta's most interesting, with more homes being renovated in all their Queen Anne glory, new restaurants, and museums like Hammonds.

Inside, you'll find two floors of handsome rooms showing special exhibits and items from the permanent collection of some 250 works. The sun porch at the back features Haitian artists. And do take a moment to examine the wonderful touches put into the restoration of the house itself—one of the oldest in the city—such as the hand-tooled craftwork of the arches over the doors.

Hammonds House presents four to six national and local exhibitions every year, and also provides resource and educational programs, such as hosting panel discussions with prominent artists and educators. These are free and open to the public. When you visit, ask them about the TransAfrican Festival and Exhibition, which is hosted every two years. You won't want to miss it if you're in town.

All this for a $2 donation for adults, or $1 for seniors and students. Hammonds House is open Tuesdays through Fridays from 10

MR. CHEAP'S PICKS

Art Galleries

Artists' Atelier—Artists at work . . . with their art for sale. Cut out the middleman for the best prices.

Atlanta Contemporary Art Center—The unofficial leader of Atlanta's modern art scene.

The Mexican Consulate—Another amazing gallery in an unexpected location.

a.m. to 6 p.m., Saturdays and Sundays from 1 p.m. to 5 p.m., and closed on Mondays.

High Museum of Art—Folk Art and Photography Galleries

- 133 Peachtree Street, N.E. (in the Georgia-Pacific Center; Gallery entrance on John Wesley Dobbs Avenue), Atlanta; ✆ (404) 577-6940 (information line)

Located at the rear of the Georgia-Pacific building at 133 Peachtree Street, the High Museum of Art's downtown galleries are solely dedicated to folk art and photography

As always, they are free and open to everyone. It's all gorgeous, both the exhibits and the rooms themselves—two long, narrow levels, outfitted with the requisite track lighting and natural wood floors. The entire place is fully wheelchair-accessible, as you can move between the upper and lower levels by elevator or by long, gradually inclined ramps.

Exhibitions featured within the past few years include "art brut" from the end of the 19th century to date, featuring some prominent artists, the likes of Pablo Picasso, Paul Klee, and Max Ernst, as well as some not so prominent art by inspired plumbers, housekeepers, religious visionaries, and psychiatric patients.

Another photography exhibition by the Nature Conservancy caught Mr. Cheap's eye. In this one, internationally known photographers were commissioned to photograph sites designated as the "Last Great Places," throughout the Americas and the Pacific Rim. And, there is always a folk art exhibition such as *Treasures of the Smithsonian American Art Museum*.

This is a comfortable, quiet oasis in the center of the bustling city. Gallery hours are Monday through Saturday from 10 a.m. to 5 p.m., and the first Thursday of every month from 10 a.m. to 8 p.m. The galleries are closed Sunday. Admission to the Folk Art and Photography Galleries is always free

The Georgia-Pacific branch also runs the High Noon series of films, lectures, and concerts on the second Tuesday of the month, also starting at 12:15 p.m. Their innovative program, Art After Work, is used for some exhibitions; call for details.

Tours are scheduled for 12:15 p.m. on the first and third Wednesdays of the month from October through April. From May through September the tour is given on the third Wednesday of the month at the same time. Reservations aren't necessary. Call ahead at least three weeks to arrange free guided tours at other times.

FIRST THURSDAYS
The Folk Art and Photography Galleries, along with 17 other galleries, participates in First Thursdays, the Downtown Atlanta Arts Walk, held each month from 5 p.m. to 8 p.m., with free food, drinks, and special events During the event each gallery provides maps to help you find your way around to other venues.

Jackson Fine Art

- 3115 East Shadowlawn Avenue; ✆ (404) 233-3739

- ✍ www.jacksonfineart.com

Located in Buckhead, Jackson Fine Art is dedicated exclusively to the art of photography, specializing in vintage and contemporary work. Considered a leading international gallery in the field of fine art photography, *Atlanta Magazine* has named it the "Best in Atlanta" over a number of consecutive years.

Here you'll find works here by emerging artists, mixed in with some of the great masters in this field, including Ansel Adams, Irving Penn, and Robert Doisneau, and more than 100 contemporary artists, such as Sally Mann and Michael Kenna.

Jackson Fine Art is open Tuesday through Saturday from 10 a.m. to 5 p.m.

King Plow Arts Center

- 887 West Marietta Street N.W., Atlanta; (404) 885-9933

- www.kingplow.com

The King Plow Arts Center, one of the premier arts centers in the city, is part of the "art corridor' being developed in the industrial area just west of Midtown. Originally a farm equipment manufacturing plant, it's composed of long, two-story brick warehouses built at the turn of the century. They've been handsomely converted into a complex inhabited by more than 65 fine tenants—artists' studios that include photographers, sculptors, writers, painters, metal smiths, printmakers, galleries, violin makers, space designed for the performing arts, and restaurants. It includes the Actor's Express theater company, as well as the Food Studio restaurant. You can wander around here, indoors and outside, enjoying the classy renovation completed in 1995. It's filled with neat little touches, like a tiny landscaped stream flowing along the narrow space between two buildings.

The Mexican Consulate

- 2600 Apple Valley Road, Atlanta; (404) 264-1240

It isn't uncommon for consulates—in Atlanta and in other cities—to display art from their native countries. The Mexican Consulate in Buckhead is unique, though, in that they have a permanent art gallery space, which stages exhibitions on a regular basis (though not all of the time). What they put into that space is truly amazing. That you can see it all for free is even more so.

Here, you can learn about Mexican art and culture and have fun at the same time. For example, one show examined the idea of fun; called *Mexican Toys,* it included over 500 items from the collection of renowned storyteller Eduardo Robles Boza, including dolls, animals, miniatures, and paper toys from many different regions of the country.

Not everything that is shown in this gallery comes from Mexico; some exhibits focus on related subjects, with works by artists from other nationalities. A recent exhibit, *Borders,* featured the work of American artist David Zeiger. His photos detailed fences and border points between the United States and Mexico.

The Mexican Consulate is involved in other artistic and cultural events as well. Give them a call for more info, or stop in to visit. You can also join the center and receive regular, advanced notification of its many art exhibits, amateur sports events, concerts, seminars, social gatherings, children's programs, and Spanish classes (though attending any of those is still free). Membership in the center is $25 a year for individuals, $30 for families, and $15 for students and seniors.

The exhibits change quarterly, so there's something to see every few months. One note: You will have to be buzzed in. Don't worry; it's just a security measure, standard at any such building.

During an exhibition, gallery hours are usually Monday through Friday from 9 a.m. to 5 p.m.

Modern Primitive Gallery

- 1393 North Highland Avenue N.E., Atlanta; ✆ (404) 892-0556

- ⌘ www.modernprimitive.com

The Modern Primitive Gallery specializes in folk art, self-taught, and something they call "outsider" art. This can best be described as work by artists removed from mainstream societal influences, such as people living in prison or suffering from mental illness. In addition to these works, MPG also features the works of trained artists.

Modern Primitive has shown work by a number of established artists, including Howard Finster, known in the avant-garde world for creating album covers for the rock group the Talking Heads. Other recent exhibits have included works by Jimmy Lee Sudduth and R.A. Miller. Exhibits change every month or so; there's often something new to see.

Modern Primitive Gallery is open Tuesday, Wednesday, Thursday, and Sunday from noon to 6 p.m., and Friday and Saturday noon to 9 p.m.

Trinity Arts Group

- 315 East Paces Ferry Road N.E. Atlanta; ✆ (404) 237-0370

Trinity Arts Group was founded over 20 years ago but moved to Buckhead in 1992. Its simple, unassuming two-story building, with a gray stucco exterior, could just as easily house a clothing store or medical office, but inside there are several large, comfortable galleries to wander through. The street level is for main exhibitions, which can feature artists and sculptors from Atlanta and around the world. There are six to eight main exhibitions a year, and each usually runs six weeks.

Occasionally the gallery displays masterworks from previous centuries, but the focus is mostly contemporary art, including creations by David Fraley and William Mize. Some of the recent exhibitions included Tuan, a Vietnamese sculptor; photographer Bob Carey, from Arizona; and Cheryl Warrick, a painter from Boston; as well as an exhibition of the late Frederick Hart, a sculptor originally from Decatur.

The upstairs gallery is outfitted with couches and chairs for a relaxed atmosphere. TAG is open from 10 a.m. to 6 p.m. Tuesday through Saturday.

TULA Art Centre

- 75 Bennett Street N.W., Atlanta; ✆ (404) 351-3551

- ⌘ www.tulaart.com

This fascinating, hidden jewel is actually several art galleries and studios under one roof. Located on a small street (just barely a street) behind the Mick's on Peachtree Street as you approach Buckhead, the TULA complex is a place where you can while away an hour or two exploring the very latest streams in the art world. This makes a delightful alternative to the same couple of hours shopping at the plaza next door along Peachtree—and far less expensive. Unless you buy one of the paintings, of course.

Wander around through galleries on two floors; the building is open at the center, with a handsome atrium. It's an art lover's heaven to look up from the lower level and be completely surrounded by galleries. There are several working studios here too; at any given time, artists may be "home" with the doors open, and you'll be welcome to drop in to chat and see their works in progress.

Among the several established galleries here are **Opus One Gallery** (✆ (404) 352-9727; ⌲ www.opusonegallery.com), featuring contemporary paintings, stained glass studio, and sculpture work of more than forty national and international artists; **Jules Jewels** (✆ (404) 355-8275; ⌲ www.julesjewels.com), where world-renown pop artist, Jules, displays her unique designs that have been featured in episodes of the television show *Friends;* **Momus Gallery** (✆ (404) 355-4180; ⌲ www.momusgallery.com) a contemporary art gallery specializing in photography and works on canvas; and **Lowe The Gallery** (✆ (404) 352-8114; ⌲ www.lowegallery.com), which alerts you to its importance simply by moving "the" into the middle of its name.

Most of these galleries are open Tuesday through Saturday only; weekday hours tend to be 11 a.m. to 5 p.m., while Saturdays begin around noon. Before you reach TULA, by the way, there is a nice cluster of antique shops that you can add to your outing.

CHILDREN'S ACTIVITIES

See also the "Museums" and "Outdoors" sections for listings of other activities suitable for children and families.

ABRACADABRA! Children's Theatre

- Suburban Plaza, 2597 North Decatur Road, Decatur; ✆ (404) 897-1802
- ⌲ www.onstageatlanta.com

ABRACADABRA!, the children's theater side of Onstage Atlanta, presents five plays a year for kids ages 3 and up. Four out of the five plays are musicals. ACT's repertoire includes classics like *Winnie the Pooh, Charlotte's Web, The Littlest Angel,* and *Aesop's Fables.* The plays are interactive, so that the kids get to participate and be in the shows. Shows run for four weeks, although a more recent production of C. S. Lewis's *The Lion, the Witch and the Wardrobe* was so successful it was repeated in the same year. (For those of you who are familiar with this play, children are invited to come on stage and be members of "the stone garden," and when they come back to life, they can pretend to be anything their little hearts desire . . .)

Some of the children's plays are original creations of Scott Rouseau, ACT's artistic director. He's written a country-western version of Cinderella, called "Cinderellie-Mae," and a rock and roll adaptation of *The Legend of Sleepy Hollow,* for the Halloween season. Another one of Scott's originals is the *Drippy Oozing Monster Thingy from Out of Space* (now that's a mouthful!), featuring lots of puppetry and special effects. In fact, in one scene hundreds of frogs fall into the audience from all directions—don't tell the kids, it's much more fun if they're surprised. (Maybe Mr. Cheap shouldn't have told the adults.)

During performance runs, plays are presented every Saturday at 10:30 a.m. and 1:30 p.m., and on

Sunday at 1:30 p.m. Tickets for children and adults are only $7. For adult fare, see the listing for Onstage Atlanta in the *Theater* section.

Atlanta-Fulton Public Library

- One Margaret Mitchell Square, N.W., Atlanta; ✆ (404) 730-1700

- And many other branches

- ✍ www.af.public.lib.ga.us

All 33 branches of the Atlanta-Fulton Public Library boast activities for children to enjoy. Many branches host story hours at regularly scheduled times each week. The Perry Homes branch has a program for toddlers, "Never Too Early to Start Reading," held every Monday, and children ages 3 to 5 can enjoy "Fun Time for Preschoolers" twice a week. The Cleveland Avenue branch once presented the "Magic of African-American History," where the storyteller was a magician.

> ### MR. CHEAP'S PICKS
>
> #### Children's Activities
>
> **Atlanta-Fulton Public Library**—With free activities that are both fun and educational, the library is a great place for kids and adults alike.
>
> **The Center for Puppetry Arts**—Fun museum exhibits and exciting performances, all rolled into one place.
>
> **The Wren's Nest**—The folks at Wren's Nest present storytellers who bring the Uncle Remus stories to life, and there are special storytelling sessions in spring and summer,

Some of the branches, such as the Central Library and South Fulton branch, sponsor craft programs for children ages six to twelve, held after school, evenings, and Saturdays.

The library is also a great place to see films for free. There are regular lineups of after-school films, back-to-back school films, and special seasonal festivals. They also have the occasional film series for grown-ups, as well as series for senior citizens.

While this may not fall under the heading of "fun," another valuable program offered at the library is "Homework Help." At the Central Library there are "homework assistants" ages 13 to 19 who are available in the afternoons to help teens in various subjects, free of charge.

Library hours and programs vary from branch to branch. Some programs require advance registration. To get more info and a calendar of upcoming events, call the central branch in Margaret Mitchell Square.

The Center for Puppetry Arts

- 1404 Spring Street N.W., Atlanta; ✆ (404) 873-3391

- ✍ www.puppet.org

There are two kinds of ways to entertain your kids here. The Museum at the Center for Puppetry Arts is home to over 350 puppets from around the world. Here, you'll see some of the most famous puppets of all time, from Punch and Judy to Jim Henson's Muppets. You'll also be introduced to less well-known examples, such as ritualistic African figures. The museum presents special exhibits, such as this year's *Winner's Circle*, which features the original Cookie Monster. And don't miss the hands-on-

ENTERTAINMENT: CHILDREN'S ACTIVITIES

exhibits that give your kids (or you) the chance to be a puppeteer.

But then, what would a place like this be without actual puppet shows? The Center's performances use a wide variety of puppetry styles and some live actors to entertain, dazzle, and delight. Recent performances included *Winnie the Pooh* and *The Velveteen Rabbit.* The CPA also offers hands-on workshops for children, such as the always popular "Create a Puppet Workshop." At the end of this class, kids ages 5 and up will have designed and made a puppet that they can take home. Give them a call regarding their special workshops for preschool children.

Tickets cost $10 and this includes the performance, Create-A-Puppet Workshop, and museum admission. Admission to the museum is just $5 when purchased individually and tykes 2 and under are free! Shows and workshops are offered Tuesday through Sunday. Times vary so give them a call, and reservations are recommended.

One last thing, ask these folks about their birthday party packages. Although these packages might not be cheap, the fun may be worth it.

The Center for Puppetry Arts is open Tuesday through Saturday from 9 a.m. to 5 p.m., and Sunday from 11 a.m. to 5 p.m.

Hobbit Hall Children's Bookstore

- 120 Bulloch Avenue, Roswell; (770) 587-0907

- www.hobbithall.com

The newsletter from this children's bookstore announces "Reading is a good Hobbit." And they've also figured out that it is a hobbit—er, habit—that is best cultivated early. Every Monday, Tuesday, Wednesday, and Saturday at 10 a.m., they present a free storytelling time for preschoolers. These hours change in summer, so call ahead.

For slightly older kids who are in school during the week, the store has free programs on Saturdays at 10 a.m. These are mostly author readings and signings, and have included Christopher Paul Curtis, author of *Watson Go To Birmingham* and *Bud, Not Buddy*; and David Wisniewski, author of *The Secret Knowledge of Grown-Ups.*

Hobbit Hall will also host birthday parties, and schools can bring in classes for story hours. Call them for more information. Located in the historic district of Roswell, within walking distance of former president Jimmy Carter's Roswell White House, store hours are Monday to Saturday 10 a.m. to 6 p.m.

Stage Door Players

- North DeKalb Cultural Center, 5339 Chamblee Dunwoody Road. Dunwoody; (770) 396-1726

- www.mindspring.com/ ~stagedoorplayers

Located about a block south of Mount Vernon Road and Chamblee Dunwoody Road in the North Dekalb Cultural Arts Center, Stage Door Players showcases the talents of up-and-coming local actors, directors, and designers. It produces a variety of plays and musicals that delight and inspire young and old alike, and encourages members of the community to participate both on stage and behind the scenes. Of particular note is Stage Door's Young Actor's Ensemble, through which budding young thespians can get some quality, professionally directed experience in the dramatic arts.

Each show has a four- to five-week run and performances are on the weekends: Friday and Saturday evenings at 8 p.m., and Sunday at 2:30 p.m. Ticket prices are $18 for adults, $16 dollars for students, and $6 for kids under 12, so you and the little ones can enjoy occasional kid-centric shows such as *Oliver*, *A Midsummer Night's Dream*, *The Just So Stories*, *Robin Hood*, and *The Red Rose*. These and others are sure to amuse small (and not-so-small) imaginations.

Give Stage Door a call to find out the current schedule.

The Wren's Nest

- 1050 Ralph D. Abernathy Boulevard S.W., Atlanta; (404) 753-7735

- www.accessatlanta.com/community/groups/wrensnest

The Wren's Nest is the historic home of Joel Chandler Harris, author of *The Uncle Remus Tales*. This beautiful Victorian home has been lovingly restored to look exactly as it did at the turn of the century. A tour of the house, complete with original Harris family furnishings, books, photographs, and memorabilia, costs $7 for adults, $4 for children 12 and under, and $6 for seniors and teens. Children under age 2 are free, and fees are reduced for groups of 25 or more.

Every Saturday at 2 p.m., the folks at Wren's Nest present storytellers who bring Br'er Rabbit stories to life, and there are special storytelling sessions in spring and summer, usually once a day at 1 p.m. (Call for details, and note that if you tour with a group of 25 or more, you'll get a discount and your own storyteller.) Tours for groups commence every hour on the half hour, with the last one beginning at 1:30 p.m.

In addition, Wren House holds a number of special events throughout the year, such as the Christmas celebration, which is always held on the second Sunday of December. This event (which also commemorates Harris's birthday) includes storytelling, choir singing, and a chance to see the home all decked out in authentic Victorian Christmas style.

Visiting hours are Tuesday through Saturday from 10 a.m. to 2:30 p.m. Walk-ins are welcome on Tuesdays, Thursdays, and Saturdays.

COLLEGE PERFORMING ARTS

The many college campuses of the Atlanta area offer a wealth of music, dance, theater, and films that don't require much personal wealth to attend (unlike the colleges themselves). Many events are free to students, of course (don't forget your ID!), but most are also open to the general public, also for free or for a very small charge. If you want to put some culture into your life on a regular basis, this is a great way to do it.

Agnes Scott College

- 141 East College Avenue, Atlanta/Decatur; (404) 471-6000; 800-868-8602

- www.agnesscott.edu

Scott College has a number of dance, theater, and music events going on each month, most of which are free or cost just a few dollars. Some of the events that have been offered for no charge include chamber music recitals, concerts by Joyful Noise Gospel Choir and the Collegiate Choral, and regular performances by the Agnes Scott College Community Orchestra. Concerts featuring the Agnes Scott College Dance Company are also free.

The school has quite a strong local reputation for the quality of its theater productions. Many of these events charge no more than a few dollars, like the recent presentation by the Blackfriars theater group of *The Vagina Monologues*, with tickets just $2 for students and $7 for the general public.

Guest performers usually bring higher ticket prices, though these are still quite reasonable.

Recent performances included a chamber music theater performance, *Tres Vidas*, celebrating the life of three Latin American women; the Kronos Quartet, "Bernstein on Broadway," and the Shapiro and Smith Dance Company. Tickets for these performances are only $10 for students and $15 general admission.

Clayton College and State University

- Spivey Hall, 5900 North Lee Street, Morrow; ℘ (770) 961-3683

- ✍ www.spiveyhall.org

Clayton State College's Spivey Hall is renowned for the wonderful acoustics of its auditorium, and the school's calendar is full of world-class musical events. Of course, such treats do not always come cheaply; some of their concerts are quite expensive. But there are plenty of opportunities to enjoy great music in a great hall and not spend a fortune.

First of all, full-time students from any school get half-price on all tickets at all times with ID. For the rest of you, Spivey presents many concerts at reasonable ticket prices. While it may cost $25 a pop to see pianist Lang Lang or jazz singer Jane Monheit, you can also hear the Atlanta Singers, an a cappella choral group, for $15. Other recent concerts in this price range have included the Morehouse College Glee Club and the Atlanta Sacred Chorale. Spivey Hall has its very own children's choir that performs concerts at Christmas time (tickets are $15) and in the spring (tickets $10).

Spivey Hall is also the place to be for a number of free concerts during the year. Faculty and students from the CSC music department present recitals throughout the school year. These are always free and open to the public. Over the course of the year, 20,000 children from all over Atlanta attend performances by classical and jazz musicians, and these are priced on the number of students attending. It's practically free when you average the price per student.

To get more information about the music department concerts, give them a call.

Emory University/Schwartz Center for Performing Arts

- Box Office, Mary Gray Munroe Theater, Dobbs University Center, 605 Asbury Circle, Atlanta; ℘ (404) 727-5050

- Box Office, Burlington Road Building, 1804 North Decatur Road, Atlanta; ℘ (404) 727-5050

- Marvin Schwartz Center for Performing Arts, 7800 North Decatur Road, Atlanta; ℘ (404) 727-5050

- ✍ www.emory.edu

If you're interested in the performing arts—whether it be music, dance, or theater—look no further than Emory University. Their calendar is jam-packed with events in all areas of performance, featuring both professional and student artists, and it even includes some literary events. Emory even has a spanking-new arts center and performance space, the Donna and Marvin Schwartz Center for Performing Arts, which was due to open in 2003. The 90,000-square-foot facility will include a world-class concert hall, a black-box experimental theater, and a dance studio.

From September through May there are at least one or two major performing arts events per week, sometimes as many as ten, and several of these are free. But even ticketed events are quite reasonably priced. Here's a quick look at some of what Emory has to offer:

Music at Emory: Professional music concerts here have presented the American Bach Soloists, the Boston Chamber Music Society, the Atlanta Winds, the Billy Taylor Trio, the Netherlands Chamber Choir, the Orpheus Chamber Orchestra, soprano Renée Fleming, and many others. Tickets to these shows usually range from $15 to $20, but are occasionally available for $4 or $8! While Mr. C thinks these are great prices already, there are discounts to be had. For example, you can also save even more money through season ticket purchases. (Call the box office for details.) The best deal, though, is for Emory students, who can save 50 percent on ticket purchases when they show a student I.D. That's like getting subscription rates, without having to commit to a full subscription. It also means that you can make up your own "series" by choosing only the concerts that appeal to you. Mr. C highly approves of this opportunity!

Emory produces a family music series, which takes place Saturdays at 11 a.m. at the Michael C. Carlos Museum. Admission is $4 for museum nonmembers.

You can also enjoy absolutely free concerts at Emory: Past performances have included The Chamber Orchestra of the San Pedro Theater, organist Peter Planyevsky, the Atlanta Youth Wind Symphony, the Emory Wind Ensemble, the Atlanta-Emory Orchestra, and the Emory Early Music Consort. For more information on music programs, call the box office at ✆ (404) 727-5050.

Theater at Emory: Tickets to professional and student and professional theater performances are very cheap: just $10 to $15 for productions such as *Man of La Mancha* and Eugene O'Neill's *Ah Wilderness.* Tickets to other productions were just $8.50.

But if even these prices don't jibe with your budget, don't despair; there are plenty of opportunities to enjoy theater absolutely for free, such as recent presentations from Starving Artists Productions.

Some productions offer "pay-what-you-can" performances, as was the case of with a Wednesday evening performance of *Agamemnon and Electra.* For more info about theater at Emory, call the box office.

Dance at Emory: While there are not as many dance offerings at Emory as theater, they are definitely worth checking out. The dance program generally offers about four concerts per year, including works with guest artists and choreographers; tickets are generally priced around $6 (what a deal!).

Creative Writing at Emory: The Reading Series of the Creative Writing Program brings celebrated contemporary authors to the campus for readings, lectures, workshops, and colloquia. Writers who have taken part in this program include Robert Pinsky, Adrienne Rich, Charles Wright, poet Nikky Finney, playwright Naomi Wallace, and novelist Chang-Rae Lee. For more information on this series, call ✆ (404) 727-4683.

Georgia State University/ The Rialto Center for the Performing Arts

- 80 Forsyth Street N.W., Atlanta: ✆ (404) 651-4727

- 🖱 www.rialtocenter.org

The school of music at Georgia State University offers dozens of concerts each semester, most free of charge at the University Recital Hall. Past free concerts have featured the Atlanta Symphony Brass Quintet, GSU Orchestra Festival, GSU Jazz Band, and the University Singers, and other (not free) concerts at GSU's Rialto Center have included the Twyla Tharp Dance and jazz pianist Dave Brubeck. GSU students can get tickets to any of the signature series concerts (usually featuring the biggest names, like Dave Brubeck) for a 50 percent discount.

A few concerts each semester do require tickets, and they're usually priced in the $20 to $25 range. However, some are cheaper (tickets to a concert by the Atlanta Brassworks were just $8), and GSU music department events—including a wide variety of concerts—are sometimes free. Call ✆ (404) 651-3676 for details.

If you are choreographically inclined, you can view one of the several dance concerts presented by GSU each year, many of which are free. For theater lovers, the GSU Players present three or four dramatic productions each year. Tickets begin at just $12 and are

> **MR. CHEAP'S PICKS**
>
> *College Performing Arts*
>
> **Emory University**—With a calendar full of theater, dance, music, and literary readings, you can't get bored—or go broke—at Emory.
>
> **Georgia State University**—The school of music at Georgia State University offers dozens of concerts each semester, most free of charge
>
> **Kennesaw State University**—Another local college with plenty to see and do, KSU has lectures, music and theater events, dance concerts, and more.

free for GSU students. Past performances have included Bertolt Brecht's *Galileo* and Eric Bogosian's *Talk Radio*. Tickets can be reserved about two weeks before opening night. Call ✆ (404) 651-2225 to get on their mailing list.

Georgia Tech Theatre for the Arts/Robert Ferst Center for the Arts

- 349 Ferst Drive N.W., Atlanta; ✆ (404) 894-9600

- 🖱 www.ferstcenter.gatech.edu

Ticket prices here are higher than those of other area colleges, but then the caliber of performances—classical, opera, jazz, dance, pop, variety, and more—is also higher. Paying $15 to $28 may seem extravagant for a campus dance concert, but to see the internationally acclaimed Dance Theatre of Harlem or the Parsons Dance Company, it is quite reasonable. You'd pay a lot more to see these dancers perform in a city like New York.

Other performers with similarly priced tickets have included the London Symphony Orchestra, comedian and actress Sandra Bernhard, magicians Penn and Teller, the unique singing group Rockapella, and Lazer Vaudeville.

If you're a real fan, you can save additional money by buying series tickets. Doing so will not only provide you with discounted prices on individual performances, but will also give you entry to exclusive wine and cheese receptions with stars such as Branford Marsalis, Gato Barbieri, and the Labeque Sisters. Discounted tickets, of course, are available for Georgia Tech students, faculty, and staff.

GT's Theatre for the Arts also sponsors a volunteer usher program, which would allow you to work at some performances and attend others for free. Call ✆ (404) 894-9200 for more info.

Kennesaw State University

- 3455 Frey Lake Road N., Kennesaw; ✆ (770) 423-6650

- ⌲ www.kennesaw.edu/arts

There's more culture going on here than you can shake a stick at! Kennesaw State University offers events in music and theater, but that's not all. They also have lectures by poets, authors, and leaders in the business world; they even have two art galleries. The best part is that many of the events here are free or only $5!

KSU's "Musical Arts Series" offers free concerts and recitals on an almost weekly basis throughout the school year. Features in this series include the KSU Jazz Ensemble, the KSU Chorale, the KSU Brass Ensemble, and the KSU Wind Ensemble. Information is available by calling ✆ (770) 423-6650.

Several "Premiere Series Concerts" each year bring in musicians from the national circuit; tickets can be as high as $20 to $45, but some great performers, such as the Atlanta Symphony Brass Quintet, can be seen for as little as $10. Call ✆ (770) 423-6742 for info. Students with an I.D. will save $10 to $20, depending on the show.

Theater events, held in the KSU Center are not as abundant as music events, but they certainly are cheap. Tickets to performances in the "Classic Theaterworks" series are just $15, and recent productions have included *The Grapes of Wrath* and *Love Letters*. Other past theatrical presentations have included *Stories for a Winter Night,* and the Ninth Georgia Performance Festival, both of which were free.

Kennesaw State has two regular lecture series. "The Chautauqua Lectures" bring distinguished guests to speak on diverse topics. This series has featured poet Maya Angelou and Native-American author Scott Momaday. For more information on this series, call ✆ (770) 423-6235. "The Tetley Distinguished Leaders Lectures" feature notable business people from a variety of industries.

For general information about music and performing arts at Kennesaw State College, call ✆ (770) 423-6742. If you ask, they'll be happy to send you a calendar of events listing all of the above info, and more.

Morehouse College

- 830 Westview Drive S.W., Atlanta; ✆ (404) 215-2601

Morehouse College doesn't have as much going on as some of the other schools around, but the offerings they do have are free and open to the public. They present about three or four music events each semester, most of which are recitals and classical music concerts, although recently a jazz festival was planned. They also have an annual Christmas Carol Concert, performed by the Glee Clubs of Morehouse and Spelman College. Call the number above for more info about music at Morehouse.

Oglethorpe University

- 4484 Peachtree Road N. E., Atlanta; ✆ (404) 364-8555 or ✆ (404) 364-8329

- 🖱 www.oglethorpe.edu

Oglethorpe University presents dozens of music concerts and lectures, plus an ambitious lineup of theater performances, for admission prices that'll make you want to do a little singing and dancing of your own.

Mad about music? Oglethorpe presents a number of concerts featuring university music students that are free and open to the public. In addition, they sponsor the "Skylight Gallery Concert Series," which presents beautiful music in a beautiful setting—the elegant, acoustically designed Skylight Gallery. These concerts are just $7 and have included performances by James Zellers, the Quintetto Barocco, and the Brookhaven Trio. Other concerts at Oglethorpe are often free, or at prices generally no more than $15; artists featured have included the Metropolitan Baroque Chamber Players, the University Singers, and the Michael O'Neal Chamber Singers. For more information, check out the Oglethorpe event site or the Singers' Web site at 🖱 www.mosingers.com. You can also call ✆ (770) 594-7974.

If you're more interested in lectures, Oglethorpe has plenty to choose from. The Rikard Lectures, which are free and open to the public, offer you the chance to hear ideas from the best and brightest in the field of business. Other free lectures take place throughout the year on the subjects of science, art, and literature.

Oglethorpe is home to the Georgia Shakespeare Festival, presented in the Miriam H. and John A. Conant Performing Arts Center. The GSF stages about five plays per year, with ticket prices running from $40 to $116 (ouch!). However, discounts are available. For details, see the listing under *Theater*.

The other theater offerings here are certainly worth checking out, especially with tickets priced at around $7. Recent presentations have included *Ernest in Love*, an adaptation of Oscar Wilde's *The Importance of Being Earnest* (yes, the spellings are purposely different); Shakespeare's *Love's Labour's Lost*; and, speaking of the Bard, a pair of original one-act comedies, *When Shakespeare's Ladies Meet* and *The Show Must Go On*. For more information about theater events, call ✆ (404) 504-1074.

And if all that isn't enough for you, check out the Oglethorpe University Museum, housed in the school's Philip Weltner Library. Along with art exhibits, this museum presents its own slate of lectures and concerts at reasonable prices, usually around $5.

Spelman College

- 350 Spelman Lane S.W., Atlanta; ✆ (404) 215-7805

- 🖱 www.spelman.edu/music/calendar.htm

The music department at Spelman College presents quite a number of concerts per semester, and almost all of them are free of charge. Pianists Dorian Ho and Nancy Paddleford have performed here, as well as jazz vocalist Audrey Skakir and the Woody Williams and the World Drum Experience. In addition to guest performances, Spelman has its own talent. You can enjoy concerts given by the Spelman College Jazz Ensemble, the Wind and String Ensemble, and the Spelman and Morehouse College Glee Club.

Spelman's Theater and Drama department produces about six shows each year; these include a mix of theater and dance events. Tickets for these shows are $8 for adults and $5 for students with I.D. Productions in a recent season have included "Ain't Misbehaving," "Antigone," "Dance 14," "Christmas in the City," "Feets Per Minute," and "A Fairy Tale: An Enchanted Journey." Sometimes Spelman puts on special performances, such as "Flying Over Purgatory," starring actress, writer and activist Ruby Dee, at up to $25 for public admission. Call ✆ (404) 526-1172 for more information.

COMEDY

For standup comedy, the best cost-cutter in the biz remains the 'Open Mike" night, when you can get in for a very low cover charge and see up-and-coming "stars of tomorrow." Guaranteed, there'll be plenty of clunkers (does the name Rupert Pupkin ring a bell, De Niro fans?), but the shows are hosted by headliners, so you're sure to get plenty of good laughs no matter what. Many clubs, some of which are listed here, have open mike shows; they tend to be early in the week. Call your favorite venue to see what they offer.

In recent years, television viewers have been introduced to the concept of "improv" through such shows as *Whose Line Is It Anyway?* The comedians ask the audience to give them ideas for characters and situations, which the players then turn into (almost always) hilarious skits. Have fun!

Dad's Garage Theatre Company

- Little Five Points, 280 Elizabeth Street, Atlanta; ✆ (404) 523-3141

- ✍ www.dadsgarage.com

It's amazing to see how this company has grown over the past seven years. Dad's Garage was founded by a small group of volunteers in 1995 and now boasts an administrative staff and actors that actually get paid for their talents. *Creative Loafing* has awarded Dad's the Best Theater and Best Improv Troupe for the past three years. Improv shows take place every Thursday, Friday, and Saturday night at 10:30 p.m.

Dad's Garage takes improv and turns it into a competitive sport. On Thursday nights at 10:30 p.m., two teams of improvisers compete against each other and are then judged by the audience. And there's also Gorilla Theatre, where improvisers compete one on one. These shows, for only $10, will always be original and never repeated. Dad's offers discounts for members and Comedy-Improv students. Another show for $10, a

ENTERTAINMENT: COMEDY

Dad's creation, is the popular soap opera *Scandals,* set in 1848 out in the Wild, Wild West.

Certain shows during the year, such as the *Lucky Yates Talk Show* and *Little John's Comedy Improv* (a Chicago-style comedy night), are offered for no more than $5. You have to roll a die to find out the price, and if you roll a six, you get in free. Comedic plays are also performed here, such as *Madonna's Obsessive Support Group,* by New York playwright, Ron Morris, at $15 for adults. And check out their Atlanta's Most Dangerous Play Festival.

For kids, a Saturday noon original creation, *Uncle Grampa's Hoo-Dilly Stew,* costs only $5 for adults and $3 for children under 12. Ask Dad's about their birthday package.

Dad's also hosts an annual fundraiser, called Improv-a-thon, which features 25 hours of non-stop comedy. The price is only $5 a show; an all-access pass is $40 paid in advance.

Laughing Matters

- Manuel's Tavern, 602 North Highland Avenue N.E., Atlanta; ✆ (404) 525-3447

- Dave and Buster's Marietta, I-75 Delk Road Exit, Marietta; ✆ (770) 951-5554

- Dave & Buster's Gwinnett, I-85 Steven Reynolds Boulevard, Exit 39, Duluth; ✆ (770) 497-1152

- ✍ www.laughingmatters.com

Laughing Matters is Atlanta's first and longest running improvisational comedy troupe. Players are involved in film, television, and radio, and some have gone on to work on shows like *The Simpsons* and *Seinfeld.* The Laughing Matters cast consists of at least 15 characters and five talented musicians.

The format employed at Manuel's is known as "Comedy Sports," which pits two teams of four comedians each against each other. They compete, with jokes, for the audience's favor. And all this fun can be had for only $10 every first Saturday of the month at 8 p.m. at Manuel's Tavern, which also has a dinner menu and full bar.

The first Friday of every month you'll find Laughing Matters at Dave and Buster's Marietta and the second Friday of every month at Dave and Buster's Gwinnett. Shows start at 8 p.m. and tickets are just $10. DAB also has a dinner menu and full bar.

For information, reservations, or to find out where else around town you can see Laughing Matters (comedians often feel the need to be moving targets), call their own telephone line: ✆ (404) 874-4050.

Punchline Comedy Club

- The Balconies Shopping Center, 280 Hilderbrand Drive, Sandy Springs; ✆ (404) 252-LAFF (5233)

- ✍ www.punchline.com

This well-established comedy venue—they've been around for 12 years—has presented superstars like Jay Leno and Jerry Seinfeld on their way up the ladder of stardom. Luckily, the club's ticket prices are very down-to-earth.

MR. CHEAP'S PICKS

Comedy

Whole World Comedy—Here's where you'll witness Atlanta's homegrown improv comedy like you've never seen it before, and at reasonable prices.

On Wednesday, Thursday, and Sunday evenings at 8:30 p.m. you can get into the Punchline for just $8, or for free if you download coupons from their Web site. There is, however, a one-item (food or drink) minimum, reservations are required, and they request men not wear tank tops. Wednesday is "open mike" night, and Thursday or Sunday is a one-man or one-women show.

The discount does not apply to special engagement shows, usually held Friday evenings at 8 p.m. and 10:30 p.m.; Saturday at 7 p.m., 9 p.m., and 11 p.m.; and Sunday at 8 p.m. These shows present some of the best comedians in the country; many of them have appeared on the *Tonight Show* with Jay Leno or the David Letterman show. Some of the recent shows include Diane Ford, nominated for "Comedienne of the Year" by the American Comedy Awards, and comic actor Pauly Shore. Prices for special engagement shows range from $10 to $20, and reservations are required. There are no Monday or Tuesday shows. Punchline also offers a light dinner menu.

Uptown Comedy Corner

- 2140 Peachtree Road N.W., Atlanta; ✆ (404) 350-6990

At this comedy club, tickets for Tuesday shows are only $5, with Wednesday and Sunday shows $10. Thursday is "Ladies Night"; women get in for $5 and men pay $10. On Fridays and Saturdays, admission is $15. There is a two-item (appetizer or drink) minimum.

Special engagement tickets are $20; national acts that have appeared here include Mike Epps (from the movies *All about the Benjamins* and *Next Friday*) and John Witherspoon (from TV's *The Wayans Brothers*).

Shows on Tuesday, Wednesday, Thursday, and Sundays get underway at 9 p.m. On Friday and Saturday, there are three shows, at 8 p.m., 10:30 p.m., and 12:30 a.m. You can obtain a discount for six people or more. Reservations are not necessary for most nights, and that's a plus for last-minute, spur-of-the-moment Cheapsters.

Whole World Comedy

- 1214 Spring Street, Atlanta; ✆ (404) 817-7529

- ✍ www.wholeworldtheatre.com

The talented members of this improv comedy troupe, in addition to being hilarious comedians, are also trained actors, and they can easily create a situation that is poignant as well as humorous. Their first performance was in 1994, and over the years they've earned awards from *Creative Loafing* and from *Atlanta City Magazine*. The troupe's artistic director, David Webster, has also received Telly and Emmy awards for his writing.

Improv shows are held at 8 p.m. on Tuesday ($10) and Thursday ($15). There are two shows on Friday and Saturday at 8 p.m. and 10:30 pm ($19.50). Each show lasts about two hours.

And since the cast are actors, you can also see about six plays a year here, such as David Mamet's Pulitzer-winning *Glengarry Glen Ross*. Tickets for plays are $15 and reservations are required; plan ahead, because they sell out early.

Whole World's cafe (not to be confused with Whole Foods) opens an hour before all shows and serves Red Brick Beer. And here's a cheapster's tip: If they sell out, the show is simulcast in the cafe for free, along with comfy furniture!

DANCE

Atlanta has several dedicated local dance companies, performing everything from classical ballet to folk/ethnic traditions to the most experimental forms of modern dance. Each of these companies produces a handful of concerts per year. These performances are held at theaters throughout Atlanta, including 7 Stages, the Saw Playhouse, the Ferst Center at Georgia Tech, the Rialto Center for Performing Arts, and other locales. Ticket prices depend on the venue, but most range from $6 to $15. Many of these companies also do site-specific works in public parks and other community settings; these may have cheaper tickets or may even be free. Check the Web sites listed here, watch the newspapers, and keep your eyes open for upcoming shows.

Atlanta Ballet

- 1400 W. Peachtree Street N.E. Atlanta; (404) 873-5811
- www.atlantaballet.com

The Atlanta Ballet has been a part of the city's life since dance visionary Dorothy Moses Alexander founded it in 1929. It's the oldest continually operating dance company in America and the official state ballet company of Georgia. Artistic Director John McFall is in his fifth season with the Atlanta Ballet, and Robert Chumbley is executive and music director.

In recent years, a big hit was *Dracula,* staged in the spectacular Fox Theatre, where performers soared in a story of passion and blood lust intriguingly scheduled during the week of Valentine's Day. However, the centerpiece of the company's productions remains *The Nutcracker,* the traditional dazzling, snowy production of Tchaikovsky's masterpiece staged by McFall.

Aside from his activities with the Ballet, McFall leads the Atlanta Ballet Centre for Dance Education, established in August 1996, which operates out of the Ballet's Midtown studios and satellite facility at 4279 Roswell Road in Buckhead. The Centre offers, among other things, classes in flamenco and yoga as well as instruction for children in a professional program of ballet, tap, jazz, or creative movement techniques.

For dance lovers with busy schedules who can't commit to a date, the Atlanta Ballet offers a Flex Pass Option that allows for attendance at performances of choice, best seating available. The passbook contains four coupons that are redeemable two weeks prior to any performance. Individual tickets range from $10 to $50.

Beacon Dance Company

- Beacon Hill Arts Center, 410 West Trinity Place, Decatur; (404) 377-2929
- www.beacondance.org

Located in downtown Decatur, Beacon is one of the Atlanta area's most innovative contemporary dance ensembles. It bills its performances as "interactive," and subscribes to the philosophy that there is dance everywhere and there

> **MR. CHEAP'S PICKS**
>
> ### Dance
>
> **Atlanta Ballet**—You'll jump for joy (maybe even pirouette) over $10 tickets for the high-class ensemble in town. Discounts for students and senior citizens, too.
>
> **Dancer's Collective**—This organization brings world-renowned modern dance troupes to Atlanta, at bargain rates.
>
> **Several Dancers Core**—This classy outfit creates and performs some heady and interesting stuff—"experimental" contemporary dance and movement—for very reasonable (sometimes even free) admission prices.

is dance in everyone. Beacon is highly respected and has received major commissions from the Arts Festival of Atlanta, the Georgia Allies, the Young Careers Guild of the High Museum of Art, the Decatur Presbyterian Church, the Atlanta Ladies Circle, and others to create numerous site-specific dance works. Beacon puts on numerous dance concerts and events throughout the year so check out their site or give them a call to get ticket information for upcoming show.

Dancer's Collective of Atlanta

- 4279 Roswell Road N.E., Atlanta, GA; (404) 233-7600

These guys are the wandering genius nomads of dance. (Hey dancers . . . Mr. C knows all about that wandering genius nomad thang!) Organized in 1980 by Joanne McGhee and three other dancers formerly with the defunct Atlanta Contemporary Dance Company, the Dancer's Collective provides Atlanta's only full-subscription season for contemporary dance. Since its inception, the Collective has brought to Atlanta more than 160 performances including the works of emerging artists Bebe Miller, David Dorfman, and Susan Marshall and more established troupes including Pilobolus, Feld Ballet, Eiko & Koma, DanceBrazil, and Urban Bush Women.

The dancers they bring in will not only give public performances, but they also teach master classes at local colleges and universities, along with conducting outreach classes with Atlanta's underprivileged youth. Each troupe generally gives two major performances during their stay, for which tickets range from $10 to $18. Subscriptions are also available.

The Dancers Collective has no home to call its own but stages its season throughout the city at diverse venues including Agnes Scott College and the Rialto Center for Performing Arts.

Full Radius Dance

- P.O. Box 54453, Atlanta; (404) 724-9663

- www.fullradiusdance.org

Performing at theaters all around Atlanta, Full Radius has a unique and worthy angle on the art of dance: This critically acclaimed company focuses on modern dance for persons with disabilities by mixing dancers on foot with dancers in wheelchairs to create choreographic works that are both technically demanding and visually exciting. From the company's perspective, their approach allows them to address the "sweep of the human experience in a world that contains a diversity of attitudes, actions, and outcomes." Sounds pretty interesting, eh? It is!

Full Radius was founded in 1998 by Douglas Scott as a modern dance company called Dance Force, Inc., and evolved as Scott saw the potential to be a catalyst for changing the way modern dance was created and supported in Atlanta. Along with a name change in 1993, a new focus developed when Scott began working with dancers with disabilities.

Full Radius Dance stages about 40 performances a year, with tickets prices from $8 to $12. This is top-notch stuff, and certainly a bargain at those prices. Call or check their Web site for upcoming performances.

Georgia Ballet

- 31 Atlanta Street, Marietta; (770) 425-0258

- www.georgiaballet.org

In existence for over 40 years, the Georgia Ballet, under the careful and excellent direction of its artistic director and founder, Iris Hensley, includes both a regional professional ballet company and a dance academy. They stage approximately nine public and 27 school shows each season, covering such works as *The Nutcracker* (presented during the holidays, of course); *Allegro Brillante,* with a score by Tchaikovsky, saluting the memory of renowned choreographer, George Balanchine; the ballet/choral collaboration, *I Never Saw Another Butterfly;* and other creative programs.

Tickets for this top-drawer entertainment run $18 to $24. Groups of 10 or more can get in for just $16 per person, and seniors get $2 off.

Ruth Mitchell Dance Theatre

- 81 Church Street, Marietta; (770) 426-0007

- http://ruthmitchelldance.com

Many people love ballet but fear they would have to mortgage their home to afford tickets to a dance concert. Well, tickets to performances by the Ruth Mitchell Dance Theatre are a remarkable $15 for adults and $10 for children and senior citizens, at all performances. If you get a group together and buy at least 10 tickets, the adult prices drop to $10 and $8.

Ruth Mitchell Dance Theater includes professional dancers and dance students; their work incorporates a number of ballet styles, from classical to modem. Past concerts have included *Cinderella, Thumbelina, A Children's Ballet, The Sapphire Collection* (a series of jazz and classical ballet concert pieces), and *The Nutcracker.* Performances usually take place at the 14th Street Playhouse or the Cobb Civic Center.

The troupe only presents three or four major concerts per season (including a *Nutcracker* holiday show), each with a run of only three or four nights. The advantage of a short season, though, is that season tickets are relatively inexpensive. For a little more than the cost of a single orchestra seat to see ballet at the Atlanta Civic Center, you can get the best seat in the house for all four Ruth Mitchell concerts. The price of $45 actually gets you four tickets for the price of three.

Ruth Mitchell also stages a number of student recitals toward the end of the season—usually in

May. These are free if you know somebody in the company and receive an invitation.

Several Dancers Core

- 131 Sycamore Street, Decatur; (404) 373-4154

- www.severaldancerscore.org

This outfit creates and performs some heady and interesting "experimental" dance and movement. Performing in Atlanta since 1986, SDC features new choreography that evolves through experimentation, improvisation, collaborations with artists from different media, and the concerns of our current world. Some recent works have included "Facing Survival," addressing the struggle against AIDS, "Aria for an Endangered Species," "The Flannery O'Connor Project," and "The Messiah Project." The latter was based on the magnificent music of Handel's *Messiah,* which inspired choreographer Sue Schroeder to explore how voice production vibrates the human form in the same way that the production of movement excites the muscles of the body. She approached the work as "an illuminated manuscript, where the dance adds color, movement and meaning to an already rich text and score." (The Cheapster couldn't have said it any better himself!)

So how much does it cost to witness one of these wonderful spectacles? Just $15 for adults and $12 for students and seniors. The company also performs a number of smaller "Lunchtime in the Studio" works in their Decatur digs, and admission to those is free! If you're at all interested in dance and expressive movement, you really can't afford *not* to check this out.

Soweto Street Beat Dance Theater

- www.sowetostreetbeat.com

This world-renowned outfit is the only professional South African dance troupe in the United States, having begun their work in 1989 in Soweto, South Africa before and relocating to Atlanta in 1992. Its mission is to teach audiences of all ages and cultural backgrounds, especially at-risk youth, about the cultural arts and history of South Africa.

SSB performed at the 1996 Olympic Festival (the only African dance company to perform in the Olympic Games), as well as at the 1993 tribute to civil rights leader Coretta Scott King and at concerts by Michael Jackson, Dionne Warwick, Stevie Wonder, and TLC. They've also performed at the Lincoln Center in New York and at many other prestigious venues.

SSB also prepares an annual performance during Black History Month, and dances at a large number of special public shows and hundreds of school appearances throughout the year. Their performances focus on the history of the Zulu Nation, and the unique dance and music styles that stem from South African ethnic groups—Zulu, Sotho, Shangaan, Venda, Swazi, and Xhosa.

In addition to festivals, the company presents formal shows at various venues around town, including the Robert Ferst Center at Georgia Tech. Tickets for these shows are usually priced from $10 to $20.

You can learn about the performance schedule on the group's Web page or on the sites of the various venues where they perform.

FESTIVALS

Atlanta abounds with cultural and music festivals dedicated to cultural pride, changes of season, music, theater, and more. Most of these are great entertainment for the entire family, and the cost usually ranges from absolutely free to about $10 per person. Of course, the accompanying food, arts, and crafts will cost a little extra. Festivals are a great way to have fun while going easy on the old wallet.

Atlanta Celtic Festival (May)

- Oglethorpe University, 4484 Peachtree Road, Atlanta; (404) 572-8045

This two-day event is held the third weekend of the month. Admission on Saturday is $15 for adults, $5 for seniors, students, and children 6 to 12. On Sunday, the adult charge drops to $10.

Atlanta Dogwood Festival (April)

- Piedmont Park, 10th Street and Piedmont Avenue; (404) 329-0501

A free outdoor festival.

Atlanta Fair (March)

- Turner Field, 755 Hank Aaron Drive, Atlanta; (770) 740-1962

Includes a midway, rides, food, and children's activities. Tickets are $3 for adults; $1 for children.

Atlanta Greek Festival (September)

- Greek Orthodox Cathedral of the Annunciation, 2500 Clairmont Road, Atlanta; (404) 633-5870

Admission is $3 for adults and $1 for children younger than 12.

Atlanta Jazz Festival (May)

- Piedmont Park, Atlanta; (404) 817-6851

Takes place on Saturday, Sunday, and Monday of Memorial Day weekend. Free.

Atlanta Lesbian and Gay Pride Festival (June)

- Various locations; (770) 876-3700

Attracts more than 300,000 people.

Atlanta Passion Play (March)

- Atlanta Civic Center, 395 Piedmont Avenue, Atlanta; (770) 234-8400

This three-hour pageant, including a chorus and full orchestra, portrays Christ's life, death, and resurrection, and draws people from around the country. Tickets range from $8 to $16.

Atlanta Virtuosi's Hispanic Festival of the Arts (August)

- Embry Hills United Methodist Church, Chamblee; (770) 938-8611

Includes lectures, storytelling, dance performances, concerts, food, and more. Admission is $15 for adults, $10 for students and seniors, and free for children younger than 12.

Buckhead Art Crawl (October)

- Various Buckhead galleries, Buckhead; (404) 467-7607

Get shuttled between fifty participating galleries, with special exhibits and receptions. Admission is $15.

Cathedral Antiques Show (January)

- Cathedral of St. Philip, 2744 Peachtree Road, Atlanta; (404) 365-1000

Admission is $10.

Conyers Cherry Blossom Festival (March)

- International Horse Park, 1996 Centennial Olympic Parkway, Conyers; (770) 918-2169

Free.

Civil War Encampment (July)

- Atlanta History Center, 130 West Paces Ferry Road, Atlanta; (404) 814-4000;

- www.atlhist.org

Mid-July recreation of the falling of Atlanta to the troops of General William Sherman. Admission is $10 adults, $4 ages 6 to 17, and free for children 5 and under.

Decatur Arts Festival (May)

- Decatur town square and other locations; (404) 371-9583

Includes art exhibits, a children's festival, storytellers, jugglers, magicians, pony rides, and more.

Fantastic Fourth Celebration (July)

- Georgia's Stone Mountain Park; (770) 498-5633

- www.stonemountainpark.org

Free.

Festival of Trees, Festival of Lights (December)

- Georgia World Congress Center, 285 International Boulevard, Atlanta; (404) 325-NOEL

Includes more than 200 trees and holiday vignettes. Free.

Georgia Renaissance Festival (April through May)

- I-85 at Exit 12, Fairburn; (770) 964-8575

Features more than 100 performances daily on 10 stages scattered across the 93-acre festival grounds. Admission is $12.95 for adults, $5.75 for kids 6 to 12. Children younger than 6 are free.

Georgia Shakespeare Festival (June-October)

- Conant Performing Arts Center at Oglethorpe University, 4484 Peachtree Road, Atlanta; (404) 264-0020

This festival usually includes three plays by the Bard and as well as other works. Tickets for the festival shows range from $20 to $26.50.

Ground Hog Day (February)

- Yellow River Game Ranch, 4525 Highway 78, Lilburn; (770) 972-6643

Admission is $6 for adults and $5 for kids 3 to 11.

ENTERTAINMENT: FESTIVALS

Independence Day (July)

- Various locations

More than 200,000 spectators watch the annual Peachtree Road Race, as well as the largest Independence Day parade in the nation, concerts, and fireworks at Centennial Olympic Park.

Inman Park Spring Festival (April)

- Edgewood and Euclid Avenues, Inman Park; (770) 242-4895

Held the last weekend of the month, this festival includes a parade, a tour of homes, antiques, food, crafts, music, and more. Free.

JapanFest (September)

- Georgia's Stone Mountain Park; (770) 498-5633
- www.stonemountainpark.org

Free.

King Week and the Martin Luther King Jr. National Holiday (January)

- 449 Auburn Avenue N.E., Atlanta; (404) 526-8900

Various tributes and activities relating to the life and work of Dr. King. Free.

Lasershow (May-October)

- Georgia's Stone Mountain Park; (770) 498-5633
- www.stonemountainpark.org

Every night May through Labor Day, and on weekends through the fall thereafter. Free.

Marietta Bluegrass Festival (May)

- Jim Miller Park, 2245 Callaway Road, Marietta; (770) 528-8875

Admission is $8 on Friday and $10 on Saturday afternoon.

Midtown Music Festival (May)

- Atlanta Civic Center, 395 Piedmont Avenue, Atlanta; (404) 233-8889

Usually held the first weekend in May. One-day admission is $25; tickets for the entire weekend are $30.

Montreaux Atlanta International Music Festival (September)

- Piedmont Park, 1085 Piedmont Avenue, Atlanta; (404) 817-6820

Jazz, gospel, and reggae acts perform at this free outdoor festival.

National Black Arts Festival

- Studioplex, 659 Auburn Avenue, Atlanta; (404) 730-7315
- www.nbaf.org

Event prices start at $5.

Oktoberfest (October)

- Helen, GA; (706) 878-2181; (800) 858-8027

Held in the alpine village look-alike town of Helen, 70 miles northeast of Atlanta. Admission is $6 on weekdays, $7 on Saturdays, $3 for children 6 through 12, or free for kids under 5.

ParkFest (April)

- Centennial Olympic Park, Atlanta; ℡ (404) 222-7275

Usually held early in the month. Free.

Springfest (May)

- Georgia's Stone Mountain Park; ℡ (770) 498-5633
- 🖱 www.stonemountainpark.org

A barbecue cook-off, live music, and a flea market. Usually held early in May. Free.

Spring Folklife Festival (April)

- Atlanta History Center, 130 W. Paces Ferry Road, Atlanta; ℡ (404) 814-4000

Admission is $10 for adults, $4 for kids 6 to 17, and free to children 5 and younger.

Sweet Auburn Heritage Festival (September)

- Auburn Avenue, Atlanta; ℡ (404) 525-0205

Takes place in the historic neighborhood around Dr. Martin Luther King Jr.'s birth home, church, and tomb. Free.

Taste of the South (Free)

- Georgia's Stone Mountain Park; ℡ (770) 498-5633
- 🖱 www.stonemountainpark.org

A great opportunity to sample okra, grits, greens, and other quintessential Southern cooking. Free.

Tour of Southern Ghosts (October)

- Georgia's Stone Mountain Park; ℡ (770) 498-5633
- 🖱 www.stonemountainpark.org

Two weeks, ghosts, monsters, and spooky storytelling at the mansion at Stone Mountain. Admission is $6 for adults and $3 for kids.

Yellow Daisy Festival (September)

- Georgia's Stone Mountain Park; ℡ (770) 498-5633
- 🖱 www.stonemountainpark.org

Arts, crafts, food, and more. Free.

MOVIES

Alas, there's not much to be done about the ever-rising prices of Hollywood movies. Some theaters do cut the price a bit from time to time. But don't despair! There are several alternative options for the budget moviegoer, the most notable of which are listed here.

AMC Buckhead Backlot Cinema & Cafe

- 3340 Peachtree Road N.E., Atlanta; ℡ (404) 816-4262

If you're getting weary of snacking only on popcorn and milk duds during the flick, note that here's a place where you can go hang out, watch a movie, and eat real grub (albeit fast-food quality). You can even get beer! Sounds to Mr. C like a good venue for a cheap date! Tickets are $5 before 6 p.m.; $7 for adults and $5 for students and seniors thereafter.

Cinefest Film Theater

- 66 Courtland Street S.E., Atlanta; (404) 651-2463

Cinefest is the movie theater on the Georgia State University campus, with ticket prices that almost make you want to go back to school. The films shown here include art-house fair, such as *Like Water for Chocolate,* recent mainstream flicks, and documentaries such as *Manufacturing Consent: Noam Chomsky and the Media.* Of course, classic campus favorites also show up on the bill, from *Snow White and the Seven Dwarves* to *Monty Python's Life of Brian* ("classics," clearly, are in the eye of the beholder).

Everyone can agree on one thing: The ticket prices here are the main attraction. Admission is just $3 before 5 p.m. and $5 thereafter. Such a deal! Call them and they'll send you a copy of their calendar, which includes show times and summaries of upcoming films. Cinefest is open seven days a week.

Goethe-Institut Atlanta

- Colony Square, Plaza Level, 1197, Peachtree Street N.E., Atlanta; (404) 892-2226

- www.goethe.de/uk/atl/enindex.htm

The Goethe-Institut is part of a program funded by the German government, which brings the culture and language of Germany to other countries. Offerings include cultural events, German language courses, and a library with books in German and English.

They have an extensive film schedule, and most screenings are free. Screenings include German films and film series. One such series, "Heimat: A Retrospective of Edgar Reitz's Acclaimed Masterpieces," included such films as *The Call of Far Away* (1919-1928), *The Highway* (1938), and *The Feast of the Living and the Dead* (1982). The center also presents some American films, such as *The Shining* and *Do the Right Thing,* shown with German subtitles. Tickets are $4 regular admission, $3 students/seniors.

You can also check out the occasional music and dance concert here. While a few of these are free, the admission price depends on the venue with which Goethe is co-sponsoring the event. Past locations have included Briarcliff Baptist Church, Stone Mountain Park, and Emory University.

The Goethe-Institut also has an art gallery, bringing German art exhibits and related lectures to the city. Call them for more information and a calendar of events.

High Museum of Art

- 1280 Peachtree Street N.E., Atlanta; (404) 733-4444

- www.high.org

Museums, particularly art museums, afford you a wonderful opportunity to see movies that don't get distributed to commercial theatres—classic films, documentaries, and foreign films. The High Museum of Art has regular offerings for which admission is just $5 for general admission; $4 for seniors, students, and museum members.

Unless otherwise noted, all films are screened at 8 p.m. in the Rich Auditorium of the Woodruff Arts Center, located next door to the High at Peachtree and 15th Streets, Arts Center MARTA stop (N5).

One popular series, "Spanish Film in the 90s," showcased the best of recent Spanish cinema, with all films in Spanish with English subtitles. Other screenings have included *Time of Favor*, winner of six Israeli Academy Awards and a riveting film that is part political thriller and part romantic melodrama; and *In Search of Famine*, a self-reflexive work about a Calcutta film crew trying to make a movie about rural poverty during the 1943 famine.

Occasionally, the High will show films in conjunction with one of its current exhibits; admission in these cases is free with your entry to the museum. For instance, the documentary *Sol LeWitt* was shown as part of an installation of that artist's wall drawings. Call the High Museum or check its Web site to get a calendar of upcoming screenings.

The High sponsors the Latin American Film Festival from late October to early-November, which includes the premiere of recent feature films from Latin America. General admission is $5; $4.50 for students and seniors. Free receptions accompany the movies.

MR. CHEAP'S PICKS

Movies

Cinefest Film Theater—A movie theater on a college campus is not only convenient, but cheap, too.

Goethe-Institut Atlanta and the High Museum of Art—If funky foreign films and avant-garde flicks are your thing, check the schedules at these museums. Not only will it be fun, it may well be free.

Lefont Plaza Theater—This sometimes funky smelling, older theater generally screens second-run art-house fare, but with a lot of fine movies in the mix.

Lefont Garden Hills Cinema

- 2835 Peachtree Road N.E., Atlanta; (404) 266-2202

This spacious Buckhead institution features award-winning foreign and limited-run independent films such as the Indian *Monsoon Wedding*. There's a lot of old-timey atmosphere here, helped along by the black-and-white pictures of classic and foreign actors surrounding the ticket counter. If you go before 5 p.m., you can get in for just $5. Otherwise, tickets cost $7.50 for adults and $6 for students and seniors.

Lefont Plaza Theatre

- 1049 Ponce de Leon Avenue N.E., Atlanta; (404) 873-1939

This sometimes funky smelling, older theater generally screens second-run art-house fare, but with a lot of fine movies in the mix. If you're game, you can even still partake in the cult classic *Rocky Horror Picture Show* at midnight on weekends. Ticket prices are $5 before 6 p.m. and $7.50 thereafter; $6 for students and seniors.

UA Tara

- 2345 Cheshire Bridge Road, Atlanta; (404) 634-6288

Indie films and art movies mix it up at this four-screen theater, which features very comfortable seating and just-less-than-standard ticket prices. Matinees run $5.25 for everybody. After 5 p.m., the general admission is $8 for adults, $6.50 for students, and $5.25 for seniors.

IMAX Theater at the Fernbank Museum of Natural History

- 767 Clifton Road N.E., Atlanta; (404) 929-6300

- www.fernbank.edu/museum

Stunning films like the documentary Everest, shown on a five-story screen, are always worth the price of admission. Tickets here are $10 for adults, $9 students and seniors, and $8 for children. On Friday evenings from January to November, that same $10 buys you an even better deal: a ticket to the museum's "Martinis & IMAX" program, featuring a movie, live music, and a place to meet and mingle, with specialty martinis and à la carte dinners for sale.

DRIVE-IN THEATERS

Ah yes! There's nothing quite so satisfying in these pre-fab, chain-dominated times as enjoying a night at the drive-in with a date or the entire family. This dying breed of theaters presents an affordable opportunity to let those summer breezes blow through your hair while you sit back in (or next to) the privacy of your own car with a good cigar and a cooler of your favorite snacks and beverages. Drive-ins these days usually feature good sound over an FM radio frequency, allowing you to run it through your car speakers, which means you can park the ol' minivan with the rear facing the big screen, open up the rear door, set up come comfy chairs, and enjoy the show. Here's a listing of the few drive-in theaters that can still be found around Atlanta.

Commerce Drive-In Theater

- 2395 Bowman Highway, Commerce; ✆ (706) 335-4505

- ✐ www.highway17theater.com

Sure, this is 60 miles from downtown Atlanta, but the drive-in movie experience is worth the trip, especially if you live northeast of town. Tickets are $6 per person, with kids under 10 admitted free.

Starlight Six Drive-in Theatre

- 2000 Moreland Avenue S.E., Atlanta; ✆ (404) 627-5786

- ✐ www.starlightdrivein.com

Tickets for second-run movies are just $6 for adults, and children under 10 are admitted free. The Starlight is open all year, seven days a week, rain or clear skies.

Storey North 85 Twin Drive-in Theater

- 3265 Northeast Expressway Access Road, Chamblee; ✆ (770) 451-4570

North 85 has two separate screens showing the latest hot releases and second-run films. Yet the admission price is only $4 for adults; and it's free for children under age 12.

MUSEUMS

Mr. C firmly believes that all museums are bargains. Consider how many treasures you can see, for less than the price of a movie! If you really enjoy a particular museum, by the way, consider becoming a member. This usually gets you free admission anytime, including perhaps your family, for the price of a couple of visits. It's a money-saver, and it helps out your beloved institution as well.

Atlanta Cyclorama

- 800-C Cherokee Avenue S.E., Atlanta; (404) 658-7625
- www.bcaatlanta.org/Page08_file/page08.html

The 1864 Civil War Battle of Atlanta revolves around you in this famous cylindrical painting, perhaps the biggest in the world. The painting was created in 1886 and restored in the 1980s.

Each viewing begins with a short film narrated by actor James Earl Jones; then the seats revolve to display the story painted on the walls of the cylindrical building.

The Cyclorama is open every day from 9:20 a.m. to 4:30 p.m., and until 5:30 p.m. from June through Labor Day. It's closed on Martin Luther King Day, Thanksgiving, and Christmas. Admission is just $5 for adults, $4 for seniors, and $4 for kids ages 6 to 12. Younger tykes get in for free.

Atlanta International Museum of Art and Design

- Peachtree Center, 285 Peachtree Center Avenue N.E., Atlanta; (404) 688-2467

One of the newer museums in Atlanta, established in 1989, this space celebrates the craftsmanship of the world's cultures through ethnographic, folk art, and design exhibits. It is a nonprofit educational organization supported by public and private funds.

Admission is free; the museum is open Tuesday through Saturday, 11 a.m. to 5 p.m.

Clark Atlanta University Art Galleries

- Trevor Arnett Hall, Clark Atlanta University, Atlanta; (404) 880-6644

This art gallery is renowned for its broad collection of African-American art. Included in the collection are examples from 20th-century masters Charles White, Jacob Lawrence, Elizabeth Catlett, and Romare Bearden. The galleries are located on the second floor. Admission is free; open from 11 a.m. to 4 p.m. Tuesday through Friday, and noon to 4 p.m. Saturday.

The Hammonds House Galleries and Resource Center of African-American Art

- 503 Peeples Street S.W., Atlanta; (404) 752-8730

Hammonds House is the only Georgia museum exclusively dedicated to African-American fine art. Housed in one of the oldest structures in the West End, what is believed to have been the first kindergarten in Atlanta once operated in one wing of this pre-Civil War home. Today the building houses a collection of more than 250 works of art, mainly by African-Americans. The collection also includes African and Haitian works. In addition to exhibitions, HH offers lectures, classes, and a resource center for scholars.

Admission is a $2 donation for adults and a $1 donation for children and seniors; the facility is closed to the public on Mondays. Hours are 10 a.m. to 6 p.m. Tuesday through Friday, and 1 p.m. to 5 p.m. Saturday and Sunday. Parking is free.

The High Museum of Art

- Woodruff Arts Center, 1280 Peachtree Street N.E., Atlanta; (404) 733-4444
- www.high.org

When the High Museum of Art opened in its new building in October 1983, the *New York Times* called it "among the best museum structures any city has built in at least a generation." Richard Meier designed the gleaming white museum with its curved glass wall overlooking Peachtree Street. Its effect is at once both classical and ultramodern. The $20 million High has won numerous design awards; in 1991 the American Institute of Architects named it one of the top ten works of American architecture of the 1980s.

You may wish to start at the top: It's fun to take the elevator all the way up, then walk through the galleries and down the ramps at your own pace. The museum's 10,000-piece permanent collection includes contemporary and classical paintings and sculpture by European and American artists plus African art, photography, and folk art.

Throughout the year, selections from the permanent collection share the space with major traveling exhibitions. The museum gift shop sells exhibition catalogs, posters, and gifts.

The Visual Arts Learning Space on the main floor offers See for Yourself, an interactive computer program designed to introduce visitors to the art disciplines including color, line, composition, and light. The walls of the space are lined with art from the museum's collection, and computers, strategically spaced, have a program that illustrates an artistic element. The goal is for participants to gain comprehension of art concepts through the computer as well as the viewing of actual artifacts.

Recent exhibits have included *Picasso: Masterworks from The Museum of Modern Art,* French Impressionists, and the works of Norman Rockwell.

The High Museum is open Tuesday through Thursday and Saturday, 10 a.m. to 5 p.m., Sunday noon to 5 p.m., and Friday 10 a.m. to 9 p.m. It's closed on Mondays and holidays. Admission is $6 for adults, $4 for students with ID and persons older than 64, and $2 for youth 6 to 17. Admission is free for museum members and children younger than 6. Occasionally a special exhibition may have a surcharge but will be free to all on Thursday afternoons from 1 p.m. to 5 p.m. Special admission prices and extended hours prevail during some exhibitions.

The 135,000-square-foot High Museum of Art is part of the Robert W. Woodruff Arts Center and is served by the Arts Center MARTA station. Paid parking is available in the Arts Center garage; there is limited on-street parking behind the Arts Center. You may also park on some streets in the Ansley Park neighborhood across Peachtree Street, but be sure to obey all posted regulations and cross busy Peachtree only at the pedestrian crosswalks. The least expensive and hassle-free transportation option is to take MARTA, exit at the Arts station, and simply walk across Lombardy Way to the museum. This is also the best way to get to the Atlanta Symphony, the Atlanta College of Art, and the Atlanta Theatre.

The High Cafe with Alon's is a basement-level eatery open at various hours throughout the museum's hours of operation. Alon's began in Virginia-Highlands and opened a branch across from the Fox Theatre. Alon's was asked to create a space at the museum. Visitors now get to take a break in this windowed-facility munching on Alon's signature sandwiches, soups, croissants, and muffins that look good and taste better.

The High Museum of Art Folk Art, and Photography Galleries

- 30 John Wesley Dobbs Avenue N.E., Atlanta; ✆ (404) 577-6940

On the ground floor of the Georgia-Pacific Center at the corner of Peachtree Street and John Wesley Dobbs Avenue, just north of Woodruff Park, the multi-level downtown branch of the High showcases photography and folk art.

Open Monday through Saturday from 10 a.m. to 5 p.m.; admission is always free. It's open until 8 p.m. the first Thursday of the month. The 51-story Georgia-Pacific Center is across Peachtree Street; the museum's main entrance is on the Dobbs Avenue side; you may also enter through the building's lobby.

Michael C. Carlos Museum

- Emory University, 571 S. Kilgo Street N.E., Atlanta; ✆ (404) 727-4282

This cavernous building on the quadrangle at the heart of Emory University was created by acclaimed architect Michael Graves. Visitors often comment on how the museum's striking design suggests a cathedral.

The design's incorporation of both ancient and classical elements is appropriate to the museum's 12,000-piece collection that is strongest in its selection of objects from antiquity. Art and objects of daily life from ancient Egypt, Greece, Rome, Africa, and the Americas are displayed inside galleries whose proportions and features honor timeless design ideals.

The museum is open seven days a week: Monday to Saturday from 10 a.m. to 5 p.m. (except Friday until 9 p.m.), and Sunday noon to 5 p.m.; it's closed on major holidays. Admission is by donation—$3 is suggested. Parking is free in a small lot right behind the museum. Paid parking is available in the Jones Building lot nearby.

Robert C. Williams American Museum of Papermaking

- Institute of Paper Science and Technology, 500 Tenth Street N.W., Atlanta; ✆ (404) 894-7840

On the outer limits of the Georgia Tech campus, this tiny museum is located on the main floor of the Institute of Paper Science and Technology. Each show lasts three months and features artifacts having to do with papermaking by hand or machine from B.C. to present times. Changing exhibitions bring in paper artists so that the entire spectrum of the paper arts from history, to art, to science are covered.

Hours are 9 a.m. to 5 p.m., Monday to Friday. Admission is free. The museum also holds papermaking and paper art workshops for children and adults.

William Breman Jewish Heritage Museum

- 1440 Spring Street N.W., Atlanta; ✆ (404) 873-1661

- ⌨ www.atlantajewishmuseum.org

The Southeast's largest Jewish museum, dedicated to collecting, preserving, studying, and interpreting the history and culture of the Atlanta Jewish community, opened in June 1996. Rotating exhibits and educational programming and two core museums as well as archives and libraries distinguish the William Breman Jewish Heritage Museum.

Housed in the Atlanta Jewish Federation, the museum was made possible by a contribution from William Breman and the Atlanta Jewish Federation. A new building on Spring Street (the land itself a gift of the Selig family) was constructed just two blocks south of Interstate 75 in Midtown adjacent to the Center for Puppetry Arts.

The first core gallery documents the Holocaust years and the second profiles the Jews of Atlanta from 1845 to the present. Rotating exhibitions for 1998 include *French Children of the Holocaust/A Memorial Exhibition*; *Jews Germany Memory*, a photo exhibit chronicling the relationship between Germany and its Jews; *Masters of Ceremony, the Second Annual Exhibition and Sale of Contemporary Handcrafted Judaica*; and *Birth of Israel/Celebrating Fifty Years of Life*.

The museum also houses the Ida Pearle and Joseph Cuba Community Archives and Genealogy Center where individual and family papers, business, and organizational records, oral histories, and visual arts reveal Atlanta's Jewish history. A library with resource materials for genealogical research and archival materials including Holocaust-related books, videos, and more is available for scholars and students, and a Discovery Center with hands-on activities related to the museum's exhibitions keeps children involved.

The Lillian and A.J. Weinberg Center for Holocaust Education at the Museum sponsors summer courses for teachers, exhibitions, school programs, teacher guides, and general public programs designed to heighten Holocaust awareness.

Security is tight at the Jewish Heritage Museum. Hours are Monday through Thursday 10 a.m. to 5 p.m., Friday 10 a.m. to 3 p.m., and Sunday 1 p.m. to 5 p.m. Parking is free. Admission is $5 for adults, $3 for students and seniors. Children younger than 6 are admitted gratis if accompanied by an adult. Group rates are available.

MUSIC

CLASSICAL

The Atlanta Opera

- 728 West Peachtree Street, Atlanta, GA; (404) 355-3311

- www.atlantaopera.org

Opera has long held an important place in Atlanta's cultural life. From 1910 to 1987, the city was a regular stop on the Metropolitan Opera's tour, and Atlantans were treated to such legendary vocal talents as Enrico Caruso, Geraldine Farrar, Olive Fremstad, and Birgit Nilsson. When the Met gave up touring for financial reasons in 1987, Atlanta was said to be the only city on the tour still meeting its financial obligation to the company.

Atlanta was the birthplace of the great diva Mattiwilda Dobbs. When she made her operatic debut in 1950 at age 25 at La Scala in Milan, Italy, the soprano was the first African-American to perform in that famous opera house. Dobbs, who graduated from Spelman College, went on to sing with the Metropolitan Opera. When her nephew, Maynard Jackson, was elected Atlanta's first black mayor, Dobbs returned to Atlanta to sing at his inauguration.

Several local companies produced a variety of operas through the years; then in 1985 the Atlanta Opera was formed. The company produces fully staged operas with an excellent chorus of local singers and principal singers from around the nation and the world. Numerous veterans of the Metropolitan Opera have appeared in recent years, including Martile Rowland, Jan Grissom, Tatiana Troyanos, Hao Jiang Tian, and Timothy Noble. The Atlanta Opera received such widespread acclaim and exceptional attendance that it added a production as well as a subscription series and a matinee series to the 1997-98 season.

All performances are given in the original language with English supertitles projected above the stage. Performances are held at the fabulous Fox Theatre. The 2000 season under the direction of artistic director William Fred Scott included such classics as *Turandot* and *Rigoletto*.

The company's Atlanta Opera Studio is an educational outreach program that brings fully staged and costumed operas into schools across Georgia. To charge season or individual tickets, call the Atlanta Opera at the number listed above or call (800) 356-7372. Individual ticket prices range from $18 to $120.

Atlanta Symphony Orchestra

- Symphony Hall, Woodruff Arts Center, 1280 Peachtree Street N.E., Atlanta; ✆ (404) 733-5000

- ✍ www.atlantasymphony.org

If you fear you'll need to refinance your house to enjoy a night of classical music with the internationally acclaimed Atlanta Symphony, Mr. C has come to the rescue. You should be aware that tickets start at just $15, and some performances are even free!

In only 50 years, the Atlanta Symphony Orchestra (ASO) grew from an inspired group of high school music students into a major orchestra with an international reputation. Since the 1976 release of its first commercial recording, the ASO's work has earned 14 Grammy Awards. The orchestra's renown grew steadily under the leadership of Robert Shaw, who passed the baton to Yoel Levi in 1988 after 21 years as music director. In 2000, Robert Spano, music director of the Brooklyn Philharmonic, was named to replace Levy, and Donald Runnicles, music director of the San Francisco Opera, was named principal guest conductor.

The ASO has commissioned and premiered works by Aaron Copland, Leonard Bernstein, Philip Glass, and Gian Carlo Menotti. In 1994, the Pointer Sisters headlined the ASO's Gospel Christmas concerts, which were taped and broadcast nationally on PBS.

The regular ASO season runs from September to May. The festive summer series, inaugurated in 1972, takes place under the stars in the 6,000-seat amphitheater at Chastain Park in Buckhead. This very popular series, attracting more than 150,000 patrons, has grown to include 30 concerts headlined by famous pop and country stars. All shows feature reserved tables for picnicking in style. In 1998, the Atlanta Symphony celebrated its 25th season at Chastain.

Also during the summer, watch for the orchestra's free concerts in Piedmont and other city parks. Here you'll find tens of thousands of Atlantans lounging on blankets amid flickering candles, transported by the magic of music as the heat of the day breaks and the evening cool sweeps through the park.

A variety of full- and partial-season subscription packages is offered; call the Season Ticket

Office ☎ (404) 733-4800. For tickets to orchestra concerts, call ☎ (404) 733-5000 or visit the High Museum Shop in Perimeter Mall, 4400 Ashford Dunwoody Road N.E. (a service charge applies). Ticket prices for individual concerts range from $15 to $90 but are reduced for family concerts and youth orchestra concerts. Public sneak preview rehearsals are held before the opening of six regular season concerts. These previews are given in Symphony Hall on the Thursday morning before the program's Thursday night premiere.

Capitol City Opera Company

- 1266 West Paces Ferry Road, Atlanta; ☎ (770) 92-4197
- ✎ www.tourmaline.com/capitolcity

Want some professional-quality opera and dinner on the cheap? The CCOC performs at the Michael C. Carlos Museum and in many area schools, boasting a seasonal program featuring traditional and modern operas. Capitol City Opera also offers a chamber series and performs arias from various operas at special Tuesday night programs at San Gennaro restaurant. The regular tickets cost around $50 each, but that includes the show, a three-course dinner, and two glasses of wine!

Music at Emory

- Glenn Memorial Auditorium, 1652 N. Decatur Road, Atlanta; ☎ (404) 727-5050
- Emory Performing Arts Studio, 1804 N. Decatur Road, Atlanta; ☎ (404) 727-5050

Emory's Flora Glenn Candler International Artists series and Music à la Carte bring international stars to Atlanta audiences. Recent performers have included the Academy of St. Martin in the Fields and "The Three Concertmasters," a program with the three renowned violinists: Cecylia Arzewski of the Atlanta Symphony Orchestra, Martin Chalifour of the Los Angeles Symphony, and William Preucil of the Cleveland Orchestra.

JAZZ/BLUES

Maybe Mr. C is getting a little older, but the fine lines that try to define musical styles have become even finer. Acid jazz, hip-hop, and house have replaced what used to be easy-to-identify genres of music. Oh well . . . that doesn't mean there aren't any bargains for the serious night crawler.

Be aware that some clubs often offer "themed" nights on different days of the week, so it's best to call your local nightspot to check on acts and cover prices. In general, you'll be able to get into hotel lounges for free, whereas the independent clubs listed here will usually charge a cover price of $5 to $15, depending on who is playing.

The Bar at the Ritz-Carlton Buckhead

- 3434 Peachtree Road N.E., Atlanta; ☎ (404) 237-2700

Puttin' on the Ritz may not be one's idea of a bargain. But what could beat a single, leisurely cocktail in such a relaxing setting while enjoying a jazz trio? Mr. C thinks not much.

Beluga

- 3115 Piedmont Road N.E., Atlanta; ☎ (404) 869-1090

Take it easy with easy listening at this cozy, upscale nightspot. There's nightly entertainment Monday through Saturday, with alternating jazz and pop/show tunes. Shows start at 10:30 p.m.

Dante's Down the Hatch

- 3380 Peachtree Road N.E., Atlanta; (404) 266-1600

Restaurateur and car collector Dante Stephenson runs this Buckhead mainstay, and runs it well. The place resembles a pirate ship, complete with multiple levels, moats, and some alligators thrown in for good measure. You can get a good fondue meal here, and Dante's claims to have "a better mixed drink," using call-brand liquor, and pouring a minimum of 1 1/4 ounces. (Now that's value!) The Paul Mitchell Trio is on board six nights a week. Other jazz and acoustic acts also appear on the Wharf. The cover charge here is $7.

Liquid

- 293 Pharr Road N.E., Atlanta; (404) 262-0604

This cool club hosts an assortment of hip thirtysomethings (and slightly more mature folks in the Cheapster's age range), with dancing on three levels to live jazz and recorded R&B music. Do enjoy a discount by calling to see if there are any drink specials or special party promotions.

Sambuca Jazz Cafe

- 3102 Peachtree Road N.E., Atlanta; (404) 237-5299

- www.sambucajazzcafe.com

If an upscale jazz supper club is your thing, and you normally don't like Mondays, swing on over to Sambuca on Mondays when swing acts take the stage. It may be part of a Texas-based chain, but you'd be hard pressed to find such a good time this early in the week anyplace else. And, there's no cover here!

FOLK/COFFEEHOUSE

Eddie's Attic

- 515 N. McDonough Street, Decatur, GA; (404) 377-4976

- www.eddiesattic.com

You've gotta check out Eddie's. This folk club is where the Indigo Girls got their start, way back when they were just Emory University students eager to play gigs anywhere. There is something going on at Eddie's nearly every night of the week, running the gamut from internationally known singer/songwriters to open mic nights (free admission) highlighting the best of Atlanta's up-and-coming talent.

And, you never know who you might run into here. Even after they made it big, Emily Saliers and Amy Ray, of the aforementioned Indigo Girls, were still stopping by to jam now and then.

Following is a listing of more informal coffeehouses held in and around the Atlanta area. These places open once a month unless otherwise noted, and have very low cover charges. Call their respective phone numbers for details on upcoming events.

Hungry Ear Coffeehouse

- Northwest Unitarian Congregation, 1025 Mt. Vernon Highway, Sandy Springs; (770) 955-1408

Performances the first Saturday of the month. Music starts at 8 p.m. A $5 donation is requested.

Grounds 'n' Sounds

- Gwinnett History Museum, 455 Perry Street, Lawrenceville; (770) 822-5178.

Performances happen on the second Friday of the month. Doors open at

8 p.m., with music and readings beginning at 8:30 p.m. $4. Beverages and light snacks available for purchase.

Lena's Place

- Central Congregational Church, 2676 Clairmont Road, Atlanta; (404) 373-0831

Open the second Saturday of the month from 8:30 p.m. to 10:30 p.m. $3 donation requested.

Fiddler's Green—3rd Saturday

- Garden Hills Recreation Center, with occasional variations; (404) 371-9371.

Doors open at 7:30 p.m. Admission is $8 to $12, though kids are free. Coffee, tea, soft drinks, and light snacks available for purchase.

Strings n' Things

- Dahlonega United Methodist Church, South Park Street, Dahlonega; (706) 864-4127; (706) 864-6439.

Open on the third Saturday of each month, offering a wide range of music with an emphasis on traditional styles. Doors open at 7 p.m.

Gwinnett History Museum Coffee-Ceilidh

- 455 Perry Street, Lawrenceville; (770) 822-5178.

Open on the fourth Friday of each month, doors open at 8 p.m. Beverages and Irish snacks are available for purchase.

Moonsongs

- Unitarian Universalist Congregation of Gwinnett, Lawrenceville; (770) 513-1968.

Open the fourth Saturday of each month. Doors open at 7:15 p.m., and a $4 donation is requested. Beverages and light snacks are available for purchase.

DANCE/DISCO

The Chili Pepper

- 208 Pharr Road N.E., Atlanta; (404) 812-9266

Neon-lit bars, cartoons on the walls, funky sofas, and more fill this hot club where DJs rule and food is out. If you get there before 10:30 p.m. you'll stand a good chance of not paying the reasonable cover charge.

CJ's Landing

- 270 Buckhead Avenue N.E., Atlanta; (404) 237-7657

Bar food and brews as well as dance music from the '70s and '80s are the attractions. That, and the 100-year-old oak tree that grows through the roof on the covered deck. Open 8 p.m. to 2 a.m. Tuesday, Wednesday, Thursday, and Sunday, and 7 p.m. to 3 a.m. Fridays and Saturdays.

Cobalt

- 265 E. Paces Ferry Road, Atlanta; (404) 760-9250

This is what Mr. C thinks of when he thinks "club." This sleek lounge/discotheque is beautifully designed. The music mix is diverse as the dancers on the two-level dance floor.

Lulu's Bait Shack

- 3057 Peachtree Road N.E., Atlanta; (404) 262-5220

Dance the night away to recorded music from 10 p.m. to 4 a.m. Lulu's Bait Shack is famous for its fishbowl size drinks; And if you're feeling game, alligator tail, catfish, and chicken are on the menu.

Metropolitan Pizza Bar

- 3055 Bolling Way, Atlanta; (404) 264-0135

Metropolitan Pizza Bar serves pizza and salad, has live music on weekends, and spins disco at the Wednesday night "Pizza a Go-Go" parties. Sometimes there's a small cover charge.

Tongue & Groove

- 3055 Peachtree Road N.E., Atlanta; (404) 261-2325

This ultra-cool venue, opened in 1994, is a drinking, dancing, pure club experience. The interior is designed to make the beautiful people look even better, with contemporary custom furnishings and flattering lighting. Sushi and lighter fare are available, but martinis and metropolitans are more likely to be consumed. There's a dance floor in the back room, where hedonistic yuppies and dedicated clubbers can be seen dancing the night away.

Dress is upscale, and there's a moderate cover charge after 10 p.m.

The World Bar

- 3071 Peachtree Road N.E., Atlanta; (404) 266-0627

The self-proclaimed "largest club in Buckhead" is open only Friday and Saturday nights, and it seems like all of younger Atlanta drops in at some point over the weekend. There's a small cover, but all drinks are $2. The atmosphere is wide open, and you should try to grab a pool table early.

ROCK/POP

The Brandyhouse

- 4365 Roswell Road N.E., Atlanta; (404) 252-7784

This English-style restaurant and pub plays pop and rock from local and national bands on a sound system that's a cut above many local live music venues.

Bar

- 250 E. Paces Ferry Road N.E., Atlanta; (404) 841-0033

"No theme, no attitude, just Bar" is the slogan at this bar without a story where patrons enjoy chugging "bobsled shooters," which are poured through an ice sculpture. Bar is open Wednesday through Saturday nights, and there's a small cover after 10 p.m. on weekends. Thursdays are college nights.

LATIN/SALSA

Asti's Terrace Lounge

- 3199 Paces Ferry Road N.W., Atlanta; (404) 364-9160

If you're looking for an intimate club experience, check out this rather small place, which is connected to Asti's Italian restaurant. Here you'll enjoy live jazz and Latin music for dancing.

Café Tu Tu Tango

- 220 Pharr Road N.E., Atlanta; (404) 841-6222

- www.cafetutuango.com/atlanta

This cafe, which features tapas appetizers, will also temp your senses with bar with its walls covered in artwork, live jazz groups for your listening pleasure, painters to interpret the scene, and even tarot card readers to look into the future.

You can Tango Monday through Thursday 11 a.m. to 11 p.m., and 11:30 a.m. to 2 a.m. Fridays and Saturdays.

Sanctuary

- 128 E. Andrews Drive N.E., Atlanta; (404) 262-1377

This is one of the oldest—and still the hottest—Latin nightclubs in the metro area. The 1,000-square-foot dance floor opens at 8 p.m. on Thursdays and at 9 p.m. on Fridays, featuring free salsa dance lessons the first hour each night. It opens at 10 p.m. on Saturdays. Moderate cover.

ECLECTIC

The Bar at the Palm

- 3391 Peachtree Road N.E., in the Swissotel, Atlanta; (404) 814-1955

After enjoying the pricey steak dinners at the lobby restaurant of the upscale Swissotel, slip into the adjacent bar for a quiet drink in a decidedly unsnooty location. The general manager has been known to boast, "I just run a saloon."

Dance City Ballroom

- 2581 Piedmont Road N.E., Atlanta; (404) 266-0166

Enjoy ballroom dancing in a smoke-free and alcohol-free environment. The Ballroom hosts public dances 9 p.m. Wednesdays and Saturdays for a small cover. Lessons are also available.

Have a Nice Day! Cafe

- 3095 Peachtree Road N.E., Atlanta; (404) 261-8898

Just like its name implies, this casual place to meet is right out of the '70s. Open Wednesdays through Saturdays; the music starts at 8 p.m.

Johnny's Hideaway

- 3771 Roswell Road, Atlanta; (404) 233-8026
- www.johnnyshideaway.com

This self-described "nightclub for big kids" showcases music from the '40s to the '80s. Dress is business casual, and the crowd tends to be 35 and older. Johnny's is open every night; there's a two-drink minimum but no cover.

OUTDOOR AND SPORTS ACTIVITIES

Agnes Scott College Tree Tour

- 141 E. College Avenue, Decatur, GA; (404) 471-6000
- www.agnesscott.edu

This college, founded in 1859, has a lovely campus with many trees more than a century old. The college offers a booklet for self-guided tours of its unique tree heritage that includes protected old trees as well as new plantings. Southern magnolias, an incense cedar, sawtooth oaks, and a white ash predating the Civil War are among the trees on this tour. With seven days notice, the college provides guided tree tours for groups of 10 to 30 people.

Centennial Olympic Park

- 265 Lucky Street N.W., Atlanta; (404) 223-4412

- www.gwcc.com

Built as a gathering place for visitors during Atlanta's 1996 Summer Olympics, this 21-acre park continues to be a great place to meet and have some fun downtown. It boasts an amphitheater, a visitor's center, picnic shelters, and landscaped grounds containing modern sculptures and memorials. Just strolling around the grounds it a fun—and cheap—activity for a sunny afternoon any time of the year. Probably the most fun thing to do in the park, however, is to visit the **Fountain of Rings**, made up of 251 computer-controlled water jets, 400 fog jets, and 487 lights. In fact, it's the world's largest fountain formed in the shape of the Olympics' famous logo of five interconnected rings! During the warmer months, the city mounts a special water show here with synchronized music, sound effects, and fabulous lights. The show takes place daily at 12:30 p.m., 3:30 p.m., 6:30 p.m., and 9 p.m. Talk about cheap thrills!

The park is open daily from 7 a.m. to 11 p.m.

Chastain Memorial Park

- 235 West Wieuca Road, Atlanta; (404) 851-1273

For years, this park has provided an oasis from downtown for all walks of life. Located about 8 miles north of downtown, CMP has a 3.5-mile jogging trail, a gym, and athletic fields for softball, soccer, football, and baseball. The park also offers picnic and playground areas plus a swimming pool. Chastain Arts Center and Gallery holds exhibits and classes regularly. The tennis facilities are the site of Atlanta Lawn Tennis Association tournaments, and the public golf course remains popular.

Perhaps the biggest attraction is the amphitheater, which seats more than 6,000 patrons. Here city dwellers revel in various entertainments, including symphony concerts, theater productions, and performances by popular musical acts. On most balmy summer evenings, locals pack a picnic dinner and head for Chastain to enjoy an evening alfresco.

Chattahoochee Nature Center

- 9135 Willeo Road, Roswell, GA; (770) 992-2055

- www.vickery.net/cnc

CNC has two trails that allow hikers to explore different environments. The woodland trail meanders through the forest near the river, which abounds with oak, hickory, and evergreen trees and supports such wildlife as hawks, jays, woodpeckers, and raccoons. The wetlands trail has a boardwalk that winds through Redwing Marsh, a habitat for beavers, muskrats, ducks, geese, red-winged blackbirds, and kingfishers.

Hike the trails Monday through Saturday 9 a.m. to 5 p.m., and Sunday noon to 5 p.m. Admission is $3 for adults, $2 for children and seniors.

Chattahoochee River National Recreation Area

- 1978 Island Ford Parkway, Dunwoody GA; (770) 399-8070

- www.nps.gov/chat

This recreation area offers more than 50 miles of trails divided into 16 land units that stretch along 48 miles of the Chattahoochee River's shoreline from Cobb Parkway on the west side of town to Buford Dam on Lake Lanier in the east. All the units offer scenic views of the river and surrounding forests; many also offer fishing and rafting opportunities. In the local lingo, rafting or canoeing down the Chattahoochee is known as "shooting the 'Hooch." The area has a 3.1-mile fitness trail beginning at the Cochran Shoals unit off I-285 at Powers Ferry Road, complete with exercise stations. This trail is suitable for walking, jogging, and biking. The trails vary in levels of difficulty; the park staff will advise you on which ones suit your needs and abilities.

At Sope Creek off Paper Mill Road in East Cobb and Vickery Creek in Roswell, you can explore the ruins of old mills. Throughout the recreation area, you will observe an array of plant life and wildlife and maybe even get in some people watching at the more popular units. Parking permits at the various recreation sites are $2 per car. The park is open daily, dawn to dusk.

Grant Park

- Georgia and Cherokees Avenues S.E., Atlanta; ✆ (404) 624-0697

Historic Grant Park is about 2 miles southeast of downtown. Take I-20, get off at the Boulevard exit, go south to Sydney Street, west to Cherokee Avenue, then south to the park entrance.

Loaded with history, Grant Park was once home to Creek Indians. Confederate artillery troops lined the park's eastern perimeter during the Battle of Atlanta.

The park was named for Lemuel Grant, a 19th-century philanthropist and former Confederate engineer who designed Atlanta's defenses against Union troops. Col. Grant donated land for the park from his sizable estate. (All that remains today are the ruins of his house in the adjacent neighborhood.)

Grant Park's athletic fields and pavilions make it a popular relaxation spot. Various amateur leagues for football, softball, and other sports use the park's athletic facilities. Perhaps its prime attractions are **Zoo Atlanta** (see the listing below) and the **Cyclorama** (see the listing under *Museums)*. Nearby you'll find Oakland Cemetery, a burial ground of famous figures such as Margaret Mitchell, author of *Gone With the Wind,* and golfing great Bobby Jones. The area abounds in lovely old Victorian homes reflecting the neighborhood's heyday. Many have been fully restored; some are still in the process of restoration. Every September, the Grant Park Tour of Homes draws crowds to view these reminders of bygone days. Much of the area is on the National Register of Historic Places.

Kennesaw Mountain National Battlefield Park

- 905 Kennesaw Mountain Drive, Marietta, GA; ✆ (770) 427-4686

- ⌨ www.nps.gov/kemo

Sixteen miles of hiking trails take you through the 2,884-acre park in which a bloody Civil War battle was fought more than a century ago. See Confederate cannon, a monument to slain Union soldiers, preserved trench works, and troop movement maps. If you don't care to study war, take in the beautiful mountain scenery instead. The visitors' center has maps for self-guided walks. The park is free and open daily from 8:30 a.m. to 5 p.m.

Laurel Park

- 151 Manning Road, Marietta, GA; (770) 794-5633

This public park on the west side of Marietta is popular with kids, who love to feed the ducks on the park's small lake. A 1-mile paved jogging trail winds alongside the water and through the woods, with exercise stations along the way. There are also 13 tennis courts; two covered picnic areas; basketball, volleyball, and shuffleboard courts; and a playground.

The park is open daily from 6 a.m. to 11 p.m. To reserve a court or picnic pavilion, call the park office at the above number.

Outdoor Activity Center

- 1442 Richland Road S.W., Atlanta; (404) 752-5385

Three miles southwest of downtown Atlanta, the Outdoor Activity Center sits atop Bush Mountain. The center has a 26-acre hardwood urban forest that's a designated National Recreation Trail. Foot traffic only is allowed on the trail. The center also has an interpretive center, an ecological playscape, a tree house classroom, and picnic tables. The Center is open Monday through Saturday, 9 a.m. to 4 p.m. Admission to educational programs is $3 per student for those in prekindergarten through high school; the center itself is free to the public.

Panola Mountain State Conservation Park

- Stockbridge, GA; (770) 389-7801

Picture Stone Mountain without the development, but with 600 acres of a preserved natural environment surrounding a 100-acre granite outcropping. The park has 6 miles of trails. You can only hike the mountain trails on scheduled hikes led by park guides, but you can take self-guided hikes on the Watershed and Rock Outcrop trails (combined length, 2 miles) adjacent to the park's Interpretive Center. Panola Mountain State Conservation Park opens at 8 a.m. and closes at dark daily.

The nature center is open from 9 a.m. until 5 p.m. Tuesday through Friday, noon to 5 p.m. Saturday and Sunday. Parking is $2 per car every day except Wednesday (when it's free).

PATH Foundation

- 1601 West Peachtree Street N.E., Atlanta; (404) 875-PATH

- www.pathfoundation.org

Since 1991, the PATH Foundation has been building a network of greenway trails throughout the city for safe walking, bicycling, and skating. This nonprofit organization relies on support from volunteers, businesses, and government agencies. By July 1, 1996, PATH had completed construction of a 35-mile, multiuse system that includes greenways connected to on-street bicycle facilities with sidewalks. The trails run from southwest Atlanta to Stone Mountain in the east. Links are planned to connect Buckhead to the Silver Comet trail and Kennesaw Mountain in Cobb County.

PATH trails are designed not only for riding, rolling, and walking enthusiasts to use in their leisure time, but also to provide quick and easy walks or bike rides to MARTA stations for commuters. Trails intersect with rail stations at West Lake, Ashby, and Vine City in the west, and East Lake, Decatur, and Avondale in the east.

The City of Atlanta, the National Parks Service, the Chattahoochee River Keeper, DeKalb County, Cobb County, and Fulton County are participating members of the PATH team. Eventually, PATH plans to construct and maintain a Greenway Trail Network of more than 100 miles. PATH membership entitles you to a quarterly newsletter, an invitation to all PATH activities, and an opportunity to participate in trail building.

Piedmont Park

- Piedmont Avenue and 14th Street N.E., Atlanta; ✆ (404) 892-0117

Atlanta's largest park and home of the Atlanta Botanical Garden, Piedmont Park is the site of numerous fairs, festivals, Atlanta Symphony Orchestra concerts, and much more.

Football and baseball games are commonplace, and softball leagues use the park's athletic fields for spring and summer competitions. Even the massive Peachtree Road Race, held each July 4, ends in Piedmont Park near the 10th Street entrance.

In this 185-acre setting, you'll find a paved jogging trail plus other trails for walking, cycling, and skating. In 1895, the Cotton States and International Exposition took place in Piedmont Park. The Olmsted Brothers firm was hired to design the landscaping for the exposition; much of the park's current design dates from this period. The exposition drew close to a million visitors during its three-month duration. Such dignitaries as President Grover Cleveland, Booker T. Washington, and William McKinley attended the event. After the exposition, an 1898 reunion of Confederate veterans camped on the grounds.

A few years later, the solemn unveiling of the Peace Monument at the 14th Street entrance drew respectful crowds. This work of New York sculptor Allan Newman symbolized the growing spirit of peace and reconciliation between the North and the South. It is said to have been built from funds collected mostly from Northern states.

Piedmont Park became a public park in 1904 when the city bought the land.

A citizens' support group called the Piedmont Park Conservancy was formed in 1989 to support and conserve the park's natural assets through citizen volunteer efforts. This nonprofit's membership sponsors guided walking tours on weekends by appointment, starting at the 12th Street entrance to the park. The group schedules regular work parties to clean and repair features of the park.

In 1996, with some of the $6.5 million already donated, the Conservancy refurbished the "ladies' comfort station" as the park's visitors center. Its showpiece is an 800-square-foot mural on the barrel ceiling, depicting the variety of activities that go on in the park.

Silver Comet Trail

- Cobb, Paulding and Polk Counties

Built with the cooperation of the Georgia departments of Natural Resources and Transportation, PATH Foundation and Cobb County, the Silver Comet Trail winds 57 miles through three counties on a former railroad bed. Bicyclists, walkers, joggers, dog walkers, and skaters—anyone without motors—enjoy the historical remains of the Silver Comet rail line as it passes through small towns and beside abundant plant life and interesting geological formations. Along the way are bridges, tunnels, forests, and farmlands. Although it is graded, only portions of the trail are paved, with other areas still packed gravel. It is wheelchair accessible.

Sweetwater Creek State Park

- Mt. Vernon Road, Lithia Springs, GA; ✆ (770) 732-5871

About 18 miles west of downtown, Sweetwater Creek State Park features a trail leading to the ruins of the New Manchester Manufacturing Company. During the Civil War, the New Manchester textile mill supplied goods to the Confederacy. Not surprisingly, the Yankees burned it down. The trail goes through a forest that contains the factory ruins and the ruins of some old homesteads from the abandoned mill village, and then proceeds along the banks of Sweetwater Creek to Sweetwater Falls. The half-mile walk to the falls is not an easy trek. You have to climb over boulders and up steep hills. You'll walk about 3 miles if you hike to the ruins, the falls, and back. It costs $2 per car to get into this park, which is open 7 a.m. to 10 p.m. daily. The trails close daily at dark.

Stone Mountain

- Stone Mountain Parkway, Stone Mountain; ✆ (770) 498-5690
- www.stonemountainpark.com

About 16 miles east of downtown, Stone Mountain is one of the best-known Atlanta area landmarks. The centerpiece of the park is the gigantic granite outcropping on which the likenesses of Confederate heroes Jefferson Davis, Robert E. Lee, and Stonewall Jackson are carved. But it's the high-tech summer laser shows that draw the crowds these days. Recreational activities include a trail to the top of the mountain, tennis, fishing, a golf course, and beach. Festivals are scheduled from May through December (see the listings under *Festivals*), with one of the highlights being the Scottish Highland Games, usually in October. Admission to the park is free, although there's usually a $2 parking fee.

Zoo Atlanta Grant Park

- 800 Cherokee Avenue S.E., Atlanta; ✆ (404) 624-5600
- www.zooatlanta.org

This world-class zoo can provide an educational, fun, and relatively inexpensive afternoon's entertainment. Check out the Giant Pandas of Chengdu, as well as gorillas, orangutans, tigers, lions, bears (oh my!), and all manner of exotic animals—large and small—from around the world. The Zoo is open Monday through Saturday from 9:30 a.m. to 4:30 p.m., and until 5:30 p.m. on the weekends. It's closed on Thanksgiving, Christmas, and New Year's Day. Admission is $15 for adults, $11 for seniors, and $10 for kids from ages 3 to 11. Children younger than three years of age get in free.

THEATER

Mr. C has the answer on how to save money on professional theater in town: volunteer to be an usher. Many theaters use regular folks to help rip tickets, hand out programs, or guide people to their seats. In exchange for your services, you can watch the show for free. Responsibilities are light; you'll have to dress nicely, arrive a bit early to learn the seating plan, and then go to it. As soon as the show begins, find a seat for yourself and enjoy the show—you're all done. Contact venues for details.

Meanwhile, here are some of the good, inexpensive theater companies around the Atlanta area:

7 Stages

- 1105 Euclid Avenue N.E., Atlanta; (404) 523-7647
- www.7stages.org

From its humble beginnings in a storefront in 1979, 7 Stages has grown into a major company operating two theaters in a former Little Five Points movie house. Risk-taking is a hallmark: An anti-Klan musical staged here in 1986 provoked the first Ku Klux Klan rally in the city in 30 years. Typical productions include experimental plays, dramas by local writers, international works, and alternative stagings of classics. The complex has a 200-seat main stage and a 90-seat black box space (entrance in the rear). A recent season featured Brecht's *In the Jungle of Cities, The Burning Lake* by Celeste Miller, *The Bald Soprano* by Ionesco, The Freddie Hendricks Youth Ensemble of Atlanta in *PSALM 13*, and *Dream Boy*, adapted and directed by Eric Rosen.

Ticket prices are $10 and $15 for the small stage productions and $15 and $20 for those on the main stage.

The Academy Theatre

- 501 Means Street N.W. Atlanta; (404) 525-4111
- www.mindspring.com/~academytheatre

The Academy produces all-original works and performs before school and community groups as well as at the playhouse. Through the spring, new plays are showcased through staged readings in the New Plays series.

Offerings in the Academy's Theatre for Youth program include "Mixin' in the Mall," a company-developed vehicle that explores conflict resolution and violence for grades six through eight, and "Fleas in the Cheese," an introduction to theater for children in preschool through second grade.

Actor's Express

- King Plow Arts Center, Atlanta; (404) 607-7467
- www.actorsexpress.com

One of Atlanta's most respected theater companies, AE presents classics, comedies, and tough psychological dramas. This troupe started way back in 1988 in a church basement. In 1991 this group produced the world premiere of *The Harvey Milk Show*, a musical based on the life of the assassinated San Francisco gay rights leader. It played to sold-out audiences and was later produced in other cities. In 1997, Actor's Express created more controversy when it modified the classic musical, *Oklahoma*. The publishers and copyright holders of the Rogers and Hammerstein work objected to the changes to the original script, so the director and cast had to make last-minute changes back to the original script to avoid having to close the show.

Agatha's—A Taste of Mystery

- 693 Peachtree Street N.E., Atlanta; ✆ (404) 875-1610

Agatha's is a mystery dinner theatre where the audience is part of the show. When guests arrive, each is given a small assignment, such as making up unusual song lyrics on the spot. The plays are all originals with names such as *An Affair to Dismember* and *Cat on a Hot Tin Streetcar*.

However, we're not just talking about a play here: The evening includes a five-course meal, wine, and beverages. (Cocktails, tax, and tip are extra.) Admission is $40 per person Sunday through Thursday and $45 per person on Friday, Saturday, and holidays. Monday through Saturday seatings are at 7:30 p.m.; on Sundays the fun starts at 7 p.m. Agatha's is across from the Fox Theatre; call for reservations.

Alliance Theatre Company

- Woodruff Arts Center, 1280 Peachtree Street N.E., Atlanta; ✆ (404) 733-5000

- ✍ www.alliancetheatre.org

The Alliance's status as a company of national importance was only enhanced when the Alfred Uhry (an Atlantan by birth) play, *Last Night at Ballyhoo*, won a Tony in 1996. Like his *Driving Miss Daisy*, *Last Night* premiered in Atlanta at this Broadway-type theater in the heart of Midtown. More recently, Elton John's *Elaborate Lives*, a retelling of the classic story of *Aida*, was premiered at the Alliance before it was retitled and taken to Broadway.

The theater was also one of only three U.S. theaters chosen by playwright Tony Kushner to mount productions of his Tony Award– and Pulitzer Prize–winning play *Angels in America: Millennium Approaches*.

The Alliance Theatre Company is a nonprofit, professional company that produces main stage, studio, and children's productions. The company has historically been a vanguard for theatrical productions with world premieres including Tennessee Williams' *Tiger Tale* and Ed Gracyk's *Come Back to the Five and Dime, Jimmy Dean, Jimmy Dean*.

More recently Atlantan Pearl Cleage's *Flyin' West* as well as her latest play, *Bourbon at the Border*, were premiered in The Studio Theatre at Woodruff Arts Center. Seasons typically include contemporary plays, classic dramas, and musicals. Recent productions include *A Question of Mercy* by David Rabe, *The Colored Museum* by George C. Wolfe, *Medea* by Euripides, and Richard Kalinoski's *Beast on the Moon*.

In addition, Alliance Theatre artists bring performing art into metro Atlanta's schools throughout the year.

Season ticket holders save 45 percent off the single-ticket price. A generous ticket exchange program exists that also means you might be able to pick up a last minute exchanged ticket. There isn't a bad seat in the house so take whatever is available. Call ✆ (404) 733-4600 for details.

Atlanta Broadway Series

- 659 Peachtree Street N.E., Atlanta; ✆ (404) 873-4300

The Fox Theatre is the setting for the American Express Atlanta Broadway Series, which presents national touring companies in topnotch productions of Broadway hits. Recent seasons included *Riverdance* at the Atlanta Civic Center and *Rent* and *Cabaret* at The Fox Theatre.

Tickets go on sale at the theater's box office six to eight weeks before a show opens. To charge by phone, call TicketMaster, ✆ (404) 817-8700; a convenience charge applies.

Barking Dog Theatre

- 175 14th Street N.E., Atlanta, GA ✆ (404) 885-1621

Barking Dog Theatre was started by two twentysomething Atlanta actors as a community of apprentices who speak about life with a collective voice that is raw, energetic, and loud. The company presents an eclectic range of works each season.

Center for Puppetry Arts

- 1404 Spring Street N.W., Atlanta; ✆ (404) 873-3391

- ✍ www.puppet.org

Founded in 1978, this unusual theater and museum annually attracts more than 350,000 visitors. Housing three separate theaters and a museum featuring authentic Muppet characters plus puppets from around the world, the center is the largest facility of its kind in North America. Programs include family-oriented shows and puppet-making workshops and classes.

The center also has two adult-oriented series: the New Direction Series, which features innovative shows by the center's company as well as national and international artists, and the Xperimental Puppetry Theater, an annual showcase for works in progress for adult audiences.

The center is closed Sundays and holidays; museum admission is $5 for adults and $4 for children 13 and younger; performances cost extra, but the museum's special exhibits are $2 with the purchase of any other ticket for the same day.

Call the above number for reservations and the ticket office, ✆ (404) 874-3089, or 24-hour hotline, ✆ (404) 874-0398, for schedules and performance prices.

Georgia Shakespeare Festival

- Oglethorpe University, 4484 Peachtree Road N.E., Atlanta; ✆ (404) 264-0020

- ✍ www.gashakespeare.org

This festival has seen its annual attendance more than double since its inaugural season in 1985. Performances are held on the campus of Oglethorpe University, whose Gothic architecture affords a fine setting for productions of Shakespeare. Originally staged in a tent, the festival now has its own $5.7 million theater. The feel of the open-air tent has been retained through the use of roll-up walls for when the evenings are pleasant. But for those typical Georgia nights rich with humidity and the occasional thunderstorm, the walls will stay in place and air-conditioning will keep actors and audience blissfully comfortable.

An evening at the festival begins at 6:30 p.m. when the grounds open for picnicking. At 7 p.m., there's cabaret-style entertainment. Performances begin at 8 p.m. The rotating repertory schedule for begins in mid-June.

Horizon Theatre Company

- 1083 Austin Avenue N.E., Atlanta; ✆ (404) 584-7450

- ✍ www.horizontheatre.com

Lisa and Jeff Adler have operated Horizon since 1983 out of an intimate, 185-seat theater in a rehabilitated school building at the intersection of Euclid and Austin avenues in Little Five Points. The professional, nonprofit company's productions range from satire to drama with a special emphasis on new plays and playwrights. In addition to four main stage productions annually, Horizon develops new writers through its New Horizons readings and cultivates new theater-lovers through its Teen Ensemble and Senior Citizens Ensemble acting and playwriting programs.

Past productions included *Abducting Hillary* by Dario Fo, Nicky Silver's *The Food Chain*, David Hare's *Racing Demon*, and *The Screened-in Porch* by Marian X.

Jewish Theatre of the South

- 14th Street Playhouse, Atlanta; (770) 368-7469

Jewish Theatre of the South presented its first musical in 1998 with *Hello Muddah! Hello Faddah!*, the Allan Sherman musical, as well as its first production of an American Jewish theater classic, Elmer Rice's *Counselor-At-Law*. In the past, the Jewish community had attempted to create an audience for theater through the now defunct Habima, which began in the '70s under the direction of attorney/actor Howard Stopeck, but the Jewish Community Center auditorium was more like a high school stage than a professional theater. Audiences will love Jewish Theatre of the South's new home at the comfortable and centrally located 14th Street Playhouse in Midtown.

Jomandi Productions

- 1444 Mayson Street N.E., Atlanta; (404) 876-6346

- www.jomandi.com

Founded in 1978, Jomandi is Georgia's oldest and largest African-American professional theater company. Jomandi has received numerous grants from prominent national arts organizations and tours more extensively than any other professional company in the Southeast. More than half its main stage productions have been premieres; the remainder have been stage adaptations of works by established black writers. Performances are given at 14th Street Playhouse, 14th at Juniper streets.

The Shakespeare Tavern

- 499 Peachtree Street N.E., Atlanta; (404) 874-5299

- www.shakespearetavern.com

Four blocks south of the Fox Theatre, this company produces the plays of Shakespeare and other classical authors. Although the setting is casual (chairs and tables for 175 people are arranged tavern-style), the productions are traditional—no need to worry that you'll find King Lear pushing a shopping cart through a post-nuclear slum. The company produces the tragedies as well as the comedies and tries hard to incorporate some of the lesser-known works.

Chef for a Night catering provides a pub-type menu before performances. You can also buy beer, wine, coffee, tea, and soft drinks before performances and at intermission. Ticket prices range from $10 to $19.50.

Theater Emory

- Mary Gray Munroe Theater, Atlanta; (404) 727-5050

Theater Emory has constructed a full-scale replica of an Elizabethan playhouse. Called "The Black Rose," both actors and studio audiences experience what it might have been like to go to a theater during the Elizabethan era.

Theatrical Outfit

- Rialto Center for the Performing Arts, 80 Forsyth Street, Atlanta; ✆ (404) 651-4727

- ⌂ www.theatricaloutfit.org

You might expect to find the type of programs produced at TO to have originated in some loft in New York's Greenwich Village. In fact, Theatrical Outfit was founded in 1976 in a space above an old laundromat in Virginia-Highland. In 1985 the company scored a big hit with a lavish production of *The Rocky Horror Show* that featured everyone's favorite Georgian crossdresser, RuPaul. Now the company stages four productions a year at the 14th Street Playhouse. The Outfit's *Appalachian Christmas*, a play written by local writer Tom Key and revised annually, has become an Atlanta holiday tradition.

WALKS AND TOURS

Atlanta Preservation Center

- 327 St. Paul Avenue, Atlanta; ✆ (404) 688-3353

- ⌂ www.preserveatlanta.com

The Atlanta Preservation Center offers tours of many of the city's historic districts, including the Fox district, Sweet Auburn, Inman Park, Ansley Park, Underground Atlanta, and historic Downtown. The cost for any one of these is $10 per nonmember adult, with students and seniors priced at $5. Atlanta Preservation Center members can take the tours for free.

APC offers tours at various times, days of the week; most of them take place on Saturdays and Sundays. Call the APC for a listing of upcoming tours and locations.

Bulloch Hall

- 180 Bulloch Avenue, Roswell; ✆ (770) 992-1731

Bulloch Hall survived the "War Between the States" by flying the French flag and confusing the Union Army; today, you can tour this antebellum house and its beautiful gardens for just $3.

But there are many other things to see and do here. Bulloch Hall also serves as a cultural center, gallery space, and reference library. Annual events include a March quilt show, a spring "Magnolia Ball," and special Christmas programs. Call for an upcoming schedule of art shows, musical and literary events, and exhibitions. Bulloch Hall also sponsors classes in various arts and crafts, including quilting, basketry, gardening, and folk art.

Tours are given Monday through Friday from 10 a.m. until 3 p.m.; appointments must be made for groups of ten or more. The cost for senior citizens is just $2, students $1, and those under 6 are admitted free.

CNN Studio Tour

- One CNN Center, Techwood Drive and Marietta Street N.W., Atlanta; ✆ (404) 827-2300

- ⌂ www.cnn.com/studiotour

So you want to find out just how the world's largest cable network really works and maybe sneak a peek at some TV news anchors? You can do all this by taking the CNN Studio tour. You'll get to see CNN's two live newsroom/TV studios, and learn about the rest of the empire built by Ted Turner and now owned by AOL Time Warner.

Tours are given daily, every hour between 9 a.m. and 6 p.m.; they sell out quickly, and you'll probably have to buy tickets for tours an hour or two away unless you plan ahead and give 24 hours notice for reservations. It's worth the wait, though, if you're starstruck. From a viewing deck above the newsroom, you can watch reporters scrambling for stories and see a live broadcast in progress, plus a few other surprises. Tour guides are well informed of the company's workings and should be able to answer almost any questions you may have about the network.

Tours last nearly an hour, and CNN makes a point of informing people that the tour involves walking down several flights of stairs (handicapped-accessible tours can be arranged if you call ahead). The cost or the tour is $8 for adults, $6 for senior citizens, $5 for children ages 6 to 12, with children under 6 not permitted. Groups of 30 people or more are asked to call in advance for arrangements.

The tour's well worth the price, though. Not only do you get an insider's view of the network, but you may just get to meet some of the stars, too.

You can also try to get day-of-show free tickets to attend the daily taping of CNN's *TalkBack Live!*

DeKalb Historical Society Tours

- Old Courthouse on the Square, Decatur; ✆ (404) 373-1098

Take a free walking tour of historic downtown Decatur. All you have to do is pick up a brochure—complete with a detailed map, historical facts, and trivia—and start walking. The brochure is available at touristy locations like Underground Atlanta, as well as visitor centers in Atlanta and Decatur.

The tour makes a total of 23 interesting stops, many of which are open to the public, so that you can also step inside and snoop around. Included on the tour are the Old Courthouse, Agnes Scott College, the Decatur Railroad Depot, and the Decatur Fire Station. The Old Courthouse even includes a free museum with more of this picturesque town's history.

The tour can be done in about two hours and, obviously, you can do as much or as little as you wish. Mr. C recommends taking your time and exploring the various sites, both historical and commercial. The best part of this tour is that you can take it anytime you want to; but do bear in mind the hours of some of the attractions themselves.

The Georgia Governor's Mansion

- 391 West Paces Ferry Road N.E., Atlanta; ✆ (404) 261-1776

The Georgia Governor's Mansion tour offers you a chance to peek into a home that not only holds social and historic value, but also serves as the home of the current governor.

On your tour you'll see the cherry paneled library, the official state dining room and drawing room, the family living room, the guest bedroom, and more. The home features a collection of priceless Georgiana, such as manuscripts by Joel Chandler Harris, Flannery O'Connor, Erskine Caldwell, and Carson McCullers. The rarest piece in the house, though, is a 19th-century French porcelain vase with a portrait medallion of Benjamin Franklin. Best of all the tour is completely free!

ENTERTAINMENT: WALKS AND TOURS

Since real people do live here, hours are limited: Tours are only offered between 10 a.m. and 11:30 a.m. on Tuesdays, Wednesdays, and Thursdays. Large groups are required to make reservations.

Georgia State Capitol Tours

- Georgia State Capitol Building, Capitol Square S.W., Atlanta; (404) 656-2844

The Capitol Guide Service provides free tours of this historic building, where the state legislature works (occasionally) to this day. You may even get a glimpse of "The Gov" dashing by. You can also sit in the Senate and House of Representatives galleries, and if they're in session, watch them wrestle bills to the ground. The first floor of the building also features a chronological display of Georgia's flags, some of which were actually used in the Civil War, the Spanish American War, and World War I. Guns and other weapons used by soldiers are also shown. You can also see how a state project—the building itself—was actually within budget!

Also on the first floor are busts of prominent figures in Georgian history, including founding father James Oglethorpe, Margaret Mitchell (author of *Gone With the Wind*), and Juliette Gordon Low (founder of the Girl Scouts). Portraits of Martin Luther King Jr., Jimmy Carter, and all the former state governors also line the wall.

The Capitol is open Monday thorough Friday from 8 a.m. to 5 p.m.

The Herndon Home

- University Place N.W., Atlanta; (404) 581-9813

This magnificent Beaux Arts classical mansion was built in the early 1900s by Alonzo Herndon. Born as a slave, Herndon founded the

> **MR. CHEAP'S PICKS**
>
> ### Walks and Tours
>
> **CNN Studio Tour**—See how the world's largest cable network operates, and maybe meet some TV stars as well.
>
> **Georgia State Capitol Tour**—History, art, and politics come together in this free tour. Added bonus: the State Museum of Science and Industry, a hidden jewel upstairs.
>
> **Martin Luther King, Jr. Center/Sweet Auburn District**—Find out how truly current history can be.

Atlanta Life Insurance Company and went on to become Atlanta's wealthiest African-American man around the turn of the century.

The home is open Tuesday through Saturday from 10 a.m. to 4:30 p.m. Admission is $5 for adults, $3 for students.

Jimmy Carter Presidential Library

- 441 Freedom Parkway, Atlanta; (404) 331-3942

- www.jimmycarterlibrary.org

This is the only presidential library in the southeastern United States, and a great place to learn about the early life, political career, and presidency of one of the most respected former presidents. Here you can stroll through the galleries, filled with thousands of historic documents, then take a break by the gardens and pond overlooking the Atlanta skyline.

The library is open Monday through Saturday from 9 a.m. to 4:45 p.m., and Sunday from noon to 4:45 p.m. It is closed on Thanksgiving, Christmas, and New Year's Day. Admission is $5 for adults and $4 for seniors. Young people age 16 and under are admitted for free.

Oakland Cemetery

- 248 Oakland Avenue S.E., Atlanta; (404) 577-8163

- www.oaklandcemetery.com

A short walk from the King Memorial MARTA station, the 88-acre Oakland Cemetery is one of the finest examples of Victorian cemeteries in the country. This is where people still lay flowers at the grave of *Gone With the Wind* author Margaret Mitchell Marsh, and golf balls at the stone of duffer Bobby Jones. Also laid to rest here are 24 past Atlanta mayors; Alexander Hamilton Stevens, who was vice president of the Confederacy during the Civil War; and nearly 3,000 Confederate soldiers.

The cemetery is a lesson in architecture, with its Gothic Revival and Neo classical mausoleums, Victorian carved tombstones, and fountain sculptures. Some of the oldest magnolia trees in the city loom over you as you walk around.

There is no admission fee. Guided tours can be arranged for a small charge of $1 for students, $2 for senior citizens, and $3 for adults. For groups of 25 or more, the charge is $2.50 per person. But it costs nothing to wander the grounds on your own; stop in at the visitor's center, a white two-story building with a small bell tower, in the middle of the cemetery. Here, you can get a free map and a few directions. The gates are open daily from 8 a.m. to 7 p.m. in spring and summer, closing up an hour earlier in fall and winter.

Martin Luther King, Jr. National Historic Site

- 449 Auburn Avenue N.E., Atlanta; (404) 526-8900

- www.thekingcenter.org

Martin Luther King Jr.'s passion for the civil rights movement lives on at this National Historic Site, with points of interest stretched along several blocks of Auburn Avenue.

King's tomb and eternal flame can be seen outside the Center for Nonviolent Social Change. Inside, the building features an audio-visual history of King's life and the development of his theory of nonviolence.

The Center is also where tours meet to visit his birth home at 501 Auburn Avenue, and where you can pick up guides to the other sites in the Sweet Auburn area. You can also see the Ebenezer Baptist Church, where both King and his father preached, just down the street at 407-413 Auburn.

Admission to the Center is free, as are the tours of MLK's birth home, though donations are accepted.

The King Center is open daily during the fall and winter from 9 a.m. until 5 p.m., and in the spring and summer from 9 a.m. until 6 p.m.

Sweet Auburn District

- Auburn Avenue N.E., Atlanta; (404) 524-1956

The entire Sweet Auburn area is rich in history, and the map obtained at the MLK Center (see listing above) can show you how to get to the houses and buildings in the area of particular interest.

The Herndon Building at 231-245 Auburn Avenue (see the description above) was named for its builder, Alonzo F. Herndon, a former slave who eventually founded the Atlanta Life Insurance Company. The Alexander Hamilton, Jr., Home at 102 Howell Street (northwest of the MLK Center), with its Corinthian columns, was the home of Atlanta's leading black building contractor in the early part of this century. The "shotgun" row houses from 472 to 488 Auburn were built at that time and are arranged in such perfect alignment that a gunshot could theoretically enter and leave the house through the doorways.

Sun Dial Restaurant Bar and View

- Westin Peachtree Plaza, 210 Peachtree Street N.W., Atlanta; (404) 589-7506
- www.sundialrestaurant.com

Check out the best view in Atlanta from the restaurant at the top of the Westin hotel. The kids will love the glass elevator ride up the side of the building (not recommended for the acrophobic!), and once you're "on top" you can relax with some good food and beverages while gazing down upon the entire Atlanta area. Admission is $5 for adults and $2.50 for kids.

Turner Field

- 755 Hank Aaron Drive, Atlanta; (404) 522-7630
- www.turner.com

The new home of the Atlanta Braves, named after Braves owner Ted Turner and converted from the 1996 Olympic track and field stadium, offers something for baseball fans of all ages. Visitors get tours of the field itself, the Braves Museum, and a behind-the-scenes view of normally restricted areas of the stadium.

The World of Coca-Cola Pavilion

- 55 Martin Luther King, Jr. Drive S.W., Atlanta; (404) 676-5151
- www.woccatlanta.com

Museum or marketing juggernaut? Whichever way you see it, you can't fail to notice the World of Coca-Cola located on the street level above Underground Atlanta.

With its many audio-visual exhibits, including a model bottling line, a 90-seat theater, and a wacky fountain that seems to shoot soda several feet before dispensing it, this shrine to soft drinks is sure to thrill the kids and impress older folks. Galleries show vintage magazine ads and commercials, and interactive television sets give a taste of how Coke's jingles sounded decades ago. You'll learn about the history of the soda from its earliest days as a headache cure to its development into the world's most recognized trademark.

Every 15 minutes, a film takes you through some of the 200 countries in which Coke is sold, from Thailand to the Philippines to Africa. At the end of your visit, free samples of Coke, Diet Coke, and Fanta are proffered, along with some unusual sodas only sold in those other countries.

The Pavilion hours are 9 a.m. to 5 p.m. Monday through Saturday, and noon to 6 p.m. on Sunday. It's closed on major holidays. Admission is $6 for adults, $4 for senior citizens over 55, $3 for children aged 6 to 12, and free for children under 6 with an adult.

Tickets may be purchased in advance by calling weekdays during operating hours The Pavilion has elevators and special assistance is available for the hearing impaired.

Restaurants

When ya gotta eat, ya gotta eat. For the dining chapters of the book Mr. C decided not to dig in alphabetically, but rather by geographical area. After all, when you're hungry, you want to eat now, no matter how appetizing some place halfway across town may sound.

The city has been divided into broad sections, so that you can just pick up the book and find the cheap choices and best values in your area.

And if you're planning a day or night out on the town, you can coordinate this section with the *Entertainment* listings.

All of the restaurants in this book are places where you can eat dinner for around $15 per person (or, in many cases, far less), not including tax and tip. Lunch prices, of course, can be even lower. Even so, all of these eateries serve filling meals of "real" food, not phony fast-food junk.

That $15 limit also does not include alcohol, which is going to be expensive just about anywhere. Have you ever pondered the fact that you can guy a six-pack of decent beer for $5 to $10, but restaurants typically charge about $5 per glass? Restaurants make a disproportionate amount of profit on alcohol—sometimes their entire profit. That doesn't mean you have to order a beer, a glass of wine, or a cocktail; politely concentrate on the cheap eats if you want the best deal.

ATLANTA NORTHEAST/DECATUR

Including Emory Village, North Druid Hills, Toco Hills

Athens Pizza House

- 5550 Peachtree Industrial Boulevard, Chamblee; ✆ (404) 452-8282

- 1565 Highway 138, Conyers; ✆ (404) 483-6228

- 1341 Clairmont Road, Decatur; ✆ (404) 636-1100

- 11235 Apharetta Highway #140, Roswell; ✆ (770) 751-6629

The Papadopoulos family has been making popular pizza in the Atlanta area since 1966. The prices are right, too; not only on the pizzas, but also on such appetizers as spinach pie ($2.50), Athens potatoes ($2.50), and fried kalamari ($6.40). (Dan Quayle might have given the owners some help with the menu.)

The pies themselves start at just $3 for a 6" cheese. But why stop there? Go all out with a 14" "Santorini Special," including feta cheese, sun-dried tomatoes, spinach, fresh garlic, artichoke hearts, and black olives—for just $15.95. You won't have to eat again for a week.

These folks also have a good selection of tasty pita wraps and hot subs, ranging in price from $4.95 to $7.95

Entrees like *moussaka,* served with spinach pie, chicken parmesan, and spinach manicotti are each served with a Greek salad and garlic bread for $8.50 to $9.75. There's a children's section on the menu, too; the kids' spaghetti dinner is just $4.50, while you can join them with the gigantic regular spaghetti plate for $7.95.

Don't pass up the baklava for desert, either. At $1.50 a slice, these nut-filled flaky pastries covered with honey are just the thing to end your meal on a sweet note.

Athens Pizza also offers many beers and wines (including Greek varieties like Kokino and Aspro), starting at $2.50 a glass.

Cafe Lily

- 308-H West Ponce de Leon Avenue, Decatur; ✆ (404) 371-9119

- ✍ www.cafelily.com

Father and son restaurant owners, Angelo and Anthony Pitillo, named this establishment after their young granddaughter/niece, Lily, and the restaurant is well regarded for its creative sandwiches and laid-back, homey atmosphere.

Special sauces and fresh bread make memorable what could be an ordinary lunch. Try the Mediterranean Grilled Cheese Sandwich, piled with a mix of fontina and parmigiano reggiano cheese, tomatoes, grilled onions, and almonds, served with soup and salad on the side ($7.95). Their Chargrilled Moroccan Jerk Chicken Sandwich is anything but everyday, made with roasted chicken breast rubbed with garlic and an array of spices topped on a toasted bun and French fries for only $6.95. The fresh salmon burgers are big sensations too, with grilled salmon, feta-dill sauce, and a side of tabouli, only $7.95. Your taste buds might also want to try the shrimp beignets ($7.95), marinated eggplant ($4.95), beer-battered Vidalia onion rings ($3.95), or salad nicoise with fresh grilled tuna, olives, field greens, and seasonal veggies for only $9.95.

Cafe Lily's "Build your own pasta meals" make dining here not only a great experience but also "an event" with choice of one pasta (capellini, penne rigate, or fettuccine), one choice of sauce (marinara, alfredo, or Aglio e Olio), one choice of veggies (peppers, mushrooms, capers, broccoli, black olives, onions, tomato) and one choice of meat (sauteed shrimp, Italian sausage, grilled chicken). Now we're talking!

Restaurant hours are Monday through Saturday from 11:30 a.m. to 10:30 p.m. They're closed on Sunday.

Cedar Tree

- Emory Village Shopping Center, 1565 North Decatur Road, Atlanta; ✆ (404) 373-2118

- ✍ www.cedartreerestaurant.com

Middle Eastern dishes are available at really cheap prices here. The breakfast selections are limited to bagels ($1), croissants ($2), and omelettes ($2.50), but Emory students and professors alike come here at lunch for super vegetarian plates, shish kebabs, and sky-high club sandwiches.

Mr. C liked the *baba ghanoush* sandwich—baked eggplant with tahini (sesame seed paste)—for just $3.25. Grape leaves and hummus wrapped in a pita is just $4.25, and the slightly spicy falafel sandwich is also $4.25.

Lamb or chicken kebab sandwiches are priced under $5. The kebab sampler platter tops the menu at $7 and comes with hummus, a salad, and pita for dipping. Student types seem to really go for the grilled pastrami, salami, and corned beef with mustard potato salad ($4.50) and the Meza Tray, a vegetarian plate with six different side orders from the menu. Enough to stuff three people, it sells for $16. Desserts include nine varieties of baklava ($1.50 each), brownies, brioche, and flan. Restaurant hours are Sunday through Thursday from 11 a.m. to 9 p.m.; Friday and Saturday from 11 a.m. to 7 p.m.

Chris's Pizza House

- Toco Hills Shopping Center, 2911 North Druid Hills Road, Atlanta; ✆ (404) 636-7544

Yeah, sure, you may think that pizza houses are a dime a dozen, but Mr. C thinks that Chris's is something special. Prices are super-cheap, and the food's quite good. This restaurant isn't what you'd call fancy, though ficus trees and skylights attempt to add a touch of class.

This is Greek pizza, by the way, not Italian (there is a difference, you know). Chris's pies come in four sizes, with prices starting at an incredibly low $3.50 for a plain individual size; a large plain 16" goes up to just $10.75. Toppings include all the basics from anchovies to sausage, plus more unusual toppings like calamata olives, salami, and pepperoncini peppers. Calzones are $6 and can be made with the same extra ingredients as the pizzas.

The menu continues past pizza, though, to more traditional ethnic foods. Go for souvlaki beef sandwiches for $5.25 and good ol' gyros for $5. Lasagna dinners, complete with Greek salad and garlic or pita bread, are only $7.75.

Spaghetti can be prepared several different ways: with butter, it's just $4, or $5.50 if you try it with one of several toppings like meatballs, peppers, mushrooms, eggplant parmesan, or sausage. Restaurant hours are Sunday through Thursday from 11 a.m. to 10 p.m.; Friday and Saturday from 11 a.m. to 11 p.m.

Coco Loco Cuban & Caribbean Cafe

- 2625 Piedmont Road N.E., Atlanta; ✆ (404) 364-0212 and ✆ (404) 261-0198

Sure, Coco Loco may have a reputation as a yuppie hangout, but its prices are surprisingly un-yuppie. The Cuban sandwich, for instance, is just $4.75 for the regular size, and $5.50 for the super. Jamaican jerk chicken sandwiches go for $5, as does the *pan con lechon* (roast pork and grilled onions). For lighter appetites, or those who can't bear the hot spices, try grilled cheese with potato sticks for $3.50, or hot dogs and quarter-pound hamburgers, each just $2.50. The spicier Cuban hamburger, with onions, paprika, and Worcestershire sauce, is also just $2.50.

On the sweet side, tropical milkshakes, in flavors like papaya or mango ($2.95), and nectars (try the tamarind, just $2.50) will douse the flames of the Cuban spices.

Even entrees are reasonably priced, served with two side dishes like yuccas, rice, or a salad. Cuban-style roast chicken with garlic and onions, fried sirloin steak, and pork chops are all just $6.95 each. Side dishes like black beans and rice ($2.75), sweet fried plantains or plantain chips (also $2.75), and homemade potato chips ($2) won't break the bank, either, so you may just have enough money left for some (not so cheap) dessert, like key lime pie ($3.75), rice pudding ($2.95), or *pastelito de guayaba* (guava pastry), just $1.50 an order. Domestic and imported beers, plus a limited wine selection, are also available.

Restaurant hours are Monday through Thursday from 11 a.m. to 10 p.m., Friday and Saturday from 11 a.m. to 11 p.m., and Sunday from 1 p.m. to 9 p.m.

The Crescent Moon

- 174 West Ponce de Leon Avenue, Decatur; ✆ (404) 377-5623

A neighborhood favorite, Crescent Moon features an extensive breakfast menu and delectable lunch entrees that won't break the bank. Their jams and preserves are homemade; so are the biscuits and buckwheat pancakes, and the syrup is pure maple.

Early risers will like the smoked chicken omelette with onions, herbs, and mozzarella ($5.50), the Italian frittata with zucchini, onions, and marinara sauce ($5.25), or the combo breakfasts, like the "Country Lane Morning" (two eggs, O'Brien spuds or stone-ground grits, toast or biscuit) for $4.50. Weekend brunch adds specials like "Eggs in Paradise"—tomatoes, basil, garlic, smoked sausage, and parmesan cheese, with choice of Irish or Cajun potatoes—for $6.50.

For lunch, half-pound hamburgers are $5.50, blackened chicken is $6.25, and a big plate of super-spicy black beans and rice with sour cream is just $4.95. Tortellini salad will fill you up for $6.25, while a pair of cheese quesadillas with homemade salsa is $4.95.

Crescent Moon sells wine and beer, along with water-filtered coffees. Restaurant hours are Monday through Saturday from 7:30 a.m. to 9:30 p.m., and Sunday from 7:30 a.m. to 3 p.m.

Dusty's Barbecue

- 1815 Briarcliff Road N.E., Atlanta; ✆ (404) 320-6264

- 🖳 www.dustys.com

Suuuuuuueeeeee! Near Emory Village, Dusty's has won awards for its pork and beef barbecue. Some locals feel that the fare has fallen a notch or two in recent years, but the place still fills almost every wicker chair in the house during peak hours. If not for the sign out front, you'd think this was just a tiny little log cabin. Pictures of pigs and cows cover the walls, while gingham tablecloths and curtains add a homey touch.

Dusty's refers to itself as "Hog Heaven," but it's the customers who think they're dreaming once they see the low prices on the lunch and dinner items here. A regular size chopped pork barbecue dinner costs only $6.60 (the larger size is $7.80). All barbecue meals come with hush puppies and two vegetables on the side. Pork tenderloins are $7.75 an order. And speaking of veggies, nonmeat eaters can come here with their carnivorous friends and dine sumptuously on the four veggie plate. It's just $5.15, with choices like green beans, corn on the cob, baked beans, fried okra, and home-cooked potato chips.

Lunch items are actually served at any time of day, like the barbecued half-chicken or roast beef au jus (both $6.80). Dinner entrees include Dusty's baby back ribs, which are $9.50 for the regular (read: Paul Bunyan) size. Combination meals run about $8.95; this gives you the chance to try pork or beef barbecue, chicken, and Brunswick stew, all in the same meal.

Dusty's is also known for its desserts, like peach, apple, or blackberry cobblers ($2.15), chocolate silk pie ($3.25), and carrot cake ($2.95). On the way out, get some Dusty's Barbeque sauce to take home to fire up on the grill. The bar-b-que sauce comes in "regular," "hot," "sweet," and "sizzlin" flavors. Prices range from $2.70 for a 12-ounce squeeze bottle, $2.95 for a pint, and $18.95 for a gallon size.

Restaurant hours are Sunday through Thursday from 9 a.m. to 9 p.m.; Friday and Saturday from 9 a.m. to 10 p.m.

Eddie's Attic

- 515-B North McDonough Street, Decatur; ℰ (404) 377-4976

- ℰ www.eddiesattic.com

If you can find Eddie's Attic (near East Trinity Place, below the courthouse), and make it up the staircase, you'll be in for a very pleasant surprise. Not only do they play super acoustic music at this tavern (the Indigo Girls got their start here), but the food is terrific, too.

Monterey chicken quesadillas are just $5.75, and a hefty basket of nachos with plenty of sour cream is $6.75. The Attic Dog, grilled up and served with lots o' fries and slaw, is $5.75, and tostada salads are $6.75. Mr. C liked his huge bowl of Attic black bean soup, garnished with green onions and sour cream, for just $3.50; while red beans and rice, served with smoked sausage, is a big seller at just $6.75.

Even if you're not there to hear the bands and poets who troop through here each week, you can have fun hanging out and playing pool on the deck.

Restaurant hours are Monday through Sunday from 4 p.m. to midnight.

Evans Fine Foods

- 2125 North Decatur Road, Emory Village;
  ℰ (404) 634-6294

Evans is one of those friendly Ma n' Pa-owned places, making their customers feel right at home from the moment they walk in the door. They've been here since 1946; and while some of the waitresses seem to have been working here since around that time, the food makes up in taste what the service lacks in speed.

For breakfast, try a stack of hot cakes for $3.40, or a cheese omelette for $3.65. Add a side of hash browns ($2), whole smoked sausage ($3.40), or corned beef hash ($2.50). Toast and jelly is $1.75, while a bowl of cereal goes for $2.50.

At lunch or dinner, there's the egg sandwich for $2.35, grilled cheese for $2.35, and a quarter-pound hamburger for $3.30. A bowl of homemade soup (like green pea or the yummy chicken gumbo) is $2.60. An open-faced roast beef or turkey sandwich with mashed potatoes is $4.95, while their famous (and tasty) chicken filet is yours for a mere $3.10. Evans also offers filet mignon ($6.95) and rib-eye steak ($8.15), breaded veal ($5.35), and fried flounder ($5.45), all served with two kinds of freshly prepared vegetables.

Don't pass up Evans's homemade desserts, especially their pies: chocolate or coconut cream, apple, or peach ($2.50). You can also take a whole pie home for a cheap $7.75. Restaurant hours are Monday through Sunday from 6 a.m. to 9 p.m.

Everybody's Pizza

- 1040 North Highland Avenue N.E., Atlanta; (404) 873-4545

- 1593 North Decatur Road, Emory Village; (404) 377-7766

Everybody loves Everybody's, not just for their great pizza, but for their starving-student prices, too. One bonus right off the bat here is that you can choose from thirty amazing toppings—including basil, shrimp, sesame seeds, rosemary potatoes, feta cheese, and sun-dried tomatoes. Put 'em all on thick or thin crusts, too. A plain individual-size pie is just $4.25, going up to $6.85 for one with any four toppings. To be totally trendy, pesto sauce is $1.25 extra on the small, and $3 more on a large pizza.

You can also order one of Everybody's own combinations, which have been getting rave reviews for quite some time. How about one with shrimp and artichoke ($11.25), Florentine (with four kinds of cheese, spinach, and tomato slices for $9.25), or spicy-sweet jerk chicken for $10.75.

Or try their lasagna ($7.25), fettucine carbonara ($7.75) or penne primavera ($7.50). Garlic-parmesan breadsticks are $2.25 for a small and $3.35 for a large order. And, just as with the pies, you can concoct your own salad, starting at $2.75.

Everybody's also serves beer and wine. Everybody got that? Hours are Sunday through Thursday from 11:30 a.m. to 10 p.m., Friday and Saturday from 11:30 a.m. to midnight, and Sunday from noon to 10 p.m.

Happy Herman's

- 2299 Cheshire Bridge Road N.E., Atlanta; (404) 321-3012

- 204 Johnson Ferry Road, Sandy Springs; (404) 256-3354

- www.happyhermans.com

Best-known as a store for imported gourmet treats and prepared foods for take-out, Happy Herman's is happy to have you sit at one of their few plastic tables near the entrance and nosh away. You can watch the traffic outside, or—much more interesting—inside the popular little shop.

Sip a tasty bowl of cream of mushroom soup ($2.89), or have them heat up a plate of cheese tortellini in tomato sauce ($6.99 per pound). Add a warm sourdough baguette or an individual-sized loaf of romano-parmesan bread, each $2. Herman's also makes an exotic array of fresh sandwiches, such as "The Smokey": smoked turkey and smoked Gouda cheese on fresh-baked bread with roasted peppers and grilled eggplant, all for $4.95. Or a New Orleans "Po' Boy" ($3.95), with layers of roast beef, turkey, ham, Swiss cheese, and thinly sliced pickles on a French roll.

And they have similarly wonderful salads, including the "Southwestern Grill" of grilled chicken breast, black beans, green peppers, cheddar cheese, and pimientos—all on Romaine lettuce, all for $4.95. There are at least a dozen different salads to choose from, and almost as many dressings to put on top; the house flavor is a ranch dressing with feta cheese mixed in.

Finish off with some very elegant cakes and pastries, baked in the store, or perhaps something from the incredible-looking chocolate confectionery counter. Such great food for a few bucks; you won't even have to leave a tip. After all this, you'll be happy too.

Hours are Monday through Thursday from 9 a.m. to 8:30 p.m., Friday and Saturday from 11:30 a.m. to midnight, and Sunday from noon to 10 p.m.

Indian Delights

- Scott Village Shopping Center, 1707 Church Street, Decatur; ✆ (404) 296-2965

How delightful—a nonsmoking, tipping-optional kind of restaurant with authentic Indian fare. Indian Delights has received kudos from *Creative Loafing*, the *Journal-Constitution*, and *Atlanta* magazine, and all for good reason.

There are only eight tables here, so lots of local business people get their grub to go. *Masala dhosa* is a wonderful grilled combination of rice, white lentils, potatoes, and onions; it's served with a lentil-vegetable soup (*Sambhar*) and coconut chutney, all of which cost a mere $4.60. Vegetable *biryani*, a rice pilaf with spicy veggies, served with yogurt on the side, is also only $4.60. The most expensive item on the menu, in fact, is the $5.50 masala dhosa with rice cake (ravioli) platter, which again is served with coconut chutney and Sambhar soup.

Appetizers will jazz up your meal for just a few bucks more. *Bhel puri*, which is fried whole wheat bread topped with potato, onions, and homemade noodles, is just $3.50. There's always the samosa, a northern Indian favorite, consisting of fried dough filled with potatoes and peas. It's served with sweet and spicy sauce, and you can get two for $2.80. Taro root leaves and chickpea pasta, topped with sesame seeds and cilantro, is $3.50. There's also the classic Mulligatawny soup ($2.50), and *ganthia* ($3.50), a spicy chickpea snack.

To cool off your taste buds after lunch or dinner, try the $2.25 *dani vada*, a white lentil ball covered in mild yogurt sauce; Mr. C prefers a sweet *lassi* (not the dog, but a sugar yogurt shake), which sells for $3.25. Nut rolls with layers of phyllo leaves are two for $2.50, and cheese balls (*ras malai*) with syrup-flavored heavy cream are also two for $2.50.

Hours are Monday through Sunday from noon to 9 p.m.

Jagger's

- Emory Village Shopping Center, 1577 North Decatur Road N.E., Atlanta; ✆ (404) 377-8888

You can't always get what you want in many restaurants, but at Jagger's you get what you need—homemade soups, salads, roast turkey, pizza, fish, you name it—there's something for everyone in the family here, and at prices that make it possible to take the whole family out more often.

This is a self-described "neighborhood place," open since 1972, so they must be doing something right. Jagger's can get crowded on the weekends with Emory students imbibing the hours away, but if you come at an off time or on a weekday, things are pretty quiet. Some professors even hold informal class discussions here.

Start off your meal with ten of Jagger's Buffalo wings ($5.95), a half-pound basket of raw vegetables ($3.25), or a cup of shrimp and crabmeat bisque ($3.95). Same price for a crock of their "Very Chunky Chili."

Dinners include such entrees as rainbow trout and roast turkey, each for $7.95. All dinners come with two choices of side dishes; choose from things like a dinner salad or cup of soup, vegetables, noodles, French fries, or mashed potatoes.

The Jagger Burger is served in a wine and mushroom sauce for $5.95; grilled chicken sandwiches, available plain, barbecued, or teriyaki style, are just $6.95 with fries. Individual-sized pizzas start at just $4.95. Desserts like French silk pie ($4.25) and amaretto cheesecake ($3.95) are big enough to share.

The children's menu features grilled cheese sandwiches and chips ($3.50), linguini ($3.25), turkey and mashed potatoes ($4.95), and Jagger's "award-winning" hot dog and fries ($2.95).

Restaurant hours are Monday through Thursday from 11:30 a.m. to 1 a.m.; Friday from 11:30 a.m. to 2 a.m.; Saturday from 12:30 p.m. to 1 a.m.; and Sunday from 1 p.m. to midnight.

Lettuce Souprise You

- 1784 Peachtree Street NW, Atlanta; ✆ (404) 874-4998

- 2470 Briarcliff Road N.E., Atlanta; ✆ (404) 636-8549

Here's a place that goes right to Mr. Cheap's heart . . . and stomach. At Lettuce Souprise You, one price gets you unlimited trips to their extensive salad bar, as well as the all-you-can-eat baked potato bar and pasta bar, plus homemade muffins, cornbread, and soups, and fresh fruit. Whew! Lettuce be thankful for places like this!

The salad bar is super-fresh and preservative-free; it features spinach, broccoli, tarragon tuna, spicy crab and pasta salad, and pineapple, along with dozens of other choices. Soups change daily but always include at least one vegetarian recipe, such as potato-leek or lentil. Egg drop, chili, and vegetable soups are featured often, too.

How can they afford to offer such a bargain, you ask? Well, they do work on keeping costs down. For one thing, Lettuce Souprise You requests that you eat only in the restaurant; they don't allow anyone to leave with more than a muffin. If you'd like something to go, they will charge you for it. Well hey, that's only fair!

Meanwhile, the price for this entire sumptuous buffet is just $6.50 at lunchtime; $7.50 for brunch and dinner. Another cheap deal: Their "frequent buyer" club entitles you to a free meal when you've had twelve lunches, six dinners, or four brunches. Can it be any surprise that Lettuce Souprise You rates so highly with Mr. C?

Hours are Monday through Thursday from 11 a.m. to 9 p.m.; Friday, Saturday, and Sunday from 11 a.m. to 8 p.m.

Lucky China

- 2179 Lawrenceville Highway, Decatur; ✆ (404) 248-1288

Lucky for you, Lucky China serves up award-winning Chinese cuisine on the cheap. The atmosphere may not be spectacular (they're in the Cub Foods shopping center), but you can't beat their food. The lunch specials are especially bargain-priced, and take-outs are prepared lightning-fast.

An order of pot stickers is $4, and their super egg drop soup is $2. Neptune soup for two, made with scallops, shrimp, and vegetables, is $6. Combinations like chicken lo mein, moo goo gai pan, mandarin ribs, shrimp with Chinese vegetables, pork chow mein, and Szechuan dishes—each served with fried rice, chicken wing, and egg roll—are priced from $5 to $6.

A puu puu tray for two (isn't that just fun to say?) gives you and your date plenty to nibble on for just $10.50. Broccoli with oyster sauce is $6.75, and curry shrimp is $9. Fried chicken with Cantonese vegetables is $9.25, and ma po bean curd with ground pork and Szechuan sauce is just $7.50. These dishes are all so big that you'll need to share, or bring a doggie bag home with you.

And, in the unlikely event that you have room for dessert, try Lucky China's jumbo orders of glazed bananas or glazed apples (a nice change from just fortune cookies), each $4.

Lucky China offers free delivery within the Decatur area on orders of $10 or more, from 4:30 p.m. to 9:30 p.m. only. They're open seven days a week, including a super Sunday brunch buffet from noon until 3 p.m. Hours are Monday through Thursday from 11 a.m. to 10 p.m., Friday and Saturday from 11 a.m. to 11 p.m., and Sunday from 5 p.m. to 10 p.m.

Madras Cafe

- 3086 Briarcliff Road N.E., Atlanta; ✆ (404) 320-7120

Near the intersection of Briarcliff and Clairmont Roads, the tiny Madras Cafe is a surefire bet for those of you who like Indian food. For those who've never cared for it, this may be the place to give it a try. If you're not into hot spices, just let the waiter know—the kitchen can adjust its recipes to fit your taste. Not only is the Indian cuisine healthy, but most dishes run in the $4 range.

Appetizers include the $2 "Mixture," a combination of chickpea noodles, peanuts, and cashews; or the Pakoda, a spicy, crispy Indian snack made from chickpea and rice flours with chilies. Steam-cooked rice cakes (*idli*) are $2.70, and *masala dhosai* (crepes filled with onions and potatoes) are $4.50.

Curried vegetable *kuruma*, a north Indian specialty, is $3, and fried *masala vadai*, a spicy, fried dish with chickpea flour, is served with *sambar* (lentil soup) and mint chutney for only $2.70.

Daily lunch or dinner specials start low as $5; a variety of dishes are served with Basmati rice, vegetable curry sauce, yogurt salad, soft bread, and soda. Traditional desserts include carrot *halwa* (made with milk, butter, and sugar, spiced with cardamom) for $2, cheese balls for $2, and sweet buttery *badhushas* for $2.50.

To wash it all down, try a mango *lassi* or sweet *lassi* (sweetened yogurt shakes), each $3, or spicy masala tea. Mango juice is just $1.60, too.

The Madras Cafe hours are Monday through Sunday from 11 a.m. to 8 p.m.

Market Cafe at Your DeKalb Farmer's Market

- 3000 East Ponce de Leon Avenue, Decatur; (404) 377-6400

- www.dekalbfarmersmarket.com

For a salad bar beyond compare, freshly-prepared stir-frys and steamed veggies, fish-n-chips, and other meals under $10, you'll find it right here in the supermarket. Huh? That's right. Not only is this one of the best supermarkets around, for both price and selection (see the listing under *Shopping—General Markets*), but over to one side of the vast interior is a sit-down cafeteria that reflects the international mix of the staff and the surrounding Decatur community.

This is a good place for meat eaters and vegetarians alike. Entrees like chicken ($4.50 fried, $5.95 baked or grilled) are served with three side dishes, as are lamb stew ($5.95) and other daily specials. A hamburger and fries is $4.50, an 8-ounce New York strip steak is $7.99, and cold deli sandwiches are just $4.

Indian *samosas*, filled with beef or vegetables, are just $2.25; they're hot, delicious, and rather greasy, just the way great food should be. Other items for vegetarians include a wonderful salad bar—a bargain at just 21 cents an ounce—and plain baked potatoes topped with broccoli and cheese for $2.50. The five veggie plate is a remarkable $4.

It's all served by a helpful, smiling staff. There is a separate bakery counter, selling delicious desserts, and that great coffee, which Your DeKalb sells so inexpensively by the pound. While the food is hard to beat, there's not much atmosphere other than people watching; and the chairs are those plastic bucket-shaped types you may recall from grade school. Even so, the cafe fills up at lunchtime, and you may have to share your big, round table with fellow diners. Mr. C recommends that you bring a sweater, by the way, since the cafe is right across from the rather chilly dairy and fresh pasta departments of the supermarket.

The Market Cafe hours are Monday through Sunday from 9 a.m. to 9 p.m.

MR. CHEAP'S PICKS

Decatur

Our Way Café—If Mr. C had his way, this homey place near Avondale Estates would be open 24 hours a day, seven days a week. Well worth going out of your way for.

Rainbow Restaurant—You won't spend much green at this hangout, tucked in the back of Rainbow Natural Foods. A favorite of vegetarians and non-vegetarians alike.

Yen Ching—It doesn't look like much from the outside, but Mr. C thinks you'll be pleasantly surprised by its Mandarin, Szechuan, and Cantonese cuisine, good prices, and attentive service.

Mary Mac's Tea Room and Restaurant

- 224 Ponce de Leon Avenue N.E., Atlanta; (404) 876-1800

- www.marymacs.com

Zell Miller and Jimmy Carter have eaten at Mary Mac's, considered to be Atlanta's oldest home cooking restaurant. Nothing's fancy here, really—you actually fill out the food slips yourself, since the waitresses are too busy carrying trays full of food for the multitudes who flock here at lunchtime.

Choose from a choice of entrees (baked chicken, country fried steak, baked fish almandine, beef tips on Creole rice, sautéed chicken livers, etc.) with two side dishes for $7.50. Sweet potato cobbler is a popular choice, but Mr. C is partial to the cheese-whipped potatoes. Included in the price are tea, coffee, or punch, Mary Mac's cornbread, and ice cream in your choice of five flavors.

Meals are served in a flash; also, half portions can be ordered for those customers "under 12 or over 90." Restaurant hours are Monday through Friday from 7 a.m. to 9 p.m.; Saturday and Sunday from 9 a.m. to 9 p.m.

Mellow Mushroom

- 30 Pharr Road N.W., Atlanta; (404) 233-3443

- 1679 Lavista Road N.E., Atlanta; (404) 325-0330

- 931 Monroe Drive N.E., Atlanta; (404) 874-2291

- 6218 Roswell Road N.E., Sandy Springs; (404) 252-5560

- 4058 Peachtree Road N.E., #B, Atlanta; (404) 266-1661

- 1715 Howell Mill Road N.W., Atlanta; (404) 350-0501

- 695 North Avenue N.E., Atlanta; (404) 524-6133

- 2150 Powers Ferry Road S.E., Atlanta; (770) 955-4311

- 5575 Chamblee Dunwoody Road, Dunwoody; (770) 396-1393

- 2950 New Paces Ferry Road S.E., Atlanta; (770) 435-5949

- www.mellowmushroom.com

This groovy, family-friendly pizza chain features 1970s shtick and some pretty compelling edible attractions: daily fresh ingredients, hand-tossed pizza, a crispy crust, and a wide and eclectic assortment of scrumptious toppings. The pies here come in the usual small (10"), medium (14"), and large (16") sizes, ranging in price from $5.20 plus 60 cents per topping to $11.50 plus $1.60 per topping. Depending on how much your stomach is growling, you can order yours by the pan or by the slice.

MM's specialty pizzas are priced from $6.40 to $20 and include the House Special (pepperoni, sausage, ground beef, peppers, "schrooms," black olives, onions, tomatoes, bacon, ham, and—my, oh my—extra cheese), Veggie (just what you'd think), Mega-Veggie (just what you'd think, even more so), Pesto, House Pesto (with spinach, mushrooms, and tomatoes), Gourmet White, Hawaiian (with ham and pineapple), Jerk Chicken (chicken, pineapple, and Caribbean spices), Mighty Meaty (sausage, pepperoni, ground beef, ham, and bacon—quick! fetch Mr. C's portable heart paddles!), and Kosmic Karma (sun-dried tomatoes, spinach, feta, fresh tomatoes, and "kosmic swirls of pesto"). Good luck finishing one of those. Meanwhile, white pizza—made without tomato sauce, and not often found in Atlanta—is just $9.95 for the small, $15.50 for the medium, and $17.50 for the large.

If pizza's not your passion, the Mushroom has other interesting and vaguely health-conscious items, such as teriyaki tofu sandwiches for $5.25, ham and cheese with sprouts for $5.95, and BLTs for $5.50. Other goodies include orders of soft pretzels for $4.35, garlic bread for $3.50, and chef salads for $6.

Mellow Mushroom has a cute animated Web site featuring animated characters, games, links, cartoons, menus, and a mini-catalog of T-shirts and hats. Still, it's much better to actually make the trek to the shop, where you can lose yourself in a '70s-style hedonistic food experience.

These mellow dudes generally keep their doors open Monday through Thursday from 11 a.m. to 4 a.m., Friday and Saturday from 11 a.m. to 3 a.m., and Sunday from noon to midnight.

In the 'burbs, the hours are generally Monday through Friday from 11 a.m. to 9:30 p.m., Friday from 11 a.m. to 10:30 p.m., Saturday from 11:30 a.m. to 10 p.m., and Sunday from noon to 9 p.m.

Mick's

- 557 Peachtree Road N.E., Atlanta; (404) 875-6425

- 2110 Peachtree Road N.E., Atlanta; (404) 351-6425

- Peachtree Center, 229 Peachtree Street N.E., Atlanta; (404) 688-6425

- Lenox Square Shopping Center, 3393 Peachtree Road N.E., Atlanta; (404) 262-6425

- Underground Atlanta, 75 Upper Alabama Street S.W., Atlanta; (404) 525-2825

- 116 East Ponce de Leon Avenue, Decatur, (404) 373-7797

- 1320 Cumberland Mall SE, Atlanta; (770) 431-7190

- 3525 Mall Boulevard, Duluth; (770) 623-1855

- 6700 Douglas Boulevard, Douglasville; (678) 715-0299

- 1070 Northpoint Circle, Alpharetta; (770) 667-2330

And other suburban locations

Get to Mick's for one of the best milkshakes in town, great burgers, super desserts, and creative drinks. Stretching from Underground Atlanta to Buckhead and beyond, this yuppie haven seems determined to make the next siege of Atlanta a middlebrow culinary one.

Prices here are not the absolute cheapest around, but you do get a lot of delicious food for the money. Start off with real fried green tomatoes ($6.75), chili-smothered French fries ($4.95), grilled carrots and broccoli ($3.50), or a cup of soup in flavors like tomato or "baked potato" ($2.95).

A half-pound hamburger, hickory grilled, with a generous side of fries or pasta salad, is $6.95. You can top it with cheddar or mozzarella cheese, guacamole, chili, barbecue sauce, or cracked pepper and mustard for $1.50 extra. Cheese-topped grilled boneless chicken is $8.50, and corn and tomato linguine with garlic bread is $7.95. Mick's chicken Reuben will completely stuff you for $8.95.

Do try to leave room for dessert, though. You'll probably want to share more of these monstrosities with a friend. Try the Oreo cheesecake ($4.95), the Giant Banana Split ($5.75), or Mr. C's favorite, the chocolate cream pie ($4.75). Yummy! Strawberry shortcake, homemade chocolate layer cake, and Heath Bar ice cream pie will all make delightful ends to your meal, and all are under $5 a piece.

Hours are Sunday through Thursday from 11 a.m. to 10 p.m. and Friday and Saturday from 11 a.m. to 11 p.m.

Nuts 'N Berries

- 4274 Peachtree Road N.E., Atlanta; (404) 237-6829

- www.nutsnberries.com

You need not be a vegetarian to love the food at this cafe, but no matter what you like, you'll love their prices.

Attached to the Nuts 'N Berries health foods and vitamins store, this little hangout serves up classic American and Mexican dishes for a pittance. Try the chicken burrito for $4.65 ($1 more with rice on the side), or a bean burrito for $4. Middle Eastern specialties include falafel burgers with tahini sauce, served with corn chips and dill pickle ($4.35), and hummus and pita bread for $4.35. If you're extra hungry, add a side of tabouli salad ($2.25), tofu salad ($2.50), or a garden salad with *miso tahini* or tofu dill dressing ($2.85).

Not to leave out the all-American tuna melt for $4.95, and a plain (but tasty, mind you) cheese sandwich piled with sprouts, tomato, and lettuce for $4.35.

Hours are Monday through Friday from 9 a.m. to 8 p.m., Saturday from 9 a.m. to 7 p.m., and Sunday from 10 a.m. to 6 p.m.

Original Pancake House

- 4330 Peachtree Road N.E., Atlanta; (404) 237-4116

- 2321 Cheshire Bridge Road N.E., Atlanta; (404) 633-5712

- 5099 Memorial Drive, Stone Mountain; (404) 292-6914

- 3665 Club Drive #104, Duluth; (770) 925-0065

- 243 Market Place Connector, Peachtree City; (770) 486-7634

The Original Pancake Houses sure won't leave you in the poor house. James Beard did name this one of the top ten restaurants in America, but you'd never know this from the prices. Quality runs high here—they use fresh juices, extra large Grade AA eggs, and pure whipping cream, plus all the cooking is done in pure butter.

The pancake recipe is a carefully guarded secret, with good reason. They're light and fluffy, and just $4.50 an order. Georgia Pecan Waffles ($5.50) are delicious. If you're truly starving, Mr. C suggests the omelettes, served with three buttermilk pancakes, plus grits or toast, all for $7.95; or a 4-ounce beef tenderloin steak for $5.50. Other good bets include French crepes with strawberry topping ($6.25). Side dishes include sweets like cinnamon applesauce ($2) and imported lingonberries in butter ($2.75).

Junior plates are available for children under ten. Two slices of French toast ($3.60) and three pancakes ($3.50) are served with milk, chocolate milk, or hot chocolate.

Meanwhile, to paraphrase the old orange juice commercials, "it's not just for breakfast anymore." OPH also serves a lunch menu of

---

MR. CHEAP'S PICKS

Druid Hills/Emory Village

Cedar Tree—It's well worth a trip to Emory Village just for this hangout's falafel sandwich alone.

hamburgers ($5.25), soups (plus soup and half-sandwich specials for $5.95), and hot dogs (two for $3.95), along with salads and chili.

Senior citizens always get a 15 percent discount here, and police and firemen also receive a discount off their meals.

The Original Pancake Houses are open Sunday through Thursday from 6:30 a.m. to 2:30 p.m., and Friday and Saturday from 7 a.m. to 3 p.m.

Our Way Cafe

- 303 East College Avenue, Decatur; ✆ (404) 292-9356

For home cooking away from home, make your way to Our Way. In the words of one server, "There's always meatloaf, some kinda chicken, and somethin' else" for main dishes, plus more veggies than you can shake a stalk at.

The scene is, as you'd imagine, pretty casual. Service is cafeteria style; patrons include lots of students from nearby Agnes Scott College, though you'll spot a few suits now and then. Our Way is decorated with pretty watercolor paintings, and there's a fireplace in the middle of the dining area.

For side dishes, try collard greens, pole beans, steamed cabbage, lima beans, sweet potato casserole, carrots, or macaroni and cheese. You'll get two or three sides with a main dish for under ten bucks, like that meatloaf with two vegetables and bread, which is just $6.25. Same price for the four-veggie plate, served with fresh bread. Some of the similarly low-priced daily specials may include pork chops, stuffed cabbage, salmon croquettes, and chicken enchiladas.

Try to save room for the yummy homemade desserts, like banana pudding or fresh strawberry pie, each only $3 a slice. At these prices, Our Way is cheaper than staying home!

Restaurant hours are Monday through Friday from 11 a.m. to 9 p.m. Closed on weekends.

Rainbow Natural Foods Restaurant

- 2118 North Decatur Road, Decatur; ✆ (404) 633-3538

See the light and try Rainbow for their super healthy breakfasts, lunches, and dinners, and especially their incredible Sunday brunch. The teeny restaurant is way in the back of the Rainbow grocery (which has prices that aren't half-bad, either—see the listing under *Food Stores*).

There's usually a line for Sunday brunch—be sure to get there early if you want a seat. A bowl of yogurt and granola is $2.95; so is a whole wheat biscuit with scrambled egg and home fries. Egg dishes can be prepared with tofu instead for $1 extra. Banana nut smoothies, made with almonds, yogurt, nutmeg, and honey, are $2.95 each—protein powder and wheat germ is extra. Mr. C tried the seven-grain French toast, topped with cinnamon, nutmeg, and honey, for $3.50 a half order (the whole order is gigantic). Huevos rancheros—made with poached eggs, beans, Monterey jack cheese, salsa, black olives, green olives, and sour cream, served with home fries—are just $5.25. Sides of tempeh bacon ($2.50) and yellow grits ($1.25) will help you fill up without flattening your wallet.

For lunch and dinner, Rainbow has "Sunburgers" (made with vegetables, sunflower seeds, and potatoes), served with carrot sticks for $4.75, and a plate of steamed vegetables and brown rice plate for $3.95. Huge guacamole sandwiches are $5.95; peanut butter, apple, banana, and honey sandwiches are $3.75; and tuna hoagies are $7.50.

Don't pass up Rainbow's super desserts, either. Eggless cheesecake is $3.75, and slices of pecan or pumpkin pie are $2.50.

Rainbow hours are Monday through Saturday from 11 a.m. to 8 p.m. Closed on Sunday.

St. Charles Deli

- Loehmann's Plaza, 2470 Briarcliff Road N.E., Atlanta; ✆ (404) 636-5201

No need to pass "Go" and collect $200 before landing on this St. Charles. Brunch, lunch, and dinner are all good deals—if you can find a seat, that is, in this restaurant that takes New Orleans streetcars for its inspiration. Things sure get crowded, especially on weekends, so you may be wise not to "board" during rush hours.

Breakfast is served from 8 a.m. to 11 a.m. and includes treats like make-your-own-omelettes starting at $5.99, and eggs with corned beef hash for $6.99. Mr. C enjoyed two eggs, with bagel, home fries, and juice (a mere $4.50); even with the busy crowd, everything was quickly delivered piping hot by one of the most unflappable waiters that Mr. C has ever seen in these parts.

Lunch features good ol' N'awlins choices like the huge muffaletta sandwich—cappicola ham, Genoa salami, mortadella and provolone cheese, topped with an antipasto salad, all on an Italian roll for $7.50. Try a softshell crab sandwich on an onion roll ($7), or the filling Philly cheese steak ($6.50). And there's always egg salad ($4.25), not to mention potato or macaroni salad, liverwurst, corned beef, and tuna salad sandwiches on pumpernickel, challah, whole wheat, Italian, or onion breads. Stanley and Stella never had it so good!

Get the office together and have a meal delivered; it's free on orders of $30 or more. Hours are Sunday through Thursday from 7 a.m. to 10 p.m.; Friday and Saturday from 9 a.m. to 10 p.m.

Surin of Thailand

- 810 North Highland Avenue, Atlanta; ✆ (404) 892-7780

- ✍ www.surinofthailand.com

Whether you're eating at Surin of Thailand or elsewhere, it seems that as far as Asian food goes, Thai food falls somewhere between Chinese and Japanese in terms of flavor.

In particular, Mr. C finds the chicken soup "lemongrass clean." S of T's double "Thai food/Sushi" menu offers fare including the *pad prik* spicy pork, spicy basil leaves with chicken and peppers, curry chicken, spring rolls, calamari, and chicken satay that are sure to please jovial crowds at $20 and under prices! You can even find things on the menu for $5 and under such as basil rolls ($4), warm chicken salad ($4.95), and edamame soy beans ($4.95). Of course, it's always worth splurging a little extra for dishes along the lines of succulent catfish for $6.50, ceviche salad made of raw tuna, salmon, and red snapper in red vinegar for $6.95, sashimi appetizer for $8.95, and— on the high end—sushi sashimi combo for $19.95.

Restaurant hours are Sunday through Thursday from 11:30 a.m. to 10:30 p.m.; Friday and Saturday from 11:30 a.m. to 11:30 p.m.

Sundown Café

- 2165 Cheshire Bridge Road N.E., Atlanta; ✆ (404) 321-1118

- ✍ www.sundowncafe.com

You have got to "like it hot" to survive eating here! If not, then

Sundown Café's spicy cuisine is not your kind of place . . .

To start, SC offers weekly specials; enchiladas suizas were recently offered for $11.95 per plate (2 chicken enchiladas with onions, tomatoes, mexican rice, and beans); or give the pescado sundown a try—it's a fish fillet flash fried in blue corn powder batter, with poblano tartar sauce and jalapeno cole slaw on the side.

Other meal options include "shrimp firecrackers" (won ton stuffed with shrimp, mushrooms, onions, garlic, peppers for $5.95—enough said!); chile relleno stuffed with jack green chili at $3.25 a bowl; or corn chowder, also $3.25. Why stop there when you can order entrees along the lines of duck fajitas for $15.95, *pescado pesto* (at market price) and pork loin with a jalapeno gravy "kick" ($12.50). Don't miss out on the margaritas; Mr. C says they're really good!

Restaurant hours are Monday through Friday from 11 a.m. to 2 p.m. for lunch; Monday through Thursday from 5 p.m. to 9:30 p.m. for dinner; and Friday, Saturday, and Sunday from 5 p.m. through 10:30 p.m. for dinner.

Taco Mac

- 1006 North Highland Avenue N.E., Atlanta; (404) 873-6529

- 5830 Roswell Road N.W., Sandy Springs; (404) 257-0735

- 2845 Mountain Industrial Boulevard, Stone Mountain; (404) 621-3601

- 2359 Windy Hill Road S.E. #100, Marietta; (770) 953-6382

- 3682 Highway S.E., Stockridge; (678) 289-0000

- 1318 Johnson Ferry Road, Marietta; (770) 552-8784

- 8879 Roswell Road, Atlanta; (770) 552-8784

- 2650 Dallas Highway SW, Marietta; (770) 795-1144

- 7397 Douglas Boulevard, Douglasville; (770) 942-0499

   And other suburban locations

- www.tacomac.com

These guys claim that Buffalo wings were invented right here. Gee, wait'll the folks in Buffalo hear that. No matter—Taco Mac's spicy wings are for real, and they've also got the biggest beer selection this side of the Mississippi to wash them down. While the service can be slow as a sloth, Mr. C still thinks that the food and the prices make Mac a hit.

Appetizers include fried zucchini, cauliflower, or mushrooms for just $5 a plate; a jumbo basket of nachos with frijoles and cheese goes for $5.75. TM's guacamole salad is a mere $3.85. Basics include soft tacos for $2.55, super burritos for $4.25, quesadillas for $6.50, and chili for just $3.50; to go with these, beers from 28 different countries are reasonably priced, even though they come from as far away as New Zealand and the Ivory Coast.

Those Buffalo chicken wings come in sizes of 10 for $5.75 or 20 for $10.95. Rustle them up in mild, medium, hot—or, for $1 extra, "Three Mile Island"–style. If you're having a party, here's an extra tip from Mr. C: You can get a 10 percent discount for platter orders of 250 wings or more.

Taco Mac has a kiddie menu too, with choices like a burger and fries for $3.50, or a mini fish and chips plate for the same price.

RESTAURANTS: ATLANTA NORTHEAST/DECATUR

Taco Mac is open Monday through Thursday from 11 a.m. to 2 a.m., Friday and Saturday from 11 a.m. to 3 a.m., and Sunday from 11 a.m. to midnight.

Touch of India

- 1037 Peachtree Street N.E., Atlanta; (404) 876-7777
- 2955 North Druid Hills Road N.E., Atlanta; (404) 876-7775

You'll wind up with a touch more money in your pocket if you eat at this restaurant, with locations in and just north of Midtown. The prices are right up Mr. C's alley; yet, the super samosas and tandoori dishes have attracted such celebrities as Mick Jagger, Sade, and Emilio Estevez.

Indian-style chicken fritters are $3.95 and prove Mr. C's theory that all ethnic groups really work from the same frugal ideas. Mild lentil soup, or spicier Mulligatawny soup, is $2.95 a bowl. Chicken curry, $7.50, is available in three spice levels; and beef kabob is $7.95. *Sag aloo* (spinach with potatoes) is $5.95; add some *chapati* bread for just $2.

Weekdays from 11:30 a.m. to 2:30 p.m. you can take advantage of the $5.50 brunch special ($4.50 for vegetarian dishes). The choices change from day to day but usually include samosas (turnovers) or pakuras (fritters), a curry dish or other main entree with rice, and the sweet of the day to quell the spices (like homemade ice cream or rice pudding).

Touch of India also sells beer and wine. Restaurant hours are Monday through Saturday from 11:30 a.m. to 11 p.m., and Sunday from 5:30 p.m. to 10 p.m.

The Varsity

- 61 North Avenue N.W., Atlanta; (404) 881-1706

Varsity Jr.

- 1085 Lindbergh Drive N.E., Atlanta; (404) 261-8843
- www.varsityjr.com

"What'll ya have?" they'll ask you at the Varsity and Varsity Jr. These drive-up, car-hop joints are throwbacks to the 1950s—and a renowned Atlanta institution. You have to come here at least once, and many people have been visiting for decades! ("Jr." is the newer "baby brother" of the established Varsity restaurant, and they both have exactly the same menu.)

You can order from the car or choose to eat inside, where you'll get to watch your burgers and fries travel along conveyor belts to your plastic orange tray. Then pick from several different dining areas, each with its own TV set showing news from CNN, sports on ESPN, or local Channel 11. Instead of tables, you sit at one of those attached desk-chair combinations we all remember so fondly from fifth grade.

Forget about your diet and get the Varsity's plain burgers for $1 (no extra charge for the grease) or double chili-cheese burgers ($1.75 each). Add some French fries for $1. Ten hot chicken wings are priced right at $3.75, while deviled egg sandwiches—just like the ones Mom used to put in your lunchbox—are $1.05. Extra toppings, like lettuce and tomato or cole slaw, are 50 cents each.

Regulars learn how to decipher the behind-the-counter names for menu items: can you figure out Chili Dog, Walking Dog, Naked Dog, Yellow Dog, or Bag of Rags?

You get one hour of free parking at the North Avenue location, and the Varsity Jr. on Lindbergh (near the Cheshire Bridge Road intersection) has a good-sized lot, too. Gosh, Susie, this'll be perfect for after the sock hop!

Yen Ching Restaurant

- Scott Village Shopping Center, 1707 Church Street, Decatur; ✆ (404) 296-0101

You may not expect much from Yen Ching, given its unimpressive strip-mall facade; but once you go inside, Mr. C thinks you'll be pleasantly surprised by its Mandarin, Szechuan, and Cantonese cuisine, good prices, and attentive service.

See for yourself and try their spring rolls ($2.50 for two), sizzling rice soup ($3.50), or shrimp toast ($4.50). Complete meals run under $10, like duck with plum sauce ($8.50), General Tso's chicken ($7.50), or pepper steak ($7). Sweet and sour shrimp is $8, while the vegetarian spicy bean curd with garlic sauce and celery, carrots, bean sprouts, bell pepper, and black mushrooms is merely $6.25. Egg foo young dishes start at $6.25. The all-you-can-eat Sunday brunch buffet, running from 11:30 a.m. to 3 p.m., is $3.75 for children under 12 (free for those under 3), and $6.95 for adults. It's a dim-sum delight.

Calm down the fire in your mouth with a cooling dessert, such as fried carmelized apples or bananas; this unusual offering is just $2.95 for a generous half order, or $4.25 for a full.

Yen Ching is open seven days a week. Delivery is free to a limited area on orders of $10 or more at lunch, or $12.50 or more for dinner. MSG-free meals can be prepared upon request, too.

Hours are Sunday through Thursday from 11 a.m. to 11 p.m.; Friday and Saturday from 10 a.m. to midnight.

BUCKHEAD

Annie's Thai Castle

- 3195 Roswell Road N.E., Atlanta; ✆ (404) 264-9546

They've really gone all out to make this a castle, with its fancy entranceway, lined with sunflower plants, and the super-polite staff. But believe Mr. C, you can have the budget of a serf and still dine like a king or queen here. Granted, some of the seafood dishes are priced over $10, but all other entrees will stuff you for $7 or so.

If you really feel like filling up, start off with appetizers like satay, the Thai chicken or beef kabobs, marinated in coconut milk. They come with peanut dipping sauce and a cucumber salad for $5. Or try the hot chicken wings, marinated and then deep-fried, for $4.

Dinner entrees are so big, they should just come with doggie bags in advance. Broccoli chicken ($11.95), curried pork ($11.95), and rama beef (with curry paste, coconut milk, and ground spinach, served on a bed of steamed spinach for $8.95) are popular choices. Spicy Thai noodles or spaghetti are $8.95 each, and the mixed vegetable stir-ry ($7.95) will fill you up without emptying your wallet.

Lunch specials are especially cheap, all served with rice, soup, or an eggroll. Pad Thai, $7.25, is a fine rendition of the popular rice noodle dish fried with bits of egg, shrimp, pork, bean sprouts, green onion, and peanuts. "Wings of the Angels," boneless chicken wings stuffed with pork, noodles, and onions, topped with sweet and sour sauce, is unique—and only $6. Curry-fried tofu and green beans, also with a choice of side dishes, is $5.50, and chili-flavored beef with basil leaves is only $6.

Annie's is open seven days a week and is easily found in Buckhead, across the street from Rocky's Pizza.

Restaurant hours are Sunday through Thursday from 11 a.m. to 10:30 p.m.; Saturday and Sunday from 11 a.m. to 11:30 p.m.

Athens Pizza House

- 5550 Peachtree Industrial Boulevard, Chamblee; (404) 452-8282

- 1565 Highway 138, Conyers; (404) 483-6228

- 1341 Clairmont Road, Decatur; (404) 636-1100

- 11235 Apharetta Highway #140, Roswell; (770) 751-6629

See the listing under *Restaurants—Atlanta Northeast/Decatur*.

Cafe at Pharr

- Pharr Road Shopping Center, 316 Pharr Road N.E., Atlanta; (404) 238-9288

The Cafe at Pharr is a no-nonsense bakery that compensates for its plain decor with incredibly fresh homemade sandwiches and desserts.

Bakery selections vary slightly from day to day but often include croissants for just $1, bleu cheese tartlettes for a mere 75 cents, and *fougasse* (the French version of the Italian flat focaccia bread) for $1.75. Cheddar and tomato crostini at 75 cents each are also priced well in Mr. C's budget.

Lunch items include French bread pizza slices for $1.75, eggpotato salad for $4.75, and walnut chicken sandwiches for $5.25. Sandwiches can be made on freshbaked white, French, or wheat bread or croissants. Whole wheat rolls, baguettes, brioche, and potato dill bread are great as lunch additions or as snacks on the go.

The cafe hours are Monday through Saturday from 10 a.m. to 5 p.m.; closed on Sunday.

Café Sunflower

- 2140 Peachtree Road, Atlanta; (404) 352-8859

- www.cafesunflower.com

When you sample a meal at Café Sunflower, you won't believe it's vegetarian! Boasting a hip, happening ambiance, you can easily find a filling meal for $10 and under.

If anything, Café Sunflower is accommodating: morning pastries are served at all hours of the day: Croissants ($1.60), bagels ($1.20), and muffins, with banana nut, blueberry, chocolate chip ($1.50).

Likewise, you can order breakfast at any time. The "Sunflower Breakfast" consists of two eggs any style served with garden vegetables, fresh orange juice, tea, or coffee for $6.50; the "Eggs Paris" meal features two fried eggs on a croissant served with veggies and beverage, also $6.95. Omelets range in price ($4.50 to $7.95) and flavors: homestyle, mushroom, smoked salmon, fine herbs, and feta cheese. Soup of the day is $3.50 and salads of any kind cost between $5.75 and $9.25.

Baked potatoes are offered with mushroom, sour cream, salmon, and broccoli toppings at $4.95. Sandwiches come in every variation you can imagine, such as roasted pepper, mozzarella, cheese, lox, and tuna cost between $5 and $6. Same concept goes for the pasta, you can order cheese, spinach or salmon ravioli for $7.95. They also have a coffee bar, "fresh squeezed" juice bar, and fruit frappes from $3 to $4. Here at Café Sunflower, you'll undoubtedly find something to sink your teeth into!

Hours are Monday through Thursday from 11:30 a.m. to 9:30 p.m.; Friday through Sunday from 11:30 a.m. to 10 p.m.

Cafe Tu Tu Tango

- 220 Pharr Road N.E., Atlanta; (404) 841-6222

- www.cafetututango.com

It may take two to tango, but it doesn't take too much money to enjoy a superb tapas meal at this beatnik Buckhead eatery. They offer "food for the starving artist," which is always music to Mr. C's ears. If Andy Warhol were still around, this would his type of artsy scene. Wild jazz music blares all around, and you may even catch the sight of an artist or two at work—be sure to check the studio area upstairs.

Many of the paintings, tables, lamps, and sculptures decorating the room were created by local artists and are for sale. But, to paraphrase the art world saying: If you have to ask how much, maybe you'd be better off sticking with the food.

It's all served in Spanish tapas style, so you start off with a pile of appetizer-sized plates at your table, and a paintbrush holder filled with utensils. Order a variety of small dishes to pass around. Each one only takes three to eight minutes to cook, and the sharp wait staff checks back frequently to see if you've got room to order more. Naturally, this is a good place to bring friends.

Mr. C liked the hummus (this kind was made with black beans), served with rosemary flat bread, for just $4.75. Chili is $5.25, and shrimp ceviche is $7.95. Grilled chicken kebabs, served with a Thai peanut sauce, are only $6.25.

All gone? Time for another round. Mr. C tried the light and flaky brick-oven baked grilled chicken pizza, with cheddar cheese and poblano peppers, priced at just $6.95. Mmmm. Other good picks include alligator bites with chutney are $6.75, and calamari is just $4.95.

The fresh-baked rolls served with herbed butter with every order are worth a trip in themselves. Daily specials during Mr. C's visit included lobster and crayfish in phyllo dough, with champagne sauce ($7.50), and grilled lamb spareribs with mint barbecue sauce ($7.25), plus grilled grouper and pasta salad ($6.50).

Tu Tu Tango's sangria is $4.95 a glass, and a full liquor selection is also available. This is a fun scene for a night out in Buckhead, yet still moderately priced; watch out though, because all those little dishes can add up.

Hours are Monday through Friday from 4 p.m. to 11 p.m.; Saturday and Sunday from 11:30 a.m. to 11 p.m.

California Pizza Kitchen

- 4600 Ashford Dunwoody Road N.E., Atlanta; (770) 393-0390

- 6301 North Point Parkway, Alpharetta; (770) 664-8241

- Lenox Square Shopping Center, 3393 Peachtree Road N.E., Atlanta; (404) 262-9221

  And other suburban locations

- www.cpk.com

There's more than just pizza to be found at this growing national chain—things like potato leek soup, fresh pastas, lasagna, and Thai chicken. Don't get Mr. C wrong; the pizza's okay, too, especially the rosemary-chicken-potato pie with white wine and lemon for $9.60 (plenty here for two to share), and the southwestern burrito, made with lime, black beans, mild chilies, cheddar cheese, tomatillo salsa, sour cream, and white sweet onions (also $9.60). All pies are available without cheese, baked on either traditional or honeywheat doughs. And unlike lots of other pizza houses in town, CPK uses no MSG.

Other entrees include angel hair, penne, or spaghetti, topped with tomato-herb sauce for $6.95, and spinach fettuccine with chicken, tri-color peppers, red onion, and cilantro in a tequila-lime sauce for $9.95. It's a large platter. Desserts are a bit pricey, in the unlikely event that you have room; try sharing a tiramisu ($5.50), Myers' Rum chocolate pecan pie ($4.95), apple crisp ($4.95), or tartufo-gelato balls rolled in chocolate chips and served with vanilla bean sauce or berry puree ($4.50).

Restaurant hours are Monday through Saturday from 11:30 a.m. to 10 p.m., and Sunday from noon to 7 p.m.

Colonnade

- 1879 Cheshire Bridge, Atlanta; ✆ (404) 874-5642

Since Colonnade has been offering classic "deep south" cuisine over the past 75 years, they must be doing something right! You certainly can't go wrong with the prices here, with fried chicken for $10.95, baked trout for $10.95, and chicken livers for $8.95 (Uh, a little FYI: You have to be a true Southern native to appreciate the chicken livers . . .!)

House salads with homemade ranch dressing and baskets of cornbread and sweet breads will get your meal started. Mr. C also highly recommends the butterfly shrimp, chopped steak, chicken pot pie, and stuffed salmon with whipped potatoes, all for around $10 per entree. Bring the family!

Colonnade will serve you Monday and Tuesday from 5 p.m. to 9 p.m., and Wednesday through Sunday from 11:30 a.m. to 9 p.m.

East Village Grille

- 248 Buckhead Avenue N.E., Atlanta; ✆ (404) 233-3345

Folks come here (from wherever) for its super-friendly service, laid-back, neighborhood meeting place atmosphere, and reasonable prices. You'll find it next to the Raccoon Lodge, another popular Buckhead hangout.

Night owls (like your humble scribe) have gotta love the Grille's late-night breakfast specials. A plate of eggs, hash browns, toast, butter, and jelly is just $2.99. Cheese omelettes are $5.50, and sausage and eggs goes for just $5.75.

The regular dinner menu, for you non-vampires, offers a dozen hot chicken wings for $5.95, or turkey Rachel (with cole slaw, Thousand Island dressing, and Swiss cheese on rye bread) for $6.95. All sandwiches come with a choice of side vegetables—the Grille's mashed potatoes are terrific. The bleu cheese burger is also popular (just $6.25, served with French fries, onion rings, or potato salad). And who could pass up the blue plate specials, all served with two veggie choices? Meat loaf, pork tenderloin, grilled fish, and rotisserie chicken are priced under $10, while the four-veggie plate with fresh baked bread's just $6.25.

The EVG menu includes almost a dozen "Heart Smart" choices, low in fat and cholesterol. But for those of you who don't care about these things, don't miss their desserts. Hot apple pie and Stone Mountain pecan pies are $3.95 a slice.

EVG hours are Monday through Sunday from 10 a.m. to 2 a.m.

Fellini's Pizza

- 2809 Peachtree Road N.E., Atlanta; ✆ (404) 266-0082
- 909 Ponce de Leon Avenue N.E., Atlanta; ✆ (404) 873-3088
- 4429 Roswell Road N.E., Atlanta; ✆ (404) 303-8249
- 1991 Howell Mill Road N.W., Atlanta; ✆ (404) 352-0799
- 1634 McLendon Avenue NE, Atlanta; ✆ (404) 687-9190

And other suburban locations

MR. CHEAP'S PICKS

Buckhead

Cafe Tu Tu Tango—It doesn't take too much money to enjoy a superb Spanish tapas meal at this beatnik Buckhead eatery.

Veggieland—A Buckhead secret that should be kept no longer! Incredible miso soup and stir-frys that are so good you won't even realize you're eating vegetarian.

White House Restaurant—This diner's not in a house, but they do make a point of making you feel at home, and you won't have to worry about going into too deep of a deficit.

While the scene at this pizza place would make for a great movie location, this is not a recommended place go take grandma or little tykes—it's loud, crowded, and the staff tends toward the slightly surly, under-employed-college-grad variety. The decor of brightly painted cinderblocks and oddball celebrity portraits (Elvis lives!) helps the wild, Felliniesque atmosphere along. The pizza's great, though, and two generously large slices can fill you up for under five bucks.

Plain slices are just $1.50 (believe it or not). Medium-sized cheese pies go for $8.50, and medium "white pizzas"—no tomato Sauce, and plenty of garlic—are $12. Extra toppings (just the basics are offered here) are $1 each. Cheese calzones are $5.50. Wash it all down with 16-ounce domestic draft beers, which will put you back just $3.

While Fellini's is a take-a-number-and-we'll-bring-your-order-to-your-table joint, they do keep tip jars at the counters emblazoned with the label "In lieu of decent wages." While it's optional, most customers do tip here, either at the counter or at their tables after they've eaten.

Fellini's is open Monday through Saturday from 11:30 a.m. to 2 a.m., and Sunday from 12:30 p.m. to midnight.

Johnny Rockets

- 5 West Paces Ferry Road N.W., Atlanta; ✆ (404) 231-5555
- Phipps Plaza, 3500 Peachtree Road, Atlanta; ✆ (404) 233-9867
- 6510 Roswell Road, Sandy Springs; ✆ (404) 257-0677
- 2970 Cobb Parkway N.W., Marietta; ✆ (404) 955-6068

- 50 Upper Alabama Street SW #130, Atlanta; (404) 525-7117

- 2050 Lawrenceville Highway, Decatur; (404) 320-1699

- 4475 Roswell Road, Marietta; (770) 955-6068

- 6700 Douglass Boulevard, Douglasville; (770) 577-2636

Go, go, go to Johnny's for huge portions of good ole American burgers and sandwiches at super value prices. The menu is limited, but you'll feel like you've been transported back in time to the 1950's.

Hamburger is the basic language spoken here. The "Original Burger," starting at $3.75, is topped with all the necessities: lettuce, tomato, mustard, pickle, mayo, relish, and chopped onion. For a quarter more, you can add Johnny's cheddar cheese and "red, red sauce." Chili and bacon will add still more to the ticket yet keep the burger under $7.

Hamburger haters can also find something for themselves here, like an egg salad sandwich ($3.45), the ever-popular BLT ($4.55), and a grilled cheese sandwich ($3.65). Throw some fries on the side for $2.45; better yet, try their chili fries for $3.75.

Johnny Rockets' "famous" malts and shakes are $3.95. For dessert, apple pie is $2.65; served a la mode, it's $3.40. It ain't like Mom's, but it's not bad. Basically, this is fast food with a bit more character than all your McChains, with its counter and stools and sparkling white tile motif-an idealized "Happy Days" kind of joint.

JR hours are Monday through Sunday from 11 a.m. to 9 p.m.

La Fonda Latina

- 2813 Peachtree Road N.E., Atlanta; (404) 816-8311

- 1150-B Euclid Avenue N.E., Atlanta; (404) 577-8317

- 923 Ponce de Leon Avenue, Atlanta; (404) 607-0665

- 1639 Mclendon Avenue N.E., Atlanta; (404) 378-5200

- 4427 Roswell Road NE, Atlanta; (404) 303-8201

Mr. C is fond of La Fonda Latina (the Latin Inn) for its incredible Mexican dishes and fun atmosphere. You can get stuffed (with food, that is) for under $8 or so; this restaurant—like most others—makes its big bucks on liquor sales.

An individual paella, the traditional Spanish casserole, is $6.95; it comes chock full of calamari, chicken, shrimp, sausage, and peppers, served over rice. Gazpacho goes for $3.75, and big cheese quesadillas with a snappy salsa on top are $4.50. La Fonda's Cuban sandwich is just $5.25. Add a side of frijoles or extra tortillas for $1.50, and finish your meal with chocolate or vanilla flan ($3.25) or sweet guava cheesecake ($3.50).

La Fonda Latina is a noisy, people-watching kind of restaurant. Don't even think about bringing a book to read with you. One recent Friday, in fact, Mr. C spotted a semi-famous band eating here before their late show at the Point; so, keep your eyes open when you eat here. Even if there aren't celebrities to check out, there are plenty of people trying to look just as interesting. Not to mention the decor of fountains, hanging beads, and statues.

La Fonda Latina's hours are Monday through Sunday from 11:30 a.m. to midnight.

Lettuce Souprise You

- 2470 Briarcliff Road N.E., Atlanta; ℘ (404) 636-8549
- 1784 Peachtree Street N.W., Atlanta; ℘ (404) 874-4998

See the listing under *Restaurants—Atlanta Northeast/Decatur.*

Maggiano's Little Italy

- 3368 Peachtree Road NE Atlanta; ℘ (404) 816-9650
- ✍ www.maggianos.com

It may come as no surprise that the décor at Maggiano's consists of the oh-so-predictable red-checkered tablecloths and family portraits of the clan hailing from back home in Italy; it's the food that delights. The fare here at Maggiano's is cooked on a "made from scratch" basis with recipes from the Old World and New World with prices for their pasta dishes ranging anywhere from $12.95 to $16.95.

Italian specialties include chicken and spinach manicotti ($12.95), homemade gnocchi with tomato vodka sauce ($14.95), eggplant parmesan for $10.95, four cheese ravioli for $12.95, and minestrone soup for $1.95 a cup. These prices won't break your piggy bank! Other menu offerings include warm chicken salad with prosciutto for $11.95, sandwiches such as salmon, bacon, and avocado for $7.50, tuna salad sandwich for $6.95. Plus veggies and side dishes include Carol's broccoli, lemon, and garlic for $4.95, garlic mashed potatoes for $4.95, and crispy onion rings for $3.95.

Hours here are Sunday through Thursday from 11:30 a.m. to 10 p.m.; Friday and Saturday until 11 p.m.

Metropolitan Pizza Bar

- 3055 Boiling Way N.E., Atlanta; ℘ (404) 264-0135

Sure it's an upscale watering hole smack dab in the center of Buckhead, but since they make such a profit on the booze (imported beers start at $4.50 a bottle), the food is relatively cheap. You can actually get a super filling meal here for under $10. Pizzas start at $6.95, and can be topped with everything from shiitake mushrooms and white clams to broccoli, pesto, roasted garlic, mixed peppers, and artichoke hearts. "Metro Lasagna," stuffed with zucchini, mushrooms, and eggplant, is $7.50. So are the calzones, packed with prosciutto, ricotta, mozzarella, and mushrooms. Finish your meal the traditional Italian way with biscotti available in honey, hazelnut, and chocolate flavors. Cappuccino and espresso are $3.50 and $2.75, respectively.

Restaurant hours are Sunday through Thursday from 6 p.m. to 2:30 a.m., and Friday and Saturday from 6 p.m. to 4 a.m.

Mick's

- 2110 Peachtree Road N.W., Atlanta; ℘ (404) 351-6425
- Peachtree Center, 229 Peachtree Street N.E., Atlanta; ℘ (404) 688-6425
- Lenox Square Shopping Center, 3393 Peachtree Road N.E., Atlanta; ℘ (404) 262-6425
- Underground Atlanta, 75 Upper Alabama Street S.W., Atlanta; ℘ (404) 525-2825
- 116 East Ponce de Leon Avenue, Decatur; ℘ (404) 373-7797
- 1320 Cumberland Mall S.E., Atlanta; ℘ (770) 431-7190
- 3525 Mall Boulevard, Duluth; ℘ (770) 623-1855
- 1070 Northpoint Circle, Alpharetta; ℘ (770) 667-2330

- 6700 Douglas Boulevard, Douglasville; (678) 715-0299

And other suburban locations

See the listing under *Restaurants—Atlanta Northeast/Decatur*.

OK Cafe

- 1284 West Paces Ferry Road N.W., Atlanta; ✆ (404) 233-2888

Open 24 hours a day, the OK Cafe is popular with students and business people during the daytime; by night, it's a haven for insomniacs and folks working the graveyard shift. You'll find it all the way over at the intersection of West Paces and the Northside Parkway.

Tropical forest print drapes, hand-painted glazed plates, and wooden cutout partitions between booths make a cozy, albeit noisy, atmosphere. Breakfast items are served any time of day—a true sign of a great all-night dinner. Be sure to try the buttermilk biscuits ($1.50), blueberry multigrain griddle cakes ($5.50), or baked ham and eggs (served with a biscuit or toast, and browns or grits, for $7). For a change of pace, sourdough French toast ($5.50) is a treat; and health food fans will love the egg white vegetable omelettes ($6.50).

In fact, the whole menu is a fun mix of traditional diner and trendy nouvelle fare. Start off your lunch with shaved fried onions ($2.50), sweet potato chips ($3.75), and a glass of the OK's incredible lemonade ($2). Tofu burgers, $5.75, joust with hefty (real) hamburgers for $5.25.

Country-fried steak is served with two incredibly fresh vegetable sides and whole-kernel peppered corn muffins, all for $9. Mr. C got stuffed on the four-veggie platter, which consisted of right-off-the-cob corn, six-cheese macaroni, broccoli, and a whole baked sweet potato ($7.50). And the OK proves that the fifties are alive and well, with their big-selling real cherry cokes and black cows.

Desserts are too big to eat alone, so bring a friend and don't be put off by the prices: Hot apple strudel goes for $4, and hot fudge sundaes are $3.50. Race you to the bottom!

Hours are Sunday through Thursday from 7 a.m. to 11 p.m.; Friday and Saturday from 7 a.m. to midnight.

Original Pancake House

- 4330 Peachtree Road N.E., Atlanta; ✆ (404) 237-4116

- 2321 Cheshire Bridge Road N.E., Atlanta; ✆ (404) 633-5712

- 5099 Memorial Drive, Stone Mountain; ✆ (404) 292-6914

- 3665 Club Drive #104, Duluth; ✆ (770) 925-0065

- 243 Market Place Connector, Peachtree City; ✆ (770) 486-7634

See the listing under *Restaurants—Atlanta Northeast/Decatur*.

The Palm

- Swissotel Atlanta, 3391 Peachtree Road N.E., Atlanta; ✆ (404) 365-0065

- ✍ www.thepalm.com

Want to impress a date or business client without breaking your budget? Try The Palm, which is cheaper by far than its Swissotel neighbor, Opus, but still quite dazzling. The post-modern art collection may be a little far out for some tastes; but the food prices, for this kind of quality, are far from out-of-this-world.

You can dine inside, or on the cafe's outdoor terrace overlooking Peachtree Road.

Lunches and dinners start with appetizer choices like butternut squash soup with smoked bacon and chives ($4.50), crispy calamari with spicy marinara sauce ($5.75), and vegetable spring rolls with plum sauce ($4.50). Tuna salad nicoise is $8.75, oriental chicken salad with soba noodles and roasted cashews is $8, and a chicken quesadilla with *pico de gallo* is $8.50.

Light menu choices include the swordfish steak with grilled vegetables ($11.75), chicken breast braised in white wine, with couscous ($11.75), and grilled salmon with yellow and green bean salad ($14). Other specialties include fettuccine pasta with shrimp and asparagus ($13.50), lump crab cake in a potato crust with papaya mustard ($11.50), and blackened mahi mahi with a citrus relish ($12).

The cafe has a select wine list, available by the glass. White wines are priced from $4 a glass, for a Monterey Vineyard chardonnay, reds start at $5 for a Napa Ridge Pinot Noir, and champagne choices include Piper Sonoma Brut 1988 for $7.

No, it ain't cheap, but Mr. C had to mention at least one place where you can afford to splurge when you've got the urge.

Restaurant hours are Monday through Friday from 11:30 a.m. to 11 p.m.; Saturday and Sunday from noon to 11 p.m.

Ray's New York Pizza

- 3021 Peachtree Road N.E., Atlanta; ✆ (404) 364-0960

Greenwich Village has this little pizzeria, called Ray's, which is legendary for classic New York-style pizza. So much so, that several chains have arrived recently, trading on very similar names. None can beat the original, but actually, they all come pretty close.

Now, this one sure looks like a typical teenager pizza-joint hangout. But Ray's makes great thin-crust pizza and sells it at very un-Buckhead prices.

Pizza slices sell for $3.50, and small pies start at only $10.50. The ingredients get quite fancy, like artichoke pesto pizzas, which start at $15.95. Other popular dishes include sandwiches like the Hawaiian chicken ($7.25), turkey burger ($6.95), and eggplant hero ($6.50); sun-dried tomato and broccoli calzones sell for just $6.95 and can be stuffed with any of the pizza toppings for 70 cents an item.

Ray's also offers an amazing selection of domestic and imported beers, from Pete's Wicked Ale, Red Stripe, and Whitebread to Guinness, Kronenbourg, Peroni, and Tecate.

Restaurant hours are Monday through Friday from 11 a.m. to 11 p.m.; Saturday and Sunday from noon to 11 p.m.

Rio Grande Cantina

- 2257 Peachtree Road N.E., Atlanta; ✆ (404) 352-8993

Not to be confused with the similarly low-priced (and ubiquitous) Rio Bravo Cantina, Rio Grande goes beyond the standard Mexican dishes and jazzes up its food with incredibly fresh ingredients and unusual combinations. The decor here does leave a bit to be desired (garish green booths and suspiciously dim lighting). But there's a hopping weekend scene at this South Buckhead spot, thanks to the good grub and popular musicians booked for no-or-low-cover shows.

Start off your meal with *sopa de polo*, a tomato-based chicken soup with rice, for $3.50 a bowl. A la carte orders, like beef tostadas ($5.50), large bean burritos ($5.50), and hot tamales for $4, will get you going. *Frijoles refritos* (that's refried beans to gringos) are just $4 an order and sides of *salsa verde, pico de gallo,* and jalapenos are just $2 each for generous sized bowls.

Lunch specials are served weekdays from 11 a.m. all the way to 5 p.m. Huevos rancheros (Mexican eggs, served with rice) are just $6.50; same price for a bean burrito and cheese enchilada plate with rice. "Arriba!" The "Speedy Gonzalez" lunch, consists of a taco, an enchilada, and rice or frijoles for a mere $5.50.

House specialties include chimichangas for $9.75 (enough for two to share), enchiladas (beef, cheese, bean, or chicken) starting at $6.25, and a half-order of chicken or burritos—with beans and jalapeno cheese sauce—for $6.50. Fajitas with rice go up to $10.75 (with shrimp for $11.50), while tostadas deluxe, filled with refried beans, chicken breast, sour cream and Rio Grande's special sauce, is $8.95.

Rio Grande also serves children's meals for those under 12, like the taco, rice, and refried bean plate, beef burrito and rice, or Mexican hamburger, each $4.95.

To end your spicy meal on a sweet note try RGC's flan ($4.50), or the *sopapilla,* a fried tortilla with honey, priced right at just $3.25 ($4.25 a la mode). RGC's fresh fruit margaritas, available in lime, strawberry, raspberry, banana, and peach, start at $5.75.

Rio Grande Cantina's hours are Monday through Friday from 11 a.m. to 11 p.m.; Saturday and Sunday from noon to 11 p.m.

Rocky's Brick Oven Pizza

- 1770 Peachtree Street N.E., Atlanta; ✆ (404) 870-7625

- 1394 North Highland Avenue NE, Atlanta; ✆ (404) 876-1111

Yo. Rocky's has fought the good fight to gain a share of Atlanta's burgeoning pizza market, and the result is lower prices for you. Brick-fired ovens produce a slightly smoky-flavored, crunchy European pizza, and there are lots of fresh, unusual toppings to jazz these up. Homemade mozzarella and impeccably fresh ingredients have helped Rocky's win international awards for their food; and it's been voted the best inexpensive restaurant in town by Fodor's Guides.

Make up your own individual pizza (prices start at $7.99) by topping it with fried breaded eggplant, Italian sausage, sautéed chicken, or other goodies for $1.25 each. Rocky's big Neapolitan (thin-crust) pie, enough for three people to share, starts at $14.97; Sicilian-styles, enough for four people, are $21.95. These gargantuan pies make this a good place to come with the gang.

Some of Rocky's more creative combinations include the Gardenia with broccoli and artichoke hearts, white glazed garlic sauce, mozzarella, gorgonzola, tomatoes, and pesto. Chicken bianca oreganato, with fresh garlic, white wine, red onions, and lemon, and eggplant florentine pizzas are also good choices.

They have great calzones here, too. All are priced at $12.50 each, such as the Beau Bock, stuffed to overflowing with salami, prosciutto ham, pepperoni, provolone, and cappicola. Rocky's offers delivery on orders over $15.

Restaurant hours are Monday through Friday from 11 a.m. to 11 p.m.; Saturday and Sunday from noon to 11 p.m.

Steamhouse Lounge Seafood Bar

- 3041 Bolling Way N.E., Atlanta; ✆ (404) 233-7980

You'll be happy as a clam with this dining choice. It's a watering hole in every sense of the word (and self-appointed as "The best little dump in Buckhead"), with bar regulars' names engraved on tiny plates and affixed to "their" seats at the bar.

To start off, try "Uncle Sherman's famous" crab dip, served with warm pita bread ($5), or the seafood nachos, laced with baby shrimp, crabmeat, bay scallops, jalapenos, and tomato ($8.25). Their super chili's a deal at $5 a bowl, as is lobster bisque at $5.25 a bowl. Fresh corn on the cob, in season, and the terrific potato salad are just $1.50 a side.

A dozen raw oysters can be shucked to order for $7.95; the "U-Shuck-'Em" bucket of two dozen oysters is $11.95; and the famous Frogmore Skillet, heaped high with steamed oysters, shrimp, Polish sausage, potatoes, and corn on the cob, all in butter sauce, is a huge bargain at $10.95. The "Steam Pot" is a popular item with groups, filled as it is with every varieties of shellfish that the Lounge sells. (Steamhouse sells shellfish sort of by the seashore . . .) It serves up to four people and is reasonably priced at $26.95.

Less daring souls (like your children, perhaps?) tend to stick to the basics like the deli salad ($7.25), turkey-bacon sandwiches ($6.95), and chili dogs ($5.25).

Reel something in for yourself. Restaurant hours are Monday through Saturday from 11:30 a.m. to 2 a.m., and Sundays from 11:30 p.m. to midnight.

Taco Mac

- 1006 North Highland Avenue N.E., Atlanta; (404) 873-6529

- 5830 Roswell Road N.W., Sandy Springs; (404) 257-0735

- 2845 Mountain Industrial Boulevard, Stone Mountain; (404) 621-3601

- 2359 Windy Hill Road SE #100, Marietta; (770) 953-6382

- 3682 Highway SE, Stockridge; (678) 289-0000

- 1318 Johnson Ferry Road, Marietta; (770) 552-8784

- 8879 Roswell Road, Atlanta; (770) 552-8784

- 2650 Dallas Highway SW, Marietta; (770) 795-1144

- 7397 Douglas Boulevard, Douglasville; (770) 942-0499

And other suburban locations

- www.tacomac.com

See the listing under *Restaurants—Atlanta Northeast/Decatur.*

Three Dollar Café

- 3002 Peachtree Road N.E., Atlanta; (404) 266-8667

- 8595 Roswell Road, Dunwoody; (404) 992-5011

- 2580 Windy Hill Road, Marietta; (404) 850-0868

- 423 Ernest W Barrett Parkway N.W., Kennesaw; (770) 426-6566

- 2166 Highpoint Road, Snellville; (770) 736-1000

The Three Dollar Café is not your average Buckhead watering hole. That's because it's much more like anywhere else's watering hole. Mr. C likes the very casual, un-Buckhead atmosphere (feel free to wear your oldest T-shirt). And while you will have to spend a little over three bucks on dinner here, alas, the name isn't all that far off. Portions are so huge, in fact, that you'll most likely get two meals out of whatever you order.

Three Dollar Café's chicken wings are real crowd pleasers at just $5.95 an order—feel free to get messy, too, since each table is thoughtfully provided with rolls of paper towels for post-pigout cleanups. Or, try an order of sautéed mushrooms for $5.75.

Mr. C got quite stuffed on the salad and steamed veggie platter, which comes with new potatoes, lots of carrots, and darn near a whole head each of broccoli and cauliflower—all for just $6.95.

Steak and cheese sandwiches are only $6.50, reubens are $6.95, and beef kabobs are $8.75. Chicken Oscar, made with crabmeat topping, white asparagus, and Hollandaise sauce, is served with squash casserole and rice and gravy, complete for $8.95.

Don't forget dessert either, with treats like key lime pie, cheesecake, and ice cream-topped brownies, each under $4.50.

Three Dollar has a children's menu, too, with spaghetti, burgers and fries, chicken wing and fries, or a grilled cheese sandwich, for just $3.95 each. Kids three and under get a free peanut butter and jelly sandwich. Now, there's a deal!

Restaurant hours are Sunday through Thursday from 11 a.m. to 1 a.m.; Friday and Saturday from 11 a.m. to 2 a.m.

Tom Tom

- 3393 Peachtree Road N.E., Atlanta; (404) 264-1163

The good news is that the food here is fab and . . . the bad news is that you have to drive to this mall restaurant to get it! Alas, another positive tradeoff is that you can easily come by a delicious meal such as ginger chicken, or desserts (chocolate mouse, ice cream, a la mode with caramel topping) for under $20 at Tom Tom's. Another win/win!

Restaurant hours are Monday through Saturday from 11 a.m. to 10 p.m. and Sunday from 11:30 a.m. to 9 p.m.

Uncle Tai's

- 3500 Peachtree Road N.E., Atlanta; (404) 816-8888

Yep, okay, this is the Uncle Tai's you may have seen advertised in *Atlanta* magazine, the one that gives those fancy cooking classes and all, right in the middle of Phipps. Granted, dinner here doesn't exactly fit into the Mr. C scheme of things, but lunch here is a relative bargain.

From 11 a.m. to 2:30 p.m. each weekday, Uncle Tai's offers a super deal: a "Cafe Platter" of shrimp with zucchini, beef with green peppers, or curried chicken. Whichever you choose, it comes with the soup of the day, a vegetable spring roll, and fried rice, all for $7.50. Not bad!

Other lunch entrees, served from 11 a.m. to 4:30 p.m. daily, include moo shu pork with bamboo shoots and tree-ear mushrooms ($7.75), sweet and sour shrimp ($8.25), fish with black bean sauce (also $8.25), and lamb with scallions ($8.25). Hunan-style noodles with shrimp and chicken are $7.25, as is eggplant in garlic sauce. Hot tea, steamed rice, and soup (hot and sour or corn) are served with all these.

Traditionally hot and spicy dishes are clearly marked; the chef can alter the spices if requested. That lunch deal may make it easier for you to impress a date, or your boss, with good food in elegant surroundings.

Restaurant hours are Sunday through Thursday from 11:30 a.m. to 9:30 p.m.; Friday and Saturday from 11:30 a.m. to 10:30 p.m.

Veggieland

- 211 Pharr Road N.E., Atlanta; (404) 231-3111

- 209 Sandy Springs Circle, Sandy Springs; ✆ (404) 252-1165

You don't have to be a vegetarian to like the food here—you'll probably never notice that there's no refined sugar or dairy products used in any of the menu items. Veggieland is a place for real purists—jars of no-salt spice mixtures and non-irradiated cayenne pepper flakes sit at each table, and even the ice cubes are made with filtered water. It's a well-kept Buckhead secret, undeservingly overshadowed by a certain (more expensive) leafy chain located right down the street.

Mr. C liked the cashew and soy strip veggie stir-fry, with its perfectly steamed snow peas, broccoli, carrots, red and green peppers, and bean sprouts sitting atop a mound of basmati rice. This was enough for two meals, really, priced at a healthy $5.50. It's also available with baked tofu and almonds, instead of the cashews and soy strips, for the same price. Whole-grain pasta primavera with pesto is another hearty entree, perfect for vegetarians and nonvegetarians alike, is just $6.25.

The Veggie Burger is made from nuts, beans, and spices, topped with tomato, lettuce, sprouts, and onion on a whole wheat bun, for $4.75; top it with soy cheese for 50 cents extra. The tofu-chicken sandwich, served with fried sweet potatoes, is just $5.25. Soup selections change daily; the potato leek soup is super, and just $2.50 for a good-sized cup.

The restaurant itself is tiny, with a small patio and a laid-back, take-your-time atmosphere. Colorful Caribbean-scene paintings and classical music make for peaceful surroundings, while the attentive service makes you feel right at home.

Veggieland hours are Monday through Friday from 11:30 a.m. to 9 p.m., Saturday from 11:30 a.m. to 8:30 p.m., and closed on Sunday.

White House Restaurant

- 3172 Peachtree Road N.E., Atlanta; ✆ (404) 237-7601

Mr. C will bet that you've driven by this treasure a hundred times without noticing, since it's wedged into a strip mall with a furniture and shoe stores, near the Buckhead IHOP. White House is the kind of diner where you get treated like a head of state—even though the food prices are more appropriate for the guy who cleans the windows.

Breakfast is served any time of the day—gotta love it! And you'll love the prices, too: Two eggs any style, grits, biscuits or toast, and butter and jelly are just $4. Hotcakes with syrup are $3.50, oatmeal is $3, and the "Working Man's Breakfast" (tsk tsk, we're supposed to say working person now), consists of a hefty-sized pork chop, with two eggs, grits, and biscuit, for $7.50.

For lunch, Mr. C tried the three vegetable platter, with whole okra, potato salad, and steamed spinach for $6, while a friend enjoyed an open-faced hot turkey sandwich with mashed spuds for $7.50. Specials change daily but include some Greek mainstays (like pastitsio or moussaka, each $8), as well as Irish beef stew, filet mignon, and barbecued pork (all under $10, including veggies and fixin's). Even seafood is inexpensive here, like fried flounder, perch, or trout dinners, all under $8.

And, if you've got room left over for dessert, don't miss the cheesecake ($3.50) or homemade peach cobbler ($3.50).

Restaurant hours are Monday through Saturday from 6 a.m. to 3 p.m.; closed on Sunday.

DOWNTOWN ATLANTA/SOUTHEAST & SOUTHWEST

Athens Pizza House

- 1959 Lakewood Avenue S.E., Atlanta; ✆ (404) 622-7911
- 246 Bobby Jones Expressway, Augusta; ✆ (706) 868-1508
- 5550 Peachtree Industrial Boulevard, Chamblee; ✆ (404) 452-8282
- 1565 Highway 138, Conyers; ✆ (404) 483-6228
- 1341 Clairmont Road, Decatur; ✆ (404) 636-1100
- 1255 Johnson Ferry Road, Marietta; ✆ (404) 509-0099
- 6075 Roswell Road, N.E., Sandy Springs; ✆ (404) 257-0252

See the listing under *Restaurants—Atlanta Northeast/Decatur*.

The Beautiful Restaurant

- 2260 Cascade Road S.W., Atlanta; ✆ (404) 752-5931

The decor may not be beautiful here (unless you like fake wood paneling, orange vinyl booths, and second-grade classroom style tables), but the bargain-priced food sure is a gorgeous deal. Servings are generously sized, and you can get a full meal for under $5. Actually, it's a great place to eat in after visiting the MLK Center down the street.

Starting with breakfast, a stack of pancakes is just $2.25, and bacon omelettes are $3.90 Grilled cheese sandwiches go for just $1.10, while the rib-eye steak breakfast tops out the menu at $7.50.

For lunch, police sergeants and other regulars file in to fill up on the house special—any three vegetables, plus fresh bread and soda or tea, for just $3.70. Choose from brussels sprouts, squash, rutabagas, turnips, okra, corn on the cob, rice, creamed potatoes, collard greens, broccoli casserole, yams, and more.

They charge you for little extras (like lemon or butter), but that helps the place keep prices down on main dishes—thus, you can get spaghetti and meat sauce for a mere $3.10.

Service is cafeteria style. The Beautiful Restaurant is open Sunday through Wednesday from 7 a.m. to 11 p.m., and Thursday through Saturday 'round the clock.

Busy Bee Cafe

- 810 Martin Luther King Jr. Drive S.W., Atlanta; ✆ (404) 525-9212

This great soul food joint draws a wide variety of patrons: politicos, cops, students, and soul food aficionados who drool over the prospect of such specialties as chitlins, giblets, ham hocks, and neck bones. Check out their "beelicious" fried chicken (try it smothered in gravy), pork chops, or meatloaf, among others. All are $7, and just $6 on Fridays. Two fresh veggies—don't miss broccoli cheese casserole or a recent Tuesday special of baby limas—come with each dinner. Desserts, especially red velvet cake and banana pudding, are great and go for around $2.50.

Open Monday through Saturday from 11 a.m. to 7 p.m.

Calypso Cafe

- 58 Walton Street N.W., Atlanta; ✆ (404) 589-0024

This noisy, popular restaurant specializes in great Jamaican food.

From Jamaican patties ($1.50) to curry conch ($10), the menu will satisfy your wildest tropical cravings. Jerk wings ($4.75) and veggie and meat patties lead to entrees such as golden brown stewed chicken ($6) and steamed flakey snapper cooked with okra, tomatoes, and onions ($7). Recommended sides are rice and peas (a mound of rice studded with black beans), plantains (roundly sweet inside, caramelized outside), and the rich homemade macaroni and cheese. Seasoned insiders opt for the oxtail marinated in brown gravy ($6.75) or curried goat ($6.50). Never-fail favorites are the tender shrimp in garlic broth and crispy fried bites of fresh conch ($7 each).

Open for lunch only 11:30 a.m. to 2:30 p.m.

Coco Loco Cuban & Caribbean Cafe

- 303 Peachtree Center Avenue N.E., Atlanta; (404) 653-0070

- 2625 Piedmont Road N.E., Atlanta; (404) 364-0212 and (404) 261-0198

- 6301 Roswell Road, Sandy Springs; (404) 255-5434

See the listing under *Restaurants—Atlanta Northeast/Decatur*.

Cowan's Sandwich Shoppe

- 124 Spring Street S.W., Atlanta; (404) 521-2190

Let's face it, folks—you expect a humble sandwich shop to have low prices. But Mr. Cheap felt he had to include this tiny diner, "sandwiched" among hulking federal buildings, because the joint is near-legendary among downtown office workers and blue-collar types.

Little more than a snack stand with just a narrow counter and a few tables inside, Cowan's has been here for over forty years. When the weather is good, picnic tables spilling into the parking lot add a few more seats.

The menu is limited, but the fare is warm and filling. Mr. C's fave is the barbecue sandwich, with a stew of pork and beans slathered onto a fresh roll for only $3.21. The "Golden Nugget," a few cents more, offers fried chicken pieces instead. Ham and cheese biscuits are another hearty homemade winner, just $1 for a single order. And pimento cheese sandwiches ($2.14) are popular, with a pile of them pre-wrapped and waiting for hurried regulars.

The atmosphere, as far as it can possibly go, is boisterous and friendly—a good place for small talk with the owner, or conversation with your coworkers (if you can get in).

Cowan's is open weekdays only, naturally, from 6:00 a.m. until about 2:00 p.m.

Mick's

- 557 Peachtree Road N.E., Atlanta; (404) 875-6425

- 2110 Peachtree Road N.W., Atlanta; (404) 351-6425

- Peachtree Center, 229 Peachtree Street N.E., Atlanta; (404) 688-6425

- Lenox Square Shopping Center, 3393 Peachtree Road N.E., Atlanta; (404) 262-6425

- Underground Atlanta, 75 Upper Alabama Street S.W., Atlanta; (404) 525-2825

- 116 East Ponce de Leon Avenue, Decatur; (404) 373-7797

See the listing under *Restaurants—Atlanta Northeast/Decatur*.

Paschal's Restaurant

- 830 Martin Luther King Jr. Drive S.W., Atlanta;
  ✆ (404) 577-3150

Located in front of the Castleberry Inn, Paschal's is a longtime landmark for down-home eating for businessmen and an older local crowd. Most of the patrons seem to be regulars from this neighborhood west of the Omni; the city's rampant development hasn't reached this far yet, and the streets around here can get pretty tough at night. Inside this restaurant, though, the folks who work and eat here go out of their way to be friendly.

The front room is your traditional luncheonette, with a counter and comfortably padded booths. To the rear, leading into the hotel, you come into a vastly different environment: a pair of darkly elegant, formal dining rooms. Whichever setting you choose, you'll find the same great soul food menu.

That food, meanwhile, is wonderful and cheap. Southern fried chicken is perhaps the house specialty; at $6, it's fantastic, and it comes with your choice of two vegetables—choices may include things like candied yams, June peas, collard greens, or rice and gravy. The crust is crunchy and tasty all by itself—the true test—with grains of black pepper mixed into the batter.

Most other lunch/dinner entrees are priced between $6 and $9, including such choices as broiled chopped sirloin, pork chops, country-fried steak, broiled catfish, flounder stuffed with crabmeat, and many others. All these come with two vegetables, as well as little bread and cornbread rolls. There is a more formal listing of steaks and chops, but these prices do rise out of The Cheapster's range.

> ### MR. CHEAP'S PICKS
>
> #### Downtown
>
> **The Beautiful Restaurant**—The decor may not be beautiful here (unless you like fake wood paneling, orange vinyl booths, and second-grade classroom style tables), but the bargain-priced food sure is a gorgeous deal.
>
> **Calypso Cafe**—This noisy, popular restaurant specializes in great Jamaican food, from Jamaican patties to curry conch.
>
> **Paschal's**—Located in the Castleberry Inn, this gem offers food that is both wonderful and cheap.

For smaller appetites, try a plate of "Paschal Style" chicken hash, served with creamed potatoes and one egg any style for $4.75; or a fried chicken sandwich, just $3.50. There are muffins and homemade soups, and salads too. One thing is certain: They won't let you leave hungry.

Paschal's is open from 7:30 a.m. to 9 p.m. Monday through Saturday.

Soul Vegetarian

- 879-A Ralph D. Abernathy Boulevard S.W., Atlanta;
  ✆ (404) 752-5194

- 652 North Highland Avenue N.E., Atlanta;
  ✆ (404) 875-0145

The very name of these restaurants sounds like a contradiction in terms. Soul food is not generally thought of as being light and healthy. One imagines some kind of tofu ribs or such. In fact, the menu does not differ much from that of any vegetarian restaurant; it's the atmosphere, complete with jazz music, a very homey welcome, and a bit of scripture on the walls that sets the place apart from the city's other sprout palaces.

Everything here is all-natural and mostly cholesterol-free, right on down to the soy ice cream that's always offered as your meal is cleared. The entrees themselves, in an unlikely turn, tend toward Middle Eastern delicacies. "Soups from Jerusalem" feature *marak alfunah*, a garlicky split-pea; it's only $1.30 a cup, or $2.45 a bowl. Add some cornbread for another buck.

Most of the entrees are salads and sandwiches, with one daily lunch ($8.45) or dinner ($10.30) special added, like spaghetti with a tomato-vegetable sauce. The dinners include salad and cornbread. Otherwise, sandwiches are all $4.00; make any one into a platter for $5.50, adding a side salad and hand-cut French fries or onion rings—however healthy those can be. The unique specialty of the house is something called kalebone, made from wheat grain (plenty of protein) into a tasty concoction that can be made into burger patties or sliced into a gyro-like pita sandwich. Flavored with a few different sauces, it's moist and filling.

Salads range from $3.45 to $7.45, in small and large sizes. These are based around carrots or tofu, along with your basic garden salad. A platter of steamed vegetables with a salad is $7.70. Finish off with the above-mentioned "ice cream"; a baked cobbler of some variety is also usually on the menu. Everything's very simple here, but done quite well.

Open Tuesday to Saturday 11 a.m. to 7 p.m., Sunday 9 a.m. to 1 p.m. and Monday 11 a.m. to 10 p.m.

Taco Mac

- 375 Pharr Road N.E., Atlanta; (404) 239-0650
- 1006 North Highland Avenue N.E., Atlanta; (404) 873-6529
- 771 Cherokee Avenue S.E., Atlanta; (404) 624-4641
- 2120 Johnson Ferry Road, Chamblee; (404) 454-7676
- 1444 Oxford Road, Emory Village; (404) 377-2323
- 1570 Holcomb Bridge Road, Roswell; (404) 640-9598
- 5830 Roswell Road N.W., Sandy Springs; (404) 257-0735
- 2845 Mountain Industrial Boulevard, Stone Mountain; (404) 621-3601

See the listing under *Restaurants—Atlanta Northeast/Decatur*.

Thelma's Kitchen

- 764 Marietta Street, Atlanta; (404) 688-5855

Located near Centennial Park, this funky little place features industrial strength white, with a steamy cafeteria line, yet it's extremely popular with a wide range of patrons from all walks of life.

Dark meat special or pork chops (around $7), rice and gravy or mac 'n cheese (about $1.50)—Thelma's is what soul food is really all about. Do you try the sweet potato pie ($1.95) or pineapple upside-down cake? These are the tough dilemmas of this consistently good soul food. The fried chicken alone is worth a trip ($7.25), as are the vegetables (don't be shy about ordering a vegetable plate ($4.15)—it's a local favorite).

Thelma's is open Monday to Friday 7:30 a.m. to 4:30 p.m. and

Thumbs Up Diner

- 573 Edgewood Avenue S.E., Atlanta; (404) 223-0690

This unassuming but handsome-looking place offers neighborhood patrons really good breakfast food and decent sandwiches for lunch—all with a scruffy soul food vibe. The food here is always fresh and delicious, and the menu boasts quite a selection for both vegetarians and meat eaters looking for a good vittles.

Enjoy the challah French toast ($2.50/slice), the Mediterranean omelette ($4.95), or the Seattle scramble ($6.95)—they're all great. Better yet, the friendly servers here will top off your coffee cup when it runs low. Mr. C thinks this place has earned its name.

Thumbs Up is open Monday to Friday 7 a.m. to 3 p.m.; Saturday and Sunday from 8 a.m. to 4 p.m.

Wall Street Deli

- Equitable Building, 100 Peachtree Street N.W., Atlanta; (404) 681-5542
   Fax: (404) 681-4652

- www.wallstreetdeli.com

It's almost as busy in here as the floor of the stock exchange, but the food they sell is not a blue-chip commodity at all. Their super-fresh salad bar has over seventy different items; it won't cost you an arm and a leg either. Each container costs up to $5.99 at the most—no matter how high you pile it with Wall Street's regular salad bar items, or even the pastas and sauces, fruits, garlic bread, veggies, and delicious mini chocolate muffins covered with confectioner's sugar. Wow!

Other popular lunch choices include the fresh sandwiches, like the "Bronx" (hot corned beef and pastrami with melted Swiss on rye) and the "Brooklyn" (hot roast beef, smoked cheddar, mild peppers with Russian dressing), each just $4.99. The "Vegetarian" (of no particular borough, apparently) is piled high with avocado, American and Swiss cheeses, sprouts, lettuce, tomato, peppers, onions, and mayo, all for just $4.49.

Soup choices include split pea, pinto bean, chicken noodle, black-eyed pea, and cream of spinach, plus chili, all starting at just $1.99 for the small size. Wall Street also offers "soup and half sandwich of the day" deals, starting at $4.65. For dessert, along with the above-mentioned muffins, Mr. C liked the peanut butter cookies (99 cents each); while cinnamon rolls, at $1.19 each, are also popular.

Many busy corporate types fax ahead their orders to save time. Mr. C has generously provided you with this insider trading info, above.

Open 7 a.m. to 3 p.m. Monday to Friday.

LITTLE FIVE POINTS

Including Ponce area, Virginia-Highland

American Roadhouse

- 842 North Highland Avenue. N.E., Atlanta; (404) 872-2822

- 1317 Dunwoody Village Parkway, Dunwoody; (404) 512-8114

Kitsch is king of the road at American Roadhouse. Heavily decorated with traffic signs, license plates, and full-size, old-fashioned gasoline pumps, these folks work hard to imbue the restaurant with a sense of nostalgic fun. Mr. C found this style a bit forced, but all this memorabilia is certainly interesting to check out.

Of course, you may simply want to ignore it all and look at the vast menu instead, which is loaded with food that's as all-American as apple pie and Chevrolet. Pull up to a plate of pecan waffles for $3.95, or a sausage and cheese omelet with home fries for $5.95. Burgers start at $5.95 and up and are made from beef or turkey. Or try the grilled chicken with cheddar for $6.95 (add $1 for bacon).

Specials—priced from $5.95 to $8.95—are all quite reasonable. Chicken pot pie, country-fried steak, and trout almandine are just some of the regular offerings. All plates come with two side dishes, from over 15 choices from Granny Smith applesauce, to sesame carrots to Waldorf salad. Oooh, yeah!

Big desserts range from apple pie (of course) to chocolate mousse pie, each priced at $3. Basically, the Roadhouse tries to cover all the bases, doing a decent job of having something for everyone.

MR. CHEAP'S PICKS

Ponce Area

Eats—Downscale becomes trendy at this cool cafeteria, from the folks who brought you Tortillas.

The Mansion—If you're looking for a good meal in a classy setting, you owe it to yourself to check this place out. If you're looking to save money, go for lunch.

Tortillas—This place takes low-maintenance dining to the max—or rather, to the Mex.

The Roadhouse is open seven days a week from 7 a.m. until 10 p.m. and an hour later on weekends.

Chin Chin

- 3887 Peachtree Road N.E., Atlanta; ✆ (404) 816-2229
- 699 Ponce de Leon Avenue, Atlanta; ✆ (404) 881-1511
- 1100 Hammond Drive, Atlanta; ✆ (404) 913-0266
- 7820 Holcomb Bridge Road, Norcross; ✆ (770) 840-9898

Enjoy delicious Chinese cuisine in this nice little shop, including entrees such as tangerine steak, golden crispy prawns, shredded pork in garlic sauce, and sautéed vegetables. Chin Chin's chef's specials and a few other entrees will take you higher than the range cited above, but you can grab a good bargain with the lunch special. You can choose from 33 items priced from $4.95 to $5.75.

Chin Chin is open Monday through Saturday from 11 a.m. to 9 p.m. On Sundays they're open from 3 p.m. to 9 p.m.

Eats

- 600 Ponce de Leon Avenue N.E., Atlanta; ✆ (404) 888-9149

This fun joint on Ponce—across from City Hall East—is something like a world-beat cafeteria, or perhaps a funky soup kitchen. The atmosphere is comfortably downscale, enough to attract a mixed crowd of yuppies and hippies alike. Antique photos and paintings by local artists hang on the walls. There is an old, upright piano, which may or may not work. It matters little, as the sound system plays an eclectic mix ranging from Billie Holiday to Bob Marley to zydeco.

Walk up to one of several stations along the side of the restaurant and grab a tray; one area serves up pastas, another meats and veggies, another is a bar where you can get a bottle of Samuel Adams or Newcastle beer for just $3 (domestics are $2.25; pitchers are available too).

Start off with the grilled chicken chili with cornbread for $2.50, a perfect complement to that ice cold brew.

The pastas begin with your choice of spaghetti, ziti, linguine, or fettucine and a number of sauce options; top this with basic marinara for a mere $3.25, to alfredo with sausage for $7. You can also add a grilled chicken breast or meatballs for $2. All come with garlic bread. Hey kids, it's chow time.

At the meat counter, the choice is even simpler: Jamaican-style jerk chicken. It's delicious, marinated with that tantalizing blend of mild spices and sweet cinnamon. Have it all by its lonesome—a half-bird for $4—or as a platter with white rice, black beans, and real cornbread (as denoted by the kernels of real corn), all for $5. This may be the largest plate of home-cooked food you'll ever get for a price like that.

There are a few other offerings, including a vegetarian plate (natch), but you have the basic scenario. For dessert, you'll have to settle with the sole offering of delicious homemade brownies for a buck.

Eats serves eats from 11 a.m.10 p.m. daily.

Everybody's Pizza

- 1040 North Highland Avenue N.E., Atlanta;
  ✆ (404) 873-4545

- 1593 North Decatur Road, Emory Village;
  ✆ (404) 377-7766

See the listing under *Restaurants—Atlanta Northeast/Decatur*.

Fellini's Pizza

- 2813 Peachtree Road N.E., Atlanta; ✆ (404) 266-0082

- 923 Ponce de Leon Avenue N.E., Atlanta;
  ✆ (404) 873-3088

- 422 Seminole Avenue N.E., Atlanta; ✆ (404) 525-2530

- 4429 Roswell Road N.E., Atlanta; ✆ (404) 303-9249

- 1991 Howell Mill Road N.W., Atlanta; ✆ (404) 352-0799

See the listing under *Restaurants—Buckhead*.

George's

- 1041 North Highland Avenue N.E., Atlanta;
  ✆ (404) 992-3649

As Mr. C always says, bars make the money on the booze, so they can afford to serve food cheap. It certainly pays to try places like George's for lunch and dinner. It has been a Vi-Hi fixture since 1961 and no wonder. They've got nearly three dozen beers to pick from, plus good food to boot.

George's is a popular watering hole for the Emory crowd (and Mr. C does mean crowd), so you may be hard-pressed to get a good seat. On weekends, it's worth a venture, though, for thick sandwiches like, the Reuben and chicken filet ($7.25). Basics like grilled cheese ($2.95), or ham, turkey, corned beef, or roast beef sandwiches ($4.50 each), can be served up with French fries for just $2 extra.

Quarter-pound hot dogs sell for $3.25, and a big bowl of cheese-topped chili is $3.95. Giant half-pound hamburgers ($6) come with fries, cole slaw, potato salad, or onion rings. Good food, good hangout.

Open 11 a.m. to 11 p.m. Monday to Thursday, and until midnight on Friday.

La Fonda Latina

- 2813 Peachtree Road N.E., Atlanta; ✆ (404) 816-8311
- 1150-B Euclid Avenue N.E., Atlanta; ✆ (404) 577-9317

See the listing under *Restaurants—Buckhead*.

The Majestic

- 1031 Ponce de Leon Avenue, Atlanta; ✆ (404) 875-0276

"Food That Pleases" are the words emblazoned in neon along the curving facade of the Majestic. It's a good thing that this is true, since the surroundings here will hardly make you feel like royalty. Little seems to have changed at this luncheonette since its opening in 1929, including quite possibly some of the staff, but before you conclude that this is going to be an unfavorable write-up, read on.

Y'see, Mr. Cheap happens to love a good dive. And this is a good one. If you feel the same way about fading, homey, come-as-you-are, leave-a-bit-heavier places, then Majestic is one for the books. Certainly this book, anyway.

For starters, the joint is open 24 hours a day. That's great already. Another plus is that you can get breakfast at any time of day or night, like freshly browned pecan waffles for $4.55; add ham, bacon, or sausage for another $1.50. Omelettes, eggs, pancakes, you know the territory.

Lunch and dinner entrees are served from 10:30 in the morning until 9:00 at night, and these are the true bargains. Most are in the $6 price range, including your choice of two vegetables on the side. Chicken breast filet with gravy is $6.50; Southern-fried chicken is $6.10, while a grilled ham steak is $4.55. Choose a pair from candied yams, fried zucchini squash, pickled beets, creamed potatoes, or even macaroni and cheese, among others, to go along with your meal.

Of course, you can always get sandwiches (hot open-face roast beef, $5.10), burgers, salads, and a variety of other entrees at all hours. Homemade vegetable soup is a winner at $2.25 a bowl. And try to save room for fresh-baked apple pie, a mere $2.25 a slice, or $3 with ice cream; you can even take home a whole pie for just $8. Alas, but then you'd miss that Majestic ambiance, which is in effect 24/7.

The Mansion

- 179 Ponce de Leon Avenue, N.E., Atlanta; ✆ (404) 876-0727

If you're looking for a good meal in a classy setting, you owe it to yourself to check this place out. If you're looking to save money, go for lunch.

This 1885 Victorian mansion sits on a hill overlooking formal gardens, a fountain, a lily pond, and a gazebo; it was originally the home of Edward Peters, whose father, Richard, was the original developer of Atlanta's Midtown neighborhood, and it opened as a continental restaurant in 1976.

The Mansion serves lunch and dinner daily and brunch on Sunday. At lunch, you may wish to start with an appetizer, such as a crab cake sandwich, for $8, then choose from entrees such as seared swordfish steak ($12), jambalaya ($11), mustard-glazed salmon ($12), or the pasta of the day ($10). The dinner entrees, which are similar, cost about twice as much, but if you're in the mood to splurge . . . go for it!

Hours here are 11 a.m. to 2 p.m., and 6 p.m. to 10 p.m., seven days a week.

Murphy's Round the Corner

- 997 Virginia Avenue N.E., Atlanta; ✆ (404) 872-0904

This Virginia-Highland landmark is open for lunch, and dinner, and offers traditional Irish fare and unique entree combinations at super prices. You'll doubtless leave here stuffed, especially if you try one of their many decadent desserts.

For breakfast, pecan waffles are $3.25, and Eggs Santa Fe (a wee bit west of the Emerald Isle) are $8 and can be made with tofu instead of eggs if you prefer.

Lunch specials, served weekdays, offer such items as boneless grilled rainbow trout for $11 and chicken quesadillas for only $7.95. And Mr. C liked the soup, salad, half-sandwich combo for $7.95.

Dieters beware: Murphy's has some of the best-looking cakes, pies, and dessert treats in the city at around $3.50. Try a trio chocolate torte, raspberry chocolate cheesecake, or sour cream apple pie. Murphy's will even buy you lunch on your birthday.

Murphy's is open Monday to Thursdays from 11 a.m. to 10 p.m., Fridays 11 a.m. to midnight, Saturdays from 8 a.m. to noon, and Sundays from 8 a.m. to 10 p.m. There's free designated parking in areas around the restaurant, and free parking evenings after 6 p.m. in the Highland Hardware parking lot at the corner of Los Angeles and North Highland Avenues.

Mirror of Korea

- 1047 Ponce de Leon Avenue N.E., Atlanta; ✆ (404) 874-6243

Two miles from downtown, this restaurant offers authentic Korean cuisine. Not many restaurants in the Atlanta area can actually say that; in many places, recipes are doctored to suit American palates.

You'll find Korean specialties such as *kim chee,* spicy marinated cabbage; *bool go ghi,* a barbecue beef dish; and *gahl bee,* a beef short rib entree, all around $8 to $10. Mirror of Korea also serves sushi, Chinese dishes, and vegetarian items.

The restaurant serves beer and wine and opens for lunch and dinner Monday through Thursday from 11 a.m. to 10 p.m., and until 11 p.m. Friday and Saturday.

Soul Vegetarian

- 879-A Ralph D. Abernathy Boulevard S.W., Atlanta; ✆ (404) 752-5194

- 652 North Highland Avenue N.E., Atlanta; ✆ (404) 875-0145

See the listing under *Restaurants—Downtown Atlanta/Southeast & Southwest.*

St. Charles Deli

- 752 North Highland Avenue N.E., Atlanta; ✆ (404) 876-3354

- Loehmann's Plaza, 2470 Briarcliff Road N.E., Atlanta; ✆ (404) 636-5201

See the listing under *Restaurants—Atlanta Northeast/Decatur.*

Taco Mac

- 375 Pharr Road N.E., Atlanta; ✆ (404) 239-0650

- 1006 North Highland Avenue N.E., Atlanta; ✆ (404) 873-6529

- 771 Cherokee Avenue S.E., Atlanta; (404) 624-4641
- 2120 Johnson Ferry Road, Chamblee; (404) 454-7676
- 1444 Oxford Road, Emory Village; (404) 377-2323
- 1570 Holcomb Bridge Road, Roswell; (404) 640-9598
- 5830 Roswell Road N.W., Sandy Springs; (404) 257-0735
- 2845 Mountain Industrial Boulevard, Stone Mountain; (404) 621-3601

See the listing under *Restaurants—Atlanta Northeast/Decatur*.

Tortillas

- 774 Ponce de Leon Avenue N.E., Atlanta; (404) 892-0193

This place takes low-maintenance dining to the max—or rather, to the Mex—and really has some fun with it. The food here is super cheap, but also super fresh; and, best of all, they have A Gimmick. When you order your food at the counter up front, they'll give you your drinks and appetizers, which you bring to your table.

They also give you a buzzing pager. When your hot food is ready, it starts vibrating in your pocket. Fun, huh? It adds an extra element of the unique to this raucous, no-frills restaurant.

The menu, geared toward fast and easy prep, could hardly be simpler. Choose a soft taco, burrito, or "super burrito" (which adds rice on the inside). Choose the filling: chicken, pork, beef, or vegetarian beans and cheese. If you wish, choose some extras, like guacamole or hot sauce.

The whole entree can cost you as little as $3, for a bean and cheese taco, and no more than $6 or so for the works. In fact, there is even a cheese and tomato quesadilla for just $2.50, grilled up nice and crunchy and folded over into something like a big Mexican slice of pizza.

All the food sampled by Mr. C and his dining companion was very fresh, especially the guacamole side order, made with chunks of avocado and topped with diced tomato ($4). Get an order with lots of salty chips, add any of these to a taco or burrito, and you've got a full meal. There's also a decent selection of not-overpriced beers on hand.

Unlike some of the other funky industrial-approach burrito joints around, Tortillas attracts a mixed young crowd of students and locals. The place was packed on a recent weeknight, and everybody was definitely having a good time. Check out the upstairs deck too, especially during good weather when they roll up the plastic screens for a lovely view of scenic Ponce. As Mr. C's friend pointed out, a cold beer and a taco up here on a warm evening can be a fine state of affairs.

Tortillas is open every day from 11 a.m. to 10 p.m.

Woody's Famous Philadelphia Cheesesteaks

- 981 Monroe Drive N.E., Atlanta; (404) 876-1939

Located just across from Grady High School on a spit of land between Monroe Drive and Virginia Avenue, this tiny, nondescript restaurant has been serving up good cheesesteaks and submarine sandwiches since 1975. Grab yourself a simulated real Philly cheesesteak for just $4.55, or chow down on one of their five or six sub varieties, which range in price from

$3.50 to 3.90. They'll also cook you some sausage ($3.85), and offer an extensive variety of ice cream for dessert.

Woody's is open 11 a.m. to 5 p.m., Tuesday through Saturday.

Zesto Drive-In

- 544 Ponce de Leon Avenue N.E., Atlanta; (404) 607-1118

- 377 Moreland Avenue, Atlanta; (404) 523-1973

- 2469 Piedmont Road N.E., Atlanta; (404) 237-8689

- 1181 East Confederate Avenue, Atlanta; (404) 622-4254

- 151 Forest Parkway, Forest Park; (404) 366-0564

This circa-1940s ice cream and burger chain offers such delicacies as the Chubby Decker hamburger ($3.37), hot dogs ($1.34), hot wings ($10 pieces for $5.34), and broasted chicken ($3.37 for two pieces), plus a selection of delicious soft ice cream ($1.50 for a basic cone.)

You can drive on up from 11 a.m. to 11 p.m. Sunday to Thursday, and until midnight on Friday and Saturday.

MIDTOWN

Bangkok Thai Restaurant

- 1492-A Piedmont Road., N.E., Atlanta; (404) 874-2514

Hidden (to the uninitiated) within the ordinary shopping center of Ansley Square, Bangkok lays claim to being the very first Thai restaurant in the entire state of Georgia. Having opened in 1977, this may well be true. Back then, Jimmy Carter was a brand-new president—doesn't that feel like a long time ago! Did any of us know back then of the Thai food revolution that was to come?

Anyway, Bangkok is a small restaurant with a surprisingly large menu, and these folks certainly know they're doing. With its natural wood decor and comfortable high-backed chairs, the place has a kind of humble elegance—proving, as some places do, that "less is more." And their service, from the moment they greet you at the door, is extra-friendly (even if you are just ordering take-out) and quick.

Most entrees are in the $6 to $9 range. These include, naturally, several different varieties of curry dishes, from Ruby curry ($8.50), made with beef or chicken, to Jade shrimp curry ($8.50). Spice is considered nice all over the menu; other piquant dishes include spicy catfish ($9.95) and Sorcerer's Apprentice ($7.95), a frighteningly hot stir-fry of chicken and veggies in chili sauce. For less spicy tastes, Gingerine ($7.50) is a zingy but not tongue-lashingly hot ginger chicken dish, and Octet ($8.50) mixes chicken, shrimp, and vegetables.

Vegetarian, rice, and noodle dishes, by the way, are even cheaper and every bit as good. Traditional pad Thai ($7.95) and curry fried rice with beef or chicken ($6.95) are heaping platters indeed. Even the *Mee-Krob* appetizer, crispy fried noodles with pork, shrimp, and bean sprouts with an orange-tamarind sauce, is huge and only $6.95. Plenty of other good appetizers and soups, by the way, as well as two dozen lunch combination specials starting at $5.50.

Bangkok is open for lunch Monday to Friday 11:30 a.m. to 2:30 p.m.; and for dinner Monday through Thursday 5:30 p.m. to 10 p.m. and Friday and Saturday 5:30 p.m. to 10:30 p.m.

Also in the Ansley Square shopping center, across from Bangkok, is another longtime Asian favorite, **The King and I** (1510-F Piedmont Road N.E., Atlanta; ✆ (404) 892-7743). The surroundings here are even less to sing about, but "getting to know you" in this case means getting to know good, filling food that's super cheap and served up super quick. The menu is a mixture of Chinese and Thai specialties.

Bobby and June's Kountry Kitchen

- 375 14th Street N.W., Atlanta; ✆ (404) 876-3872

Bobby and June's is a true family-run roadside diner. It's a working-class version of the Silver Skillet just a few blocks down the street, which is so downscale as to be considered trendy. There's no kitsch at the Kountry Kitchen, where lifelong waitresses in beehive hairdos make sure you are well taken care of. The building itself is a wooden cabin whose interior is divided into a small counter and a couple of rooms filled with booths. Several of Bobby's prize fishing catches are stuffed and mounted on the walls, along with steer horns (which, presumably, he did not catch himself), old gee-tars, and vintage soda bottles.

The Kitchen starts up early—5:30 a.m., six days a week. Have a couple of eggs—"Any way you want 'em, honey"—with several strips of bacon, two biscuits, and grits, for $5.63 with coffee and $4.56 without coffee. Lots of folks also stop in for a variety of "breakfast sandwiches" to go; everything here is made up right quick.

For lunch (the place closes up at 3 p.m., 2 p.m. on Saturday), the specialty is barbecued ribs. On Thursday and Saturday they serve beef ribs with one vegetable for $6.42, with two for $7.23, three for $8.30, or all by their lonesome for a paltry $7.77.

The rest of the week it's pork ribs with two vegetables for $9.61 and just add another $1.24 for additional vegetables and pork ribs all alone for $7.77. All barbeque entrees include garlic bread.

Other meat platters also vary as daily specials, like steak and gravy, beef tips and rice, fried chicken . . . you know, the basics. These tend to be a bit less than the ribs, starting at $5.90 a plate with one side. The sides change daily but may include rice and gravy, turnip greens, fried okra, green beans, pinto beans, stewed squash, corn on the cob, cream potatoes, macaroni and cheese, tossed salad with fresh tomatoes, pickled beets, and a cucumber, onion, and tomato salad.

Homemade soups are heart-warmingly cheap at $2.42 per bowl, and of course there are sandwiches and burgers as well. And don't forget a slice of pecan pie afterwards, just $1.61, or apple or peach cobbler or banana pudding for a mere $1.07. Can you beat that for homemade desserts? Mr. C doubts it.

The restaurant is open Monday through Friday from 5:30 a.m. to 3 p.m., and Saturday from 5:30 a.m. to 2 p.m. It's closed on Sundays.

California Pizza Kitchen

- Lenox Square Shopping Center, 3393 Peachtree Road N.E., Atlanta; ✆ (404) 262-9221

RESTAURANTS: MIDTOWN 299

- 4600 Ashford Dunwoody Road N.E., Atlanta; ✆ (770) 393-0390

- 6301 North Point Parkway, Alpharetta; ✆ (770) 664-8246

See the listing under *Restaurants—Buckhead*.

Cha Gio

- 132 10th Street, Atlanta; ✆ (404) 885-9387

This Vietnamese restaurant in the midst of Midtown is a hit for its fantastic spring rolls. Come here for Cha Gio's lunch and dinner specials, which make it easy to sample several dishes without spending your life savings.

Start off with a pair of those spring rolls for just $2.25, available in meat or vegetarian varieties; and six fried chicken wings are just $1.95, and Vietnamese-style wonton soup is only $2.50.

You won't break the bank with main dishes like sliced chicken with ginger root and snow peas, sweet and sour chicken, or lemongrass pork chops, all priced at $7.95. Marinated red snapper and shrimp dishes served with vegetables and rice are $9.95.

Daily lunch specials include a $6.31 buffet, with fried rice or steamed rice, steamed vegetables, and a choice of two meat dishes. Cha Gio's chef will be happy to prepare any special dish request, or tone down the spices in the hotter menu items.

Cha Gio is open from 11 a.m. to 3 p.m., Mondays through Saturdays, and from noon to 9 p.m. Sundays.

C. W. Long Cafeteria at Crawford Long Hospital

- 449 Peachtree Road N.E., Atlanta; ✆ (404) 686-2497; ✆ (404) 686-1959

MR. CHEAP'S PICKS

Midtown

Bobby and June's Kountry Kitchen—Lifelong waitresses in beehive hairdos serve up good n' cheap food here, with no concessions to yuppie culture.

Cha Gio—Here you won't break the bank with main dishes like sliced chicken with ginger root and snow peas, sweet and sour chicken, or lemongrass pork chops, all priced at $7.95.

Red Light Café—Claiming to present "righteous California cooking," this is indeed a very West Coast mix of coffeehouse, restaurant, and music club, all at the same time.

Touch of India—Add a touch of spice to your life without burning a hole in your wallet. In Buckhead, too.

Who says you have to stay there to eat there? As far as hospital food goes, this stuff is actually good, and the staff sees to it that there are actually some healthy menu items. The clear-your-own-table cafeteria setting also means there's no tipping necessary, saving another buck or two. All told, you can get in and out of this place for about $5 per meal. (And that's certainly better than the room rates at this place!)

Breakfast features items like omelettes, biscuits, and pancakes. You can even make your own breakfast combo with, say, grits, turkey patties, hash browns, and sausage links.

For lunch, help yourself to the salad bar, soups, barbecued pork ribs, fried chicken, hamburgers, pizza, and more. Sandwiches and burgers go for around $2, and side orders are even cheaper. The lunch menu changes daily so call the menu number ✆ (404) 686-2497 to hear the choices.

The cafeteria serves breakfast every day from 6:15 a.m. to 9:30 a.m., lunch from 11 a.m. to 2:30 p.m., and dinner from 4:30 p.m. to 7:30 p.m.

Lettuce Souprise You

- 1784 Peachtree Street N.W., Atlanta,: ✆ (404) 874-4998

- 2470 Briarcliff Road N.E., Atlanta,: ✆ (404) 636-8549

See the listing under *Restaurants—Atlanta Northeast/Decatur.*

Mary Mac's Tea Room and Restaurant

- 224 Ponce de Leon Avenue N.E., Atlanta; ✆ (404) 876-1800

See the listing under *Restaurants—Atlanta Northeast/Decatur.*

Mick's

- 557 Peachtree Road N.E., Atlanta; ✆ (404) 875-6425

- 2110 Peachtree Road N.E., Atlanta; ✆ (404) 351-6425

- Peachtree Center, 229 Peachtree Street N.E., Atlanta; ✆ (404) 688-6425

- Lenox Square Shopping Center, 3393 Peachtree Road N.E., Atlanta; ✆ (404) 262-6425

- Underground Atlanta, 75 Upper Alabama Street S.W., Atlanta; ✆ (404) 525-2825

- 116 East Ponce de Leon Avenue, Decatur, ✆ (404) 373-7797

- 1320 Cumberland Mall S.E., Atlanta; ✆ (770) 431-7190

- 3525 Mall Boulevard, Duluth; ✆ (770) 623-1855

- 6700 Douglas Boulevard, Douglasville; ✆ (678) 715-0299

- 1070 Northpoint Circle, Alpharetta; ✆ (770) 667-2330

And other suburban locations

See the listing under *Restaurants—Atlanta Northeast/Decatur.*

Original Pancake House

- 4330 Peachtree Road N.E., Atlanta; ✆ (404) 237-4116

- 2321 Cheshire Bridge Road N.E., Atlanta; ✆ (404) 633-5712

- 5099 Memorial Drive, Stone Mountain; ✆ (404) 292-6914

- 3665 Club Drive #104, Duluth; ✆ (770) 925-0065

- 243 Market Place Connector, Peachtree City; ✆ (770) 486-7634

See the listing under *Restaurants—Atlanta Northeast/Decatur.*

Red Light Café

- 553 Amsterdam Avenue. N.E., Atlanta; ✆ (404) 874-7828

- ✍ www.redlightcafe.com

Whether you need to fortify yourself after a day of shopping at the Midtown Outlets, or you've discovered this place as a worthy hangout on its own, the Red Light—both a restaurant and a nightclub—is a great place to stop. Yes, it's next to the shops; yes, with such cavernous high ceilings it might have been a warehouse too. But its owners have managed to turn the space into an artfully cozy room, with Mission-style wooden tables and chairs, a counter offering today's newspapers, and darkly atmospheric lighting.

Claiming to present "righteous California cooking," this is indeed a very West Coast mix of coffeehouse, restaurant, and music club, all at the same time. Sip a cup of strong Sumatra roast or espresso; have a sandwich, a full meal, or some homemade pastry; and peruse the artworks by local artists on the walls. Pick up a book or a board game from one of the side tables. Whatever, it's, you know, cool.

The food itself is phenomenal. Every ingredient is fresh, from the crisp and colorful garden vegetable salad to delightfully creative and delicious entrees. Mr. C was ecstatic over Angel Hair Alla Checca, thin spaghetti tossed with wedges of tomato, basil, and fresh garlic; it's topped with mozzarella and fresh romano cheeses, all of which make a wonderfully tasty combination.

Pastas are the only real entrees; otherwise, the menu consists of interesting nouvelle sandwiches and salads, like "corn-fed ham" with pesto, on wheat or sourdough bread, served with a garnish of fresh fruit for $5.25; the Garden sandwich, like, totally California, a mix of fresh vegetables in a Parmesan vinaigrette not to mention pesto boboli pizza ($4.25) and turkey black bean chili ($4.50). Oh, and peanut butter and jam sandwiches with apple or banana for $2.25.

Red Light also serves bottled beer, draft beer, wine, tea, and coffee. As well as desserts, such as homemade cookies and cakes, ice cream, too.

So what about the club scene here? Tuesday night is comedy with such shows as "Ken the Cookie Man and Friends" and "Lynn van Lier." Wednesday is open mic night. Dogwood Thursdays means bluegrass music at 9 p.m. Whether you prefer Grateful Dead or more traditional roots music, you'll find some satisfaction here for a cover of only $3—and you get a good deal on the local Dogwood Brew.

Food is served from 5 p.m. to 2 p.m. on Tuesday, Wednesday, and Thursday; from noon on Friday and Saturday. The cafe is usually open until 3 or 4 in the morning—and that includes the kitchen! If you haven't heard about this place yet, or have been meaning to check it out, what are you waiting for?

Rocky's Brick Oven Pizza

- 1770 Peachtree Street N.E., Atlanta; (404) 870-7625
- 1394 North Highland Avenue NE, Atlanta; (404) 876-1111

See the listing under *Restaurants—Buckhead*.

Silver Grill Restaurant

- 900 Monroe Drive, Atlanta; (404) 876-8145

The Silver Grill may be the quintessential Southern roadside diner. It's been around for 40 years or more, and it's simply staggering to think of how much hash has been slung by this meal-a-minute joint in that time. Actually, what gets served up here the most seems to be good ol' Southern-fried chicken—plump, meaty breasts of it, deep-fried to a crackly crunch. For $7.50, one of these will be the centerpiece to a platter, along with your choice of three cooked vegetables. Plus a basket of fresh baked rolls or cornbread. Plus tea or coffee. Full yet?

Every day they have real mashed potatoes and gravy, cole slaw, potato salad, and pickled beets. Otherwise the veggies change daily. You'll usually see things like black-eyed peas, creamed white corn, mustard greens, okra and tomatoes, and perhaps their "Pear and Cheese Salad." You can even get a platter of just sides, your choice of four, for $6.25. Mainly, though, people go for the basic "meat and three." In addition to the chicken that may include country-fried steak, veal cutlets, or pork chops, all for the same $7.50. Or shoot the works with filet mignon for $9.50 and three vegetables.

If you have a smaller appetite than these hearty and heavy meals would suggest, perhaps you should look elsewhere. Well, that's not entirely true; there are sandwich versions of the fried chicken or steak, each $3.85; as well as hamburgers for $3.50, cheeseburgers $3.85, and grilled cheese sandwiches are only $2. French fries are $1.50 and a half order of onion rings is $2.25, whole order $3. These may possibly help you save room for dessert. Peach, apple, or cherry cobbler is the specialty of the house for only $1.50. Throw a scoop of ice cream on it for just $3 and you may bust a gut here, but you sure won't bust a wallet.

Sit at the old-style counter and you can watch what appears to be a culinary circus moving in fast-forward mode. Service can be brusque at times, like the lunch rush, but it never fails to be brisk as well. When they can catch their breath, the staff can be quite friendly. The place may not win any prizes for decor, but it's clean, bright, and definitely funky.

Open for weekday lunch and dinner only, Mondays through Fridays from 10:30 a.m. to 9 p.m.

Silver Skillet

- 200 14th Street N.W., Atlanta; (404) 874-1388

Here's another of Atlanta's great greasy spoons, serving up hot breakfasts and meat-and-vegetable lunches in a setting of yellow and olive green. It's a particularly hot spot on weekends for a mixed crowd of dress-down yuppies, students from Georgia Tech, and older folks who've been finding the Skillet a comfortable and dependable place for over thirty years.

The place opens at 6 a.m. on weekdays and a bit later on weekends. You can belly up to the counter, into a booth, and begin your day with a couple of biscuits and gravy ($2.75); add two scrambled eggs and the price is $3.50. The gravy is thick and creamy, with just a dash of black pepper. Two eggs and bacon, any way you like 'em, are $4.50 and just about all breakfast dishes include grits, toast, and gravy, or a biscuit on the side.

For lunch, all the classics are here: country-fried steak, baked or fried chicken, chicken and dumplings, broiled Cajun catfish (the only concession to the yupsters), and more. With two vegetables, the price range is $5.75 to $6.50. Vegetables vary, with choices including baked or mashed potatoes and gravy, cole slaw, macaroni and cheese, cabbage, and broccoli casserole. And if you're just looking for a quick (but equally heavy) bite, Skillet burgers and cheeseburgers are $4; with fries, $6. A Skillet country ham sandwich is $5.25. Add a cup or bowl of homemade vegetable soup, or finish off with a slice of ice box pie (lemon or coconut) and you shouldn't have to eat again for a week.

The Silver Skillet is open for breakfast and lunch Monday to Thursday 6 a.m. to 3 p.m.; and Friday 6 a.m. to 2 p.m. Saturday is breakfast-only from 7 a.m. to 1 p.m. and Sunday, breakfast-only from 8 a.m. to 2 p.m. During the week, you can also eat in "The Little Skillet," which is part of the same building; it too has a counter and tables, not to mention some actual silver in its decor.

Touch of India Tandoori Restaurant

- 1037 Peachtree Street N.E., Atlanta; ✆ (404) 876-7777

- 2955 North Druid Hills Road N.E., Atlanta; ✆ (404) 728-8881

See the listing under *Restaurants—Atlanta Northeast/Decatur.*

The Varsity

- 61 North Avenue N.W., Atlanta; ✆ (404) 881-1706

See the listing under *Restaurants—Atlanta Northeast/Decatur.*

PERIMETER SUBURBS

American Roadhouse

- 842 N Highland Avenue N.E., Atlanta; ✆ (404) 872-2822
- 3060 Peachtree Road N.W. Atlanta; ✆ (404) 266-1177

See the listing under *Restaurants—Little Five Points.*

Anne & Bill's Restaurant

- 424 Forest Parkway, Forest Park; ✆ (404) 366-4477

Anne & Bill's is one of Mr. C's favorites. You'd be foolish to miss this gem on the way to or from the airport. All types of folks—produce growers from the nearby farmer's market, businesspeople, and locals—crowd into the lobby to wait for a table. But service is swift, even during rush times, and once you taste Anne & Bill's apple betty, homemade cornbread, super fresh veggies, or fried chicken, you'll be glad you stayed.

For you jumbo-sized appetite types, try the Texas breakfast: An 8-ounce steak, two eggs any style, and grits, toast, or biscuits, all for $6.95. Scrambled eggs and salmon, with grits or bread, is $5.05; and the frisbee-sized hot cakes are $2 each. Three-egg omelets served with grits start at just $3.75. And you've gotta love their coffee, just $1 a cup with a free refill.

Show up early to beat the lunch crowd, and try the veggie plate for just $2.95, which comes with as many of Anne & Bill's cornbread mini muffins and yeast rolls as you can eat. Choose from such sides as incredible mashed potatoes, rutabagas, spinach, macaroni salad, carrot salad, and fried squash.

Hot roast beef with mashed potatoes, gravy, and sliced tomato, served on light bread, is $5.50. Quarter-pound burgers are only $2.15, hash browns, home fries, or French fries are $1.50, and turkey sandwiches go for only $3.30. And the half-bird fried chicken with salad, fries, and rolls is a bargain at $6.

The most expensive item on the menu is the rib-eye steak, priced at $8.25; with it, you also get French fries or two vegetables, tossed salad, and homemade rolls.

If you don't have room for dessert (and believe Mr. C—you probably won't), you should definitely get something for later. Homemade pound cake is $1.15 a slice, peach cobbler is just $1.25, and pies are only $1.35 a slice, including sweet potato, lemon meringue, banana, coconut and chocolate cream pies, key lime, or pecan pies.

Anne & Bill's opens bright and early at 5:30 a.m. weekdays, and closes up around 3 in the afternoon. On Saturdays, they're open 7 a.m. to 2 p.m. They're closed Sundays.

Athens Pizza House

- 5550 Peachtree Industrial Boulevard, Chamblee; (404) 452-8282

- 1565 Highway 138, Conyers; (404) 483-6228

- 1341 Clairmont Road, Decatur; (404) 636-1100

- 11235 Apharetta Highway #140, Roswell; (770) 751-6629

See the listing under *Restaurants—Atlanta Northeast/Decatur*.

California Pizza Kitchen

- 6301 North Point Parkway, Alpharetta; (770) 664-8241

- Lenox Square Shopping Center, 3393 Peachtree Road N.E., Atlanta; (404) 262-9221

And other suburban locations

- www.cpic.com

See the listing under *Restaurants—Buckhead*.

Carrabba's Italian Grill

- 2999 Cumberland Circle S.E., Atlanta; (770) 437-1444

- 1887 Mount Zion Road, Morrow; (770) 968-3233

- 6395 Spalding Drive, Norcross; (770) 582-0336

- 3580 Sweetwater Road, Duluth; (404) 935-7600

- 1160 Ernest W. Barrett Parkway N.W., Kennesaw; (770) 499-0338

- www.carrabbas.com

This chain features a variety of fresh Italian dishes cooked to order in an "exhibition kitchen" within view of the diners. (Now that's entertainment!)

House specialties including crispy calamari ($6.79), chicken marsala ($13.99), and a variety of pasta dishes and handmade pizzas ($8.99 to $9.99) baked in their wood-burning oven. They also specialize in grilled food—fresh fish, seafood, and meats basted with special seasonings and cooked over a wood-fired grill ($11.99 to 15.99).

The pizzas include the Margherita, with Roma tomatoes, basil, extra virgin olive oil, and fresh mozzarella; Italian Chicken, featuring grilled chicken breast in an Italian-style sweet and sour sauce with pine nuts, scallions, and romano, fontina, and mozzarella cheeses; Chicken Gratella, fire-roasted chicken breast basted with olive oil and herbs, served with vegetables and garlic mashed or roasted rosemary potatoes; as well as "classic favorites" with pepperoni and sausage.

For kids, Carrabba's offers a special menu including pasta, chicken fingers, and kid-size pizzas, as well as pizza dough that they can use like Play-Doh!

Carrabba's is open Monday and Tuesday from 4:30 p.m. to 10 p.m. On Wednesday through Friday they open at 11:30 a.m., and close at 10 p.m. on Wednesday and Thursday and 11 p.m. on Friday. On weekends, they're open Saturday 4 p.m. to 11 p.m., and Sunday 3:30 p.m. to 9 p.m.

Fellini's Pizza

- 2809 Peachtree Road N.E., Atlanta; ✆ (404) 266-0082
- 909 Ponce de Leon Avenue N.E., Atlanta; ✆ (404) 873-3088
- 4429 Roswell Road N.E., Atlanta; ✆ (404) 303-8249
- 1991 Howell Mill Road N.W., Atlanta; ✆ (404) 352-0799
- 1634 McLendon Avenue NE, Atlanta; ✆ (404) 687-9190

And other suburban locations

See the listing under *Restaurants—Buckhead*.

Fujita

- 5495 Jimmy Carter Boulevard, Norcross; ✆ (770) 441-3663

Winner of the *Creative Loafing* Reader's Poll as "Best Japanese Restaurant" and "Best Sushi," Fujita specializes in the highest-quality fresh sushi, served in a friendly, bright atmosphere.

As is customary in real sushi places, you can check off your a la carte sushi preferences on one of the order forms provided at each table, or you can look at the menu for a wide variety of sushi dinners, combos, and other (cooked) offerings.

Mr. C recommends the special sushi or sashimi lunches—both $9. You can also get a tuna roll and sushi for the same price, or enjoy the *tempura udon* (noodles) for just $7. If you order the sushi a la carte, Cheap-san recommends the albacore tuna sushi and the "Fujita Roll."

If cooked food is more to your liking, you'll like the chicken or beef teriyaki, or the pork ginger, for an easy-to-swallow $5.75. All these selections include soup, salad, and rice. You can also get the combination lunch box: shrimp tempura and sashimi, sashimi and chicken teriyaki, and other delectable combos (complete with soup, salad, and rice) for $7.25.

The dinner menu offers basically the same choices, priced between $6.95 and $15. The difference is slightly larger portions, plus soup, salad, rice, dumplings, sesame chicken, and a California roll! A sushi regular dinner ($10.95) includes a California roll and seven pieces of sushi; with the sushi special dinner ($14.95), you get an eight-piece California roll, a six-piece tuna roll, and seven pieces of sushi. Talk about a feast!

If you're really hungry, you also might want to try the lobster combination box ($14.95 to $15.95), which includes lobster with teriyaki, lobster with sushi, lobster with tempura . . . you get the idea!

Beer, wine, and sake are all available here.

Fujita is open seven days a week from 11:30 a.m. to 2 a.m.

MR. CHEAP'S PICKS

Suburbs

Anne & Bill's—Down home cookin' doesn't get much better than this Forest Park eatery, y'all.

Fujita—Award-winning sushi and other Japanese fare at reasonable prices.

Hemingway's—This jammin' joint brings a little Key West atmosphere to the heart of Marietta.

The Village Corner—Situated in Stone Mountain Village, in the shadow of the big rock itself, sits one of the finest German restaurants you're likely to find in the Atlanta metro area.

Hemingway's

- 29 West Park Square, Marietta; (770) 427-5445

- www.hemingwaysmarietta.com

"Wasted away again in Mariettaville" is a lyric that you would never, *ever* hear Cap'n Cheap belt out. Nevertheless, when he is in the mood to loosen up with some decent food and libations, his sun-deprived mind wanders north of town, not south, to this oasis of good times. Located on the historic downtown Marietta square, Hemingway's brings a little Key West atmosphere to the suburbs. In fact the *Atlanta Constitution* has called it Atlanta's "Parrothead Paradise."

This a fun place, featuring live music on the weekends and the obligatory Hawaiian-shirted, good-times crowd. However, this jammin' joint probably wouldn't have made it into this guide if not for its plentiful, tasty, and reasonably priced grub. So grab a table or pull a stool up to the bar. Order you favorite beverage and start perusing the menu for some satisfying munchie food.

You may want to start out with a platter of conch fritters, chicken quesadillas, or Nachos Supreme (all $6.95). Or perhaps the coconut fried shrimp ($6.95) or chips and salsa ($4.95) strike your fancy. You can also order some delectable sweet plantains ($2.95) to satisfy your lower-latitude cravings.

For the next course, you can select from a range of half-pound burgers, served with a side of cole slaw, pasta salad, potato salad, or chips, and priced at $5.45 to $6.45. Or, order a sandwich—a wide variety is available from $3.95 for you basic grilled cheese to $8.95 for a fried oysters po'boy!

For dinner courses, Hemingway's offers fried basket meals ($6.95 to $8.95), as well as a number of entrees in two-size portions: Check out the Captains Fried Seafood Platter (fresh catch, shrimp, oysters, and clams), priced at $17.95; full- or half-rack baby back ribs ($9.95 or $13.95); boneless blackened chicken breast ($7.95 or $10.95); or perhaps Masas de Puerco (chunks of slow roasted seasoned pork, deep-fried and topped with sautéed onions; a Cuban specialty served with sweet plantains), available for $6.95 or $9.95.

There's also a kid's menu here, with the usual assortment of chicken fingers, hot dogs, grilled cheese, and the like for $3.75 to $4.75.

The desserts go for $3.45 to $4.75, and of course include key lime pie, as well as mud pie, flan, Oreo cheesecake, and other goodies.

Hey . . . if you can't get enough of a good time—or good food—think about stopping by for Sunday brunch, served from 11:30 a.m. to 2:30 p.m., where for a mere $6.95 you can take your pick of eggs Benedict and home fries, or a ham, cheese, and onion omelette with bacon, home fries, and toast. (Coffee, tea, or soda is included.)

Hemingway's is open Tuesday through Thursday from 11:30 a.m. to 1 a.m., Friday and Saturday from 11:30 a.m. to 2 a.m., and Sunday from noon to 5 p.m.

Now, about that margarita . . .

Johnny Rockets

- 2970 Cobb Street, Marietta; (770) 955-6068

- 4475 Roswell Road, Marietta; (770) 955-6068

- 6700 Douglas Boulevard, Douglasville; 770) 577-2636

- www.johnnyrockets.com

See the listing under *Restaurants—Buckhead*.

Joli-Kobe French Bakery and Restaurant

- The Prado, 5600 Roswell Road, Sandy Springs;
  (404) 843-3257

If you can find a parking spot in the super-busy Prado complex, be sure to try the super-big deli sandwiches and homemade soups at Joli-Kobe. The place itself is nothing fancy, with a casual, local hangout feel; but the fare is healthier than you'll find at most typical delis. All sandwiches are piled high with fresh lettuce, tomato, and sprouts, plus fresh fruit and a pickle on the side. Joli-Kobe's shrimp sandwich is a bargain at $5.50, served on your choice of croissant, baguette, or whole wheat bread. The almond curry chicken and sauteed chicken are also $5.50 each; egg salad sandwiches are $3.95; and you can also get any of these choices on a child-size croissant for $2.95.

Joli-Kobe is known for its creative and value-sized salads, like pasta ham, teriyaki chicken, and turkey salads, served with vinaigrette or ginger dressing. Needless to say, the cafe is good to know about for quality take-out food; you can even bring an 8-ounce bottle of those delicious dressings home for $1.50.

At press time, Joli-Kobe was in the midst of renovation but was expected to reopen very soon. Call for hours!

Kobe Steakhouse of Japan

- 5600 Roswell Road, Atlanta;
  (404) 256-0810

Here at Kobe Steakhouse of Japan, you might consider bringing a large group of people as the chef will "stop and chop" as well as "slice and dice" food at your very own table; it's always fun to watch as food is prepared to individual's orders!

So if you're craving anything stir-fry for about $12 a plate, then this is the locale to try. The chef will serve up anything your heart desires in a matter of minutes—fried rice, grilled shrimp, meat, fish, or sauteed bean sprouts, zucchini, mushrooms, anything!

Restaurant hours are Monday through Thursday from 1:30 p.m. to 9 p.m., Friday and Saturday from 11:30 a.m. to 10 p.m., and Sunday from 4:30 p.m. to 9 p.m.

The Mad Italian

- 2092 Cobb Parkway South, Marietta; (770) 952-1806

- 2197 Savoy Drive, Chamblee; (770) 451-8048

- www.maditalian.com

They're crazy about high quality at this South Buckhead and suburban eatery. The prices on Italian sandwiches, pasta, and calzones, in fact, are downright foolish. The Mad Italian is so nuts about fresh ingredients that his bread is flash frozen and trucked in all the way from New York; the folks here say that the Atlanta humidity and altitude are "improper" for good bread baking.

Anything you say, guys—the effort certainly pays off. Sandwiches, available in three sizes priced from $4.85 to just $6.50, include tuna hoagies, Italian sausage, meatball and cheese, cheese steak, and chicken salad varieties, along with the vegetable sauté with cheese. Pickles and potato chips come with sit-down orders (too bad for you take-out lovers). Whether you eat in or out, for just $1.50 more, you can enjoy the Mad Italian's house salad or spaghetti, or a cup of his soup of the day (Mr. C recommends the minestrone, but the pasta e fagiole is also highly touted by those in the know.)

Cheese or meat calzones go for just $5.95; if you really feel like stuffing yourself, go for the baked cheese ravioli ($7.50), served with fresh bread and butter and house salad; or the pasta trio (cannelloni Florentine, spinach and cheese shells, and ricotta cheese shells) for $7.95, or fettucine Alfredo for $6.95.

Keep the kids happy with items like the kids' spaghetti plate (just $3.50). The Mad Italian is perfect for family dining, with a casual, wood-paneling, wicker-chair, gum-at-the-cash-register kind of atmosphere.

Restaurant hours are from 11 a.m. to midnight.

Mellow Mushroom

- 1570 Holcomb Bridge Road, Roswell; ✆ (770) 998-8260

- ✍ www.mellowmushroom.com

See the listing under *Restaurants—Atlanta Northeast/Decatur*.

Mick's

- 116 E Ponce de Leon Avenue, Decatur; ✆ (404) 373-7797

- 3393 Peachtree Road N.E., Atlanta; ✆ (404) 262-6425

- 1320 Cumberland Mall S.E., Atlanta; ✆ (770) 431-7190

- 3525 Mall Boulevard, Duluth, ✆ (770) 623-1855

- 1070 Northpoint Circle, Alpharetta; ✆ (770) 667-2330

- 6700 Douglas Boulevard, Douglasville; ✆ (678) 715-0299

See the listing under *Restaurants—Atlanta Northeast/Decatur*.

Original Pancake House

- 5099 Memorial Drive, Stone Mountain; ✆ (404) 292-6914

- 3665 Club Drive, Duluth; ✆ (770) 925-0065

- 243 Market Place Connector, Peachtree City; ✆ (770) 486-7634

- ✍ www.originalpancakehouse.com

See the listing under *Restaurants—Atlanta Northeast/Decatur*.

Pho 79

- 4166 Buford Highway N.E., Atlanta; ✆ (404) 728-9129

This little place, situated in the "Oriental Mall" on Buford Highway, boasts three large banquet-sized tables, seven or eight four-person booths, a large-screen TV playing Vietnamese MTV and other programs, and food delicious enough (or perhaps spicy enough) to bring tears to the eyes of a suitably hungry patron.

"Pho" means "noodles" in Vietnamese, and it is the specialty of the house—truly a creative masterpiece of complex flavors and presentation. Check out the *phi sate*, a noodle bowl of stir-fried beef morsels in a tangy and rich tomato/chili broth; or perhaps *mi quaint*, made up of crisp rice cake pieces, pork, boiled egg, shrimp, sausage, red cabbage, onions, bean sprouts, and basil in bowl full of wide flat yellow noodles and broth. *Pho tai Gao*—a rice noodle soup with spicy beef broth and sliced meat and garnishes such as bean sprouts, basil, *rah gai* (a crunchy slender green), and sliced green chili pepper—is both filling and tasty. All the Pho dishes, priced from $5.75 to $5.95, come in a large bowl with a side dish of cilantro, sprouts, jalapenos, and limes to mix with the noodles, and man, are they good!

You can also make a dinner of egg rolls dipped in *nukmaum* (a sort of fermented fish sauce) or a variety of hot sauces ($2.75 for two).

The menu also includes several exotic fruit drinks, as well as *cafe sua da*, iced French coffee with sweetened condensed milk ($1.95).

Pho 79 open every day at 10 a.m. On Sunday through Thursday they close at 9:30 p.m.; on Friday and Saturday, they keep their doors open until 10 p.m.

Provino's

- 3606 Satellite Boulevard, Duluth; (770) 497-8841

- 1255 Grimes Bridge Road, Roswell; (770) 993-5839

- 2911 Chapel Hill Road, Douglasville; (678) 838-0630

- 2252 East Main Street, Snellville; (770) 972-8411

- www.provinos.com

Provino's offers a wide variety of well prepared and filling Italian choices, including a wide variety of pasta, fish, veal, and more. The antipasto starters, priced from $3.95 to $5.95, include calamari, clams oreganato, artichoke hearts, mozzarella sticks with marinara, stuffed mushrooms, and more, but they only whet the appetite for the delicious main courses. In that department, you might want to try the Pasta Lover's Special, including four different pastas with meat sauce, meatball, sausage, and sautéed mushrooms; or the Cannelloni Genovese, pasta stuffed with ground veal, spinach, cheese, and Rosatella sauce—both of which are priced at $10.95. You vegetarians will appreciate the eggplant vegatale (like eggplant Parmigiana, only without meat sauce) for $9.95.

If pasta isn't your *thang* on a particular night, you can get to work on any number of other typically Italian offerings, including chicken Florentine (or Francese, or Romano, or Marsala), priced from $11.95 to $13.95; veal prepared as Parmigiana, marsala or Diana, ranging from $13.95 to $14.95; that old standard, sausage and peppers, at $10.95; Cioppino—an array of clams, shrimp, crab, scallops, mussels, and snapper simmered in a spicy tomato garlic sauce and served over linguine ($16.95); or perhaps the Red Snapper Francese ($13.95), or the Seafood Trio, composed of shrimp, scallops, and chopped clams, sautéed with herbs and garlic in a Marinara or Rosatella sauce ($13.95). Whatever direction you go, you're either going to be asking for a doggie bag or waddling very slowly out the door at the end of the evening. All dinners are served with a family salad bowl, fresh-baked garlic rolls, and pasta.

If the main course isn't enough for you, then you can wade into the somewhat decadent Italian desserts: cannoli, cheesecake, tiramisu, chocolate mousse cake, and other sweet delights ranging from $3.95 to $4.75.

On the busier weekend nights, you may have to wait for a table—sometimes up to 35 or 40 minutes, but rarely any longer. No worries: just relax with a glass of Chianti, Valpolicella, or other fine wine from Provino's bar. (They even have Italian beer!)

The amount of food (or at least the number of calories) you get here for the money is already a darn good value, but there are at least two ways in which you can save even more money: First of all, Provino's offers a birthday special—just show them your I.D. on that special day, and you will get any entree priced at up to $10 for free! Otherwise, show up any day before 6:30 p.m. for the restaurant's early bird special and you'll be able to get any pasta dinner valued up to $10.95 for just $8.95.

Provino's is open Monday through Thursday from 4:30 p.m. to 10 p.m., Friday and Saturday from 4:40 p.m. to 11 p.m., and Sunday from 4 p.m. to 10 p.m.

Pappasito's Cantina

- 2788 Windy Hill Road, Marietta, 770-541-6100

- www.pappasitos.com

This place is another one of those "hey amigo, let's party!" kinds of Southwestern-themed chains that have become so popular these days. Pappasito's even boasts that it is known for its "sizzling fajitas, margaritas and the best chips and salsa north of the Rio Grande!" Well, as a connoisseur of mass-market Tex-Mex food, Mr. C can't argue. The fixin's here are satisfying and, if not exactly cheap, worthy of the "good value" seal of approval.

Appetizers include chile con queso, tortilla soup, tamales, ceviche, Pappasito's salad, and quesadillas—all offered in the range of $4.15 to $12.

Enchiladas come in many stripes and combinations, including chicken, beef, and seafood, and range from $8.45 to $9.85 for a two-enchilada combo platter.

Shrimp Diablo—spicy jumbo shrimp, broiled and served sizzling—is $16.55. However, Pappasito's is most renowned for those sizzling fajitas. The fajitas al carbon—tender marinated grilled beef or chicken breast sliced and served with tomato, peppers, and grilled onions—go for $13.25; and the shrimp fajitas are priced at $18.55. If you're in the mood for lighter fare, you might try the grilled chicken salad ($10.25).

Desserts include flan, capirotada (rich chocolate bread pudding served with cinnamon ice cream), sopapillas, and other Southwestern goodies—all ranging in price from $3.95 to $6.15.

Really, really hungry? On Wednesday evenings you can immerse yourself in P's "All You Can Eat Fresh Lobster Feast" for $29.95. Okay, that's not cheap, but Mr. C thought you just might want to know.

Pappasito's boasts an open-air patio that actually stays open all year 'round, thanks to a nifty heating system, so you can sit out there, sip your margarita, and pretend you're in Mexico instead of Marietta. At times, men in Southwestern attire will even stroll by the tables playing music, adding some additional atmosphere to the good food and drink. So what's not to like about this place? Nada!

Pappasito's is open Sunday through Thursday from 11 a.m. to 10 p.m.; Friday and Saturday from 11 a.m. to 11 p.m.

Ray's New York Pizza

- 3201 Peachtree Rd, Atlanta; (404) 364-0960

- 6309 Roswell Rd, Atlanta; (404) 252-9888

See the listing under *Restaurants—Buckhead*.

Swallow at the Hollow

- 1072 Green Street, Roswell; (678) 352-1975

- www.theswallowatthehollow.com

Just as the name suggests, the Swallow at the Hollow is way out in the boondocks, but the restaurant's rustic barn and tin-roof setting makes for a worthwhile trip. Plus, the barbeque is the best you can possibly come by in the greater Atlanta vicinity!

To start, green, leafy "Swallow Salads" with a mix of romaine, red leaf, spinach, tomatoes, carrots, cucumbers, onion, red pepper, and smoked gouda cheese goes for $6.95 and an extra $2.50 for sides of sliced beef, pork, turkey, or portabella mushrooms. For an appetizer, you can try "Hollow Munchies" such as marinated BBQ pork pizza for $8.95, Baby Back Ribs (at market price), Brunswick stew for $3.95 a bowl, and biscuits for $1.95. Be sure to "Get to the Que" and choose a pork, beef, sausage, or turkey sandwich with the fixin's for only $5.25.

The Banana Chocolate Chip Pudding is "outta this world!" at $4.50 per serving. Plus, with an extensive wine and beer list and barbeque "to go" . . . you'll be glad you came!

Restaurant hours are Wednesday through Saturday from 11 a.m. to 10 p.m., Sunday from 5 p.m. to 9 p.m.; closed on Monday and Tuesday.

Taco Mac

- 5830 Roswell Road N.E., Sandy Springs; (404) 257-0735
- 2359 Windy Hill Road S.E., Marietta; (770) 953-6382
- 2845 Mountain Industrial Boulevard, Tucker; (770) 621-3601
- 3682 Highway 138 S.E., Stockbridge; (678) 289-0000
- 1318 Johnson Ferry Road, Marietta; (770) 977-4467
- 8879 Roswell Road, Sandy Springs; (770) 552-8784
- 2650 Dallas Highway S.W., Marietta; (770) 795-1144
- 7397 Douglas Blvd, Douglasville; (770) 942-0499
- 2615 George Busbee Parkway N.W., Kennesaw; (770) 426-1515
- 3334 Highway 78 West, Snellville; (770) 736-1333
- 685 W Crossville Road, Roswell; (678) 795-0080
- 3545 Peachtree Industrial Blvd, Duluth; (770) 814-7388
- 4305 State Bridge Road, Alpharetta; (770) 754-9290
- 9020 Highway 92, Woodstock; (770) 517-0030
- 2003 Riverside Parkway, Lawrenceville, (770) 682-7189

And other suburban locations

- www.tacomac.com

See the listing under *Restaurants—Atlanta Northeast/Decatur*.

Three Dollar Cafe

- 2580 Windy Hill Road S.E., Marietta; (770) 850-0868
- 423 Ernest W Barrett Parkway N.W., Kennesaw; (770) 426-6566
- 2166 Highpoint Road, Snellville; (770) 736-1000
- 38595 Roswell Road, Dunwoody; (404) 992-5011

And other suburban locations

See the listing under *Restaurants—Buckhead*.

Veggieland

- 211 Pharr Road N.E., Atlanta; (404) 231-3111
- 209 Sandy Springs Circle, Sandy Springs; (404) 252-1165

See the listing under *Restaurants—Buckhead*.

The Village Corner/Basket Bakery and Cafe

- 6655 Memorial Drive, Stone Mountain; ✆ (770) 498-0329

Situated in Stone Mountain Village, in the shadow of the big rock itself, sits one of the finest German restaurants you're likely to find in the Atlanta metro area. The Village Corner is a family business that is owned by Hilde and Claus Friese, natives of Munich and Hamburg. Their son Carl is executive chef; their niece Krista the general manager.

The assortment of freshly baked breads they bring before the meal is impressive enough—white, honey, wheat, rye, pecan, pumpernickel—and the quality of the food goes up from there. The dinner menu features a selection of authentic, carefully prepared German and Continental cuisine, beers, and wines, and nightly specials include fresh seafood or wild game. The portions are renowned for both their size and quality—and amazingly, most dinner entrees are $16 or less (lunch is cheaper, of course).

Try the *wiener schnitzel* (veal) or *sauerbraten* (beef), served with potatoes and vegetables, for $15; or, dive into the *Wurstplatte*, at $15 a choice of *bratwurst, weisswurst, knockwurst,* or smoked sausage on applekraut with parsley potatoes.

They also offer Chicken Cordon Bleu ($16), New York Strip Steak ($18), Appalachian Rainbow Trout ($18), as well as Deutsche Platte fur Zwei ($24), filled with a variety of sausages and potatoes that serves as a filling dinner for two, which is what a *platte fur zwei* is supposed to do.

The typical portion is more than most folks can eat in one setting. Even so, try to save room for the desserts, which include an assortment of cakes, pies, and pastries, apple fritters, and German chocolate cakes.

At lunch, the Village Corner provides a selection of those same German specialties, plus delicious sandwiches, salad plate, and (of course) German potato salad—all perfectly suited to box and take on a hike in the woods around the mountain. Lunch choices tend to run from $5.95 to $13.95.

If you're here for a more-than-hearty breakfast, check out the potato or apple pancakes, plus other typical breakfast dishes, as well as a selection of muffins and pastries. Overall, the combination of setting, portion, and food quality here is hard to beat!

The Village Corner is open Tuesday and Wednesday from 8 a.m. to 10 p.m.; Thursday, Friday, and Saturday from 8 a.m. to 11 p.m., and Sunday from 10 a.m. to 10 p.m.

Lodging

Mr. C finds it very difficult to fall asleep if he thinks he paid too much for his hotel room; he ends up counting dollars all night.

Luckily, Mr. C has found ways to navigate the tricky waters of the hotel biz to find rooms in Atlanta where you can stay for under $100 a night. In fact, some offer rooms for under $50 a night. He's also found a few that cost more than that but deliver good deals.

Remember, though: hotel rates ebb and flow with the seasons. And don't forget that taxes are always going to be added on top of any quoted price. Be sure you understand other policies of the hotel, too: Do they charge extra for additional persons in the room? Do they charge extra for local calls and toll-free calls? (Mr. C heads for the pay phone in the lobby if they do.) Is free parking included?

When it comes time to *negotiate* for a room rate, always ask about discounts. I've never seen an instance where a hotel room ever has only one price. Take advantage of any discounts you can—including corporate, AAA, military personnel, American Association of Retired Persons, and others. Furthermore, if you're going to be in town long enough, ask about weekly rates.

Keep in mind that The Cheapster has included descriptions of certain properties belonging to national chains, and that you'll probably be able to find other local properties with similar amenities and rates by checking that company's national reservation number or its Web site, both of which are provided.

Also, keep in mind that Atlanta is convention central. If you're planning to stay in a hotel, motel, or bed and breakfast, be sure to make reservations—and make them early. Convention business also means that many rooms are empty come Friday, so you can get a great weekend package deal at almost any hotel in the city. Even ritzier places like the Westin may run under $100 a night with one of these deals.

Finally, the peripatetic Mr. C strongly recommends that you peruse lodgings on one or more of the travel-oriented Web sites, such as Orbitz.com or Travelocity.com. These companies usually have the best connections to discounted room rates, which can change minute to minute. They also offer frequent promotions that can save you even more money. Once you have their best rate, try calling the hotel directly to see if they have an even better deal; hotels pay commissions to travel agents and online sites and sometimes they retain their very best rates for those who call them directly.

HOTELS/MOTELS

AmeriSuites

- 330 Peachtree Street N.E., Atlanta; ✆ (404) 570-1980
- National Reservations Number: ✆ (800) 833-1516
- ⌨ www.amerisuites.com

Part of a growing national chain, this 94-room hotel is located on the site of the former Quality Inn Halbersham. What has been lost in charm is not inconsiderable, but the rooms are clean and the rates are still pretty reasonable. Singles and doubles start at $99 and you get the usual benefits of a large chain: good, consistent service and efficiently designed living spaces. There's no restaurant or pool here, but downtown is full of good places to eat and there is an exercise area.

The Underground, the Omni, and the Peachtree Center are right near by, and the MARTA is two blocks away. It's easy to get around and there are lots of things to see. This is not a cheapster special, but it is a good, dependable hotel in an excellent location.

Amerisuites is part of the Prime Hospitality Corp., which also operates Wellesley Inn & Suites.

The Castleberry Inn

- 186 Northside Drive, Atlanta; ✆ (404) 893-4663
- ⌨ www.castleberryinn.com

Located less than a mile from the Georgia Dome in downtown Atlanta, this 200-room hotel has single rooms starting at $65 and double rooms starting at $75, plus *free* parking. Mr. C. likes the rates so much that he doesn't mind doing without a free continental breakfast, room service, a pool, and in-room computer ports. There is a workout area. What the heck, a shower afterward will do just fine.

Mr. C knows he can use the money he saves on his room to pay for a wonderful meal at Paschal's, the classic soul food restaurant that is located on the premises. (See the listing under *Restaurants—Downtown Atlanta/Southeast and Southwest*). Room service is overrated. This is food worth leaving the room for.

At these rates and at this location, Castleberry is a bargain worth considering.

Cheshire Motor Inn

- 1865 Cheshire Bridge Road N.E., Atlanta; ✆ (404) 872-9628; or ✆ (800) 827-9628

A bit cozier than your typical motor lodge, the Cheshire Motor Inn has modern rooms that start as low as $64 a night. Even at such low prices, these rooms have a double bed and color TV with cable. They are clean, comfortable,

LODGING: HOTELS/MOTELS 315

and well kept. There are two rows of these cottage-style rooms.

Conveniently located just north of Piedmont Park, CMI is central to the northern half of the city. There is bus service, but it's better to have a car here. You can go downtown or out to the northern suburbs in 20 minutes or so.

Cheshire is located on the same premises as the Colonnade Restaurant, a popular and moderately priced dining spot that is as well known for its traditional Southern cuisine as for the crowds that make it hard to get a table. (See the listing under *Restaurants—Buckhead.*) Many other good restaurants, stores, and a movie theater can also be found up and down Cheshire Bridge Road.

Comfort Inn Buckhead

- 2115 Piedmont Road N.E., Atlanta; ✆ (404) 876-4365; or

- National Reservations Number: ✆ (800) 228-5150

- ✎ www.choicehotels.com

Singles run from $59 to $79, and doubles can go as low as $69, at this Spanish villa-style motel. There's not much doing on this stretch of Piedmont, unless you count the Denny's down the street; but business travelers like the easy access to 1-75/85 and the late (noon) checkout time. Lenox Square is just a short drive away, as is the Buckhead Diner and the hopping Buckhead Avenue/Bolling Way area of town.

Want a free paper first thing in the morning? *USA Today* is waiting for you at the desk in the lobby. Read it during your free continental breakfast, which is served in the first floor breakfast room. And all your local and 800 calls are free! It's a nice deal for a weary traveler looking for comfort and cleanliness at a terrific price.

Days Inn Peachtree

- 683 Peachtree Street N.E., Atlanta; ✆ (404) 874-9200

- National Reservations Number: ✆ (800) 325-3535

- ✎ www.daysinn.com

Days Inn is a name people trust, and this one, located almost directly across the street from the Fox Theatre, is quite a bargain for a hotel in town. Single rooms start around $59 and can go up to $79 during peak season. Doubles start at $69, with even better corporate rate deals for business travelers. You get complimentary coffee with that too.

This is a distinctive, classic Southern-style brownstone building, with an ornate exterior and fancy chandeliers in the lobby. Such graceful elements are holdovers from its pre-Days days. Don't let this overwhelm you, though; rooms are decorated simply and tastefully. An added bonus is the security system at the front door. This is Atlanta's entertainment district and you should be aware that there are a few unsavory characters wandering around at night.

In addition to being centrally located to both the business district and the fun of Midtown clubs, this Days Inn is within walking distance of the North Avenue MARTA station. There is a parking garage in the rear and it costs $7 a night to park your car there.

Days Inn Atlanta Downtown

- 300 Spring Street, Atlanta; ✆ (404) 523-1144

- National Reservations Number: ✆ (800) 325-3535

- ✎ www.daysinn.com

This 260-room Days Inn is located downtown. Though it's slightly more expensive than its Peachtree cousin, this is still a good place to

> **MR. CHEAP'S PICKS**
>
> *Hotels/Motels*
>
> **Castleberry Inn**—This 200-room downtown hotel has single rooms starting at $65 and double rooms starting at $75, plus *free* parking.
>
> **Cheshire Motor Inn**—Super-cheap, yet comfy and modern.
>
> **Comfort Inn Buckhead**—Well, it's near Buckhead, but not even close to Buckhead prices.

stay when you're budgeting. A single or double room can run as low as $89 (with an additional 20 percent discount available through AAA) and parking is only $10 a night. This is a very reasonable deal at a hotel whose location couldn't be more convenient.

Emory Inn

- 1641 Clifton Road N.E., Atlanta; ✆ (404) 712-6700 or ✆ (800) 933-6679

- ⌨ www.emoryconference center.com

Affiliated with world-renowned Emory University, the Emory Inn is far from the bustle of downtown, yet still within easy access of Interstates 95 and 20. Ponce de Leon Avenue is just a few blocks away, which can take you either straight into midtown or out to Stone Mountain. The Lenox Square Shopping Center, Phipps Plaza, and central Buckhead are short drives away.

Of course, you can stay right where you are and explore the Emory campus itself, including the Michael C. Carlos Museum, Theatre Emory (see the listings in the "Entertainment" section), and the Glenn Memorial Auditorium.

The Inn is where many dignitaries stay when visiting the university, and it's also preferred by researchers working with the nearby Centers for Disease Control and the national headquarters for the American Cancer Society.

Rooms in the three-floor inn run about $145, which includes use of the pool, whirlpool, and exercise room. (A note to handicapped individuals: There are no elevators at the Inn.) This is definitely at the high-end of Mr. C's budget, but if you can afford it, a lovely place to stay.

Fairfield Inn Atlanta Airport

- 2451 Old National Parkway, Atlanta; ✆ (404) 761-8371 or ✆ (800) 228-2800

- ⌨ www.fairfieldinn.com

Sure, it's not the most convenient location for downtown and the roar of the 747 may invade you living space now and then. Still, at rates of $53 to $79, this 132-room hotel—part of Marriott's award-winning economy chain—could be worth a stay. You'll be only 5 miles from Turner Field, 17 miles from Six Flags Over Georgia, and just 3 miles from the Georgia Trade and Convention Center.

Hampton Inn

- Hampton Inn Buckhead, 3398 Piedmont Road N.E., Atlanta; ✆ (404) 233-5656

- Hampton Inn Hotel, 3400 Northlake Parkway, Atlanta; ✆ (770) 493-1966

- Hampton Inn-Druid Hills Road, 1975 North Druid Hills Road N.E., Atlanta; ✆ (404) 320-6600

- Hampton Inn Marietta, 455 Franklin Road, Marietta; ✆ (770) 425-9977

- Hampton Inn Southlake, 1533 Southlake Parkway, Morrow; ✆ (770) 968-8990

- Hampton Inn-Atlanta Airport, 1888 Sullivan Road, College Park; ✆ (770) 996-2220

- National Reservations Number: ✆ (800) 426-7866

- ⌨ www.hamptoninn.com

With single and double rooms for as low as $89 a night in the off season, this national chain is definitely a bargain. Mr. C especially enjoys the Hampton Inn continental breakfast, which consists of the usual coffee and danish, but also offers cereals, bagels, toast, and juice. Mr. C also likes the fact that some Hampton Inns provide free parking, free local phone calls, and free cable television. Business travelers will appreciate rooms that are equipped with data jacks to attach to personal computers. Some Hamptons even have outdoor swimming pools; open in season, of course. Plenty of nonsmoking rooms are also offered, and kids and the third and fourth adult in each room stay for free at some hotels. What a deal! Hampton Inn's are all well located, whether you want to stay near the airport or enjoy the trendy Buckhead shopping at Phipps Plaza and Lenox Square.

Don't forget the Hampton Inn guarantee: If you're not happy with your stay for any reason, you don't have to pay. But since Hampton Inns tend to be immaculately clean and comfortable, with staff to accommodate your every need, it's an unlikely scenario.

Holiday Inn Atlanta-Decatur Conference Plaza

- 130 Clairmont Avenue, Decatur; ✆ (404) 371-0204

- National Reservations Number: ✆ (800) 465-4329

- ⌨ www.hiselect.com/atl-decatur

This is a great place for the whole family to stay, since it's well removed from the noise and crowds of downtown and midtown, and away from Buckhead's traffic, yet still close to lots of fun spots. It's handicapped-accessible, with non-smoking rooms available. There's an indoor swimming pool and an exercise room too. Of course, this place is a favorite of business travelers, thanks to the 25,000-square foot conference plaza that adjoins the hotel.

Downtown is just 5 miles away, a short and easy drive. The Decatur MARTA station is an even shorter distance by foot. There are lots of flea markets and salvage shops in the area, not to mention Your DeKalb Farmer's Market (see the listing under *Shopping—Food Stores*), Emory University's cultural life and museums, plus the historic downtown Decatur area. The lively Little Five Points and Virginia-Highland neighborhoods are surprisingly close, too.

The Citrus Grove restaurant is located in the hotel, and it provides room service for those who don't want to change out of their pajamas. During the week the hotel provides complimentary van service from 7 a.m. to 3 p.m. to business destinations within a five-mile radius.

With all these amenities, not to mention the fancy marble decorations, you'd expect to pay a lot more than the going rates, which range from $78 to $159 a room on weekdays or weekends. Not cheap, but definitely reasonable.

The Inn at the Peachtrees

- 330 West Peachtree Street, Atlanta; ✆ (404) 577-6970 or ✆ (800) 242-4642

- 🖱 www.atlantahotels.org

Normal rates are $79 for a single and $89 for a double room at this cute little downtown motel, and that includes a free breakfast buffet seven days a week, and free cocktails between 5 and 7 p.m. Monday through Thursday. Corporate rates, government rates, and AAA discounts can lower the cost of a room even more. Since it's just a couple of blocks from the Civic Center and Peachtree MARTA station, the Inn is a real favorite for school tours and business travelers (on-site parking is limited, so keep this in mind).

Underground Atlanta, Macy's, Peachtree Center, and the World Congress Center are also right nearby. There's no pool, but visitors do have access to a health club down the block.

The 100 rooms are far from huge, but they do have a warm, homey atmosphere. Cable TV is included in the room price, and pay-per-view movies are also available.

Radisson Hotel

- 2061 North Druid Hills N.E., Atlanta; ✆ (404) 321-4174

- National Reservations Number: ✆ (800) 333-3333

- 🖱 www.radisson.com

Radissons are everywhere and everywhere includes Atlanta. Located in the Executive Park District, this chain hotel is clean, convenient, and relatively inexpensive. Single rooms start at $89 a night, and doubles are the same, with single, double, queen, and king-sized beds available. At these prices you wouldn't expect a pool, but this hotel has one. With an exercise room and a restaurant, the Druid, this place has many of the extras of the more expensive hotels without the extra charges, including free parking.

Ramada Limited

- 3403 Memorial Drive, Decatur; ✆ (404) 284-5722

- National Reservations Number: ✆ (800) 345-8025

- 🖱 www.ramada.com

They call this place "limited" because they don't offer room service and other high-end amenities. Still, there's nothing limited about the many amenities you get at this rather new, 80-room place for a mere $57 to $64 per night. Located near Decatur's theaters, nightclubs, restaurants, and shopping, and only about 6 miles from both downtown (east) and Stone Mountain (west), there's plenty here to make you comfortable: microwaves and refrigerators in most of the rooms, standard hair dryers and coffee machines in all of them, a complimentary continental breakfast, a fitness room, and two swimming pools. Not bad.

Sleep Inn Buckhead

- 800 Sydney Marcus Boulevard, Atlanta; ✆ (404) 949-4800

Located in the heart of Buckhead, this six-floor, 142-room chain property offers comfortable digs at reasonable prices. For a standard rate of $89, you get a queen or two doubles, computer hookup, desk, a free continental breakfast, and an outdoor pool! The hotel also has a guest laundromat on the premises, so you can pack light!

Of course, there are Sleep Inns all over the metro area with similar amenities and rates. Check their

LODGING: ALTERNATIVE LODGING 319

Web site or one of the online reservations services for details.

The Travelodge, Atlanta Downtown

- 311 Courtland Street N.E., Atlanta; ✆ (404) 659-4545
- National Reservations Number: ✆ (800) 578-7878
- ⌘ www.travelodge.com

For those who don't mind the noisy downtown area, the Travelodge offers low rates—about $89 for a single room and $99 for a double—in a convenient, central location. Add in free parking, rooms that open up onto balconies, and a free continental breakfast and you've got a bargain too good to pass up. It's just blocks away from the Civic Center, SciTrek, Underground Atlanta, the CNN Center, and the MARTA.

Villager Lodge

- 144 14th Street North West, Atlanta; ✆ (404) 873-4171 or ✆ (800) 328-7829

Villager Lodge is part of a chain of independently franchised motor hotels. These are establishments that have been taken over from previous operators, renovated, and run separately. "Extended stay lodging" is the special angle here, meaning the Villager offers weekly rates as well as daily. Many of the rooms include microwaves and refrigerators to further the cause of saving money while visiting Atlanta.

There is an outdoor swimming pool open during the warmer months and cable television. The motel's location, at the nicer, northern end of midtown, is convenient whether you have a car or not. It's right off of the 1-75/85 highway. If you're traveling on foot, the Woodruff Arts Center and the similarly named MARTA station are right around the corner.

Rates for a double occupancy room, when Mr. C inquired, were about $50 per weeknight, $60 on weekends, and $223 per week—a big discount on the daily rate. This is truly a cheapster special!

ALTERNATIVE LODGING

Atlanta Youth Hostel

- 223 Ponce de Leon Avenue N.E., Atlanta; ✆ (404) 875-2882 or ✆ (800) 473-9449
- ⌘ www.hostel-atlanta.com

Welcome to the Hostels of America network, where travelers (mostly college age or so) from as far away as Australia know they can stay for almost no money. You can do the same, whether you're visiting from Athens, Greece, or Athens, Georgia, even if you're not a member of the network. The cost for members is a

microscopic $17 per night, $19 for nonmembers. That, plus a one-time linen rental fee of $1 if you didn't bring your own (savvy hostelers do), is the entire cost. Can't beat it.

These, of course, are no-frills accommodations, dormitory-style. You'll be sharing your room with other folks. Bathrooms are shared as well.

The common areas aren't as no-frills. There's a TV lounge, and there are kitchen facilities so you can save more money by doing your own cooking. It's all tastefully decorated and quite lively. Part of the charm of a hostel, obviously, is meeting foreign travelers and exchanging stories about faraway places. The folks who work here are also ready to provide tons of information about local attractions and transportation.

The Atlanta Youth Hostel has ninety beds, which can easily fill up during peak times. It's always a good idea to call ahead and make reservations. You can even use a credit card. The North Avenue MARTA station is just a few blocks away.

Bed & Breakfast Atlanta

- 1001 Saint Charles Avenue, Atlanta; (404) 875-0525 or (800) 967-3224

- www.bedandbreakfast atlanta.com

This isn't a bed and breakfast in itself, but rather a matchmaking service that can place you in any of the over eighty B&Bs in the Atlanta area. Bed and breakfasts can sometimes be even cheaper than discount-rate hotels and motels, since they don't have to pay a staff to remain on duty 24 hours a day. Size, location, and amenities also lead to a wide variety in prices.

MR. CHEAP'S PICKS

Alternative Lodging

Bed & Breakfast Atlanta—Why stay in a standard hotel room when you can have someplace with all the comforts of home, plus a hearty breakfast? This reservations service can place you in any of the over eighty B&Bs in the Atlanta area, often at rate even cheaper than discount-rate hotels and motels.

These folks are members of the Georgia Hospitality & Travel Association and the Georgia Bed & Breakfast Council. Many of the participating inns are actually private homes that make you feel at home by allowing you full use of the living room and other areas of the house. All are near public transportation and offer private baths, air-conditioning, and continental breakfasts. Because of B&B Atlanta's detailed information, special needs, such as allergies to pets or foods, can be factored into your request for accommodations.

Rates run anywhere from $75 to $125 a night for single rooms and $80 to $125 for a double, with a $20 charge for the third person over the age of three in a room with parents. Weekly and monthly rates are also available. A small service fee is worked into the cost.

You can even purchase gift certificates for the service; just keep in mind that B&Bs usually cost $80 to $125 for two people. B&B Atlanta's business hours are Monday through Friday from 7:30 a.m. to 6:00 p.m.; you can leave a message for a callback at other times.

guestsAtlanta

- 811 Piedmont Avenue N.E., Atlanta; (404) 872-5846 or (800) 724-4381

- www.guestsAtlanta.com

This is a nice alternative to hotels and motels, especially if you're staying for a week or longer. Formerly Midtown Manor, guestsAtlanta (that is the right spelling) is, in fact, a group of individual Victorian-era houses on a tree-lined street just a couple of blocks from Peachtree Street. That short walk makes quite a difference; at once, a commercial (and somewhat rundown) area gives way to a pleasant, quieter residential neighborhood.

Rooms at guestsAtlanta are fully furnished in turn-of-the-century style. They are all carpeted and include a color TV with cable. Laundry and microwave ovens are also available in each building. Some quarters have their own bathrooms, but the more inexpensive rooms require you to share a hallway bathroom. You also get a private phone, and local calls, incoming and outgoing, are free.

Daily rates start at $80 a night and range up to $200, depending on the size of the room. Weekly rates begin at $180, though these spaces tend to be occupied on very long-term schedules. The average room rents for $200 per week. Prices include a continental breakfast, available in the lobby each morning. When you register, you get a set of keys, one for your room and one for the front door of the house, so you have 24-hour access, as well as 24-hour security. A manager also resides in each building, and there is a front office open during business hours. The staff is very friendly, taking care of any little needs very promptly. Off-street parking is available too.

Alphabetical Index

7 Stages, 247
79th Street Rug Shop, 51, 52–53
A Cappella Books, 29–30
A Flea An'Tique, 12, 99
A&R Discount Electronics, 92
AA Ideal Used Appliances, 18, 20
AAA-ALL American Appliance, 18
Abbadabba's, 168
ABRACADABRA! Children's Theatre, 209–10
Academy Theatre, The, 247
Actor's Express, 247
Adams Farms, 118
Agatha's—A Taste of Mystery, 248
Agnes Scott College, 212–13
Agnes Scott College Tree Tour, 241
All-American Package Store, 144
Alliance Theatre Company, 248
Alpha Business Interiors, 130, 131
AMC Buckhead Backlot Cinema & Cafe, 228–29
American Roadhouse, 291–92, 303
AmeriSuites, 314
Ann Jacobs Gallery, 203
Anne & Bill's Restaurant, 303–4, 305
Annie's Thai Castle, 274–75
Antique City, 12, 49, 121
Antiques and Beyond, 12–13, 99
Appliance Warehouse, 18–19
Army Surplus Sales, 168
Arthur's Ladies Sportswear, 56–57
Artists' Atelier, 203, 205
Artlite Office Supply, 185–86
Ashby Discount Sewing Machines, 19, 164–65
Asti's Terrace Lounge, 240
Athens Pizza House, 258, 275, 287, 304
Athlete's Foot, The, 168–69
Atlanta Arts Hotline, 199
Atlanta ballet, 221, 222
Atlanta Book Exchange, 30
Atlanta Braves, 255
Atlanta Broadway Series, 248–49
Atlanta Celtic Festival, 225
Atlanta Contemporary Art Center, 203–4, 205
Atlanta Cyclorama, 232
Atlanta Dogwood Festival, 225
Atlanta Fair, 225
Atlanta Greek Festival, 225
Atlanta International Museum of Art and Design, 204, 232
Atlanta Jazz Festival, 225
Atlanta Lesbian and Gay Pride Festival, 225
Atlanta Opera, The, 235–36
Atlanta Passion Play, 225
Atlanta Photography Gallery, 204
Atlanta Preservation Center, 251
Atlanta State Farmer's Market, 102, 114–15, 159–60
Atlanta Symphony Orchestra, 236–37
Atlanta Vintage Books, 30
Atlanta Virtuosi's Hispanic Festival of the Arts, 225
Atlanta Youth Hostel, 319–20
Atlanta-Fulton Public Library, 210
Atlantic Office Furniture, 130–31
AtlanTIX, 200
ATZ Salvage, 99
Aviarium, The, 159

B. Dalton Booksellers, 32
"Baby Depot" at Burlington Coat Factory, 64
Backstreet Boutique, 66, 68–69
Ballard's Thrift Store, 128–29
Bankok Thai Restaurant, 297–98
Bar, 240
Bar at the Palm, The, 241
Bar at the Ritz-Carlton Buckhead, The, 237
Barking Dog Theatre, 249
Barnes & Noble Booksellers, 31, 36
Basket Bakery and Cafe, 312
Baumann's Home Appliance Center, 19

Beacon Dance Company, 221–22
Beautiful Restaurant, The, 287
Beaver's Book Sale, 32
Bed & Breakfast Atlanta, 320
Bed Depot, A, 23–24, 25
Beluga, 237–38
Bennies Discount Shoes, 169–70
Bentley's Luggage & Gifts, 148–49, 150
Berry Patch Farms, 118
Best Buy, 19–20, 81–82
Best Buy Mattress, 24
Best Fashions, 59–60
Better Menswear, 54
Beverly Bremer Silver Shop, 13, 15
Big Kmart, 85–86
Big Lots, 82–83
Big Shanty Antiques/Flea market, 13–14, 15
Bijar Oriental Rugs, 49
Bill Stanton's Health Food Market, 118–19
Binders Art Center, 186–87
Blooming Earth Florist/Greenhouse, A, 102–3
Bob Carroll's, 20
Bobby and June's Kountry Kitchen, 298, 299
Book Nook, The, 30, 32–33, 36–37
Boomerang, 195
Borders Books & Music, 34–35, 37
Brandyhouse, The, 240
Brownlee's Furniture, 121–22
Buckhead Art Crawl, 226
Buckhead jewelry, 136–37
Buford Highway Flea Market, 99, 100
Bulloch Hall, 251
Burlington Coat Factory, 64, 83–85, 134
Business Furniture Liquidators, 131
Busy Bee Cafe, 287

C. W. Long Cafeteria at Crawford Long Hospital, 299–300
Cafe at Pharr, 275
Cafe Lily, 258–59
Café Sunflower, 275–76
Café Tu Tu Tango, 240–41, 276, 278
California Pizza Kitchen, 276–77, 298–99, 304
Callanwolde Fine Arts Center, 200–201
Calypso Cafe, 287–88
Camera Bug, 44–45
Camera Country USA, 45, 46
Canco, 49–50, 51
Capitol City Opera Company, 237
Carpet Liquidators, 50, 51
Carrabba's Italian Grill, 304
Castleberry Inn, The, 314, 316
Castleberry's Treasure for Your Home, 122–23
Casual Image Furniture, 123
Cathedral Antiques Show, 226
Cato, 57
CD Warehouse, 37–38
Cedar Tree, 259, 269
Centennial Olympic Park, 242
Center for Puppetry Arts, The, 210–11, 249
Cha Gio, 299
Chamblee Antiques Row, 14
Chapter 11 Books, 30, 35
Chastain Arts Center, 201
Chastain Memorial Park, 242
Chattahoochee Nature Center, 242
Chattahoochee River National Recreation Area, 242–43
Cheers Beer & Wine, 144–45
Cherian's, 21–22, 21–22
Cheshire Motor Inn, 314–15, 316
Chickibea, 69–70
Chili Pepper, The, 239
Chin Chin, 292
China Cabinet, 195
Chris's Pizza House, 259
Cinefest Film Theater, 229, 230
Circles Unlimited, 70
Circuit City, 21, 38–39, 89
Circuit City Express, 39
Civil War Encampment, 226

INDEX

CJ's Landing, 239
Clayton Appliances, 20, 21
Clayton Big & Tall Men's Clothing, 54–55
Clayton College and State University, 213
Clothing Warehouse, The (Atlanta), 72
Clothing Warehouse, The (Decatur), 72–73
CNN Studio Tour, 251–52
Cobalt, 239
Coco Loco Cuban & Caribbean Cafe, 260, 288
Coffee Plantation, 110–11
Colonial Bakery Outlet Store, 106–7
Colonnade, 277
Color Tile and Carpet, 50–51
Comfort Inn Buckhead, 315, 316
Commerce Drive-In Theater, 231
CompUSA Superstore, 45–46, 92–93
Consignkidz Inc, 64, 70
Consignshop, The, 51, 69, 70–71
Container Store, The, 132–33, 134
Contemporary, The, 203–4, 205
Conyers Cherry Blossom Festival, 226
Conyers Mattress Outlet, 24
Cooper Music Superstore, 151–52, 154
Corner Compact Disc, 39
Corporate Office Furniture, 131–32
Costco Wholesale, 85
Cowan's Sandwich Shoppe, 288
Coyote Trading Company, 196
Crescent Moon, The, 260
Criminal Records, 40
Crystal Blue, 196
Cumberland Diamond Exchange, 137–38

D & K Discounters, 55, 57, 60
Dad's Garage Theatre Company, 218–19
Dance City Ballroom, 241
Dancer's Collective of Atlanta, 222
Dan-Dee Sales, 156
Dante's Down the Hatch, 238
Days Inn Atlanta Downtown, 315–16
Days Inn Peachtree, 315
Decatur Arts Festival, 226
DeKalb Historical Society Tours, 252
Delta Computers, 93, 94
Designer Furniture Source, 122, 123–24
DHS Sell-Out Center, 129
Discount Appliances, 20
Discount Electronics, 90
Discount Mattress Zone, 24–25
Dress Barn, 57–59
Dusty's Barbecue, 260–61

Earwax Records, 40
East Village Grille, 277–78
Eastside Office Furniture, 132
Eat More Records, 39, 40–41
Eats, 292–93
Eddie's Attic, 238, 261
Emile Baran Instruments, Inc., 152, 154
Emory Inn, 316
Emory University, 213–15
Emory Village Flowers/Gifts, 103
En Vogue Shoe Warehouse, 170–71
England Piano & Organ Warehouse Showrooms, 152–53
Evans Fine Foods, 261–62
Everybody's Pizza, 262, 293

Factory Stores at Adel, 95–96
Fairfield Inn Atlanta Airport, 316
Famous Bargain Music, 153
Famous Footwear/Factory Brand Shoes, 171–74
Fantastic Fourth Celebration, 226
Fay Gold Gallery, 204–5
Fellini's Pizza, 278, 305
Fernbank Museum of Natural History, 230–31
Festival of Trees/Lights, 226
Fiddler's Green—3rd Saturday, 239
Flintwood Farms, 118

Flora Dora, 103–4
Florsheim Factory Outlet Store, 170, 172
Flowers Baking Company Thrift Stores, 106, 108
Foot Locker, 172–74
Forsyth Fabrics, 165
Freedman Men's Shoe Outlet and Suits, 54, 55
Friedman's Jewelers, 138–39
Friedman's Shoes, 170, 174–75
Fujita, 305
Full Moon Records, 41
Full Radius Dance, 222–23

Galaxy Music Center, 153–54
Galyan's, 175, 180
Gardner Farms, 118
Gateway IV Real Solid Oak Furniture, 124–25
George's, 293–94
Georgia Antique Center/International Market, 14
Georgia Ballet, 223
Georgia Governor's Mansion, The, 252–53
Georgia Lighting Clearance Center, 133, 134
Georgia Renaissance Festival, 226
Georgia Shakespeare Festival, 226, 249
Georgia State Capitol Tours, 253
Georgia State University, 215
Georgia Tech Theatre for the Arts, 215–16
Gilbert House, The, 201
Goethe-Institut Atlanta, 229, 230
Gold and Diamond Gallery, 139–40
Golf Discount, 180–81
Goodwill Thrift Stores, 74–75
Grant Park, 243
Great Gatsby's Auction Gallery, 100
Great Western Emporium, 137, 140
Green's Beverage Stores, 144, 145
Ground Hog Day, 226
Grounds 'n' Sounds, 238–39
GuestsAtlanta, 320–21

Guitar Center, 154, 155
Gwinnett History Museum Coffee-Ceilidh, 239

Habersham Vineyards/Winery, 144, 145
Hammonds House, The, 205–6, 232
Hampton Inn, 316–17
Hancock Fabrics, 165–66
Happy Herman's, 262–63
Harp's Farm Market, 118
Harry's Farmers Market, 112–13, 115, 145–46
Harry's In A Hurry, 113
Have a Nice Day! Cafe, 241
Haverty's Fine Furniture, 125
Hemingway's, 305, 306
Henri's Bakery, 107–8
Herndon Home, The, 253
Hi-Fi Buys, 90–91
High Museum of Art, 229–30, 232–33
High Museum of Art—Folk Art/Photography Galleries, 206, 234
Hill Street Warehouse, 14, 134
Hill Street Warehouse Sample Store, The, 136
Hobbit Hall Children's Bookstore, 211
Holiday Inn Atlanta-Decatur Conference Plaza, 317
Home Sore Futon Gallery, 25
Horizon Theatre Company, 249–50
Hungry Ear Coffeehouse, 238
Identified Flying Objects, 196–97
IMAX Theater/Fernbank Museum of Natural History, 230–31

In Any Event . . . , 156
Independence Day, 227
Indian Delights, 263
Inman Park Spring Festival, 227
Inn at the Peachtrees, The, 318
Inner Space & Hoot Owl Attic, 197
International Bakery, 108–9

INDEX

International Farmer's Market, 114, 115, 146
It's About Time, 138

Jackson Fine Art, 206–7
Jagger's, 264
JapanFest, 227
Jax Beer & Wine, 146
Jewish Theatre of the South, 250
Jimmy Carter Presidential Library, 253–54
Jo-Ann Fabrics & Crafts, 166
Johnny Rockets, 278–79, 306
Johnny's Hideaway, 241
Joli-Kobe French Bakery/Restaurant, 307
Jomandi Productions, 250
Jules Jewels, 209
Junkman's Daughter, The, 74, 175, 197

K & G Liquidation Center, 60–61, 80
Kaminski Jewelry, 140
K-B Toys, 192, 193
KEH Camera Brokers, 46
Kennesaw Mountain National Battlefield Park, 243
Kennesaw State University, 216
Kiddie City, 192
Kids 'R' Us, 65
King Plow Arts Center, 207
King Week/Martin Luther King Jr. National Holiday, 227
Kobe Steakhouse of Japan, 307

La Fonda Latina, 279, 294
Lady Foot Locker, 172–74
Lake Park Mill Store Plaza, 98
Lakewood Antique Market, 14–15, 100–101
Lasershow, 227
Last Chance Thrift Stores, 75
Laughing Matters, 219
Laurel Park, 244
La-Z-Boy Furniture Galleries, 125–26
Leather & Luggage Depot, 149, 150

Lefont Garden Hills Cinema, 230
Lefont Plaza Theatre, 230
Lena's Place, 239
Lettuce Souprise You, 264–65, 280, 300
Lewis & Sheron Textile Company, 166–67
Liquid, 238
Loehmann's, 61–62, 175
Lowe The Gallery, 209
Lucky China, 265
Lulu's Bait Shack, 239–40
"Luxury Linens" at Burlington Coat Factory, 134

Mabelton Mattress Liquidators, 25–26
Mad Italian, The, 307–8
Madras Cafe, 265–66
Maggiano's Little Italy, 280
Maggie Lyon Chocolatiers, 109
Main Street Antique Market, 15
Majestic, The, 294
Mansion, The, 292, 294–95
Marietta Bluegrass Festival, 227
Market Cafe at Your DeKalb Farmer's Market, 266
Market Grocery at Atlanta State Farmer's Market, 114–15, 159–60
Marshalls, 86–87
Martin Luther King, Jr. National Historic Site, 254
Martin Luther King Jr. National Holiday, 227
Mary Mac's Tea Room and Restaurant, 267, 300
Mattress Firm, The, 25, 26
Mattress King Discount Sleep Superstores, 27–28
Mattress Liquidators, 25, 26–27, 126
Maud Baker Flower Shoppe, 104–5
Mellow Mushroom, 267–68, 308
Men's Wearhouse, 54, 55–56, 175–76
Metropolitan Pizza Bar, 240, 280
Mexican Consulate, The, 205, 207–8

Michael C. Carlos Museum, 234
Michael's Arts & Crafts, 187
Mick's, 268–69, 280–81, 288, 300, 308
MicroSeconds, 93–94
Midtown Designer's Wearhouse, 57, 59, 140–41
Midtown Music, 154
Midtown Music Festival, 227
Midtown Outlets, 95
Mirror of Korea, 295
Modern Primitive Gallery, 208
Momus Gallery, 209
Monroe Power Equipment Company, 22
Montreaux Atlanta International Music Festival, 227
Moonsongs, 239
Morehouse College, 216–17
Mori Luggage & Gifts, 150
Murphy's Round the Corner, 295
Music at Emory, 237
Music Trader, The, 154
My Favorite Place, 15, 129–30

National Black Arts Festival, 227
New Natalie's Bridals, 57, 63–64
Norcross Furniture Outlet, 126
North Georgia Premium Outlets, 97–98
Nuts 'N Berries, 119, 269

Oakland Cemetery, 254
Office Depot, 186, 187–89
Office Max, 186, 189
Oglethorpe University, 217
OK Cafe, 281
Oktoberfest, 227
Old New York Book Shop, 35–36
One Price and More Clothing Store, 62–63
Opus One Gallery, 209
Original Pancake House, 269, 281, 300, 308
OshKosh B'Gosh, 65–66
Our Way Cafe, 266, 270
Outback Bikes, 177, 181

Outdoor Activity Center, 244
Outrageous Bargains, 136, 167

Palace Bakery, 109
Palm, The, 281–82
Panola Mountain State Park, 244
Paper Parlour, 156–57
Pappasito's Cantina, 310
Park Avenue Rugs, 51
ParkFest, 228
Parkway Used Appliances, 22
Party City, 157–58
Paschal's Restaurant, 289
PATH Foundation, 244–45
Payless Shoe Source, 170, 176–77
PC Warehouse, 94–95
Peachtree Road Liquor Store, 146–47
Pearl Artist and Craft Supply, 186, 189–90
Perfumania, 78
Perfume Outlet, The, 78–79
Pet Set, The, 160, 161
Pet Supermarket, 162–63
Petco, 163
Pete's Little Idaho Tater Farm, 118
Pets Etc., 160–61
PetsMart, 161–62
Phidippides, 177, 181–82
Pho 79, 308–9
Phoenix and Dragon, 198
Piedmont Park, 245
Pike Family Nurseries, 103, 105
Play It Again, 71
Play It Again Sports, 182–83
Preferred To-Go, 115
Pride of Dixie Antique Market, 15–16
Prime Outlets at Calhoun, 96
Prime Outlets at Darien, 97
Pro Golf, 183
Provino's, 309–10
Punchline Comedy Club, 219–20

Rack Room, 176
Radio Shack, 91
Radisson Hotel, 318
Rainbow Natural Foods, 109–10, 111, 119–20, 266, 270–71

INDEX

Ramada Limited, 318
Ray's New York Pizza, 282, 310
Recycle Electronics, 90, 91–92
Red Baron's Antiques, 16
Red Light Café, 299, 300–301
Return to Eden, 120
Rhodes Furniture, 28, 122, 126–27
Rialto Center for Performing Arts, The, 215
Richard's Variety Store, 192–93
Rich's Furniture Clearance, 28–29, 127–28
Rio Grande Cantina, 282–83
Robert C. Williams American Museum of Papermaking, 234
Robert Ferst Center for the Arts, 215–16
Rocky's Brick Oven Pizza, 283, 301
Ruth Mitchell Dance Theatre, 223–24

S & H Shoes, 177–78
Sally Beauty Supply, 79–80
Salvation Army Thrift Store, 75–76
Sambuca Jazz Cafe, 238
Sam's Club, 87
Sanctuary, 241
Sara Lee Bakery Group, 106–7
Scavenger Hunt, 101
Scentsations, 80
Schwartz Center for Performing Arts, 213–15
Scott Antique Market, 16
Sears, 22–23
Sensua Gallery, 198
Sevananda Community Owned Natural Foods Market, 120–21
Several Dancers Core, 222, 224
Shakespeare Tavern, The, 250
Shoe Depot Warehouse, 178
Shoemaker's Warehouse, 170, 178–79
Showcase, Inc, 46, 47
Silver Comet Trail, 245–46
Silver Grill, 301–2
Silver Skillet, 302–3
Singer Sewing Products, 23

Sleep Inn Buckhead, 318–19
Soccer & Sports Warehouse, 183–84
Soccer Alley, 183
Solomon Brothers Diamonds, 137, 141
Soul Vegetarian, 289–90, 295
Southeast Arts Center, 201–2
Southern Candy Company, The, 110
Soweto Street Beat Dance Theater, 224
Spelman College, 217–18
Sports Authority, The, 179, 184–85
Spring Folklife Festival, 228
Springfest, 228
Spruill Center for the Arts, 202
St. Charles Deli, 271, 295
St. Vincent de Paul, 76
Stage Door Players, 211–12
Staples: The Office Superstore, 186, 190–91
Starflight Drive-In Theater, 231
Steamhouse Lounge Seafood Bar, 283–84
Stefan's Terrace, 66, 73–74
Stone Mountain, 246
Stone Mountain Handbag Factory Store, 66, 98
Storehouse, 122, 128
Storey North 85 Twin Drive-In Theater, 231
Strings n' Things, 239
Suburban Picture Frames, 190
Sun Dial Restaurant Bar/View, 255
Sundown Café, 271–72
Sunglass Hut International, 66–68
Surin of Thailand, 271
Swallow at the Hollow, 310–11
Sweet Auburn Curb Market, 111–12
Sweet Auburn District, 254–55
Sweet Auburn Heritage Festival, 228
Sweet Repeats, 66, 69, 72
Sweetwater Creek State Park, 246

Taco Mac, 272–73, 284, 290, 295–96, 311
Tanger Factory Outlet Center, 98
Tanger Factory Outlet Center 1, 96

Tanger Outlet Center, 96–97
Tara Antiques, 16–17
Target, 41, 47, 88
Taste of the South, 228
Terrell Mill Shoe & Luggage, 150
Textile Warehouse, 167
Theater Emory, 250–51
Theatrical Outfit, 251
Thelma's Diner, 290–91
Three Dollar Café, 284–85, 311
Thrift House of the Cathedral of St. Philip, 76–77
Thumbs Up Diner, 291
Tiny Tots Consignment, 64–65
Toco Hills Giant Package Store, 147
Toddler Outlet, 65
Tom Tom, 285
Tongue & Groove, 240
Tortillas, 292, 296
Touch of India, 273, 299, 303
Tour of Southern Ghosts, 228
Tower Beer & Wine Stores, 147–48
Tower Records, 41–42
Toys 'R' US, 193–94
Travelodge, Atlanta Downtown, 319
Treasure Mart, 129
Trinity Arts Group, 208
Tuesday Morning, 51–52, 80–81, 134–35, 141–42, 151, 191, 193, 194
TULA Art Centre, 208–9
Turner Field, 255

UA Tara, 230
Uncle Tai's, 285
Uptown Comedy Center, 220

Value Village Thrift Store, 77
Varsity Jr., 273–74
Varsity, The, 273, 303
Veggieland, 278, 285–86, 311
Village Corner, The/Basket Bakery/Cafe, 305, 312
Villager Lodge, 319

Wall Street Deli, 291
Wallpaper Atlanta/Dwoskins, 135

Wallpaper Plus, 135–36
Wal-Mart, 88
Walter R. Thomas Wholesale Jewelers, 142
Wax'n'Facts, 39, 42
Westbury Carpet One, 52
Wherehouse Music, 39, 42–43
White House Restaurant, 278, 286
Whole Foods Market, 112–13, 115, 116–17, 145–46
Whole World Comedy, 220
Wholesale Office Furniture, 131, 132
Wildside Pet and Aquarium Connection, 163–64
William Breman Jewish Heritage Museum, 234–35
Winn Dixie, 158
Wolf Camera & Video, 47–48
Woody's Famous Philadelphia Cheesesteaks, 296–97
World Bar, The, 240
World of Coca-Cola Pavilion, The, 255
Worth the Weight, 143
Worthmore Discount Jewelers, 137, 142–43
Wrecking Bar, The, 17
Wren's Nest, The, 210, 212
Wuxtry Records, 43

Yellow Daisy Festival, 228
Yen Ching Restaurant, 266, 274
Your DeKalb Farmer's Market, 115–16, 148
Yule Forest Christmas Tree Farm, 118
Yule Forest Highway 155, 118

Zesto Drive-In, 297
Zoo Atlanta Grant Park, 246

Subject Index

Accommodations. *See* Lodging
Antiques/gifts, 12–17, 21–22
   shows, 226
   silver, 13
Appliances, 17–23
   outdoor equipment, 22
   sewing machines, 19, 23
   used, 18, 20, 22
Art galleries, 202–9
   African-American, 205–6
   contemporary, 203–5, 208–9
   First Thursdays, 206
   folk, 206, 208
   Mexican, 207–8
   photography, 204, 206, 206–7
   studio, 205, 207, 208–9
Art museums. *See* Museums
Arts centers, 200–202
Art supplies, 185–91
Atlanta Arts Hotline, 199
Auctions, 100

Bakeries, 106–9, 312
   French, 107–8, 307
   international, 108–9, 312
Baseball, 255
Beds/mattresses, 23–29. *See also* Furniture
Beer. *See* Liquor/beverages
Books, 29–36
   rare, 35–36
   Southern author, 29–30
   used, 30, 32–33

Cameras/photo supplies, 44–48
   photo classes, 47
   used, 44–45, 46, 47
   See also Electronics
Candy/nuts, 109–10
Carpeting/rugs, 48–53
   antique, 49, 51
   oriental, 49, 51, 52–53
   used, 51

Cassette tapes. *See* Compact discs, tapes etc.
Children's activities, 209–12
   puppetry, 210–11
   reading, 210, 211
   storytelling, 212
   theater, 209–10, 211–12
Christmas trees, 118
Clothing, new, 53–68
   accessories, 66–68
   bridal/formal wear, 63–64
   children's, 64–66
   handbags, 66
   men's, 54–56, 59–63
   women's, 56–63
Clothing, used, 68–77
   consignment/resale, 68–72
   thrift store, 74–77
   vintage, 72–74
Coffees/teas, 110–11
College performing arts, 212–18
Comedy shows, 218–20
Compact discs, tapes etc., 36–43
   records, 40–41, 43
   used, 40, 40–41, 42
Computers. *See* Electronics
Cosmetics/perfumes, 77–81
Craft supplies, 185–91

Dance performances, 221–24. *See also* College performing arts
Dancing, 239–41
Decorative items. *See* Home furnishings
Digital cameras. *See* Cameras/photo supplies
Discount department stores, 81–88
Drive-in theaters, 231

Electronics, 89–95
   audio/video equipment, 81–82, 89–92
   computers, 81–82, 89, 92–95
   used, 91–92, 93–94

Fabrics. *See* Sewing and fabrics
Factory outlets, 95–98
    Adel, 95–96
    Atlanta, 95
    Calhoun, 96
    Commerce, 96
    Dalton, 96–97
    Darien, 97
    Dawsonville, 97–98
    Lake Park, 98
    Locust Grove, 98
    Stone Mountain, 98
Farmer's markets, 102, 114–16, 117–18
Festivals, 225–28
Flea markets/emporia, 12, 13–14, 99–101
Flowers/plants, 101–5
Furniture
    new, 121–28, 140
    office, 130–32
    used, 128–30
    See also Beds/mattresses
Futons, 25. *See also* Beds/mattresses; Furniture

Games, 191–94
General markets/prepared food to go, 111–17
Gifts. *See* Antiques/gifts; Unusual gifts
Greeting cards. *See* Party supplies
Grocery stores. *See* General markets/prepared food to go

Health food/vitamins, 118–21
Home furnishings, 132–36, 140
    kitchenware, 132–33, 134
    lighting, 133, 134
    linens, 134–35
    wallpaper, 132–33, 135–36
Hotels. *See* Lodging

Information, Atlanta Arts Hotline, 199

Jewelry/crafts, 136–43

Linens. *See* Home furnishings
Liquor/beverages, 112–13, 114, 116–17, 143–48
Lodging, 313–21
    alternative, 319–21
    hotels/motels, 314–19
Luggage, 148–51

Mattresses. *See* Beds/mattresses
Movies, 228–31
Museums, 231–35
    African-American, 232
    art, 232–34
    historical, 212, 232, 234–35
    Jewish heritage, 234–35
Music, live, 235–41
    classical, 235–37
    dance/disco, 239–40
    eclectic, 241
    folk/coffeehouse, 238–39
    jazz/blues, 237–38
    Latin/salsa, 240–41
    rock/pop, 240
Musical instruments, 151–55
    guitars, 153–55
    piano/keyboard, 151–53
    school, 152–54
    violins/stringed, 152

Office supplies, 185–91
Organic food markets, 116–17, 118–21
Outdoor/sports activities, 241–46

Paint. *See* Home furnishings
Parks. *See* Outdoor/sports activities
Party supplies, 155–58
Performing arts. *See* College performing arts; Dance performances; Theaters
Perfumes. *See* Cosmetics/perfumes
Pet supplies, 159–64
Photo supplies. *See* Cameras/photo supplies
Picture frames, 190
Plants/flowers, 101–5
Power equipment, 22

INDEX

Records. *See* Compact discs, tapes etc.
Restaurants, bars/taverns, 261, 293–94, 300–301
Restaurants, breakfast, 269, 281, 298, 300, 303–4, 308
Restaurants, cafe, 258–59, 270, 271–72, 275, 281–82, 284–85, 296–97, 311
Restaurants, delis, 115, 262–63, 271, 291, 295
Restaurants, dessert shops, 285
Restaurants, diners, 261–62, 264, 267, 277–78, 286, 287, 290–91, 292–93, 294, 298, 299–300, 303–4
Restaurants, ethnic
   American, 260–61, 268–69, 273–74, 278–79, 280–81, 285, 291–92, 298, 300, 303, 306, 308
   Caribbean/Cuban, 260, 287–88
   Chinese, 265, 274, 285, 292
   French, 307
   German, 312
   Indian, 263, 265–66, 273, 303
   Irish, 295
   Italian, 280, 304, 307–8, 309–10
   Japanese, 305, 307
   Korean, 295
   Mexican, 271–73, 279, 282–83, 284, 290, 294, 295–96, 310, 311
   Middle Eastern, 259
   tapas, 276
   Thai, 271, 274–75, 297–98
   Vietnamese, 299, 308–9
Restaurants, pizza, 258, 259, 262, 267–68, 275, 276–77, 278, 280, 282, 283, 287, 293, 298–99, 301, 304, 305, 308, 310
Restaurants, sandwich shops, 288, 298, 299–300
Restaurants, seafood, 283–84, 294–95
Restaurants, soul/southern, 260, 267, 277, 287, 289–90, 294–95, 295, 301–3, 306, 310–11
Restaurants, soup/salad, 264–65, 280, 300
Restaurants, tip-free, 299–300
Restaurants, vegetarian, 264–65, 266, 269, 270–71, 275–76, 280, 285–86, 289–90, 295, 300, 311
Rugs. *See* Carpeting/rugs

Sewing and fabrics, 19, 23, 164–67
Shoes, 167–79
   athletic, 168–69, 171–74, 175, 177, 179
   men's, 55, 169–70, 171–72, 174–76
   repairing, 150
   women's, 170–75, 176–78
Silverware, 13
Sporting goods, 180–85
   bicycles, 181
   golf equipment, 180–81, 183
   running apparel, 181–82
   soccer, 183–84
   used, 182–83
Sports activities. *See* Outdoor/sports activities
Stationery, 185–91
Stereo equipment. *See* Electronics
Tapes. *See* Compact discs, tapes etc.

Televisions. *See* Electronics
Theaters, 246–51
   African-American, 250
   Jewish, 250
   mystery, 248
   professional, 248–49, 250
   Shakespeare, 249, 250
   See also Children's activities; College performing arts
Tickets, 200
Tours/walks, 251–55
Toys, 191–94
Trees. *See* Plants/flowers

Unusual gifts, 194–98

VCRs. *See* Electronics
Videos. *See* Compact discs, tapes etc.
Vitamins. *See* Health food/vitamins

Walks/tours, 251–55
Wallpaper. *See* Home furnishings
Watches. *See* Jewelry/crafts
Wine. *See* Liquor/beverages

About the Author

Corey Sandler is the author of more than 150 books on consumer issues, travel, business, and computers. Among his bestsellers: the *Econoguide Travel Book* series (Globe Pequot Press), *Buy More Pay Less* (Prentice Hall Direct), and *Fix Your Own PC* (John Wiley). Sandler is a former correspondent for the Associated Press and a newsman for Gannett Newspapers. He was also editor-in-chief of *Digital News* and executive editor of *PC Magazine*.

THE *MR. CHEAP'S*® SERIES:

Today's consumers aren't cheap . . . but we all know the importance of a bargain—and the thrill of the hunt for getting quality at a good price. From neighborhood shops to outlet centers, from cheap bites to fancy dinners, from free activities to high quality lodging for a low price, *Mr. Cheap's*® offers all the information to find it and get it.

Also Available in the Series:

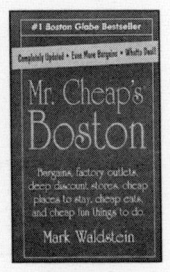

| 1-55850-556-3 | 1-58062-374-3 | 1-58062-271-2 |
| $9.95 | $9.95 | $9.95 |

| 1-55850-388-9 | 1-55850-445-1 | 1-58062-693-9 |
| $8.95 | $9.95 | $9.95 |

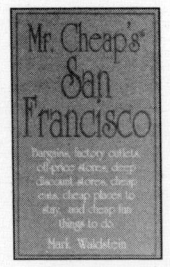

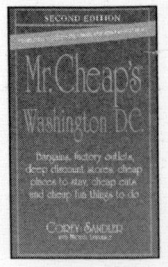

Available Wherever Books Are Sold!
For more information, or to order, call 800-872-5627 or visit
www.adamsmedia.com
Adams Media Corporation, 57 Littlefield St., Avon, MA 02322